# ENVIRONMENT AND SOCIETY

*Fifth Edition*

# ENVIRONMENT AND SOCIETY

## HUMAN PERSPECTIVES
## ON ENVIRONMENTAL ISSUES

### Charles L. Harper
*Creighton University*

**Pearson**

Boston   Columbus   Indianapolis   New York   San Francisco   Upper Saddle River
Amsterdam   Cape Town   Dubai   London   Madrid   Milan   Munich   Paris   Montreal   Toronto
Delhi   Mexico City   Sao Paulo   Sydney   Hong Kong   Seoul   Singapore   Taipei   Tokyo

**Publisher:** Karen Hanson
**Project Manager:** Elizabeth Gale Napolitano
**Editorial Assistant:** Christine Dore
**Executive Marketing Manager:** Kelly May
**Marketing Assistant:** Janeli Bitor
**Production Manager:** Fran Russello
**Cover Administrator:** Jayne Conte
**Editorial Production and Composition Service:** Jogender Taneja/Aptara®, Inc.
**Cover Designer:** Karen Noferi
**Cover Image Credit:** Fotolia: © Petersen

Credits appear on page 289, which constitutes an extension of the copyright page.

Many of the designations by manufacturers and seller to distinguish their products are claimed as trademarks. Where those designations appear in this book, and the publisher was aware of a trademark claim, the designations have been printed in initial caps or all caps.

**Library of Congress Cataloging-in-Publication Data**
Harper, Charles L.
    Environment and society: human perspectives on environmental issues /
Charles L. Harper.—5th ed.
        p. cm.
    ISBN-13: 978-0-205-82053-5
    ISBN-10: 0-205-82053-0
    1. Human ecology.   2. Environmental policy.   3. Environmentalism.   I. Title.
    GF41.H383 2012
    304.2'8—dc23

                                                                    2011018692

10 9 8 7 6 5 4 3 2 1—DOC—15 14  13 12 11

ISBN-10:    0-205-82053-0
ISBN-13: 978-0-205-82053-5

# CONTENTS

# PREFACE

*Environment and Society: Human Perspectives on Environmental Issues* is intended to provide students and interested readers with an introduction to environmental issues. More specifically, it is about human connections and impacts on the environment—and vice versa. There are many specialized research reports and monographs about particular environmental topics and issues, but I intend this book as an integrative vehicle for many different human and environmental issues.

Stimulated by the enormous growth of interest in environmental issues and problems in higher education, my own classes have a yeasty mix of students from biology, environmental science, the social sciences, and others from education, philosophy, and marketing. I have tried to write a book that is at least understandable to them all. Perceptive readers will note that in some places the book alternates between more elementary and advanced discussion. That is deliberate, because social science students know some things that natural science students do not, and vice versa. This book discusses blocks of material that incorporate contemporary environmental concerns, controversies, and discourses. A pervasive theme is that people and scholars bring very different intellectual views (*paradigms*) to the understanding of human–environmental issues. I think that these different views are not ultimately irreconcilable, but if you do not like attention given to different points of view, this is probably not the book for you.

The fifth edition is different from earlier editions because there are new data and ideas added in many places. Here are some examples: The first chapter uses food to illustrate the relationship between environmental science and social science, and the discussion of environmental resources and human impact. There is new information and the environmental impacts of the world economic recession of 2008; the gulf oil spill of 2010; and new data and material about soil, water, and coral reefs. Sections on climate change include discussion about newer ideas to address climate change (wedge analysis), and the section after discussing climate problems is followed by a discussion about scientific uncertainty and risk (included at the suggestion of manuscript reviewers). There are new scientific discussions about the possibilities of biofuels and the ethical tradeoff between current ethanol biofuels and food prices, about trade and material requirements for manufacturing wind turbines, about producing energy efficiency by using combined heating and power systems, and about many ideas to increase the efficiency of contemporary economic processes. There is newer data about population growth and global migration as related to relation to social and environmental sustainability, a new discussion about different perspectives on globalization and environmental consequences. There is a new discussion of the environmental implications for evolving social and environmental "resiliency," new perspectives about globalization and social and environmental sustainability, an updated discussion of evidence related to two major conceptions about the future trajectories of human–environmental relations as this century emerges, and an enhanced discussion of the "levers for progress in human–environmental relations. There is new material on "green consumerism," and the weakening of American environmental regulation between 2000 and 2009. Finally, there is a more in-depth discussion of the irony of the overwhelming popularity of concern for the environment and significant environmental activism from the evidence of the Gallop firm and the growing antienvironmentalism in American attitudes and politics.

To make this a more user-friendly book, each chapter is followed by some review questions, and some questions and issues that attempt to help you make macro–micro links between large-scale issues and the lives of persons (Personal Connections). These personal connections are *not* review questions that summarize chapter content, but opportunities for dialogue between the book and its readers and between readers. They may be points of departure for discussion and argumentation. At the end of each chapter, there are some sources (both print and electronic) for further exploration of each topic. There is a glossary at the end of the book that defines social and environmental terms used that you may not be familiar with.

It is only fair that you have an idea of what kind of book you are going to be reading and how it is organized. It is about environmental problems themselves, but it has a *social science perspective,* and will be more concerned with how these problems relate to human behavior, culture, and social institutions. The book also examines suggestions for changing the human–environment relationship to a more "sustainable" environment, society, and world order. Finally, it is important for you to know that this book will provide a broad overview that focuses more on the interconnections among a variety of issues rather than on any particular issue in great depth. *Many* other books and research papers provide in-depth coverage of specific topics. (At the end of each chapter, I provide a few suggestions for books and Web sites.)

Chapter 1 introduces basic concepts about environments, ecosystems, and human social systems, and various ways that people have understood and interacted with their biophysical environment. It examines how human–environment relations have come to be understood and studied by social scientists, and ends with a summary of the driving forces of human activity that impact the biophysical environment. Chapter 2 is a reading human "footprint" on the planet, which discusses some resources, resource depletion, and pollution issues. Chapter 3 is about climate change and particularly about the contentious issue of global warming. Chapter 4 is about the energy systems that underlie all human economic activity, and the prospects for their transformation in the near future. Chapter 5 is about human population growth with special reference to food issues. Chapter 6 examines globalization and the prospects for more sustainable human–environment relations from several contemporary perspectives. Chapters 7 and 8 continue to examine the prospects for greater sustainability by examining economic markets, politics, policy, and environmental movements.

An important theme that I try to develop with progressive clarity is the importance of *worldviews* and *paradigms* that have implicit basic assumptions about the "way the world works." People in cultures have them, and they shape the scholarship of experts in different fields. These are embedded in our thinking in subtle ways that often make good communication difficult.

I am a sociologist by training, and my outlook on environmental issues is informed by environmental sociology, a subdiscipline that has developed rapidly over the last 30 years. Even so, no single scholarly discipline has a corner on truth about such a multifaceted and important topic. I have therefore attempted to give attention to the work and perspectives of economists, political scientists, anthropologists, geographers, and policy analysts as they address environmental and ecological issues. That makes this book as much a social science work than a narrow treatise about environmental sociology. But of these fields, the book will draw most heavily on environmental sociology and economics.

## SCIENCE, VALUES, AND LANGUAGE

I have tried to write an objective book about the human causes of and reactions to environmental problems and issues. But the book will not ignore scholarly or public controversy and disagreement. It addresses some outrageously difficult and multidimensional issues as reasonably as possible but—obviously—will not do so to everyone's liking. Like all good social science or indeed, all good science of any kind, sooner or later it connects objective "facts" with things that people find important (values), and with criteria for making normative choices among them. As Thomas Dietz put it while speaking about the prospects for a new "human ecology":

> We must become a normative as well as a positive science. I don't mean that human ecologists, as scientists, need continually to be engaged in advocacy. I do mean that we must use our analytical skills to develop arguments for the proper criteria for making decisions. We must help individuals and collectivities make better decisions by offering methods for handling value problems. (1996/1997: 50)

There is, in truth, no completely value-free social science or any other kind of science. So, the book will talk about facts and data, but it also exhibits my own values, hopes, and fears about the human predicament. It is impossible (and I think undesirable) to eliminate one's own opinions and values from scholarly work. But they should be labeled as such, so I have tried to be careful in putting "I think . . ." statements in front of those places where I am particularly aware that not all would agree.

It's fair to warn you that you will be reading a book that details a lot of bad news about human–environment interactions. Reading sustained fare about problems can be very depressing and can generate fatalism. But it is also important to note that I find some compelling reasons for hope (if not optimism) about the possibilities for a more positive future. Those reasons occur mainly in the later chapters of the book, so if what you read initially depresses you, *read on*. The book moves, after the early chapters, from the more physical to the more social dimensions of environmental issues, and from the more depressing litany of facts and problems to examining some possibilities for positive change. I discovered in writing the book, somewhat to my surprise, that if I am a pessimist, I am a hopeful one.

I should mention one other thing that should be obvious to you by now. As much as possible, this book is written in an informal and, I hope, unpretentious style. I have often tried to write as if I were carrying on a conversation with you as an individual rather than communicating with an anonymous group of people. It's the way I like to communicate, and I hope it makes the book more engaging to read.

## SUPPLEMENTARY MATERIALS FOR INSTRUCTORS AND STUDENTS

**Instructor's Manual and Test Bank (ISBN 0205022642)**    The Instructor's Manual and Test Bank has been prepared to assist instructors in their efforts to prepare lectures and evaluate student learning. For each chapter of the text, the Instructor's Manual offers different types of resources, including detailed chapter summaries and outlines, learning objectives, discussion questions, classroom activities and much more. Also included in this manual is a test bank offering multiple-choice, true/false, fill-in-the-blank, and/or essay questions for each chapter.

**MyTest (ISBN 0205022634)**    The Test Bank is also available online through Pearson's computerized testing system, MyTest. MyTest allows instructors to create their own personalized exams, to edit any of the existing test questions, and to add new questions. Other special features of this program include random generation of test questions, creation of alternative versions of the same test, scrambling question sequence, and test preview before printing. Search and sort features allow you to locate questions quickly and to arrange them in whatever order you prefer.

**PowerPoint Presentation (ISBN 0205022359)**    Lecture PowerPoints are available for this text. The Lecture PowerPoint slides outline each chapter to help instructors convey sociological principles in a visual and exciting way.

All supplementary materials are available online to adopters at www.pearsonhighered.com

**MySearchLab**    MySearchLab provides a host of tools for students to master a writing or research project. It provides online access to reliable content for internet research projects, including thousands of full articles from the EBSCO ContentSelect database, a complete online handbook for grammar and usage support, a tutorial on understanding and avoiding plagiarism, and AutoCite, which helps students correctly cite sources.

## ACKNOWLEDGMENTS

Every intellectual work is in some sense autobiographical. My early college education (of many years ago!) was in biology and the physical sciences. But I subsequently pursued graduate studies in sociology, and for years I have been engaged in a professional life that has dealt only peripherally with environmental and ecological issues. This book attempts to put together the pieces of my education as a coherent whole in a way that addresses some important human and intellectual concerns of our times.

Intellectual works are not just autobiographical. They involve the insights, encouragement, forbearance, and constructive criticisms from many others, and I need to thank them, particularly my colleagues and students at Creighton University. They contributed substantially to this work and tolerated me while I was working on it. Thanks especially to James T. Ault, who had the patience to read and critically comment on many parts of the book. Thanks to a succession of Graduate School Deans at Creighton University who provided modest but important material support.

I also want to thank an amazing network of environmental social scientists at other institutions who encouraged me through various editions. They include Fred Buttel (University of Wisconsin) before his recent untimely death; Eugene Rosa, Thomas Dietz, Robert Brulle, J. Allen Williams, Paul Stern (National Research Council); and Bruce Podobnik. I am especially indebted to William Freudenburg (University of California-Santa Barbara) and Riley Dunlap (Oklahoma State University) for their friendly criticism and encouragement over the years. I do not, of course, hold any of them responsible for errors of commission or omission. Those are mine alone.

I thank anonymous reviewers for their useful comments about this edition at various stages who can now be named. They were Monica Snowden, Wayne State College, Peter Korsching. I owe an enormous debt of gratitude to former Prentice Hall sociology editor and publisher Nancy Roberts, who was an encourager in the early editions, as well as Karen Hanson, current publisher for sociology at Pearson, for her kind support, and especially Liz Napolitano, senior production project manager for Pearson social sciences. They were the human voices of a large, and to me, anonymous organizations, who patiently helped to bring order to a complex project. I thank my copyeditor Khumanthem Seilesh Singh, who had the formidable task of making order and sense from sometimes messy prose. Finally, for her patient and loving support, I thank my wife, Anne, to whom this book is dedicated.

If you would like to contact me, I would be happy to hear your comments and reactions to the book and its uses.

*Charles L. Harper*
*Department of Sociology and Anthropology*
*Creighton University*
*Omaha, Nebraska, 68178*
*charper@creighton.edu*

# ABOUT THE AUTHOR

Charles Harper is a professor of sociology at Creighton University in Omaha, Nebraska. As a member of the faculty there since 1968, he has developed and taught numerous courses in the sociology department. Dr. Harper's teaching and scholarly interests involve the study of social change, globalization, the sociology of religion, social theory, and environmental sociology. He has published papers in a variety of academic journals.

Along with *Environment and Society*, Dr. Harper is the author of two other textbooks. Coauthored with Kevin Leicht, his book *Exploring Social Change: America and the World* (Prentice Hall, 2011) is now in its sixth edition. Another book, *Food, Society, and Environment*, originally published by Prentice Hall is now in its second edition (Tafford Press, 2007). As an undergraduate, Dr. Harper studied biology and the natural sciences. He received a bachelor's degree from Central Missouri State University, a master's degree in sociology from the University of Missouri, and a Ph.D. in sociology from the University of Nebraska at Lincoln.

He and his wife, Anne, live close to Creighton's campus near a "clan" of adult children, stepchildren, and grandchildren. He enjoys traveling, bicycling, and reading.

# CHAPTER 1

# Environment, Human Systems, and Social Science

The impact on our environment is so extensive that we live in a "socialized environment."

To begin, here is an illustration that links the environmental sciences and the social sciences. Food, for instance, is clearly of paramount importance to maintain human life, and thus a supremely important resource. You can consider food by raising two kinds of concerns. *First,* "Is there enough food to support a healthy life?" If not, humans live with malnutrition or hunger. If there is too much, humans may live with an epidemic of obesity. Either can be fatal. Are there enough fertile soil, water, and varieties of plant and animal species to enable humans to produce the required food by farming, raising livestock, hunting, or fishing? Is there enough energy to cultivate, irrigate, or transport an adequate amount of food? These concerns about having enough food for a large and growing population are most obviously related to nature and the natural world—and to natural and environmental science. *Second*, "What about the *kind* of food and its distribution within a human community?" Is it the kind of food that is not only nutritious, but also which people like because it satisfies their emotional needs, as well as their needs for social belonging and participating in a human society and culture? Do economic markets, political or cultural rules, and subsistence technologies produce an adequate distribution of the food that is produced? Is that distribution just? Who owns the resources and systems that produce food? Do particular people have the money or political power to acquire enough food in a given human community or nation? These concerns are more obviously related to the social world—and to the social sciences.

Although each group of concerns is "most obviously" related to either the natural or the social sciences, that is an oversimplification. Both natural and social science concerns—about food and other environmental issues—are closely connected. Those connections are not always obvious because they have different perspectives, definitions, and histories. News about the broader connections between the natural and social worlds has not been good in recent decades. Begin with news about the obvious: wilderness and soil and water resources are under stress, forests are disappearing, we are awash in pollution and garbage of our own creation, and the earth's climate is changing significantly. Add to these, in no particular order, concerns about indoor air pollution, landfill overcrowding, low-level nuclear wastes, urban sprawl, unsustainable consumption and population growth, environmentally induced diseases, and the variety of energy issues that we face. This list could continue for a long time, and you have probably heard of them. They are, I think, measures of how rapidly and pervasively environmental issues and problems have entered the popular consciousness and political discourse of our times.

This book is about the connections between the natural and social worlds, described from the points where the natural sciences (especially environmental science) and the social sciences (especially sociology and economics) intersect. This chapter begins by introducing, in broad strokes (1) ecosystems, (2) human sociocultural systems, (3) some parallels and differences between the evolution of ecosystems and human systems, (4) environmental social sciences, particularly economics and sociology, and (5) some of the human driving forces of environmental and ecosystem change.

## ECOCATASTROPHE OR ECOHYPE?

Are all the problems listed earlier just alarmist stuff? How *real* are these problems? Sure, everyone knows that there are environmental problems—with pollution and the rainforests, nuclear energy, and the possibility of global warming. But is ecocatastrophe really around the corner, or are the problems greatly exaggerated? Like me, you probably don't spend much time or energy thinking about these problems. The world seems okay: I get up and go to work and enjoy my family life, farmers continue to grow food that is plentiful and normally tasty, and drinking tap water has not made me ill (not yet, anyway). After 2000, and particularly after September 11, 2001, many of us have a sense of unease, for many reasons. Even so, to many in the richer nations, the biophysical world still seems okay. Perhaps, if you are like me, it is hard to experience directly the environmental devastation depicted here. We are aware, of course, that there *is* human suffering, poverty, disease, and terrorism in the world; and to most of us, the economic, political, and individual causes of human problems and misery seem more direct and obvious than the environmental ones. Surely you realize that I have been talking about extremely complicated issues and controversies for the human future—if not for you, then certainly for your children and grandchildren. Not "merely" scientific and academic debates, they have become issues and policy dilemmas that reverberate in the political arenas of the United States and the world, where they compete with more traditional ones.

## ECOSYSTEMS: CONCEPTS AND COMPONENTS

The most fundamental concept for ecological understanding is the notion of a *system* as a network of interconnected and interdependent parts. An *ecosystem* is the most basic unit of ecological analysis, which includes all the varieties and populations of living things that are interdependent in a given environment. Ecosystem and environment are not the same, even though they are often used interchangeably. The environment includes the earth (rocks, soil, water, air, atmosphere, and living things), but an ecosystem means the "community" of things that live and interact in parts of the geophysical environment. Ecosystems are composed of structural units that form a progressively more inclusive hierarchy:

| | |
|---|---|
| *Organism* | Any individual form of life, including plants and animals (Felix, Fido, you, and me) |
| *Species* | Individual organisms of the same kind (e.g., dolphins, oak trees, corn, humans) |
| *Population* | A collection of organisms of the same species living within a particular area |
| *Community* | Populations of different organisms living and interacting in an area at a particular time (e.g., the interacting life forms in the Monterey Bay estuary in California) |
| *Ecosystem* | Communities and populations interacting with one another *and* with the chemical and physical factors making up the inorganic environment (e.g., a lake, the Amazon basin rainforest, the High Plains grasslands in the United States) |
| *Biome* | Large life and vegetation zones made of many smaller ecosystems (e.g., tropical grasslands or savannas, northern coniferous forests) |

In addition, ecologists speak about the *biosphere* as the entire realm where life is found. It consists of the lower part of the atmosphere, the hydrosphere (all the bodies of water), and the lithosphere (the upper region of rocks and soil). Combined, the biosphere is a relatively thin, 20-kilometer (12-mile) zone of life extending from the deepest ocean floor to the tops of the highest mountains (Miller, 1998: 92).

Exchanges (or *cycles*) of energy, chemicals, and nutrients are the interconnections that bind the components of ecosystems and subsystems with the physical environment. Among important cycles are the flows of carbon, nitrogen, oxygen, phosphorus, and water. See Figure 1.1, which illustrates the carbon cycle.

These cycles are symmetrical in terms of energy. The ultimate source of the earth's energy is solar radiation, which is built up into complex forms of energy and used by living things. Then it is eventually emitted into the environment, mostly as low-quality heat energy near the earth's surface. Similar to the conservation of matter, the *first law of thermodynamics* says that energy cannot be created or destroyed, only changed into different forms. So, like matter, you can't get something for nothing—energy input always equals energy output. But wait! When you use energy, you can't even break even. Unlike matter, energy can't be recycled over and over. Respiration or burning gasoline in your car permanently degrades useful complex forms of energy (such as that stored in carbohydrates or petrochemicals) to low-grade forms, such as heat,

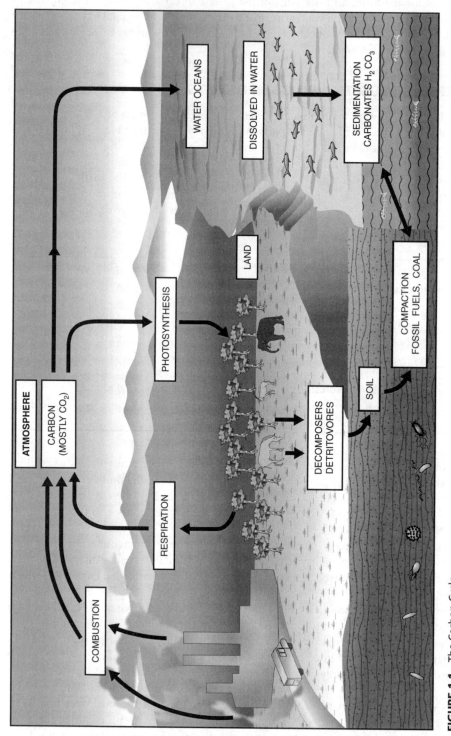

**FIGURE 1.1** The Carbon Cycle

*Source:* Based on T.G. Miller, Jr., 1998: 114–115.

that can't be reused. The *second law of thermodynamics* states that we can't recycle or reuse high-quality energy to perform useful work again. This tendency for energy to run downhill is called *entropy*. Thus, the heat produced from combustion and the respiration processes of living things is eventually diffused over the earth and radiates back into space. Useful energy is never to be recovered until solar radiation builds more over eons of time, and the material remains from combustion and respiration aren't really disposed of, but accumulate in various *sinks* (like air and water). The human implications of this are profound.

The transfer of food energy from its primary producer sources (green photosynthetic plants) through a series of consumer organisms where eating and being eaten is repeated a number of times is called a *food chain*. The greater the number of feeding (or *trophic*) levels, the greater the cumulative loss of usable energy. That explains why larger populations at lower trophic levels are required to support smaller populations at higher levels, and particularly at the top of food chains. Food chains are thus *food pyramids*. This energy-flow pyramid explains why larger populations of people can be maintained if they eat mostly at lower levels on the food chain (by eating vegetables or grains) than at higher levels (by eating cattle fed on grains) (Cunningham et al., 2005: 58–60).

A *habitat* is the location of an organism within an ecosystem, whereas its *ecological niche* is its role in a community of organisms that comprise an ecosystem. Sometimes niches overlap, and two species compete for the same resources. But often different kinds of *resource partitioning* make it possible for different species to share the same habitat without much competition. For instance, species inhabit and feed from different layers of rainforests: Some are ground feeders, some feed on short shrubs, some live and feed in the shady understory, and others live in the high canopy. The droppings of all of these species feed the detritovores that recycle nutrients to the otherwise fragile tropical soil. There are other ways that species "share the wealth" in a given ecosystem. Hawks and owls feed on similar prey, but hawks hunt during the day and owls hunt at night.

Every organism has nutrient needs that the ecosystem and its physical environment must provide for it to thrive. If a population gets too large, the ecosystem is overloaded and cannot provide the basic needs of every organism. If this overload occurs, populations become stressed and may begin die back. The concept of ecosystem *carrying capacity* and the possibility that population growth can produce an *overshoot* of available resources is illustrated by Clark's analogy of bacteria in a petri dish. When bacteria are introduced into a nutrient-rich petri dish, exuberant growth follows. But in the limited world of the petri dish, such growth is not sustainable forever. "Sooner or later, as the bacterial populations deplete available resources and submerge in their own wastes, their initial blossoming is replaced by stagnation and collapse" (1990: 1). But you don't have to rely on analogies like this; there are many real cases in which species have outgrown ecosystem carrying capacity, and after such overshoot, population size has collapsed. For example, David Klein's study of reindeer tells of the introduction of 29 animals, minus wolves—their natural predators—to remote Matthew Island off the coast of Alaska. In the next 19 years, they had multiplied to 6,000 animals and then, through starvation, had crashed to 42 in the following 3 years. When discovered, the 42 reindeer were in miserable condition, all probably sterile (1968: 350–367).

Like other species, humans need space, clean air, water, food, and other essential nutrients to survive and maintain a quality existence. If human population gets too large relative to its environment, however, the carrying capacity of that ecosystem may be overtaxed, and human welfare may be threatened. Also like animal species, there are numerous real cases of human local and regional overshoot disasters and population crashes in various countries throughout history. (I will return to some of these cases later in other chapters. See Box 1.1.)

---

### BOX 1.1

#### Environmental Degradation and Social Change

Many people who understand human social evolution as a story of continual progress fail to appreciate the role that environmental degradation has played. Commonly, people believe that the change from food foraging to horticulture and then to agriculture happened because people traded a precarious and insecure way of life for one that was more secure and satisfying. Little evidence exists to support this view. Rather, climate changes that "shrank" livable environments, human population growth, the exhaustion of edible plant and large animal populations, and the discoveries and innovations that made dependence on agriculture possible *all* combined to cause this transformation. Furthermore, fossil records and archaeological evidence confirm that hunter-gatherers did not abandon their lifestyle until forced to do so by the problems, and did so at different times and in widely scattered areas around the world (Lenski and Nolan, 1999; Sanderson, 1995). A similar combination of environmental problems, scarcities, and technological possibilities caused the decline of ancient empires (like the Mayans, Mesopotamians, and Romans) and stimulated the emergence of industrial societies. The growth of innovations and technologies produced more complex and inclusive human systems having ever-larger productive capacities to support human populations. Elites may have benefited from an enhanced ability to extend their control and powers of taxation across larger systems. Non-elites, however, often did not change their lifestyles from positive attractions but rather to survive when they had no other choices (Tainter, 1998; Homer-Dixon, 2006). In the nineteenth and twentieth centuries, established farmers often did not *willingly* move to cities seeking urban employment, but the story of rural to urban migration is also one of progressive rural poverty, bankruptcy, and foreclosed farm mortgages.

---

The human consequences have included widespread malnutrition, disease, starvation, all kinds of social stress, outmigration, and sometimes war as people compete for scarce resources.

### Ecosystem Change, Evolution, and Human–Environment Interaction

Today most scientists think that biological species evolve, and that *natural selection* and *rare genetic mutations* are important mechanisms for the evolution of species. Ecosystems also evolve, and have done so since long before humans arrived on the scene. *How so?* Alfred J. Lotka, one of the founders of ecological science, provided important leads to this question beginning in the 1920s. Viewed ecologically, the competition among species is fundamentally about sources of energy. Competition for available energy (nutrients and food) in their environment triggers changing relationships among different species, often causing ecosystems to evolve into more inclusive systems. When energy is available in the environment, the species with the most efficient energy-capturing mechanisms has a survival advantage. Organisms with superior energy-capturing devices will be favored by *natural selection,* increasing their numbers and their total energy consumption throughout the ecosystem (Lotka, 1922; 1945: 172–185). These processes often result in *ecological succession,* whereby species may replace one another in gradual changes.

Over the earth's long 3-billion-year geological history, ecosystems have evolved by (1) *natural selection,* as described earlier, and (2) *coevolution,* or the reciprocal natural selection that forms relationships between different species, called *symbiosis*. Symbiosis can be mutually beneficial (*mutualism*), or as (*parasitism*), only beneficial to one species but not mutually beneficial, as when fungi or micro-organisms infect humans and other species. Interestingly, there are micro-organisms that live in human digestive tracts that appear to be in a mutualistic relation with humans by aiding in the digestive process (Odum, 1971: 271–275).

This relies on the work of renowned ecologist and ecological theorist E. P. Odum, and I note of some of his ideas about the relevance of ecological evolution and human–environment interactions. Odum understood the relationships between different kinds of environments and ecosystems as a *compartment model* in which four broad types of natural settings are partitioned according to their biotic function and life cycle criteria. There are (1) environments with young, relatively immature, and rapidly growing ecosystems; (2) ones with more mature, diverse, or climax ecosystems that tend toward protective equilibrium; (3) compromise or multiple-use environments and ecosystems that combine both types and functions; and (4) urban-industrial environments that are relatively *abiotic* in relation to the other types. You can see these four types represented schematically in Figure 1.2.

The important point is that the growth of human settlements and communities obviously decreases the proportion of other types of environments and ecosystems at the expense of the more mature, protective ones. Human activity creates urban-industrial environments, with their vast sprawling growth and their great expansion of simplified growth ecosystems. This happens through the cutting of forests, the expansion of land for agriculture and other uses, and the increase of multiple-use ecosystems that combine some wilderness with fields, towns, or highways, among other factors.

The impact of human activity usually creates simplified-growth ecosystems by producing virtual *monocultures* (areas where primarily one type of organism grows). Whether cutting trees, plowing prairies for crops, or cultivating grass in a lawn, humans reduce the biological diversity of living things that exist in "wild" ecosystems. A field of corn or soy beans and your lawn (if it is mainly of one kind of grass) is such a monoculture. If you have had to maintain such a monoculture, you know that it takes a great deal of effort in weed pulling and requires herbicides and pesticides to keep other life forms from invading it. The *loss of biodiversity* in monocultures has its price, not only by the addition of chemicals that are very difficult for nature to recycle, but also by the fact that monocultures are much less robust and hardy than more diverse systems. They are notoriously more susceptible to damage by drought and diseases, such as sod webworm that kills blue grass, or the whole range of insect, fungi, and microbe infections that can decimate grain

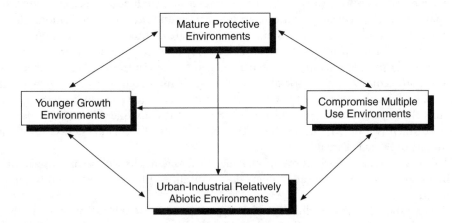

**FIGURE 1.2**   Compartment Model of Environments and Ecosystems According to Function and Life Cycle Criteria

*Source:* Based on Odum, 1971: 269.

crops and livestock monocultures. The Irish Potato Famine of the 1840s is an example of the devastation that can be caused by the collapse of an agricultural monoculture. A fungus ("blight") infection killed the Irish potato crop for several years, resulting in widespread starvation and civil disorders, and—importantly—triggering massive waves of Irish emigration to countries such as the United States, Canada, and Australia (Harper, 2007: 60, 203).

Odom's observations of the 1970s are still relevant: "Until we can determine more precisely how far we may safely go in expanding intensive agriculture and urban sprawl at the expense of the protective landscape, it will be good insurance to hold inviolable as much of the latter as possible" (1971: 270).

Is there a "saturation limit" for what, how, and how much of the biophysical environment can be appropriated for human use and still provide broadly positive conditions for social life for most of humanity? To what extent can we do this and still value and respect for its own sake the earth's rich and diverse genetic inheritance of species and ecosystems that resulted from 3 billion years of evolution? *Tough questions,* but important ones.

## SOCIOCULTURAL SYSTEMS

I noted the Irish Potato Famine of the 1840s to illustrate the biotic vulnerability of agricultural monocultures. The fact that a large number of persons of Irish descent are in the United States, Canada, and Australia partly because of this catastrophe demonstrates in a very graphic way the important connections between humans and the natural world. Humans and human societies are certainly embedded in the ecosphere, but, as is often noted, humans are also unique creatures among all others. Humans are social animals, a characteristic they share with other species, such as bees, gorillas, and dolphins.

For sociologists, a basic abstract organizing concept is the *social system,* which is like *ecosystems* for ecologists. You could simply note the structural units of social system, from small to large and inclusive (e.g., individuals, small groups, communities, bureaucracies, societies, world order), but that wouldn't be very enlightening, particularly because it ignores a whole dimension of human systems that most differentiate *Homo sapiens* from other species: *culture.* Even though the social animals mentioned live in social systems, they lack a cultural dimension. A *sociocultural system* is a network of interdependent actors (individuals, organizations, subsystems) that are in relatively stable patterns of interaction and intercommunication. They share cultural patterns (both material and symbolic), which are distinguishable from those of other such systems. If you are suspicious that I am not exactly on new ground, you are right; a human system is another specific version of the general system concept introduced earlier that is fundamental to both ecology and the social sciences. This is important because it means that for humans as well as other species (1) everything is ultimately connected to everything else, and therefore, (2) you can't ever do *just* one thing without some consequences for other parts of the systems in which you live. Table 1.1 shows the components of human systems, distinguishing some clusters of related elements.

This is a useful and fairly conventional analytical scheme. As will become apparent, however, things are not divided so neatly; others do it a bit differently; see Lenski and Nolan (1999) and Sanderson (1995).

Because the relevance of these human system elements or subsystems may not be quite obvious to you, I need to say a few things about them, particularly as they relate to understanding environmental issues. *First,* you may be wondering how some are different, particularly the difference between a nation state and a society. Today we usually think of them as the same, but they

| **TABLE 1.1** | Elements of Sociocultural Systems |
|---|---|
| *Culture* | worldviews<br>paradigms<br>Ideologies<br>knowledge, beliefs, values<br>symbols, language |
| *Social structure* | world-system<br>society<br>nation state<br>complex organizations (bureaucracies)<br>social stratification systems (based on economic class, ethnicity, kinship, or gender)<br>small groups<br>kinship systems<br>status-roles |
| *Material infrastructure* | wealth (tokens, wives, cattle, money)<br>material culture, subsistence technologies (plows, computers)<br>human population (size and characteristics)<br>human–environment relations<br>biophysical resources (land, forests, minerals, fish) |

really are not. Real nation states did not even exist much before the 1500s, but *society,* the most inclusive structural unit of human systems, is as old as are *H. sapiens.*[1] There are people, such as the Berbers of North Africa, who comprise a coherent society but who live in several North African nation states (Algeria, Mauritania), as do the Mohawks (whose "territory" straddles the U.S.–Canada border). *Second,* these elements are really not an evolutionary or developmental sequence. For the earliest known *H. sapiens,* and among the few scattered indigenous peoples of the world today, there *is* no operating society beyond the level of families or kinship systems, no larger communities, and no inequality beyond elementary status roles based on age and gender. Furthermore, an authentic world order that has the potential to knit nations and societies into a truly global system of sorts has been emerging for only about the last 500 years, and its features are not yet very clear. *Third,* there are some things left out. There are, obviously, *individual* human organisms, and there are *social networks* that are somewhere in between populations and organized groups in the number and strength of the system bonds between actors.

## Culture

Surely the most important distinction between *H. sapiens* and other species is the extent to which humans are cultural creatures. Nonhuman animal social behavior is more shaped by the behavioral instructions or codes carried in their genetic makeup—which interact with their environments in complex ways. Human behavior and environmental adaptation is more flexible, open-ended, and shaped by learning; in other words, it is cultural. *Culture* is the total learned way of life that people in groups share. You can think of it as a sort of humanly constructed software (to use a computer analogy) for what the world is like, for how people should relate to each other, and for how they ought to adapt and "make a living" in the biophysical environment. Since our genetic equipment gives us very little specification about any of this, it is fair to say that much of our behavior and social patterns are shaped by culture rather than by biology. Exactly how much is debatable, and this issue has been at the core of an intense—but not very productive—debate between evolutionary biologists, anthropologists, and sociologists for about a decade.[2] People do not always conform to cultural norms, but we all experience powerful social pressures to conform and often face social sanctions if we don't.

But culture is hard to classify by this three-part scheme (Table 1.1) because it has both symbolic and material dimensions. *Material* technology, for instance, includes the tools, factories, weapons, and computers that relate to economic subsistence. Underlying these "things" are ideas, plans, recipes for doing things, and the innovative processes that are part of *symbolic* culture. To continue the computer analogy, if material culture is the hardware or mainframes, symbolic culture is the software programs of human systems. Such technologies include all the ideas, formulas, tools, and gadgets that people use to convert raw biophysical material resources into goods and services that humans find useful. Viewed as part of the material infrastructure, they relate to "making a living" in the elemental sense of providing sufficient food, shelter, and clothing. But they also include a lot of other "stuff" unrelated to basic subsistence like pet rocks, toenail clippers, computers, and sociology texts, which have economic utilities that would be quite baffling to most humans who ever lived.

## Social Institutions

Social institutions are both left out *and* hard to classify by the foregoing scheme. They are nearly universal sociocultural formations, like families, economies, political systems, judicial systems, healthcare, and so on. Social institutions are both structural and cultural. That is, they include broadly established ideas, values, beliefs, technologies, and structural systems that address some enduring human concern related to collective survival. You can get a sense of the structural *and* cultural sides of institutions by thinking about families (groups organized around kinship). The operative structural units of American families, established by law and custom, are parents and their children (even though other relatives have an important legal and cultural standing). On the cultural side, again established by both law and custom, married spouses are two (only two) people of the opposite sex. They *ideally* exhibit an interaction style shaped by the values of positive affection (love) and trust, rather than by economic utility or relations of domination-submission. Children, normatively now not more than two or three, are to be valued intrinsically, and not as utilities for family economic or sexual exploitation. Does this picture represent the empirical reality of all families in the United States? Of course not. But social institutions are imperative normative "shoulds" that most people find hard to disagree with, supported as they are by powerful cultural customs and laws. Furthermore, this institutional template is very different from that of families in other cultures (as anthropologists have studied extensively). The point is that social institutions are as much cultural as structural.

## Social Structure

Elementary structural units of human systems are statuses and roles. Your *status* is the position or "rank" you occupy in a social system. *Status* is a structural term, and *role* is a behavioral or cultural one. The status-role concept is somewhat analogous to the way ecologists use the ideas of *ecological habitats* and *niches*—as the structural locations and functioning of organisms within an ecosystem. Furthermore, it is important for you to note that some other social animals, particularly primates, have almost human-like status-role systems. As our evolutionary cousins, primates (and some other mammals) live not as unorganized mobs but in relatively structured *rank-dominance hierarchies,* usually with the older males in charge of things.

## The Duality of Human Life

The cultural uniqueness of human beings has a profound implication. It results in what I take to be an existential dualism that underlies much of the debate about human–environment relationships, including quarrels about the seriousness of environmental problems. This duality, inherent in the human condition, can be stated simply:

> *On the one hand*—humans and human systems are unarguably embedded in the broader webs of life in the biosphere. We are one species among many, both in terms of our biological makeup and our ultimate dependence for food and energy provided by the earth.
>
> *On the other hand*—humans are the unique creators of technologies and socio-cultural environments that have singular power to change, manipulate, destroy, and sometimes transcend natural environmental limits. (Buttel, 1986: 338, 343)

Biologists and ecologists usually emphasize the first part of this duality, and social scientists typically place more emphasis on the second part. You probably recognize that *both* statements are true in some complicated and partial sense. Yet it makes a great deal of practical difference which assumption we use as a guide to action, choices, and policies. Since the industrial revolution, the second assumption—*humans as an exceptional species*—has been the dominant assumption and viewpoint. It is important to note that humans act on the basis of such viewpoints rather than on the basis of what the world "really is." This is a subtle but important point that requires some elaboration.

## Worldviews and Cognized Environments

There is obviously a reality external to human beings that we live within. But human choices and policies are more directly related to our *definitions* of that reality than to what reality "really" is. In other words, human social behavior is more directly related to symbolic constructions and definitions of situations than by external environments per se. People *exist* in natural environments, but they *live and act* in worlds mediated and constructed by cultural symbols (Berger and Luckmann, 1976; Schutz, 1932/1967; Thomas, 1923).

Yes, there is an external biophysical environment independent of how people think about it, but people act on the basis of what they *think* the environment to be. To differentiate this imagined environment from the "real environment," scholars have invented a rather awkward term, *cognized environment*, to mean their human definitions and interpretations of the biophysical environment. The very notion of nature itself is a way of *cognizing* the environment that didn't exist much before the eighteenth century. As a cultural conception and idea, nature was invented mainly by English intellectuals in the eighteenth century, particularly Romantic artists, writers, poets, and literati (such as Wordsworth and Ruskin). They sought a metaphor to contrast the "good" pristine natural state with the (presumed) evil artificiality of the cities, mines, and factories of the industrial world. Thus the notion of nature that has come down to us was originally part of the Romantic discourse and critique of the invasion and destruction of all that was "natural" by the barbaric machines of the industrial system (Harrison, 1993: 300; Fischer, 1976, chap. 2). "Mother Nature" is a more obviously gendered and anthropomorphized cognition of the biophysical environment (*anthropomorphized* means that something nonhuman is understood in human terms).

The *worldview* that people share is their totality of cultural and beliefs and belief systems about the world and reality. It is a broader concept than their *ideologies*, meaning the parts of worldviews that people purposely use to justify action and choices. Examples of ideology would include individualism, nationalism, or environmentalism. *Cognized environments* are also components of worldviews that are obviously related to ideologies about the environment.

## ECOSYSTEM AND SOCIOCULTURAL EVOLUTION: HUMAN ECOLOGY

This chapter began by discussing the components of human systems and continued to discuss some distinctive things about human experience of themselves in relation to their biophysical environments: their dualistic perception of themselves as a species in nature and capability of transcending environmental limitations, the importance of worldviews, ideologies, and cognized environments. Continuing the parallel with ecosystems, I turn to the evolution of human systems, and will highlight some similarities and differences between biological and sociocultural evolution. After long neglect, some scholars are reviving evolutionary thinking about human systems that has the potential to link large- and small-scale processes, explain the emergence of complexity, and link social science to biology without misleading reductionism (Dietz et al., 1990: 155; Maryanski, 1998).

Ecological theorists (Lotka and Odum) argued that ecosystems evolve as different species compete for available energy in the physical environment and selectively survive. If uninterrupted, the result, over time, is a larger, more complex, and inclusive structure of species connected in food chain niches and often in symbiotic relations that range from mutualistic to parasitic. In a parallel way, sociocultural evolution proceeds when humans compete for control over limited resources. As they do so, some persons and groups develop more efficient material infrastructures. Complex relationship systems of statuses and roles emerge that parallel niches in ecosystems. These relationships, and the exchanges of goods, labor, control, loyalty, and symbols on which they are based, parallel, it seems to me, *symbiotic relationships* in the biological world. *First,* there are social *exchanges of reciprocity*, which produce egalitarian, mutual benefit relationships in nonhierarchical contexts like mutualism. *Second,* there are social *exchanges of redistribution,* wherein goods and services are shifted "upward" to persons or centers that reallocate them (like profits, plunder, and taxes). These exchanges result in relationships that are asymmetrical in terms of power and equity, and stratified relationships (Polanyi, cited in Rogers, 1994: 45). Reciprocal exchanges predominated among hunter-gatherers, whereas redistributive exchanges became more pronounced as human systems evolved in more complex systems (what we called "civilizations"). Redistributive exchange bears some resemblance to the asymmetry of parasitic and predator–prey relationships.

With the emergence of industrialism, a *third* kind of exchange transformed social systems. Production for *use* became progressively eclipsed by production for exchange for other goods and services. Even human labor became a "commodity for exchange" at a fixed monetary rate. Money as finance capital became the premier material resource of industrial societies. These processes happened within the third form of exchange, in *exchange markets.* Unlike the two mentioned earlier (reciprocity and redistribution), in exchange markets social relationships became embedded in the economy instead of vice versa (Polanyi, cited in Rogers, 1994: 45).

Moving from hunter-gatherers to industrialism, the growing complexity of human technological systems exhibits another parallel with the evolution of ecosystems. Large-scale and complex market exchanges, particularly in industrial societies, dramatically increased occupation specialization (the "division of labor") and other kinds of social differentiation. That is analogous to *speciation,* the evolution of different biological species that use different niches of an environment. Social differentiation represents a kind of *quasispeciation*. In this process, we H. *sapiens,* though remaining a single biological species, use the environment as if we were many species. Different institutions, industries, and occupations use the same biophysical environment in different ways for resources important to their specialized purposes. Thus in a highly complex social order equipped with modern technology, human beings become a *multiniche* species (Hutchinson, 1965; Stephan, 1970; Catton, 1993/94). Why is knowing this important? Because it should enable you to understand why people in modern societies have difficulty cooperating on problems of truly common interest without becoming sidetracked by their "special interests."

I hope you can see some parallels between the evolution of ecosystems and sociocultural evolution, but you can't carry these parallels too far, because there are important differences as well. While all animals communicate—that is, transmit behaviorally relevant information—only humans do so extensively through the use of *cultural symbols*. *H. sapiens* share this symbolic capacity with our evolutionary primate cousins, but that of humans is of such greater magnitude that it makes us, in effect, unique among animals. The communication mechanism of other species is largely genetically programmed and innate, unlike the meaning of human symbols, which are *arbitrary* and depend on a consensus of symbol language users (Sanderson, 1995: 32–33).

In biological evolution, the units of transmission and selection are individuals and particular genes that survive (or do not) between generations. In sociocultural evolution, however, the units of transmission and selection may be individuals, a society, or its subsystems. But the generation of sociocultural novelty along with its intergenerational selection and transmission is Lamarckian rather than genetic (Jean Baptiste Larmarck, Darwin's most famous predecessor, argued that animals could inherit learned behaviors and characteristics). Moreover, "symbol systems can blend, and components can be added to or subtracted from culture, thereby making it difficult to predict what is being inherited or transformed" (Maryanski, cited in Freese, 1998: 29). In this sense, Maryanski argues that human systems do not evolve, but they do change and develop. Most scholars retain the idea of sociocultural evolution but emphasize the accumulation of complex contingencies (such as the generation of novel forms, their transmission and selection over time), which is closer to the biological meaning of the term rather than fixed "stages" of development, common in the early history of the idea (Burns and Dietz, 1992).

These considerations led scholars to abandon earlier strongly deterministic approaches to the evolution of human systems in which environmental and material forces were thought to determine everything else. Earlier generations of anthropologists and geographers coined the notion of *environmental possibilism* for more flexible approaches. These models posit that material and biophysical factors are broad limiting factors for particular human systems, but the most immediate and particular causes of many social and cultural changes are *other* social and cultural factors. Anthropologist Julian Steward, who rekindled interest in sociocultural evolution, used the term *culture core* to describe a society's technology and subsistence economy (what I earlier referred to as material infrastructure). The biophysical environment has direct interacting effects solely on this culture core, but only indirectly with other elements of human systems. Relationships are two-way interactive ones with feedback, or *cybernetic* ones (Kormondy and Brown, 1998: 45–47). See Figure 1.3.

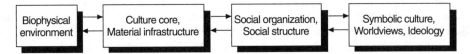

**FIGURE 1.3**  Human Ecology Theory: Relationships Between the Biophysical Environment and Sociocultural System Elements

It is important to note that sociocultural evolution is not a uniform story of more inclusive and technically complex systems. *Devolution* occurred periodically when complex systems like early civilizations collapsed and resulted in smaller, simpler systems. This discussion of ecosystem and sociocultural evolution is not a thorough discussion of sociocultural development, but it has mentioned hunter-gatherer and industrial societies. In what follows I discuss industrial societies in more depth, both because we live in industrial societies and because they are so important in understanding contemporary environmental problems.

## Industrial Societies

Industrialization began about 300 years ago in Europe. Like the invention of agriculture, industrialization depended upon some key discoveries and technologies—first in the textile industry in England—that substituted machine production for human and animal labor. Industrial production depended not only on new machines, but also on new energy sources to power them—water power, steam engines, hydroelectric power, petroleum, and so forth. Like the agricultural revolution, the *industrial revolution* eventually produced a quantum leap in the power to accumulate economic surpluses, and in the scale and complexity of human societies.

Because the new engines and machines were large and expensive, centralized production in factories began to supplant the decentralized "cottage" craft production of earlier times. People began to migrate to cities in unprecedented numbers, not only because the factory jobs were located there, but because the application of industrial techniques to agriculture—such as the introduction of farm machinery and new inorganic chemical fertilizers—reduced the demand for labor in rural areas. In industrial cities, wealth and power began to be associated not so much with control of land—as in agricultural societies—but with ownership and control of industrial enterprises. A new class system based on industrial wealth rather than the ownership of land began to emerge. Increasingly labor became a cash commodity rather than a subsistence activity, with shares as taxes. Work became increasingly separated from family life and bound up with emerging bureaucratic systems of production. Modern complex organizations (bureaucracies) and nation states were significant new social formations of industrialism.

Like the agricultural revolution before it, industrialism stimulated a whole basket of cultural and economic innovations, in transportation and communication, and in medicine, sanitation, and disease control. Prominent among these innovations was the acceleration of the rate of scientific discovery and the application of science-based technologies to economic production. These developments, particularly improved disease control and the rapid accumulation of food stocks, allowed unprecedented population growth and an extension of the human life span. Unlike agricultural societies, in which overpopulation, ecological collapse, and plagues kept global population rates modest (up to about the 1600s), in industrial societies rapid improvements in economic technology and disease control resulted in positive feedback between population growth and accumulating wealth. I will return to population-environment issues in Chapter Five.

However, as with the agricultural revolution, it is arguable whether industrialism improved the life of the ordinary person, at least until after the turn of the twentieth century. Early industrialism as observed by both Charles Dickens and Karl Marx was, for the vast majority, an uprooting from farm life into a bleak new life of misery, industrial hazards, and exploitation in early industrial sweatshops. But, in the longer term, improvements in health and living standards diffused from social elites to ordinary people in the large middle and working classes of industrial societies, if not to those at the bottom. Some scholars argue that after the turn of the twentieth century, industrial societies became more equalitarian than historic agricultural societies in terms of both political rights and the distribution of material well-being (Lenski and Nolan, 1999). Yet this is a slippery argument. Most people live longer, are materially better off, and have more individual freedoms. But have they traded overt forms of social domination and oppression for more subtle forms of control and pervasive alienation unique to the industrial world? Critics of urban industrial societies argue that they have separated humans from nature, destroyed or weakened the bonds of traditional communities (neighborhood, kin), weakened our sense of civic community, and made us dependent on vast international systems (like market economies and treaty organizations) that elicit neither our loyalty nor comprehension. Critics argue urban industrialism produces fragmented ("autonomous") individuals and families with little connection to community at several levels (Young, 1994).

For some time now, a *world-system* of nations with its connected *world market economy* has been evolving. These developments, along with shared cultural traits and aspirations among people in many parts of the world, constitute what is commonly called *globalization*. The important point is that because a world-system of sorts is emerging, there are few hunter-gatherers or agricultural people anywhere on the earth who remain untouched by the expansion of the industrial societies. Although the diffusion of industrial technologies, consumer goods, and culture has been uneven, it is now found everywhere. For better or worse, Coca-Cola and Marlboro cigarettes are found in every Chinese village. The polar Eskimos (Inuit people)—those that weren't killed off by smallpox and measles—now zoom around the tundra hunting with snowmobiles and repeating rifles. Gone forever are igloos and dogsleds (except for sport), and their children are now plagued by dental caries from refined sugar in their diets, a problem virtually unknown when they were pristine hunter-gatherers.

**HUMAN–ENVIRONMENT RELATIONS IN INDUSTRIAL SOCIETIES**   Like agricultural societies, industrialism dramatically increased human use and withdrawals from the biophysical resource base. The key change in the human–environment relationship was the use of relatively cheap fossil fuels that supported industrialization, more intensive agriculture, and urbanization. This involved much more extensive exploitation of the physical and biotic resource base. It also produced more, and more difficult, pollution as production gradually shifted from natural materials (wood, paper, cotton), which are environmentally benign compared to synthetic materials that break down slowly in ecosystems and may be toxic to humans and wildlife (such as stainless steel, DDT, dioxin, and plastics—chemicals that Mother Nature never knew!).

No evidence yet exists of the weakening or total collapse of an industrial society—for ecological reasons (abundant such evidence exists for historic agricultural societies). This is because the industrial environmental degradation has so far been more than offset by increased investment and technological inputs. Whether this state of affairs will continue to be true in the future is arguable. It is the "big question" I return to in Chapter Six. Here, I note that it took the Copan Mayans more than 400 years to collapse, and much longer for Mesopotamians. By comparison, industrial societies have only been around for about 300 years, and the growth of world population and technological prowess means that our biophysical impacts are on a much larger scale than in historic agricultural systems.

**THE DOMINANT WORLDVIEWS OF INDUSTRIAL SOCIETIES**   If the main cognized environment of agricultural societies was that of a garden to be tended, modified, and dominated by

Creating an agricultural monoculture by spraying herbicides on a winter wheat crop in the United Kingdom.

humans, that of industrial societies is a dramatic extension of this concept. It was amplified particularly by cultural developments of the European Enlightenment period (seventeenth and eighteenth centuries), which emphasized empirical reasoning, science, the world as a giant cosmic mechanism, and the ability of humans to rationally control nature through systematic innovation and experimentation. The earth and other species became cognized as a huge *resource base* and facility to be used, developed, and managed for human needs and desires. Unlike agriculturalists, industrial people not only tended the garden, they also attempted to remake it.

Many scholars have attempted to describe the Dominant Western Worldview (DWV) of industrial societies. Although they differ about the details, they agree that industrial DWVs amplify the second part of the human duality already mentioned: that humans, by virtue of culture and technology, have a unique power to change, manipulate, and sometimes to transcend natural environmental limits. In one way or another, most scholars think that DWVs of industrial societies have the following themes:

- Low evaluation of nature for its own sake.
- Compassion mainly for those near and dear.
- The assumption that maximizing wealth is important and risks are acceptable in doing so.
- The assumption of no physical ("real") limits to growth that can't be overcome by technological inventiveness.
- The assumption that modern society, culture, and politics are basically okay.
  (Milbrath, 1989: 119).

For other versions see Dunlap (1983, 2000a); Harman (1979); Olsen, Lodwick, and Dunlap (1992: 18); and Pirages (1977).

Some described this worldview as the DWV of free-market or capitalist industrial societies. But it is obvious that the former communist nations of Eastern Europe and the USSR damaged their environments to a much greater degree than did Western market economies.

Most now believe that it applies generically to industrial societies. In view of the emergence of the world-system of nations and world market economy, it is also fair to note that this DWV does not affect only the more developed countries of the northern hemisphere. Hardly anyone in the world today is immune from it. People in the less developed countries want the things of industrialism (TV, autos, vaccinations, Coca-Cola, and cigarettes). The industrial DWV is diffusing rapidly around the world, where the *desire* for progress is defined largely in terms of increasing material consumption, security, and well-being. This is true even in the poorest less developed countries, where material and health standards are now very low and misery is widespread.

But, it is also important to recognize diversity and change. The DWV does not control everything—there are competing worldviews—and now it is obviously in some kind of flux and transition. Since the beginning of the twentieth century, there *was* concern in the United States about maintaining natural environments (for both utilitarian and aesthetic reasons), which produced turn-of-the-century conservation movements. These movements led to the establishment of protected public lands, national forests, and parks. Similarly, there was concern among agricultural agencies about soil preservation and erosion, which continues today. But increasing popular environmental and ecological awareness was stimulated most directly from environmental problems and *environmental social movements* beginning in the 1960s, in the United States as well as other nations. I will return to environmental movements in Chapter Eight. They are connected with a rise in "ecological thinking" and a change in the DWV just described.

## ENVIRONMENTAL SOCIAL SCIENCES

Ecology has been a part of biology since the 1930s, but environmental and ecological social sciences are newer. Their contemporary forms grew mainly in the 1960s and 1970s as scholarly responses to the environmental problems, conflicts, movements, and popular consciousness of those decades. But in fact the social sciences have a long and ambivalent intellectual history in how they think about the environmental embeddedness of human systems. Today almost all social science fields deal meaningfully with environmental issues, almost all contribute to "environmental social science," including anthropology (e.g., in this chapter and Chapter Four), demography and human geography (e.g., in Chapters Five and Six), social psychology and behavioral science (e.g., in Chapters Four and Six), and political science (e.g., in Chapter Seven). Here I discuss only two, beginning with economics, because economic analysis is so central to contemporary discourses, and then sociology, which has important integrating perspectives to frame human-environmental issues.

### Economic Thought

The founders of the field of economics all assumed that the earth's biophysical resources (land, minerals, and living things) were the necessary basis for the economic production of useful goods and services. But, beginning with *Adam Smith* (1723–1790), they argued that *labor*, not nature, was the major source of economic value. Smith argued that the operation of private unregulated *markets* was the best natural mechanism to determine the *economic value* of goods and services and wages. Smith distinguished between market value and moral or social value, separating the latter from economics and thereby initiating the tendency of economic thought to treat the economy in abstraction from the rest of the sociocultural world.

Smith argued that the desire for profits and the "unseen hand" of unregulated markets would produce the best possible economic and social world. It would create a system that reflected "real" economic values and encourage the use of investment, labor, and technology in ways that increase production in response to consumer desires. Smith's view was buoyant and optimistic, reflecting a bustling and successful nation of English traders, shopkeepers, and merchants on the eve of the real industrial expansion that was to come. In the next decades, that optimism would fade. *David Ricardo* (1772–1823), for instance, argued that economic growth and the desire for profits would lead people to bring even marginal resources, such as poor and infertile land, into production. As population grew, it would "become necessary to push the margin of cultivation further" (Heilbroner, 1985: 95). His message was ecological but also moral, for he argued that in the long term only the fortunate landlords stood to gain as their holdings rose in value—not workers struggling to make a living or enterprising capitalists laboring to maintain profits.

*Thomas Malthus* (1776–1834) argued that increasing production and improved living conditions would lead to population growth. But he argued that population grows exponentially, while material resources such as food supplies increase in an arithmetic way.[3] Malthus predicted that after the bloom of initial growth would come the inexorable regression to scarcity, bringing with it the "population checks" of misery, famine, pestilence, war, and social chaos. Malthus not only was an influential figure in economics but also provided an early link among economic, demographic, and ecological thinking.

*Karl Marx* (1818–1883), like others, argued that nature was an important factor in production but that social factors, in particular, the "ownership of the means of production" (land, capital, factories) was more important. Like Ricardo and Malthus, he saw chaos at the end of the capitalist era. But he argued that its sources were to be found not in the demographic-economic calculus of Malthus, but in inherent and eventually unmanageable conflicting material interests between economic classes of workers and the owners of the means of production. He believed that their struggle over wages and profits would eventually be resolved in the apocalyptic and revolutionary transition to socialism. The creative intellectual accomplishment of these classic thinkers was to move from anecdote to science, to comprehend economic markets as law-abiding systems whose dynamics could be understood and—perhaps someday—predicted. In this quest, they were only partly successful.

As prophets, one has to admit that they were all a bust: We have not realized the capitalist paradise of Smith; Ricardo's landowners do not dominate the industrial world (certainly not at the expense of finance capital); capitalism has been able to politically contain the apocalyptic demise that Marx predicted (which ironically happened to state socialism in our time); Malthus certainly underestimated the amount of food that could be produced and the number of people who could be supported. But the greatest irony of all was that even though their views gave shape to modern economic thought, they all failed to comprehend the expansionary dynamic of industrial capitalism. They all thought that the growth they were witnessing would be short-lived and that a "dull" steady state economy or systemwide collapse was only a few decades away (Heilbroner, 1985: 305–306). In that assumption, they were dead wrong.

More than the classic thinkers, contemporary economists emphasize the second part of the human-environmental dualism previously described. *Neoclassical theory,* the dominant perspective, views the economy as a circular flow of investment, production, distribution, and consumption, understood in abstraction from the natural environment and rest of social life as well. To put it starkly, in the neoclassical view the economy contains the ecosystem (as resource bases and pollution sinks). Surely a natural scientist would put it the other way around—that the ecosystem contains the economy as well as other human institutions. Neoclassical theory implies that environmental and resource problems cannot be very important ones because the economy is a closed system with a pendulum-like movement between production and consumption. This model is abstracted from the environment: within which the money economy is actually embedded, and there are no connections between money flows and biophysical reality (Rees, 2002: 254).

This prevailing economic model relies on the mechanics of free and open markets to ensure environmental sustainability. The late professor Julian Simon was the most ebullient proponent of the doctrine of "near-perfect sustainability," whereby

> Technology exists now to produce in virtually inexhaustible quantities just about all the products made by nature . . . We have in our hand now . . . the technology to feed, clothe, and supply energy to an ever-growing population for the next seven billion years. (1996: 342)

They maintain that the technological advance will outpace resource scarcity over the long run and ecological services can be replaced by new technologies. Economic markets work the same to make money and determine prices whether resources are plentiful or scarce. Nor do social values or questions of justice intrude: Markets work whether you are growing corn, producing health services, selling heroin, cleaning up toxic wastes, or selling slaves. Neoclassical economics deals extensively with "efficient" allocation, secondarily with distribution, and not at all with matters of scale. Although construing the world in narrow and abstract terms, neoclassical economics has become enormously influential in industrial societies in shaping debates about social, political, and environmental policy. This is true partly, I think, because the theory appears more objective by deliberately ignoring questions of human values and political and ethical considerations. But these, I think, are important human questions and considerations that really ought not to be "ruled out of court" (Costanza et al., 1995: 60, 80; Daly and Townsend, 1993: 3–6).

Some economists were concerned with environmental resources issues for several decades without recasting the neoclassical theory significantly. But by the 1970s, a small and growing band of economists were trying to recast economic theory by finding ways of incorporating both *nature* and *human values* into their economic calculus. They began by viewing the economy not as a separate isolated system but, rather, as an inextricably integrated, completely contained, and wholly dependent subsystem of the ecosphere. In contrast to neoclassical economics, *ecological economics* sees the economy as an open, growing, wholly dependent subsystem of a materially closed, not-growing, finite ecosphere.

> The biophysical fact is that through the technology-driven expansions of the economy, human beings have become the dominant consumer organism in the world's major ecosystems . . . This poses a serious challenge to the mainstream belief that economic activity is not seriously limited by biophysical constraints. (Rees, 2002: 259)

See Figure 1.4.

Ecological economists have addressed a new set of problems and dilemmas that are outside the boundaries of conventional economic analyses. Here are two illustrations: (1) How can values ("prices") be assigned to goods that are held in common (the "commons") that are used by many and owned by none, such as the atmosphere, rivers, oceans, and public space? They cannot be privately owned in small pieces that can be meaningfully bought or sold, hence there *is* no market

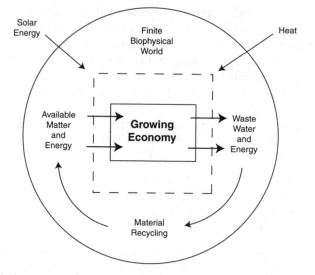

**FIGURE 1.4**  Ecological Economics: Growth in a Finite World

for them, and therefore no prices to limit use. The widely recognized problem is that we tend to overuse common as opposed to privately held goods (Hardin, 1968, 1993). (2) How can economic analysis incorporate and assign responsibility for the variety of environmental and social *externalities,* that is, the real overhead or human costs incurred in the production process that are borne not by particular producers or consumers but by third parties, the larger social community, or the environment (Clark, 1991: 404)?

Ecological economics challenges the article of faith of neoclassical economists that human ingenuity and technology will always overcome environmental limits and ecosystem capacities. It also recognizes important matters of value that can't be reduced to price efficiency: "A good distribution is one that is *just* or *fair,* or at least one in which the degree of inequality is limited within some acceptable range" (Costanza et al., 1995: 80). How much inequality is just? As you can see, not only *nature* but also *human values* and *culture* have been reintroduced center stage.

Ecological economists are busy tinkering with ways to "price" social and esthetic externalities, finding ways of circumventing "commons problems" and producing measures of human well-being broader than those that simply measure how much money a nation produces (e.g., gross national product figures). They are also rethinking tax and subsidy policy to reverse their historically damaging environmental impacts and ways of avoiding onerous regulation.

Beyond these efforts economists have contributed two major ideas. First, *emissions trading schemes* are useful for making policy: Producers of wastes and emissions are assigned tradable "credits" for less environmentally damaging production. These credits can then be traded or auctioned (for money) to greater polluters (per unit of product). Emissions trading systems try to reverse the usual economic benefits that go to polluting firms, which make money by simply dumping pollutants into the environment. Such schemes have significantly induced producers to reduce the production of some toxic wastes in the United States, and are under discussion as a method to address global climate change by rewarding nations for reducing their production of greenhouse gases (known as "cap" and "trade" policies) (Tietenberg, 2002). Second, *ecological modernization* is a broad theory arguing that while modernizing, firms could become more efficient by mimicking an ecosystem with lots of feedback systems and recycling, for instance by using wastes from one process to supply or fuel another economic process. It is an alternative to only extracting raw materials, consuming them, and throwing them away. Ecological modernization, originated among economists and business leaders and elaborated by ecological economists and environmental sociologists, is now an important framework for research and policy (Mol, 2003; Mol and Sonnenfeld, 2000). I will return to these issues in Chapters Six and Seven.

## Sociological Thought

By the 1880s sociological thinking was taking shape across the English Channel in France and Germany. In vast oversimplification, the classic formulations in sociology can be understood in the work of three paramount figures: Karl Marx, Emile Durkheim, and Max Weber. Like the classical thinkers of economics, they sought to establish social analysis by *dissociating* it from the fashionable biological determinism of the day that used biological analogies to understand social phenomena (Buttel, 1986: 340). Classic sociological thinkers did not totally ignore natural and environmental factors, but were ambivalent and cautious about their influence on social structure and processes.

But when the environment became a widely recognized American problem in the 1960s and '70s (such as with air and water quality, urban pollution, and toxic wastes), some analysts turned to the sociology of environmental issues, and about how people perceived and related to them. Some wondered why sociologists were so reluctant to treat physical and environmental variables as important influences on society and culture. In a series of groundbreaking papers, Dunlap and Catton maintained that sociologists had unwittingly adopted a scientific paradigm that prevented them from doing so.

Philosopher of science Thomas Kuhn developed the notion of scientific paradigms to describe the mental image of scientists that guided their theory and research in particular fields (1970). A *paradigm* is a set of implicit assumptions about the "way the world works" or a "lens" through which scholars view their subject and practice their craft. It is not a theory (about relationships between variables) but rather a "fundamental image of the subject matter representing a broad consensus within a discipline"(Ritzer, 1975: 7). Catton and Dunlap suggested that the dominant paradigm in sociology was shaped—not surprisingly—by their own classical theories and the DWV of industrial and Western society (Catton and Dunlap, 1978; Dunlap and Catton, 2002: 332). They called it the *Human Exemptionalism Paradigm* (HEP) because it assumed that humans are unique among species and that we are exempt from the power of environmental forces.

- Humans are unique among the earth's creatures, for they have culture.
- Culture can vary almost infinitely and can change much more rapidly than biological traits.
- Thus, many human differences are socially induced rather than inborn; they can be socially altered, and inconvenient differences can be eliminated.
- Thus, cultural accumulation means that progress can continue without limit, making all social problems ultimately solvable.

Critical of the notion of human exemptionalism, Catton and Dunlap urged sociologists to "get over it" and move toward another paradigm that would facilitate taking environmental variables seriously in their studies, which they termed the *New Ecological Paradigm* (NEP), with the assumptions contrary to HEP:

- Humans have exceptional characteristics, but they remain one among many species that are interdependent in ecosystems.
- Humans are shaped not only by social and cultural forces, but also by cause, effect, and feedback linkages in the web of nature.
- Humans live in a finite biophysical environment that imposes potent restraints on human affairs.
- Although the powers derived from human inventiveness may seem to extend carrying capacity limits, ecological laws cannot be repealed. (Catton and Dunlap, 1978: 42–43)

When sociologists began to create an environmental sociology, they "mined" the ideas of their classical thinkers (where else could they begin?). Classic sociological theorists, even though underemphasizing the role of natural world as potent in the shaping and containing of social phenomena, nonetheless created perspectives that had seminal ideas for environmental sociology. For *Marx*, there was a materialist view of reality, which included the notion of a nature–society "metabolism" (Foster, 1999). *Durkheim* used biological analogies to understand societies, even though he rejected the biological and psychological determinism of social phenomena. *Weber* conducted research about natural-resource (or "environmental") factors as shaping differences in power among social groups and classes (Buttel, 2002: 39; Buttel, 1986: 340–343). How did environmental sociology develop?

## The Greening of Social Theory and Sociology

*Karl Marx* was an influential scholar whose ideas are today claimed—or *disclaimed,* as the case may be—by scholars in many fields. Among his multiple critiques of early capitalism, Marx noted that pervasive social conflict processes resulted in growing concentration of ownership of land and productive resources (including money), as well as classes of wealthy and poor, with decisive political control by the wealthy. In his view, the dominant ideas and values, laws, philosophies, and worldviews—in other words *culture*—simply represent the material interests of the dominant economic classes. It is fair to mention again that, like the other early political-economic thinkers discussed, Marx was a failure as a prophet. His notion of the impending utopia through triumphant worker revolutions was in obvious error, given the events of our times. Even so, his ideas about the nature and dynamics of human societies retain considerable appeal.

Shorn of utopian prophecies, the contemporary heirs of Marxian thought typically identify their perspectives as *conflict theories,* which argue that the most important societal dynamics are diverse processes by which the subsystems and classes in society come into conflict over control of limited material resources *and* the symbolic rewards of society. In many developing societies, material resources still mean biophysical resources like land and minerals, but in industrial societies, they become *money* as an abstract indicator of economic value. Moreover, as Max Weber pointed out in his critique of Marx, conflict can be about control of the symbols of prestige and social honor (who wins Academy Awards, Olympic Gold, or Nobel Prizes?), as well as material interests.

Through various forms of conflict and power struggles, society's subsystems attempt to protect or enhance their control of resources and values. These processes periodically exhibit visible tensions and conflict, resulting in inequalities of power and resources that biologists would call a *dominance hierarchy* and social scientists would call a *social stratification system.* Even so, the ability of one part to dominate the system is limited by the others with which they must contend, and society itself is likely to be controlled by a coalition of the most powerful subunits. Both social stability and change derive from such ongoing competition and conflict (Collins, 1975; Olsen, 1968: 151).

Observing that large corporate organizations are important features of modern free market societies, Allan Schnaiberg and his colleagues developed a *conflict theory* of human–environment interaction. They argue that many social analyses of environmental problems have paid too much attention to consumption and too little to the dynamic of production. Competition makes higher profitability a key to corporate survival, and firms must continually grow to produce profits and attract investments. This imperative for continual growth becomes a *treadmill of production* in which each new level of growth requires future growth, and growth in production requires the stimulation of growth in consumption. The contradiction is that *economic expansion is socially desirable, but ecological disruption is its necessary consequence.* Environmental disruption limits further economic expansion. New technology may introduce efficiencies that reduce the environmental impacts per unit produced, but continued increase in total consumption offsets this effect. The deeper threat of the treadmill may not lie in technologies that pollute, but in the competitive logic of economic growth without limit (Schnaiberg and Gould, 1994: 53). Governments are in the ambivalent situation of being expected to encourage economic growth, pay the costs of environmental disruption, and regulate environmental abuse. The first of these outcomes is of overwhelming *political* importance.

Schnaiberg and colleagues propose a *societal-environmental dialectic* as the most likely pattern of change:

1. *The economic synthesis:* The system of addressing the contradiction between economic expansion and environmental disruption in favor of maximizing growth without addressing ecological problems.
2. *The managed scarcity synthesis:* In which there is an attempt to control only the most pernicious environmental problems that threaten health or further production by regulation; governments appear to be doing more than they really are (the situation of U.S. environmental regulation policies since the 1970s).
3. *The ecological synthesis:* Major efforts to reduce environmental degradation through specific controls over treadmill production and consumption institutions directed specifically to that end. Curtailment would produce an economy so that production and consumption would be sustainable from the use of renewable resources. This is a hypothetical case with no known examples; it would emerge only when the disruption of the environment is so severe that the political forces would emerge to support it. (Buttel, 1986: 346–347; Buttel, 2002; Schnaiberg, 1980; Schnaiberg and Gould, 1994)

Conflict-based processes that result in such agreements or syntheses may result in different outcomes: (1) the most powerful entities perpetuate the status quo and enhance their domination, (2) a prolonged stalemate occurs between dominant and contending parts of the system, or (3) significant change takes place that redistributes power, wealth, and privilege. *In most historic moments, the first outcome is most likely.*

You can see the relevance of this, as a NEP-oriented conflict theory of human–environment relations. There are others. See, for instance, Roberts and Grimes (1999) and Goldfrank, Goodman, and Szaz (1999). The titles are telling; for instance, the paper by Roberts and Grimes is entitled "Extending the World-System to the Whole System: Toward a Political Economy of the Biosphere."

Unlike Marx, *Emile Durkheim* (1858–1917) was engaged in establishing sociology as a distinct academic field. The distinctive element of Durkheim's sociology was his emphasis on culture and cultural values (that he came to call "collective representations") as the basic integrative and binding moral force in human societies. He was greatly influenced by the evolutionary thinking of Darwin and the used analogies between biological system and social systems to understand social relations; but, as noted earlier, he vehemently rejected the fashionable "biolologism" of his day (which alleged that biological factors determined everything else), as well as geographic and other environmental determinisms. Durkheim also rejected "great man" theories of history, arguing that society and culture were "sui generis," that is, self-generating systems with their own structure and dynamics. In doing so, he undoubtedly contributed to the dominance of the HEP among later sociologists.

For Durkheim, culture was the most basic force for solidarity in the social world, and he understood human social evolution abstractly as a transition from simple and homogenous systems with powerfully binding cultural rules (*mechanical solidarity*) to complex and heterogeneous systems with weaker and less binding cultural rules (*organic solidarity*). You can get a concrete sense of this by considering the long evolutionary history of the transition from hunter-gatherers to agricultural "empires," and then to complex industrial societies.

Yet there is a germ of ecological thinking in Durkheim's ideas. Writing at a time when the ideas of Malthus and Marx were in fashion, Durkheim rejected both of their apocalyptic predictions. He argued, to the contrary, that increased population density and the intensification of the struggle over scarce resources were important antecedents to industrialism and the complex division of labor in industrial societies. This increasingly complex division of labor would, he thought, increase the adaptability of more populous and dense societies to their environments by decreasing direct competition over resources and causing cultural innovation—such as science and bureaucracies—that would redefine and effectively expand resources. "The oculist does not struggle with the psychiatrist, nor the shoemaker with the hatter or the cabinet maker, nor the physicist with the chemist, etc." (1893/1964: 262). Occupational specialization in industrial capitalism would produce a "quasi-speciation" much like bottom dwellers and canopy dwellers in tropical rainforest ecosystems, which would not directly compete for the same resources. He thought, in contrast to Marx, that industrialism would mitigate class conflict by reducing scarcity. In his view, the major problems of industrialism would stem from the weakening (cultural) bonds between groups in an increasingly complex division of labor—resulting in rootlessness and cultural confusion (anomie).

Sociologist William Catton contends that Durkheim misread both Darwin and contemporary ecology. The result of the growth of social complexity Durkheim could observe in his time was not a "mutualism of interdependent specialists," but rather a web of unequal power-dependent class relations more akin to "parasitism" that Marx observed (Catton, 1997: 89–138). I'm not sure how devastating this critique is to Durkheimian thought. Although class relations in modern capitalist societies are vastly unequal, they are more equalitarian with regard to both resources and rights than preindustrial ones, as in the empires of the ancient world. Perhaps the point is moot: Predator–prey and host–parasite relations can be symbiotically stable, even if not equitable. Well-adapted predators do not decimate their populations of prey, and a well-adapted parasite doesn't quickly kill its host.

*Functionalist theories* are the descendents of Durkheim's ideas. They assume that humans live in sociocultural *systems* that, like all systems, have parts or *subsystems* that work or *function* to keep the entire system going (as the complex division of labor sustains industrial capitalism). To get a sense of this, try a mental experiment: What kinds of processes (functions) are critical to the viability and survival of *any* social system? Some are obvious: (1) producing enough individual people through reproduction, immigration, or organizational recruitment;

(2) socializing individuals well enough to be able to live in particular systems; (3) producing enough goods and services to maintain individuals and organizations; (4) maintaining sufficient order and authority to resolve conflicts and allocate goods; and (5) generating enough shared culture to facilitate communication and consensus (see Mack and Bradford, 1979). The particular ways in which such functions are accomplished differ greatly among human societies. Furthermore, note that a sustainable relation between humans and their biophysical environment was *not* a part of this list of functional processes (as understood in the 1950s). Nature was only implied to be "out there" as a resource for economic functioning.

Dunlap and Catton described the functions of the environment differently by suggesting *three functions of the environment* for human society (as well as other species). Ecosystems function as a *supply depot* for human material sustenance. Ecosystems and environmental sinks (like rivers and the atmosphere) function as *waste repositories* for wastes and pollution. In addition, ecosystems provide *living space* for all activities, and overuse of this function produces crowding, congestion, and the destruction of habitats for other species. Moreover, Dunlap and Catton argue that overusing the environment for one function may impair the other functions (as when a waste site makes a neighborhood undesirable for living, or pollutes groundwater resources). Human impacts may become so large that they threaten to be *dysfunctional*, threatening human social viability on a global scale. This impairment may be of such magnitude as to impair the environment's ability to fulfill all three functions, for humans or other species (Catton and Dunlap, 1986; Dunlap and Catton, 2002). See Figure 1.5.

*Max Weber* (1864–1920) is hardly ever regarded as an ecological thinker, but he was an important early sociological theorist whose ideas have influenced environmental sociology. In contrast to Marx, Weber thought the basic force in society was power itself (not simply the control of wealth). In modern societies, Weber observed, power is increasingly wielded by large-scale organizations and bureaucracies. But, unlike Marx, Weber gave considerable weight

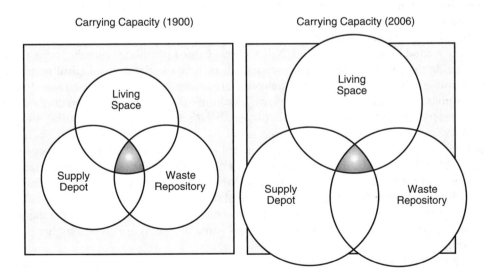

**FIGURE 1.5**  The Social Functions of the Environment

*Source:* Adapted from Dunlap and Catton, 2002, "Which Functions of the Environment Do We Study?" *Society and Natural Resources,* 15, 245. Used with permission of Taylor and Francis Group, L.L.C., http://www.taylorandfrancis.com.

to the role of ideas, legitimating ideologies, and myths (broadly, "culture") in historical change and development (Humphrey, Lewis, and Buttel, 2002: 45). Weber argued that the main thrust of Western social development could be understood as the progressive development and diffusion of the cultural complex of *"rationality"*—about linking means and end efficiently—in Western societies, which underlies the development of capitalism, as well as bureaucracy, and empirical science.

Weber's ideas have been extended to environmental sociology in two different ways. One focuses on managers of bureaucratic organizations. Environmental protection involves the government managers and administrators in the process of exercising their power to carry out the intent of environmental protection legislation. Ken Gould, for instance, studied this process by examining the ability of municipalities to enforce water pollution regulations in Canada and the United States. Municipalities differ in size, access to environmental organizations, and dependence on a single local employer—for instance, a paper mill or nuclear fuel processing facility. If single industry communities also lack access to active environmental organizations, or municipal or state regulators, they will have more limited ability to enforce or manage pollution regulations.

Gould found that communities with a more diverse employment base had more political autonomy and, thus, greater managerial control capacity. This was especially true of communities that gained employment from summer and fall tourism. Greater control capacity meant that regulatory agency managers had more political legitimacy in the community and more effective authority to exercise in environmental management (1991).

In a similar environmental extension of Weber's ideas, Canadian sociologist Raymond Murphy's *Rationality and Nature* examined the other side of the coin: why environmental movements pressure bureaucratic organizations (including transnational corporations) in a wide variety of settings to develop new accounting procedures that reflect the NEP. In doing so, they often target state managerial agencies, because only the state has the resources necessary to force information out of private companies and to set and enforce the rules needed to ensure that knowledge (about risks) is not concealed (1994: 143). Given that states depend considerably on the money and influence provided by large corporations, whether or not the state has the power to act independently is an important question.

The second kind of extension of Weber's ideas helped stimulate *symbolic interactionism* emphasizing the role of symbols, culture, and ideas. It is a social psychological perspective that maintains that self-concepts and behavior are critically shaped by language, symbols, and people's "definitions of the situations." As humans interact, they constantly create, defend, rearrange, and negotiate their identities, social relationships, and cultural meanings (Mead, 1934). An implication of this is that social and cultural reality are, in fact, social constructions, and this gave rise to what were termed *social constructionist* perspectives (Alfred Schutz, 1967; Berger and Luckmann, 1976). They do not deny that real environmental problems exist, but focus on "the process through which environmental claims-makers influence those who have power to recognize environmental problems and accept responsibility for their solutions" (Hannigan, 1995:55). Social constructionism enables us to understand how environmental concerns vary over time, and how some problems are given a higher priority than others.

This is easily illustrated by the media attention that frames novel problems like rainforest destruction, or climate change, (Leon-Guerrero, 2009: 378). What we take as "things" like organizations, society, culture, social institutions, and even "nature," are really shorthand ways of describing particular historical outcomes of interaction episodes between real human actors. Social construction is a form of social action in which competing groups seek to define issues in terms that support their material interest and thereby reshape underlying material and social processes. The most common application of these perspectives by environmental sociologists is in the study of environmental movements. Robert Brulle, for instance, has extensively analyzed the American variety of environmental (and antienvironmental) movements in terms of how they embody different kind of "discourses" in American culture about the human–environment relationship, to which I will return in Chapter Eight (2000).

Seeing the world, and even the environment ("nature"), as a social construction is a subtle but important point. There is, of course, an external biophysical world that exists quite apart from human awareness and perceptions. Humans live in this world and its constraints, but importantly, they do so in terms of how they understand and define it. Furthermore, as noted earlier, people *cognize* the natural world and environment in very different ways, and I have described in some depth the ways that people have cognized and constructed the environment variously at different stages of human development. It should be obvious that the *culture of nature*—that is, the ways we think, teach, talk about, and construct the natural world—is as important a terrain for action as nature itself (Ciccantell, 1999: 294–295; Hannigan, 1995; Wilson, 1992: 87).

## Conclusion: Environment, Ecosystems, and Human Systems

This chapter ends by summarizing how environments/ecosystems and human systems impact each other, and by emphasizing that every environmental problem is also a social issue.

### THE HUMAN DRIVING FORCES OF ENVIRONMENTAL AND ECOLOGICAL CHANGE

Instead of a balance of nature or a "static equilibrium," ecological theory now emphasizes that some change and flux is the normal state of affairs. But environmental and ecological changes today differ from those of the past in at least two ways. The pace of global environmental change has dramatically accelerated, and the most significant environmental changes are now *anthropogenic,* caused by human impacts (Southwick, 1996: 345–348; Stern et al., 1992: 27). Indeed, everywhere you look there are signs of human modifications of the natural world: buildings, roads, farms, human-modified lakes, rivers, and oceans. Even the gaseous envelope surrounding the earth is becoming littered with human refuse—bits and pieces of satellite "junk" now in orbit. As nature recedes into the interstices of the

planet, pristine wilderness is becoming so rare that there is concern with preserving the last natural refuges unmodified by human civilizations.

Four types of human variables are *proximate causes* or *driving forces* of environmental and ecosystem change: (1) population change; (2) institutions, particularly political economies that stimulate economic growth; (3) culture, attitudes, and beliefs—including social constructions and environmental problems; and (4) technological change (Stern et al., 1992: 75). Chapter Six discusses another way of understanding environmental impact, as a joint product of population, the level of affluence, and technology (the $I = PAT$ model).

### SYSTEM CONNECTIONS

These human "causes" of environmental change are themselves a complex system that not only produces changes in global ecosystems, but causes changes in each other through complex feedback mechanisms. They are distinct but interdependent, and I am unwilling to argue that any is a "more basic" cause, as some scholars do.[4] It seems to me that given their interdependent character,

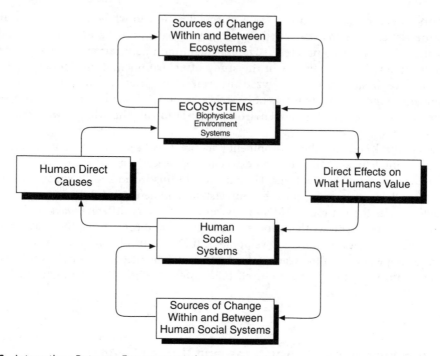

**FIGURE 1.6**   Interactions Between Ecosystems and Human Social Systems
*Source:* Based on Stern et al., 1992: 34.

doing so raises a number of chicken-and-egg arguments (which came first?) that are not very productive. I *do* think it is important to distinguish between more proximate causes (such as a particular technology or social forces that produce hunger or civil war) and more distant or underlying levels of causation (such as population pressure or global climate change). Which is more important depends on the time horizons and purposes of analysis.

Within the physical environment, ecosystems and human social systems are interconnected and interdependent, and the scope of human activity is now so vast and powerful that hardly any ecosystem in the world is free from human impacts. But each ecosystem has its own internal dynamics of equilibrium and change quite apart from human systems. Similarly, each human system has its own sources of change apart from being embedded in ecosystems. The important thing is to understand the connections by which

the dynamics of human societies become the proximate causes of ecosystem change, and the parallel connections between ecosystem change and the things that humans depend on and value. These relationships are summarized in Figure 1.6.

## INTELLECTUAL PARADIGMS ABOUT HUMAN–ENVIRONMENT RELATIONS

Scholars from different disciplinary backgrounds have different assumptions about the "way the world works" and thus pose questions a bit differently. Here are three main scholarly paradigms about human–environment issues.

1. Natural scientists emphasize the implications of continuing *growth in scale in a finite world*.
2. Neoclassical economists "frame" the causes of human–environment problems in terms of more proximate causes of *market failure and resource allocation problems*.

3. Other scholars, including some economists, sociologists, and political scientists, frame human–environment problems broadly in terms of other proximate causes, seen as *social inequality and maldistribution.* These include, for instance, national and global patterns involving the vastly unequal distribution of wealth, political power, information, technology, and so forth.

This chapter ends where it began by illustrating the connection between natural science and social science as related to environmental concerns. The varieties of science are also connected to different paradigms. Illustratively the problem of world hunger can be framed as (1) too many people making demands on limited natural and agricultural resources, (2) the overregulation and failure of free markets that make producing food unprofitable compared to other investments, or (3) an adequate total food supply, but hungry people so poor that they cannot afford to buy food and so powerless that governments are unresponsive to their needs. (I will return to this issue in Chapter Five). Such paradigmatic differences are keys to understanding many debates about the seriousness and causes of human–environment problems. Reconciling them as legitimate but different points of view is difficult, but I don't believe it is impossible. Subsequent chapters will return to these paradigmatic differences in various places. *Stay tuned.* Let me end by reiterating what should now be an obvious point. Natural environmental/ecological phenomena and problems are social issues as well. Social questions and controversies arise about, for example, natural resources like fertile land, mineral deposits, pristine forests, and fresh water. Who owns them? Will they be used or left alone? If used, for what, and how fast? Who benefits and who pays the costs? Which people or organizations have a stake in these questions, and whose preferences will prevail? If there is an environmental/ecological problem such as pollution, species extinction, or climate change, who, if anyone, bears the costs of doing something about it? How are such costs distributed? Put more abstractly, "what are called 'natural' resources are in fact social as well as natural; they are products of historical contingent sociocultural definitions just as much as they are products of biochemical processes" (Freudenburg and Frickel, 1995: 8). Now, most scholars are aware that environmental problems and change cannot be understood, much less dealt with, in the absence of substantial contributions of the social sciences (Stern et al., 1992: 24).

## Personal Connections

*Questions for Review*

1. What does it mean to say that environmental problems are also social issues? Illustrate concretely.
2. What are the "Dominant Western Worldview" (DWV) and the "Human Exemptionalism Paradigm" (HEP)? How do you see them operating in our world?
3. How did Malthus and Marx have different views of the causes of environmental problems?
4. What are some differences in environmental perspectives of neoclassical and ecological economists? Similarly, how do the functionalist, conflict, and interactionist perspectives in sociology point to different things and problems about the environment?
5. What are three important functions of the environment for humans? Illustrate concretely. What do these have to do with the notion of an environmental carrying capacity?
6. What are the main human "driving forces" that produce environmental change? Explain.

*Questions for Reflection*

1. What are some of the layers of culture and civilization that tend to insulate you from the natural world? How do they illustrate your embeddedness in nature? Think, for instance, about buying food in a supermarket: That which you normally understand as a consumer actually makes you a participant in vast food chains, energy, and resource transfers that nature never knew. What are some other examples?

2. When do you think about the natural world—when you see it on TV or in books (you know, breathtaking pictures of distant mountains)? Does your daily routine include being in the natural world? Do you normally experience nature with aesthetic appreciation, as a resource to be used, or as an intrusion to be minimized in an otherwise comfortable life?

3. The notion of worldviews is abstract. But look again at the description of the worldview of Western industrial societies in this chapter. Can you see any connection between it and your or your friends' perceptions about "the way the world works," or values about what is good and bad? How might this be reflected in the behavior of those around you?

4. What kinds of personal inducements are there to keep you or your friends consuming? Pressures from the expectations of others? Time? The media and advertising? What kinds of forces are there that inhibit you and others from adopting more environmentally frugal behavior? What's the connection among recreation, consumption, and waste in your life? How do you "have a good time"?

## What You Can Do

"Think globally, act locally" has become a slogan (mantra?) of the environmental movement. If you are concerned about environmental problems, you do need to think globally about them. You also need to act locally, in your own corner of the world. But, you also need to act in ways that have larger-scale relevance. Including a list of things you can do to "walk lighter on the earth" is common in books about environmental issues, and I mention some of these ideas in later chapters. Changing individual lifestyles is important, but not sufficient to address the environmental problems that beset us; powerful institutions and organizations operate beyond individual behaviors. But it does not follow that the actions or attitudes of individuals are irrelevant for larger-scale change. For now, I want to leave you with the notion that the individual matters. This was well put in the novel *Middlemarch*, by the famous British writer George Eliot: "The growing good of the world is dependent on individual acts." Renown anthropologist Margaret Mead had similar thoughts: "Never doubt that small groups of thoughtful, committed citizens can change the world; Indeed, it is the only thing that ever has." Think about how your life does, or could, embody this environmental ethos.

## Real Goods

Let me tell you about something I have lately come to value, although I didn't for years: *Anne's garden*. My wife, Anne, likes to grow things. We live in an ordinary, older urban neighborhood, with brick and wood-frame houses and big established trees. The trees that shade the backyard are not fancy ones; in fact, a landscaper would call them "weed trees." There's an alanthus (sometimes called the tree of heaven), a mulberry tree, several Chinese elms, and a big cottonwood. I cut the grass—whatever grows, some blue grass and rye grass, but also a variety of weeds and clover that have taken root. By contrast, some of my neighbors spend lots of money having their lawns regularly doused with fertilizer, herbicides, and pesticides, and they have beautifully manicured bluegrass and zoysia monocultures.

Since we first lived there, Anne kept planting and tending flowers and vegetables. There are irises, day lillies, roses, crocuses, and tulips and other flowers, and in various years a mixture of green beans, snow peas, cabbage, brocolli, peppers, and tomatoes. The yard has attracted a variety of creatures: a tribe of entertaining and contentious squirrels, a multitude of bees and pollinators, summer cicadas and other bugs, garter snakes that nest under an upturned corner of an old driveway slab, a variety of birds that nest and feed, bats that hunt bugs on summer evenings. Sometimes—if you are very quiet after dusk—a family of hoot owls show up on their nocturnal prowl through the city. Oh yes, there's Jake, a feisty Jack Russell Terrier, who has pretensions to becoming a vicious top carnivore (but not as good at climbing trees as the squirrels).

*What's the point?* For a long time I just thought it was weird. But more recently it dawned on me that our whole backyard has become a mini-ecosubsystem of its own. A green leafy, vibrant, buggy urban polyculture (compared to the backyard of some neighbors) where something is always blooming and dying. I have come to appreciate why the English word *paradise* derives from a word in an ancient Mideastern language meaning "a small green garden." It is a small corner of the world that I have come to cherish as beautiful in its own right. Every winter I wait for its return.

Can you think of a place you know about that people experience similarly?

## More Resources

Dunlap, R.E., Buttel, F., Dickens, P., and Gijswijt, A. (2002). *Sociological theory and the environment: Classical foundation, contemporary insights.* Lanham, MD: Roman & Littlefield Publishers.

Dunlap, R. E., and Marshall, B. (2006). Environmental sociology. In C. Bryant and D. Peck (Eds.), *21st century sociology: A reference handbook,* vol 2 (pp. 329–340). Thousand Oaks, CA: Sage.

Kormody, E., and Brown, D. (1998). *Fundamentals of human ecology.* Upper Saddle River, NJ: Prentice Hall.

McNeill, J. (2000). *An environmental history of the twentieth century world.* New York: W. W. Norton.

Miller, T., and Spoolman, S. (2009). *Living in the environment: Concepts, connections, and solutions* (16th ed.). Belmont, CA: Brooks/Cole.

Pointing, C. (1991). *A green history of the world.* London: Sinclair Stevenson.

## Electronic Resources

**www.usee.org**
Economists study environmental issues: news, ongoing research, papers, meetings and events, people. The newsletter of the U.S. Society for Ecological Economics

**www.socio.ch/evo/index_evo.htm**
A wealth of research, books, and reports about the evolution of societies by the Sociological Institute from Zurich University in Switzerland (available in English and German).

**www.wri.org**
The World Resources Institute's accessible and up-to-date reports on various environmental topics (continuously updated)

**http://earthtrends.wri**
Information and papers about a variety of environmental topics from the World Resources Institute

**http://www.eldis.org/go/topics/resource-guides/ environment**
Information about 2,115 topics

## Endnotes

1. There were, of course, kings and political empires throughout much of human history. But these were different from modern nation states—with their greatly expanded social functions (e.g., economy subsidy and regulation, public education, and social welfare). Perhaps as important, modern nation states emphasize *sovereignty* as involving the right, not just the coercive power, to rule. Similarly, organizations in the bureaucratic sense are relatively new social inventions that arose at about the same time as nation states. The major difference between modern organizations and those of antiquity is that in modern bureaucratic organizations, accountability and authority are vested in organizational statuses and structures rather than in persons. The importance is that modern organizations have greatly enhanced stability and continuity. The army of Attila the Hun and the pyramid-building crews of the Egyptian pharaohs were both personal empires that did not long survive their founders (the classic formulation of the features of bureaucratic organizations can be found in Weber, 1922/1958).

2. While you should not overdraw the similarities between *Homo sapiens* and other animal species, it would be an equal error to dismiss human rootedness in the biotic world. The relative weights given to biological/genetic programming versus cultural learning as causes of the behavior of humans and other species is a perennial debate that surfaces about every decade in new guises. But this is surely a matter of degrees of difference rather than sharp differences of kind. It is, I think, a matter of "both–and" rather than "either–or." To say that, of course, only concedes an abstract principle and gives no help in knowing specifically how much of which to emphasize in what circumstances. New versions of this heredity–environment debate have been shaped in the subdiscipline of biology that has come to be called *sociobiology*. For more about this, see Barash (1979), Maryanski (1998), Van den Berghe (1977–1978), and Wilson (1975).

3. Linear (arithmetic) growth is additive (1,2,3,4,5,6,7 . . .), while exponential growth squares each new number (2,4,8,16,32,64 . . .). If Malthus was correct about this, you could see his point about the inexorable tendency for population to outstrip supply.

4. In what has come to be called the Ehrlich–Commoner debates among environmental scientists, biologist Paul Ehrlich has argued that population growth is the most important driving force for environmental change and problems (1974, 1992), while zoologist Barry Commoner has argued that advanced industrial technology is a more important and powerful cause (1971). Among many others, sociologist Alan Schnaiberg emphasizes the importance of the institutional arrangements, and in particular the political economy (1980). Other analysts, including social theorist Talcott Parsons, view culture, values, and paradigms as the most basic forces that sanction and limit the other variables.

# CHAPTER 2

# Humans and the Resources of the Earth: Sources and Sinks

Clear-cutting trees for lumber like this is a major cause of deforestation.

In the 1960s, when I was a young man, I took a canoe trip with a friend down the Current River in southeast Missouri. The water was clear and cold, and while the surrounding land was hilly, rocky, and not much good for agriculture except for grazing a few cattle, the river was lined with magnificent forests in the Ozark National Scenic Riverways and the Mark Twain National Forest. Tourism and outfitting canoeists was one of the major industries in the surrounding counties. My father told me that when he was a young man living near the area in the 1920s, the trees had been clear cut by lumber companies and soil erosion had turned the clear spring-fed river into a muddy mess. I marveled at the contrast between the merciless exploitation of resources that had taken place around the turn of the century and the restoration that I witnessed by the 1960s. Although the landscape was certainly not like it was before human settlement, the net effect of human activity over time had in some ways compensated for the damage done at an earlier time, at least in that particular area.

In Chapter One, I noted the contemporary litany of environmental problems—to frame some concerns of this book. This chapter returns to some of these problems in more depth and begins to sketch their connections with humans and societies. As an obvious disclaimer, this chapter is not an exhaustive compendium of the state of the planetary resource system. If you need to know more, there are many other sources (texts and scholarly writings, and huge professional literatures) to which you may turn. Some of the more accessible of these are noted at the end of this chapter.

The planet is a huge system of natural capital, which also serves as a vast recycling system for humans (and other living things). So that you don't view natural capital as free and unlimited, I will note some important economic and ecosystem *services* that the earth provides, and, sometimes, their estimated monetary value—if natural capital were priced, as done by biologist Gretchen Daily and others in the late 1990s (1997). The dollar value of the economic and ecosystem services of "nature" would obviously be *much* greater after a decade of currency inflation.

In narrow anthropocentric terms, you can conceptualize the earth as a series of *sources* (from which resources are drawn) and *sinks* (into which human wastes and effluents go). The chapter will discuss the current state and human use of *physical resources:* soil, water, biotic resources (forests and species diversity). Later chapters discuss climate and energy resource issues in greater depth. I will also discuss *pollution sinks* (of solid wastes and chemical pollutants): in simpler words, the "supply depots" and "waste repositories" depicted in the previous chapter (Dunlap and Catton, 2002). To tie this chapter with the previous one, think about how each particular resource problem is also a *social issue* and how it is connected to the four sociocultural driving forces of environmental and ecological change noted at the end of Chapter One.

## LAND AND SOIL

Soil is formed from the minerals derived from the breakup and weathering of rocks combined with decaying organic material derived from wastes and the dead and decaying remains of plants and animals. Since soil contains microbes and other detritovores, it is not only a variable mix of inorganic and organic compounds, but also a "living layer" of the biosphere. Topsoil layers are particularly rich in the nutrients necessary for primary producers to carry on photosynthesis. We are utterly dependent upon the land for food: 98% of human food is produced on the land. Worldwide, food and fiber crops are cultivated on 12% of the land surface, 24% is pasture used for grazing livestock that produces meat and milk, while forests cover another 31%, most of which is being exploited for fuel, lumber, paper, and other forest products. The remaining land, less than one-third, is desert, mountains, tundra, and other land unsuitable for agriculture (Buringh, 1989).

Land can be degraded and eroded so that it is less productive or even useless for human cultivation. In fact, land is always eroding naturally; topsoil is being dissolved or carried away by water or wind; and the rate of this natural erosion varies with local geology, climate, and topography. The *critical question* is the rate of erosion and degradation in relation to the rate of soil formation, and in particular the impact of human activity on the relationship between these two processes. The arrival of humans practicing agriculture increased the volume of soil and silt being carried into the ocean by at least two and a half times the original rate (studies cited by Craig et al., 1988: 353). Agriculture has without doubt led to the accelerating erosion of topsoil and soil nutrient loss, and subsequently to declining crop and livestock yields. This often, as noted in Chapter One, shaped the fate of agricultural societies. Think about how soil problems have obvious connections to the "driving forces" mentioned in the previous chapter: Population growth? Social institutions that stimulate economic growth? Human culture, attitudes and beliefs? New technologies? An obvious way to begin thinking about this is the connection between soil and food.

## Soil and Food

If human intervention produced a net degradation of soil, how can we explain the enormous increase in food production in recent times—which grew faster than human population? From the beginning of agriculture until about 1950, nearly all the growth of food output came from expanding cultivated land area. Since 1950, at least four-fifths of the increase in food output came from increasing *productivity* (Brown et al., 1992: 36).

While modern "intensive" agriculture dramatically increased productivity, it all but destroyed the traditional methods of preserving soil productivity that farmers everywhere had learned to practice, such as terracing, contour plowing, crop rotating, using fallow years, using organic fertilizer, and—in the tropics—shifting agriculture and herd migration. Intensive agriculture encouraged continuous cropping of monocultures without rotation or fallow periods, cropping on hilly and marginal land, and overgrazing in confined pasturelands. Since 1950, manufactured inorganic chemicals, capital, and energy inputs made it possible to expand food supply. As a consequence, since 1950 the *net area* of cultivated land area has not grown much (Brown, 1999b). Thus copious food production overdraws and degrades natural resources (both water and soil) to maximize production. In fact, for such reasons, food production is not now increasing. Grain production was virtually flat in 2005–2006. Grains dominate the world's diet and agricultural landscapes, which is planted on half the world's cropland. But per capita consumption increased slightly as countries drew down stocks (what is "left over" between harvests). World cereal stocks continue their long-term decrease (Halweil, 2006: 22).

Experts have been concerned about the global soil situation for some time (e.g., Eckholm, 1976). In the 1980s, studies of the earth's soils suggested that we could adequately feed the world's population, because there was a lot of good land that could be brought into food production (Crosson and Rosenberg, 1990). However, this optimistic view weakened. Experts more recently estimate that about one-third of the world's soil that ever existed has been lost (Southwick, 1996: 347). In 1992, a joint study by the U.N. Environmental Programme and the World Resources Institute found that soil was eroding on 38% of the world's cropland, and another study found that soil erosion and degradation had reduced food production on about 16% of the world's cropland (Miller, 2005: 279). These declines partly explain declining yields on some lands despite the extensive use of costly fertilizers. "Because fertilizers are not a substitute for fertile soil, they can only be applied up to certain levels before crop yields begin to decline" (Pimentel, 1992b: 331).

Responding to massive soil erosion during the dustbowl of the 1930s, the United States was among the few nations to make soil conservation a national priority. The Conservation Reserve Program (CRP), part of the 1985 farm bill, encouraged the conversion of erodible land to grassland or woodland and penalized farmers who didn't manage soil responsibly by denying them the benefits of government farm programs (price supports, crop insurance, and low-interest loans). The good news was that soil losses on erodible cropland were cut by about 65%—reprenting the greatest short-term reduction in erosion in U.S. history. Even with this progress, the Natural Resources Conservation Service (of the U.S. Department of Agriculture) estimated that American soil is eroding 16 times faster than it can form, and the Great Plains states have lost half their topsoils since agriculture began there (Miller, 2005: 280). Experts estimate that the world loses 24 billion tons of topsoil per year (Montgomery, 2010).

## Addressing Soil Problems

A major reason to be concerned with soil problems is obvious. To feed a growing global population on increasingly degraded and expensive agricultural resources, we will need to increase the productive yield of agriculture while protecting the fertility of cropland soils. That's easy to state, but it is a *formidable* goal, particularly on a world basis. Erosion can be reduced by encouraging terracing, contour plowing, multiple cropping (planting ground cover crops in between rows of corn, for instance), and using low-tillage methods (which leave crop residues on the land for soil binders and organic fertilizer). Using more organic fertilizer, which reduces the need for chemical fertilizers, can increase nutrient recycling. The use of organic wastes for fertilizer is growing. Many Asian cities systematically recycle human wastes onto the immediately surrounding farmland. By the 1980s, Shanghai was virtually self-sufficient in producing vegetables grown this way (Brown, 1988: 50). Moreover, communities in the more developed countries (MDCs) were returning organic material to soils at a growing rate by the 1990s (Gardner, 1998).

Contrary to global trends, some propose land reforms that encourage smaller privately owned farms because, compared with very large ones, they are more productive since they are more labor and less capital and technology intensive. Small farmers with secure land ownership are also more likely, other things being equal, to care for the land sustainably than are landlords or corporations operating remote large estates. But others suggest addressing problems of soil (and food) through the application of technology and the advantages of large-scale management. Many nations need food price policies that encourage the profitability of agriculture. But these ideas about land reform and price policy are *political dynamite* because they involve changing the rules about land ownership and often raising the price of food; you can understand why few governments have been willing to tackle them. Preserving the soil and increasing the world food supply will require the best efforts not only of agricultural scientists and geneticists, but also of energy planners and economic and political policy makers of all sorts. Addressing soil problems would trigger a basket of thorny economic and political problems where land is privately owned and used (or abused!). This underscores the point made in closing Chapter One: All environmental problems are also social issues. I will return to food issues in Chapter Five, in connection with population issues.

## Economic and Ecosystem Services: Pricing Soil Degradation

Lest you think that the costs of soil degradation are only abstract and long term, consider some efforts to price them. Direct costs of soil erosion, as measured by the costs of replacing lost water and nutrients on agricultural land, amount to about $250 billion per year globally. Additional costs, including damage to recreation, human health, private property, navigation, and so on, amount to about $150 billion globally, and $44 billion in the United States alone. Soil erosion is extremely costly in the short term, but the benefits of many prevention measures would greatly outweigh the costs. Even so, the political and economic barriers to implementation of such measures are formidable (Daily et al., 1997: 127–128).

## WATER RESOURCES

Even more clearly than soil, water is the lifeblood of the biosphere. Life is only possible because of the solar-driven circulation of water through the hydrological cycle from the ocean to the atmosphere, from the atmosphere to the land, and back to the ocean. Water is a renewable resource, but most water circulates from the ocean to the atmosphere and back. A much smaller fraction falls as precipitation over land, and of that, much reevaporates or runs off back to the ocean so that an even smaller fraction is available for human agricultural, industrial, and household use. Usable water is *very* unevenly distributed over the earth's surface, so getting enough water has often been a source of political conflict. Because water is renewed within the water cycle, we tend to treat it as a renewable, free, and unpriced common good. It is not, however, the volume of water that determines how much is available for use over time, but its renewal or "recharge" rate for groundwater, lakes, and rivers. Worldwide, surface water and groundwater each supply about half of the needed freshwater, but the recharge rate for groundwater is *very slow,* about 1% per year (W. Cunningham and M. Cunningham, 2010: 372–373; Miller, 2005: 307–309).

Unlike many resources, there are relatively fixed minimum requirements for water needs. To assure adequate health, people need a minimum of about 100 liters of water (about 26.5 gals.) per day for drinking, cooking, and washing. Many times, this amount is necessary to support the economic base of communities, and affluent persons in more water-rich societies use many times this personal daily minimum. Agriculture accounts for the most water use, about 70% worldwide, and it is also the most inefficient use. It requires 1,700 liters (about 400 gallons) of water in a growing season to grow 1 kilogram (about 2.2 pounds) of corn. Accounting for runoff, evaporation, waste, and other factors, a hectare of corn (about 2.4 acres) requires on average 10 million liters of rainfall, spread evenly over the growing season. It is not uncommon for 70% to 80% of the water in irrigation systems to be lost by evaporation or to seep into the ground before reaching crops. Industry accounts for about 20% of global water use. It takes over 400,000 liters of water to produce an automobile, and industrial societies produce about 50 million cars every year. A nuclear reactor needs 1.9 cubic miles of water a year, and together all U.S. reactors use up the equivalent of one and a third Lake Eries each year. Of all water uses, cities and residences consume only about 10%. Still, that adds up to a lot of water. You probably use more water each day than you think you do, particularly in relation to the 26–27-gallon daily minimum need (Miller and Spoolman, 2009: 317; Miller, 2005: 309–310; Pimentel et al., 2004; Falkenmark and Widstrand, 1992: 14).

### Growing Water Use and Its Problems

Water usage tripled since 1950, and by 1992 humans used more than eight times the flow of the Mississippi River—about 4,400 cubic kilometers per year (Postel and Carpenter, 1997: 197). Planners met this growing demand by so-called water development projects: dams, irrigation, and river diversion schemes. But limits to this ever-expanding consumption are swiftly coming to light. Around the world, water tables are falling, lakes are shrinking, and wetlands are disappearing. When water tables sink in coastal regions, salt water often seeps in, making the groundwater unusable for drinking or agriculture. About one out of six people around the world do not have access to clean and affordable water, which could increase to one out of four by 2050. As a rule of thumb, hydrologists define water scarce areas as those in which annual supplies are less than 1,000 cubic meters (Miller, 2005, 312; Postel, 1992a.).

Because it takes 1,000 tons of water to produce 1 ton of grain, it is not surprising that 70% of world water use is devoted to irrigation, and that raising irrigation efficiency is central to raising water productivity (Brown, 2008: 179). Given this, farmers are pumping groundwater from aquifers out faster than nature can recharge it. This "groundwater deficit" is widespread, and as a result water tables are falling in the nations of the world that hold more than half of the people and produce more than half of the grain (including the United States, China, and India). Groundwater overdraft and aquifer depletion is serious in most of the world's intensive agriculture and urbanized regions (Liu, 2006: 104).

Since irrigation has grown rapidly as a cornerstone of modern agriculture, groundwater supplies are particularly critical. Water is being pumped from wells much more rapidly than the recharge rates. The effects of such aquifer depletion vary depending on whether is it a renewable one (replenished from rain and rivers) or a fossil one (which is in the ground but never renewed). Renewable aquifers may eventually recover from overpumping, but for nonrenewable ones it means the end of pumping. In China the shallow northern aquifer that supports that nation's agriculture dropped 15 meters in the last 30 years. In the United States, groundwater depletion has been a concern in California and the Southwest, along the Atlantic coastal plain, and the Gulf plain. In the United States, the aquifer that supplies water to the nation's "salad bowl" in California's San Joaquin Valley has dropped 10 meters in many places in the last 10 years. The High Plains Ogallala Aquifer under the Great Plains from Texas to South Dakota supplies 30% of the country's groundwater used for irrigation, and it is being depleted eight times faster than nature can replenish it. (Liu, 2006:104–105; Postel, 2010). At this rate of water consumption, much of the Ogallala Aquifer will be barren in several decades, diminishing the 40% of the United States's beef and grain supplied by that region. As that happens, ripple effects will be felt in High Plains economies and communities as they begin to deal with slow depopulation and search for economic alternatives to their traditional agricultural bases. As you might imagine, since I live in Nebraska, this issue hits pretty close to home.

The good news is that the United States used 30% less water per capita than it did in 1975, according to the data of the U.S. Geological Survey. The lower per capita use was produced mainly by increasing the efficiency in agricultural irrigation and industries—but not lower household water use. That is still increasing, in spite of regulations that require more efficient toilets and showers. During that time Americans migrated from water-rich areas (the Northeast and Midwest to water-short regions (the West and Southwest). This reduction in per capita water use is astonishingly good news, but as the U.S. population and economy has grown, there are still water problems, and water use still grows robustly even with such efficiencies (Gleick, 2009).

Water problems generate social and political conflict. It has long been brewing in California between farmers (who use 80% of its water but produce only about 3% of its economic wealth) and the huge cities of Southern California (Los Angeles, San Diego), which draw water not only from California but also from the Colorado River. The social consequences of water shortages in the United States are that litigation simmers among states, regions, and urban and rural water users—and water management proposals proliferate.

## Water and Political Conflict

The water conflicts in a wealthy nation like the United States will be mild compared to those in poorer, drier nations, which have neither the economic wealth nor technological resources to address water problems as do Kansans or Californians. Squabbles over water have been rapidly escalating, for instance, between Ethiopia and Sudan (which control the Nile headwaters and plan to retain most of it) and downstream Egypt (which is totally dependent upon the Nile flow). The decades-long conflict between India and Pakistan over Kashmir is partly about

---

### BOX 2.1

#### Water and Middle East Conflicts

Of all the world's regions, the Middle East is most likely to erupt in "water wars." The national, religious, and ideological conflicts in the Middle East are well known, and water is certainly not the most obvious cause of these, but a hydrological time bomb of sorts underlies and amplifies those intense historic conflicts (Miller and Spoolman, 2009: 313). The Jordan River Basin is by far the most water-short region, with fierce competition for its water among Jordan, Syria, Palestine (Gaza and the West Bank), and Israel. Neither Israel nor Jordan nor Palestine has a large enough supply of water to meet the World Health Organization's minimum standard of 500 cubic meters per capita day potable water supply (Deconinck, 2004). In 1964 Israel dammed the southern outlet of the Sea of Galilee and began diverting water to its "national water carrier" pipeline to the south. In response, the Arab League agreed to divert the northern Jordan River's two tributaries and impound water for use by Jordan and Syria. Israel launched air attacks on the diversion project and set off a chain of events that led to the 1967 Arab-Israeli war (Wolf, 2000). Whether water is at the base of the political conflict in the Middle East or is more a mask to underlying tensions, it is clear that conflict over water contributes to the tensions. On the other hand, states' mutual vulnerability to water scarcity could be a source of future cooperation rather than war. (Coles, 2004)

---

control of the water-rich region at the foot of the Himalayas. India is damming up the river that ties the whole region together, and the Pakistanis fear that the Indians might turn off the floodgates in the middle of some hot summer and parch that part of Pakistan. On the eastern border of India, the poverty-stricken Bangladeshis had similar fears, because India was damming the Ganges only miles from the border. Bangladeshi officials viewed this act as a matter of life or death, and demanded that the matter be brought before the World Court in the Hague (*Der Spiegel*, 1992).

## Addressing Water Problems

As with soil problems, solutions to water shortages involve improved efficiency and conservation. And the most obvious place to start is to replace today's wasteful irrigation systems with more efficient systems, such as drip irrigation. With the tools and technologies now available, technically farmers could cut their water needs by 10%–50%, industries by 40%–90%, and cities by one-third with no sacrifice of economic output or quality of life (Postel, 1992a: 2333). When water is made so cheap by governments, there is no real incentive for growers to invest in more efficient systems, and the ability of nations to invest in technologies and conservation varies considerably. A rich society with willing neighbors, such as in Southern California, can construct canals, pipelines, and pumps to import water. Poorer societies must develop severe ration and regulation schemes, and often experience famine and/or conflict over water (Meadows et al., 1992: 56).

Even while these water shortages are going on, there is an important water issue about the growing habit of affluent people everywhere to consume bottled water for "safety," taste, or as a substitute for other beverages, even though most municipal water is effectively regulated in industrial nations. The difference in cost between bottled and tap water is staggering: the bottled version costs $500–$1,000 per cubic meter, compared with 50 cents per cubic meter for quality tap water. Many tests show that it is not safer to drink than tap water. Most of the costs go into production, packaging, transportation, advertizing, and corporate profits—not the water itself. Bottled water generates a waste stream of plastic that is often not recycled. The taste for bottled water is often a matter of prestige and taste (culture), not safety, and raises enormous social justice as well as environmental concerns (Li, 2007).

One policy to address water shortages has generated controversy. Is access to enough clean water to meet human needs a basic human right, or is water a commodity to be sold in the marketplace? Currently, most water resources are owned by governments and managed as public resources for their citizens. However, increasingly governments are hiring private companies to manage water supplies. Moreover, three large transnational companies based in Europe—Vivendi, Suez, and RWE—have a strategic plan to buy up as much of the world's water supplies as possible, especially in Europe and North America. Their argument is that private companies have the money and expertise to manage water resources better and more efficiently than government bureaucracies. Experience with this public–private partnership approach is mixed. Some companies have done a better job, but others have not. Some government officials, particularly in cash-strapped less developed countries (LDCs), actually want to sell water resources to private companies, but many oppose the full privatization of water because they believe that it is an essential resource that is too important to be entirely in private hands (Miller, 2005: 312).

To address water supply problems, we can substantially conserve existing supplies and increase efficiency, but, given the nature of the hydrological cycle, we cannot expand the total supply much. Nor can we rely only on conservation and technological strategies. Addressing water supply and distribution problems requires a combination of regional cooperation in allocation, slowed population growth, improved efficiency, higher water prices to improve irrigation efficiency, and—sometimes—imported grain or food to reduce water needs. Obviously, producing this complex combination of factors will not be easy (Miller, 2005: 305).

## Freshwater Economic and Ecosystem Services

Rivers, lakes, aquifers, and wetlands provide myriad benefits to human economies. They provide water for drinking and hygiene, irrigation and manufacturing, and such goods as fish and waterfowl, as well as a host of "in-stream" nonextractive benefits including recreation, transportation, flood control, bird and wildlife habitats, and the dilution of pollutants. Such in-stream benefits are particularly difficult to quantify, since many public goods are not priced by the market economy. Thus the total global value of all services and benefits provided by freshwater systems is impossible to gauge accurately, but would certainly measure in the *several trillions of dollars* (Postel and Carpenter, 1997: 210).

# BIODIVERSITY AND FORESTS

We live in a world with economic capital, social capital, and natural capital. Of these, we understand the importance of the first two very well, because they are the substance of our everyday lives. The biological dimensions of nature (natural capital), particularly the diversity of plants and animals, is probably underappreciated (Wilson, 1990: 49). Thus, I will discuss them in a bit more depth than I did soil and water issues.

## Forest Resources

Two-thirds of the forests that existed historically around the world are gone now. Of the three major intact and unfragmented forest biomes that cover about 12% of the earth's surface, *boreal* forests that circle the northern latitudes (e.g., in Canada, Russia, and Scandinavia) are the largest (about 30% of the remaining forests). These are followed by *temperate zone* forests (in the United States and Europe) and *tropical* forests, which cover only about 6% of the earth's surface (about the size of the lower 48 of the United States), and just four countries—Brazil, Indonesia, Zaire, and Peru—contain more than half of the world's tropical forests. Even with this small area, tropical forests receive more than 50% of the world's rainfall and provide habitat for the vast majority of the world's known species of other plants and animals. This gives them a unique and strategic importance on the earth as a global system (Myers, 1997: 215–216).

Humans are rapidly destroying both boreal and tropical forests. In the north this is caused mainly by commercial logging, but in the tropics it is caused in various proportions by commercial loggers, farmers, and ranchers (both peasant and corporate). Chances are that the next hamburger you eat or cup of coffee you drink—a cup is sitting by my computer right now—was produced on land that was formerly a tropical forest. Pollution and climate change also take their toll on forests, and the impacts of both will likely increase in the future.

In the temperate zone, forests are now roughly stable in *area,* but in the United States much of the forests are regrown secondary forests after clear-cutting in the Northeast, Midwest, and Southeast before the turn of the twentieth century. They are much more fragmented and less biodiverse. Europe has virtually no primary forests left. In both the United States and Europe, a primary reason for reforestation—even more important than deliberate reforestation programs—has been urbanization, which left only a small fraction of the population on farms. As agriculture and livestock operations became concentrated on productive soils, the pressure on many previously forested lands decreased. This same pattern of reforestation occurred in Japan (Spears and Ayensu, 1985: 301). Even though temperate forests are now roughly stable in area and are often being "sustainably" managed, many temperate zone forests exhibit declining growth rates, soil nutrients, and wood quality (W. Cunningham and M. Cunningham, 2010: 255). Two decades ago, eminent biologist Norman Myers commented that "if we carry on business as usual, today's young people may eventually look out on a largely deforested world" (1989).

**TROPICAL DEFORESTATION**    Will the history of temperate zone forests be repeated in tropical zones? Probably not, because they have different climates, soil types, and ecosystems. In general, tropical forests are richer in species, faster growing, more fragile, and more vulnerable. To a much greater degree than temperate forests, tropical jungle ecosystems depend on nutrient recycling within the forest itself rather than in the (typically) nutrient-poor tropical soil. Moreover, when cleared of tree cover, heavy tropical rains quickly leach and erode existing soil nutrients, making agriculture unsustainable and forest regrowth long and difficult. Thus, at their present rate of destruction, tropical forests are nonrenewable, not renewable, resources (Meadows et al., 1992: 57–58; Cunningham et al., 2005: 245–246).

Globally, half of the original tropical forests remain, but they are rapidly disappearing because they are being cut, logged, and degraded. The U.N. Food and Agriculture Organization estimates that about 13 million hectares of tropical forest are being cleared every year. Since about 5.7 million hectares are regrown by planting or new growth, the net forest loss is about 7.3 million hectares per year. Put another way, that's an area about the size of a football field cleared every second (W. Cunningham and M. Cunningham, 2010: 251)! At present rates, experts estimate that sometime between the years 2020 and 2090, virtually all of the world's tropical forests will be gone.

The basic causes of tropical deforestation are population growth, poverty, government policies, expanding agricultural land, urbanization, lumber exports, and not valuing the economic and ecological services of standing forests (Miller, 2005: 212). More concretely, deforestation involves a mix of actors and agencies, including multinational lumber and paper companies seeking profits, LDC governments anxious to pay off international debts, and peasants scrambling for firewood (Meadows et al., 1992: 60–61).

## Forest Economic and Ecosystem Services

Standing forests supply various human and ecosystem services, stabilizing landscapes, protecting soils from erosion, helping them retain moisture, and storing and cycling nutrients. They serve as buffers against pests and diseases. By preserving watersheds, they regulate the quantity and quality of waterflows, and they help prevent or moderate floods and store water against drought in downstream territories. They help keep rivers and seacoasts free from silt. They are critical to the energy balance of the earth and modulate climate at local and regional levels by regulating rainfall. They shape the sunlight reflectivity of the earth (the "albedo" effect). At planetary levels, they help contain global warming because they store and sequester carbon as part of the earth's carbon cycle (see Figure 1.1). While all forests do these things, many of these functions are more prominent in tropical forests (Myers, 1997: 215–216).

Consider the costs of some particular forest ecosystem services, as their loss or modification affects or might affect humans. In Nepal between 30 and 75 tons of topsoil is washed away from each deforested hectare of land (about two and a half acres) each year, much of it unwittingly "exported" to India, where it winds up as turgid streams of mud in the Ganges and other rivers. The economic costs are substantial, particularly to Nepalese agriculture and to the Indians, where rivers have about 14 times the silt sediment as does the Mississippi, and rising riverbeds aggravate floods in densely populated regions. The on-site soil conservation benefits of India's tree cover have been estimated at between $5 billion and $12 billion per year, while the value of flood control has been assessed at $72 billion. Perhaps most mind-boggling, what would the value of such forest services be in the year 2025, when at least 3 billion people in the LDCs are suffering from water shortages? If forests disappear, there would be a decline in nonwood products such as foodstuffs, wild game, fruit, Brazil nuts, and latex that are of great value to local populations and sometimes in trade. In the Mediterranean basin (Greece, Italy, Spain, France, Morocco, and others), trade in cork, resin, honey, mushrooms, wild fruit, and trees used in livestock production had an estimated value of between $1 billion and $5 billion in 1992. The old-growth forests of North America's Pacific Northwest protect habitats for 112 fish species—and the salmon industry alone is worth $1 billion per year (Myers, 1997).

## Declining Biodiversity

We do, of course, appreciate the value of the species of things that provide our food, fiber, and wood products, but the value of the diversity of species itself in ecosystems is largely unappreciated by people (Wilson, 1990: 49). As noted, tropical forests and the world's wetlands (e.g., swamps, mangrove swamps, and saltwater marshes) are particularly rich repositories of species biodiversity, and they are now widely threatened. Moreover, the problem is not just in tropical forests. In 1997, the World Conservation Union (IUCN) coordinated a study of 240,000 plant species around the world and found that one out of eight plant species surveyed is potentially at risk of extinction, and that more than 90% of these at-risk species were endemic (found only in a single country and nowhere else in the world) (Tuxill, 1999: 97). Many animal species are threatened also. Corals, for instance, are in steep decline, which form the world's magnificent coral reefs. These unique assemblages of tiny coral animals and symbiotic plants cover less than 0.1%

| TABLE 2.1 | Declining Diversity |
|---|---|
| *Plants* | In 2005 data from the World Conservation Union (IUCN) estimated that 70% of plant species it assessed and 3% of *all* plant species are threatened with extinction. Equally alarming was the loss of genetic diversity among domestic (crop) plants. |
| *Reptiles* | For the 1,277 species assessed by the IUCN, 26% were either threatened with or in danger of immediate extinction. Of the world's 270 turtle species, 42% are rare or threatened with extinction. |
| *Birds* | BirdLife International estimated in 2005 that 12% of *all* bird species fell in the "threatened" category. Among the main threats to birds were intensive agriculture, overexploitation, and pollution. |
| *Fish* | One-third of North America's freshwater fish stocks are rare, threatened, or endangered; one-third of U.S. coastal fish have declined in population since 1975. Introduction of the Nile perch has helped drive half the 400 species of Lake Victoria, Africa's largest lake, to or near extinction. Of 2,158 species assessed by the IUCN, 39% were either threatened with or in danger of immediate extinction. |
| *Mammals* | Of the 4,355 species assessed by the IUCN, 39% were either threatened with or in danger of immediate extinction. |
| *Carnivores* | Virtually all species of wild cats and most bears are declining seriously in numbers. |
| *Primates*[a] | The IUCN considers primates the most imperiled order of mammals—50% are threatened with extinction, and another 20% are "near-threatened." While many species are threatened, one species (human beings) continues unprecedented expansion, with a world population of more than 6 billion. |

[a]An order of mammals that includes monkey, apes, lemurs, and humans.
*Sources:* Carrus, 2006: 96; Eckerele, 2006: 98; Tuxill, 1997: 13; 1998: 128.

of ocean area but are among the earth's most complex and productive ecosystems. As late as 2005, an estimate 20% of the world's coral reefs had been "effectively destroyed" with no immediate prospects for recovery. They have been lost mainly by human pressure—from fishing, mining of coral, coastal development, waste dumping, oil spills, and runoff from inland deforestation and farming. But, the biggest threat today is climate change, which exacerbates other stresses. Besides providing food for some 30 million people, they generate significant tourism revenue. Florida's reefs were estimated to bring in $1.6 billion annually (Mastney, 2006: 94). You can see some illustrations of declines or threatened declines of diversity in Table 2.1, which summarizes findings from more than 25 studies.

To me it is particularly poignant that so many primates, our closest biological relatives, are threatened with extinction—sort of like deaths in the family tree. These particulars about species extinction add up to quite an impressive general picture. But compared to the data noted earlier about soil degradation and water problems, these estimates are even more uncertain. They are uncertain because nobody knows exactly how many species of living things there really are and therefore nobody can calculate with any precision what the *rate* of extinction actually is (Simon and Wildavsky, 1993; Wilson, 1990: 49). There have been at least four waves of species extinction in the history of the planet. Even so most scientists think the present human-induced wave of extinction surpasses anything since the wave of extinction that took place during the Cetaceous Age (65 million years ago) that ended the age of dinosaurs. Previous mass extinctions probably caused 50%–90% of the earth's species to become extinct. After each wave, biodiversity made a comeback, but it took many millions of years (Miller and Spoolman, 2009: 185).

**THE HUMAN CAUSES OF DECLINING BIODIVERSITY**    Conservation biologists use the acronym HIPPCO to summarize threats to biodiversity, which stands for Habitat destruction, Invasive species, Pollution, Population (human), Climate change, and Overharvesting (Miller and Spoolman, 2009: 193). Let me examine in more depth three of these. *First,* the greatest threat to all kinds of wild species is the destruction and fragmentation of habitats as humans occupy and control more of the planet. According to conservation biologists, tropical deforestation is the greatest eliminator of species, followed by the destruction of coral reefs and wetlands. To reiterate: Tropical forests alone cover only 5% of the earth's surface, but contain more than 50% of all terrestrial species (and even higher proportions of arthropods and flowering plants). Wilson estimates that the current rate of species disappearance from tropical forests is about 4,000 to 6,000 species per year, which is about 10,000 times greater than the natural "background" rate of extinction before humans arrived (1990: 54). The two other great genetic storehouses of species—wetlands and coral reefs—are also under severe stress from human intrusion and both land and waterborne pollution.

*Second,* modern agriculture is a powerful cause of declining biodiversity. People have historically used more than 7,000 plant species for food, now reduced to largely 20 species around the world. These are mainly wheat, corn, millet, rye, and rice. Humans encountered these plants haphazardly at the dawn of the agricultural revolution, but they are now selectively bred into a few strains with greatly reduced genetic variability. In Sri Lanka, farmers cultivated some 2,000 varieties of rice as late as 1959. Today only five principal varieties are grown. India once had 30,000 varieties of rice; today most production comes from only 10. In a trip through your supermarket fruit section, you can purchase perhaps five or six varieties of apples; in North America alone, more than a hundred varieties were grown and marketed in the late 1800s. The same sort of reduction in genetic variability has taken place in the herds of cattle, sheep, and horses that humans raise. The U.N. Food and Agriculture Organization estimated that by the year 2000 two-thirds of all seeds planted in LDCs were of uniform genetic strains. In addition to the destruction of habitats and the impact of agriculture, humans have reduced biodiversity in other ways. These include overfishing, commercial hunting and poaching, predator and pest control, the sale of exotic pets and plants, and deliberate or accidental introduction of alien or nonnative species into ecosystems. Nonnative species—usually highly adaptable plants and animals that spread outside their native ranges, often with human help—do well in disturbed habitats (Miller, 2002: 565–70; Tuxill, 1998: 129; Wilson, 1990: 85).

*Third,* the extent to which the earth's climate warms (the *"greenhouse effect"*) will cause reduction in biodiversity. Climate change is a planetary geophysical process, but as the next chapter argues, it has substantial human causes. It will mean changes in seasons, rainfall patterns, ocean currents, and other parts of the earth's life-support systems. Climate change could cause an increased die back and decomposition of forest biomass, triggering the release of more $CO_2$ and other greenhouse gases into the atmosphere that would magnify warming trends. Since the largest forests are the boreal forests located in the northern high latitudes (e.g., Canada and Siberia), where temperatures would rise the most in a greenhouse-affected world, they could quickly start desiccation and die off, except in areas offset by increased precipitation. By one estimate, such warming could increase Canada's forest fires by 20% and their severity by 46%

(Myers, 1997: 223). Although species responded to past climate changes by migrating or shifting their ranges, such adaptive responses will be more difficult in today's degraded habitats. How many species would be able to migrate or adapt to changing climate is not known (Tuxill, 1998: 129). Neither are successes in potentially moving much agriculture from the world's "breadbaskets" into regions with different soils, nutrients, water resources, and across political boundaries. In sum, the earth's "wild things," both plants and animals, are caught in a vise between declining diversity of agricultural species, habitation destruction, and the threats of global climate change.

**CONCERN FOR BIODIVERSITY: WHO CARES ABOUT WILD CREATURES?**    We should care about declining biodiversity for at least three reasons. They are (1) the natural diversity of living things has great actual and potential value as food, medicines, and other substances commercially important for humans; (2) biodiversity provides ecosystem services that play important roles in different niches in ecosystems upon which all life, including human, ultimately depends; and (3) as the earth's evolutionary and biological heritage, the diversity of species is irreplaceable and valuable in itself. Let me expand on each of these points a bit.

*The first reason,* in the most anthropocentric terms, is the great actual and potential economic value of natural species diversity. From tropical forests alone, we get essential oils, gums, latexes, resins, tannins, steroids, waxes, acids, phenols, alcohols, rattans, bamboo, flavorings, sweeteners, spices, balsam, pesticides, and dyes. Many wild plants bear oil-rich seeds with potential for the manufacture of fibers, detergents, starch, and edibles. Plants called euphorbias contain hydrocarbons rather than carbohydrates; hydrocarbons make up petroleum. Of the species that are candidates for "petroleum plantations," some can grow in areas made useless by strip mining. Several tree species—including beech, elm, oak, sycamore, willow, and elder—can clean up urban pollution, particularly sulfur dioxide. They act as air coolants. A 20-meter shade tree can mitigate enough heat to offset three tons of air-conditioning costing $20 a day in the United States.

This highly abbreviated list is just the beginning. Consider chemicals from "wild things" in medicine and pharmaceuticals. More than half of all modern medicines are either derived from or modeled on natural compounds from wild species. "The United Nations Developmental Programme estimates the values of pharmaceutical products derived from developing world plants, animals, and microbes to be more than $30 billion per year" (W. Cunningham and M. Cunningham, 2010: 228). Pharmaceutical companies are busy prospecting for useful products in many tropical countries, often without compensating them (a practice called *biopiracy*). Merck, the world's largest biomedical company, paid an institute in Costa Rica $1.4 million for plant, animal, and microbe samples to be screened for medicinal applications. Two cases are most famous: *Taxol,* a compound in the bark of the Pacific Yew, which loggers called a "trash tree." It can help people with breast and ovarian cancer, not by curing the disease, but by enabling patients to live longer with less pain. Second, the *Rosy Periwinkle* found only in Madagascar that enabled 9 of 10 children with leukemia to survive a normally fatal disease (Myers, 1997: 263–267). The U.N. Convention on Biodiversity has called for a more equitable sharing of gains from rich and poor nations (W. Cunningham and M. Cunningham, 2010: 229).

Among animals, amphibians have been a good source of medicine and pharmaceuticals, since they are beset by all kinds of predators and diseases. Medicine from an Australian tree frog protects against infections. An Ecuadorian rainforest frog secretes a painkiller with 200 times the potency of morphine. Insects secrete substances that promote wound healing and that fight viruses. An octopus extract relieves hypertension, seasnakes produce anticoagulants, and the menhaden (a fish) produces an oil that helps atherosclerosis. A Caribbean sponge produces a chemical that acts against diseases caused by viruses, much as penicillin did for bacterial diseases.

Even lowly barnacles, the bane of sailors, produce a chemical that could be adapted for cement for tooth fillings and could replace the binding pins now used to set broken bone fractures (Myers, 1997: 265).

Consider the value of biodiversity for food and agriculture. Although farmers can now purchase and plant genetically engineered seeds, the productivity of our food supply still depends on the plant diversity maintained by wildlands and traditional agricultural practices. Wild relatives of crops continue to be used to maintain the resistance to disease, the vigor, and other positive traits that produce billions of dollars in benefits to global agriculture. The previous chapter noted the vulnerabilities inherent in such agricultural monocultures with reduced biodiversity. Remember the Irish potato blight famine and its social consequences? There are more recent illustrations. By 1970, when 70% of the seed corn grown in the United States owed its ancestry to six inbred lines, developed commercially by seed companies, a leaf fungus infected ("blighted") cornfields from the Great Lakes to the Gulf of Mexico, and American's great corn belt was threatened. Fifteen percent of the entire crop—as much as half in parts of the South—was destroyed, increasing costs to consumers of more than $2 billion. The damage was halted with the aid of various kinds of blight-resistant germ plasm from a "wild" genetic ancestor that derived from Mexico. Wild species have great potential to help address the world's food problems. For example, a species of wild corn was discovered in the mid-1970s and preserved from extinction—just in the nick of time. Only a few thousand stalks were surviving in three tiny patches in south central Mexico that were about to be cleared by loggers and farmers. This strain was found to have built-in genetic resistance to four of the eight major viruses that affect corn, which heretofore breeders had not been able to breed into commercial varieties (Miller, 2002: 278).

Think about the value for humans of *pollinators,* including honey bees and many other species. Pollination services are provided to cultivated food crops both by wild (feral) and managed insects that nest in habitat adjacent to croplands and orchards. For example, the activities of honey bees and wild bees are essential in pollinating about $30 billion worth of U.S. crops in addition to pollinating natural plant species. One scientist estimated that in New York state alone bees pollinated about *1 trillion* blossoms on a single summer day (Pimentel, 1992a: 219). The number of honey bee colonies in the United States has been declining since 1947 for reasons that are not clearly understood, but probably has to do with organophosphate insecticides and diseases. By 2009, wild bees have become valuable and hard for growers to buy. As biologist David Pimentel commented sardonically, "Humans have found no technology to substitute for the natural service of bees, or many others supplied by wild biota" (1992a: 219).

The important point of these illustrations is that humans clearly cannot survive by depending only on a few livestock and crop species. The diversity of wild species, whose role is not often appreciated, is also vital for humans and to maintain ecosystems themselves.

Beyond direct human benefits, a *second important reason* for valuing biodiversity is its *ecosystem services,* that is, how it influences the supply of ecosystem goods and services. Ecosystem services include the important roles in particular niches that a diversity of species play in maintaining the food chains, energy and matter cycles, and population balances of entire ecosystems. Diversity is fundamental to all ecosystems, and its decline has raised numerous concerns, including the possibility that the functioning and stability of the earth's ecosystems might be threatened by the loss of biological diversity (Schulze and Mooney, 1993).

The rapid expansion of human activities across the earth and the subsequent modification of natural ecosystems produced much lower diversity within managed ecosystems. As we destroy, alter, or appropriate more of these natural systems for ourselves, ecosystems and their services are compromised. At some point, the likely result is a chain reaction of environmental/ecological

---

### BOX 2.2

### Who Cares About Bats, Anyway?

Worldwide there are 950 known species of bats—the only mammals that can fly. They have two traits that make them vulnerable to extinction: They reproduce slowly, and many live in colonies in caves or abandoned mines that are likely to be closed off by people. Bats play important ecological roles. About 70% feed on crop-damaging nocturnal insects and other insect pest species such as mosquitoes. This makes them a major nighttime SWAT team for such insects. In tropical forests, some fruit-eating bats distribute plants throughout tropical forests by excreting undigested seeds. As a keystone species, such bats are vital for maintaining plant biodiversity and for regenerating areas of tropical forests cleared by people. If you enjoy bananas, cashews, dates, figs, avocados, or mangos, you can thank bats. Mistakenly, many people fear bats as filthy, rabies-carrying bloodsuckers, but most bats are harmless to humans and livestock. In the United States, only 10 people have died of bat-transmitted disease in decades of record keeping. More Americans die each year from falling coconuts (Miller and Spoolman, 2009: 192).

---

decline. When such thresholds will be reached, no one can say, "few would argue that every beetle or remaining patch of natural vegetation is crucial to planetary welfare, but the dismantling, piece by piece, of global life-support systems carries grave risks" (Ryan, 1992: 10).

A *third reason* for valuing species diversity is very different than for human utility or ecosystem services. Preserving biodiversity is important to many people for esthetic and spiritual reasons. The diversity of existing species is an irreplaceable product of an eons-long evolutionary process. Every living thing contains from 1 to 10 billion bits of information in its genetic code, brought into existence by an astronomical number of mutations and episodes of natural selection over the course of thousands or millions of years. This process has enabled life to adapt to an incredible diversity of physical environmental circumstances. But as species diversity declines, natural speciation will not refill the gap left by extinction in any meaningful human time scale. Biodiversity—the world's available gene pool—is one of the earth's most valued and irreplaceable resources. Species diversity is also a meaningful source of mystery and great beauty to many people. These reasons obviously *transcend* viewing the world in narrowly anthropocentric terms as "sources and sinks" related to human uses of the earth and its creatures. I think that each nation should value the diversity of living things as a part of its planetary heritage as well as its resource base; it is the product of millions of years of evolution centered on that particular place. Hence, there is as much national reason for preserving biodiversity as for concern and preservation of the nation's history, language, and culture (Wilson, 1990: 50, 58).

## Addressing Deforestation and Declining Biodiversity

As with soil and water resources, there are many ways that the nations of the world could slow or halt unsustainable forest use. One of the most significant ways of reducing tree harvest rates is by greater efficiency in use, eliminating waste, and recycling. The United States, for instance, has the world's highest per capita paper consumption, of which fully half is quickly discarded packaging and only about a third is recycled. Much of U.S. wood consumption could be saved by increasing the efficiency of sawmills, plywood mills, and construction. Similar steps could be taken in the LDCs by the introduction of more efficient cooking stoves to reduce the world's demand for fuelwood. These methods would reduce the economic "throughputs" of forest products and thus deforestation rates.

Let me note some specific initiatives to preserve forests and biodiversity:

1. *Promoting sustainable use:*   The sustainable exploitation of forests by local and indigenous people is often worth more than commercial exploitation (e.g., logging). From sub-Saharan Africa's relic forests, people derive almost 80% of their dietary protein. In Amazonia, the harvest of mammals, birds, medicinals, fish, nuts, and the like can generate as much as $200 per hectare compared with commercial logging, which generates (unsustainably) less than $150 per hectare (Myers, 1997: 227). The main barrier is political: Big companies and national governments can turn lumber, cattle, or gold into hard currency (for debt payment) more easily than forest products, which offer more benefit to local people.

2. *Debt for nature swaps:*   Participating nations act as custodians for protected forest reserves in return for foreign aid or debt relief. Typically a private organization pays a portion of the debt and supervises the swap. By 1987, there were 31 debts for nature among 13 nations, reducing debt by more than $187 million (Humphrey et al., 2002: 247). Critics charge that such swaps do little to change the circumstances that led to environmental destruction in the first place, and don't eliminate debt. To address these criticisms, in 2000 Conservation International bought long-term logging "rights" for 81,000 hectares (200,000 acres) of tropical rainforest in Guyana so that the government is getting the same benefits it would get if the land were actually being logged (Cunningham et al., 2005: 249).

3. *Preserving nature in place:*   Conservationists have long sought to set aside parks and nature preserves. Such nature preserves now account for about 8% of the earth's surface. Such wilderness preserves cause problems when they conflict with cultural and economic uses. Some are protected from poachers in name only. To date, the best job of protecting tropical forests is in Costa Rica, which in the 1970s set aside 12% of its land (6% for the exclusive use of indigenous people). In comparison, the United States has only 1.8% of its land as wilderness reserves not used for any commercial purpose. Such conservation paid off for Costa Rica. Tourism (especially "ecotourism") provides most of its revenues from outside the country.

4. *Gene banks and conservatories:*   A major approach to preserving plants and animals has been to remove them from their habitats and protect them in specialized institutions, such as zoos, botanical gardens, nurseries, and gene banks. By one estimate, nearly 25% of the world's flowering plants and ferns are now so protected. Gene banks focus almost exclusively on storing seed of crop varieties and their wild relatives. They arose from plant breeders' needs to have readily accessible stocks of breeding material, particularly after the near disaster of the American corn crop in 1970, noted earlier (Tuxill, 1999: 107).

5. *Bioprospecting:*   In 1991, Merck & Company paid the Costa Rican Biodiversity Institute $1 million to search for and locate tropical organisms as sources of pharmaceuticals. In the event that marketable product results, the company will retain the patent and pay the institute an undisclosed royalty (rumored to be 1% to 3% of sales). Critics of such arrangements argue that most of the money should go to local or indigenous people, from whose land (and often from whose folk knowledge) such products were developed, rather than only to corporations in industrial nations.

6. *International treaties:*   The 1973, Convention on International Trade in Endangered Species of Wild Fauna and Flora (CITES) provides a powerful legal tool for controlling international trade in threatened plants and animals. It requires that signatory nations issue permits for a limited number of species exports and imports. As you can see, there is a potentially powerful combination of strategies that could be used to slow or stop the process of species extinction.

## WASTES AND POLLUTION

Human economies generate enormous amounts of waste. You probably think of *solid wastes* as municipal garbage, but that is only a small but highly visible portion of the solid wastes produced by industrial societies. The U.S. Environmental Protection Agency and the Bureau of Mines estimate that 75% of solid wastes are produced by mining and oil and gas production, 13% by agriculture, 9.5% by industry, 1.5% by municipal garbage, and 1% by sewage sludge (Miller, 2005: 533). The solid waste produced by nonfuel mining alone amounts to more than a billion tons per year, at least six times that produced by municipalities. Yet even the 1.5% of total solid wastes from homes, businesses, and municipalities represent a *significant* amount of discarded junk. Consider that Americans throwaway:

- Enough aluminum to rebuild the country's entire commercial airline fleet every three months. The airlines alone threw away enough aluminum cans in 2004 to build 58 Boeing 747 Jets.
- Enough vehicle tires to encircle the planet almost three times.
- About 2.5 million nonreturnable plastic bottles each hour.
- Enough disposable diapers per year that, if lined up end to end, would reach to the moon and back seven times.
- 1.5 billion pounds of edible food per year.
- Enough office paper to build a wall 11 feet high across the country from New York City to SanFrancisco.
  (Miller, 2005: 534; National Resources Defense Council, 2006)

Electronic or *e-waste* consisting of discarded TVs, cell phones, computers, and other electronic devices is the fastest-growing solid waste problem in the United States and the world. It is a source of toxic and hazardous wastes such as polyvinyl chloride (PVC) and compounds with lead and mercury that can contaminate the air, water, and soil. In the United States, only 2% of e-waste is currently recycled (Miller, 2005: 534).

Garbage and urban waste on the street in a neighborhood in Los Angeles, California.

## Chemical Pollution from Agriculture

Agriculture, particularly intensive or industrialized agriculture, is an important source of pollution and toxic substances. Agriculture generates chemical pollutants in the residues from pesticides and herbicides, from the nitrates and phosphates remaining from the use of chemical fertilizers, and from the salt that accumulates in soil from irrigation water.

Modern synthetic pesticides and herbicides do indeed increase the productivity of crops. Since 1950 pesticide use increased more than 50-fold, and most of today's pesticides are more than 10 times as toxic as those of the 1950s. Most such agrochemicals are used in the MDCs, though their use is spreading to LDCs. Since 1980 nonagricultural uses have increased, and today about 25% of pesticides and herbicides are used on places like lawns, gardens, golf courses, and parks. The average American lawn is doused with 10 times as much pesticide as a hectare of American cropland (Miller, 2005: 521).

Because they were first introduced after World War II, these pesticides have been found to have toxic effects on humans and other species. Among the most noxious is the wide variety of herbicides, fungicides, and pesticides (mainly insecticides) applied to croplands, which leave residues in the soil and water—as well as on the fruits and vegetables you buy in grocery stores. Although some of the most dangerous chemicals with long-lasting residues (the chlorinated hydrocarbons such as DDT and chlordane) have been banned from use in the United States, they have been replaced with others with equally high toxicity levels but shorter-lived residues (organophosphates such as parathion). Swedish researchers found that exposure to glyphosate (the active ingredient in Monsanto's widely used Roundup herbicide) nearly tripled people's chances of getting cancer (non-Hodgkins lymphoma) (Miller, 2002: 508). Use of the more dangerous agrochemicals has merely shifted overseas, particularly to the LDCs, from which the United States increasingly imports food. Ironically, the world market economy completes a *circle of toxins* as well as one of goods and services.

The World Health Organization estimated that each year 25 million agricultural workers in LDCs are seriously poisoned by pesticides and at least 20,000 die (Cunningham et al., 2005: 204). In the United States, the effects are particularly severe among Hispanic migrant farmworkers, who have very high levels of exposure. In fact, partly because of exposure to agrochemicals, farming was named the nation's most hazardous occupation, ahead of construction, mining, and manufacturing. Furthermore, every year about 20,000 Americans—mostly children—get sick from home misuse or unsafe storage of pesticides (National Institute for Occupational Safety and Health, 1992, cited in Miller, 1998: 623). More than 20 years ago the U.S. Environmental Protection Agency ranked pesticide residues in foods as the third most serious environmental health threat in terms of cancer risk (Miller, 1998: 625).

As if this weren't bad enough, mounting evidence indicates that in the long run, pesticides are not effective in protecting crops from losses. The reason is that while insect pests may initially be suppressed by insecticides, they breed and mutate rapidly and tend to develop chemically resistant strains that then require *more* or different chemicals to suppress. Chemicals can also produce more insects by killing the predators (birds) that feed on them.

Since the 1940s, the world has been on a *herbicide and pesticide treadmill* that was very profitable for the agrochemical industry. But it is of dubious long-term value in increasing food security and is surrounded by evidence of pervasive long-term health hazards (Halweil, 1999). Synthetic agrochemicals accumulate in living tissues through various levels of food chains (called *bioaccumulation*). Because of these characteristics they are termed *persistent organic pollutants* (POPs). The "endocrine disruption hypothesis" is widely known, which

---

## BOX 2.3

### Breaking the Circle of Toxins

Agrochemical companies in the United States and other MDCs manufacture and sell to other countries, usually LDCs, pesticides and herbicides that have been banned, restricted, or never even approved in the country of origin. But what "goes around, comes around" via imported foods. Scientists have tried—without much success—to get the U.S. Congress to ban such exports. In 2000, more than 100 countries developed an international agreement to ban or phase out the use and international sales of 12 especially hazardous organic chemicals. Nine of these were chlorinated hydrocarbon pesticides like DDT. In 2004, this treaty went into effect, an agreement which the United States has not signed (Miller and Spoolman, 2009: 298). Even so, DDT is still used in LDCs because it is one of the few chemicals that effectively suppresses the mosquito that spreads malaria.

---

suggests that POPs can mimic hormones in people, specifically estrogen hormones causing behavioral and reproductive pathologies than can be transferred from mother to child by breast milk (Adeola, 2004; Baskin et al., 2001).

Another category of agricultural pollutants consists of residues from the application of *inorganic chemical fertilizers* to croplands. These fertilizers unquestionably boost crop yields, but they leave large concentrations of nitrates and phosphates that wash into streams, rivers, lakes, and groundwater. During warm weather, this stepped-up nutrient level produces rapid growth of aquatic plants, such as algae, water hyacinths, and duckweed, which for their own respiration use most of the dissolved oxygen in the water. These plants then die and sink to the bottom to decay, along with most of the oxygen-consuming fish and aquatic animals. This process, called *cultural eutrophication,* may leave a body of water that is essentially dead except for the decomposers and the few scavenger species that can live in such an oxygen-depleted environment. A river ecosystem that undergoes cultural eutrophication from a specific point may recover miles downstream, but it is more damaging when it does not derive from a specific point. The 221-square-mile Florida Everglades illustrates this, as this area is being degraded by broad water flows containing nitrates (and pesticides) from the sugar fields and orange groves to the north (Miller, 2002: 651). In the United States, many medium to large lakes, and more than half of the large lakes near major population centers, suffer some degree of cultural eutrophication. The long-term health risks for adults of exceptionally high nitrates in drinking water are not well understood, but there is some evidence that they are related to high rates of female breast cancer and miscarriages. There is clear evidence that in very young children nitrates can react with oxygen-carrying hemoglobin in blood, producing a serious illness known as the "blue baby" syndrome (World Resources Institute, 1993: 40–41).

The *salinization* of land from long-term irrigation is the third important cause of chemical pollution. Freshwater contains between 200 and 500 parts per million (ppm) of salt. Crops take up the freshwater but leave salt in the soil, and daily irrigating a plot of land can add literally tons of salt to the soil each year, eventually exceeding the salt tolerance limits of crops. Unless soil is flushed with freshwater periodically—an expensive process in water-short irrigated areas—soil eventually becomes barren and useless. Remember that this was part of the plight of the ancient Mesopotamia, Rome, and other agricultural civilizations discussed in Chapter One. Since World War II, growing irrigation around the world increased agricultural productivity, but the long-term consequences of soil salinization may now be decreasing it (Postel, 1992b). It is a growing problem in California's fertile valleys in the United States.

## Addressing Solid Waste Problems

In the MDCs, modern sanitary landfills are state-of-the-art constructions vastly different from historic town dumps. They have many technical improvements like barriers and caps to keep *leachate* (dangerous liquid waste residue from the degradation of solid wastes) from seeping into soil and drainage pipes. Still, there are problems: Most eventually *do* leak. Tree roots can perforate the barriers and caps. Leachate, which contains over 100 toxic chemicals, does seep out. Many of America's landfills have wells close by, and most municipalities do not test for leachate. Measurable health problems are correlated with proximity to landfills. If, as noted earlier, mineral production and distribution is related to global social inequality, there is a similar national linkage here. Pervasive evidence shows that landfills are more likely to be found close to lower-income and minority populations (Bryant, 1995; Bullard, 1990, 1993).

In addition to the environmental, health, and social justice issues that surround solid waste dumps, there is a host of other pressing concerns. One is that the dumps are rapidly filling up. Furthermore, people don't want them, and communities have become more effective in blocking the construction of new waste disposal facilities for both industrial and municipal wastes. NIMBY issues ("not in my back yard") have been prime organizing issues for grassroots environmental activists. Governments and industries responded by seeking to reduce the volume of the solid waste stream by either incinerating (burning) it or recycling it. But there are problems with both.

*Incineration* does reduce the volume of solid wastes, by about 90%. Although it removes many harmful chemicals from wastes and has a potential to produce energy, the capital construction costs of incinerators are very high. Incineration produces ashes that are rich in other chemicals in significantly toxic amounts (dioxins, furnans, hydrocarbons, lead, cadmium, chromium, mercury, and zinc). It does little to discourage the production of such wastes and transfers many of them from one sink (the landfill) to another (the atmosphere).

*Recycling* has been the most publicized solution to reduce the solid waste stream. Switzerland and Japan recycle about half of their municipal solid waste. The United States recycles about 30%, up from 6.4% in 1960. Taken together, the proportion of glass recycled between 1980 and the mid-1990s rose from less than 20% to over 50%. The recycled proportion of metals Americans used rose from 33% to 50% between 1970 and 1998. Furthermore, around the world, the proportion of paper and cardboard recycled grew from 38% to 41% between 1975 and 1995 and may reach 46% by 2010 (Gardner and Sampat, 1999: 45). Even with many practical difficulties in recycling municipal solid wastes and resistant lifestyles—particularly American ones—studies show that with greater economic incentives and more efficient waste management systems, the MDCs could boost their recycling of municipal waste to 60% to 80%. Recycling is being transformed from a gesture to help the environment into an industry. The causes of this change are economic growth's increased demand for raw materials and the construction of plants that can process recycled materials (Miller, 2005: 540; Scheinberg, 2003). It is good that recycling has become a part of modern economies but, as critics note, profitability rather than health or environmental threats often determine whether something is recycled or not (Weinberg et al., 2000).

*Reuse* of materials is even more effective. It extends resource supplies and reduces energy use and pollution more than incineration or recycling. Obvious examples are beverage bottles.

Unlike throwaway or recycled cans or bottles, refillable beverage bottles create local jobs related to collection and refilling. But few U.S. bottles are refilled, and by the mid-1990s only 10 states sold refillable bottles. In Germany, 95% of the soft drink, beer, wine, and spirits containers are refillable. But Denmark led the world in reuse of beverage containers, banning all that cannot be reused (Miller, 2002: 528).

The problem is that it is difficult to deal with solid waste (or any other pollutant) after it has been created. The most effective way of dealing with wastes is source reduction or, as it is sometimes called, the *dematerialization* of production and consumption (more about this in Chapters Six and Seven). In other words, the most effective reduction of the solid waste stream could be realized by introducing efficiencies in extraction, production, or consumption so that the economic cycle simply doesn't generate as much solid waste. For consumers, this would mean manufacturing more durable, long-lasting goods (rather than disposable ones), reuse of things like glass bottles (rather than recycling them), and source reductions such as reducing the layers of packaging (rather than recycling them). Roughly, a hierarchy of more effective ways to address solid waste problems would begin with source reduction, followed by reuse, recycling, incineration, and landfills, in that order.

All of this would require significant modifications in the *throwaway economies* of many industrial nations. In the current system, neither producers nor consumers bear the real costs of the solid wastes they generate. Governments (or aggregated taxpayers) do. This means that there are no real incentives that encourage the reduction of material "throughput" because there are no real market signals to particular producers or consumers. As Chapter One noted, the economic process should internalize and particularize the real costs of production, or make the industrial system function more like a biological ecosystem.

Many American cities have undergone environmental "remediation" for such toxic materials in urban areas, paid for by EPA grants and "superfund" money deriving from fines levied against industrial polluters. The responsible industries consistently oppose doing this, and conservative national politicians allowed the superfund to become virtually exhausted by 2007. My home town (Omaha, NE) is engaged in an expensive program to replace lead-contaminated soil of residential areas in a whole section of the city that was adjacent to an urban lead refinery operating from 1910 until 2000.

## Municipal Pollution

Because industries are usually in human settlements and cities, they directly contribute to the water and air pollution around cities, but municipal pollution also includes pollution from municipal wastes and sewage as well as air pollution from the combustion of fuels in autos, factories, and homes.

In LDCs, much of the sewage from human settlements is not treated and is highly contaminated with raw sewage and micro-organisms that carry waterborne diseases such as dysentery, typhoid, and cholera. Poverty often means malnourishment and exposure to soil and water that carry disease. This high incidence of diarrheal diseases in LDCs reflects the lack of safe drinking water and the ingestion of food- and soil-borne microbes that cause disease. One of the most important things that could be done to improve health and nutrition in LDCs would be to provide clean drinking water to more people so that they could absorb the food they have. The problem, of course, is that most LDCs do not have the capital resources to build sewage treatment plants for towns and growing urban areas. Even in wealthier MDCs, the poor often have greater exposure to such hazards. Partly for such reasons, disadvantaged populations everywhere have lower life expectancies.

Most MDCs have long invested in sanitation and water treatment facilities that reduce the risk from these water-related diseases. *Primary treatment* involves filtration that removes the suspended junk, while *secondary treatment* uses settling basins where aerobic bacteria degrade organic pollutants. Sewage treatment leaves a toxic, gooey sludge that must be dumped or recycled as an organic fertilizer. About 54% of such municipal sludge is applied to farmland, forests, highway medians, or degraded land as fertilizer, and 9% is composted. The rest is dumped in conventional landfills (where it can contaminate groundwater) or incinerated (which can pollute the air with toxic chemicals) (Miller, 2005: 511). Yet, conventional sewage treatment does not remove many toxic chemicals, nitrates, or phosphates. Special treatment can deal with many of these problems, but because of their costs (twice as much as conventional treatment facilities), they are rarely built.

Chapter One described carbon dioxide as the by-product of all respiration and combustion of carbon-based fuels. But there are *many* other chemical by-products of the combustion of fuels. One is suspended carbon particles (soot), which can remain in the air for a long time and can contribute to respiratory disease. Another is carbon monoxide (CO), which is the result of incomplete combustion, particularly from cars and trucks. CO is an odorless gas that interferes with the body's ability to absorb oxygen and can exacerbate heart and respiratory disease or even cause death. Sulfur dioxide ($SO_2$) is produced from the burning of coal and oil. It can cause respiratory problems. More important from an ecosystem perspective is that $SO_2$ combines with water in the atmosphere to form acids (e.g., sulfuric acid) to form acid rain, which kills forests (miles away from the sources) and pollutes soil by making it too acidic for optimum plant growth. Wide areas of the United States and Central and Eastern Europe have been affected by acid rain from urban and industrial sources. Nitrous oxides ($NO_x$) and other volatile organic compounds (VOCs) are also produced from the incomplete combustion of fuels and hydrocarbon compounds from autos and a wide variety of commercial and industrial sources. More important, in the presence of sunlight, $SO_2$, $NO_x$, ozone, and VOCs react to form *smog,* a hazy, dirty brown, toxic witch's brew of more than 100 exotic chemicals

A thermal inversion keeps a thick layer of mid-winter smog over Beijing, China.

that hangs in a bubble over most cities when the weather is right. Smog is particularly a problem in cities such as London, Los Angeles, and Mexico City, where topography and inverted thermal layers of air (warmer aloft than on the surface) often hold smog to the surface in more concentrated forms. But look for it if you fly into any major large metropolitan center.

## Pollution Trends

The awareness of environmental problems that developed in the 1960s began with an awareness of toxic wastes and water and air pollution, and since that time many MDC governments have instituted antipollution programs.[1] But there have been successes. The United States passed the Safe Drinking Water Act of 1974, and from 1972 to 1992 the organic material from sewage and industrial sources dumped into rivers declined significantly. Drinking water generally became safer except that from broad flow runoff of agrochemicals (like nitrates from fertilizer), private wells, and very small water systems (World Resources Institute, 1993: 38, 41).

The good news is that about 95% of people in MDCs and 74% of people in LDCs now have access to clean water (the shrinking supply is a different matter, noted earlier). But there are still problems. According to the World Health Organization, there are still about 1.4 billion people in LDCs without access to clean drinking water. As a result, about 93,000 people die prematurely from infectious diseases spread by contaminated water, or by lack of water for adequate hygiene. The U.N. estimates that it would take $23 billion over about a decade to bring water and sanitation to those people. If the MDCs paid for half of that, it would amount to about $19 a year for each person in LDCs (Miller, 2005: 495).

Even in the United States, water quality is still mixed and controversial, for esthetic reasons as well as fears about water quality by the proliferating sales of bottled water and home water purification systems (both highly promoted and advertized by industries). Both are of questionable health value. Some bottled waters have been found to be not as pure as tap water. By 2000, Congress was being pressured by water-polluting industries to weaken the Safe Drinking Water Act in various ways, while environmentalists were calling for it to be strengthened (Miller, 2002: 499).

In the United States, Congress passed Clean Air Acts in 1970, 1977, and 1990 that required the EPA to set national standards for ambient air quality and emission standards for toxic air pollutants. The legislation was successful because between 1970 and the mid-1990s, levels of air pollutants decreased nationally by almost 30%, even though both population growth and economic growth continued in those years. Requiring industries to make public their annual and release of toxic chemicals promoted their more effective management. The mandatory Toxic Release Inventory (TRI) provides such data. By 2002, release of 300 chemicals tracked since 1988 had been cut in half (Assadourian, 2005). Lead, in particular, has virtually disappeared from air pollution because it was removed from gasoline. The result has been that 50 million people now breathe cleaner air, and the economic benefits have greatly exceeded the costs. The United States spent about $346 billion between 1970 and 1990 to comply with the Clean Air Acts, whereas the human health and ecological benefits in that same period were estimated at between $2.7 and $14.6 *trillion* (in 1990 dollar values). Even so, since the middle of the 1990s, Congress was under intense pressure from polluting industries to weaken the 1990 Clean Air Act, and in 2006 the Bush administration proposed legislation that would do precisely that.

Even with obvious progress in the United States, air is probably not clean enough and problems remain. Nitrogen dioxide levels have not dropped much since 1980 because of a combination of inadequate automobile emission standards, and more vehicles traveling longer distances. Urban smog remains a problem in many areas. In 1994, 100 million people in 43 metropolitan regions continued to live under ground level ozone and smog conditions that violated federal air safety standards. The worst offender for unhealthy air was—surprise—the Los Angeles basin (Associated Press, 1994: 19). Similar trends exist in other MDCs. But air pollution continues to exceed health guidelines in many cities in LDCs, including Beijing, Calcutta, Teheran, and Cairo (O'Meara, 1999: 128).

## Conclusion: The Resources of the Earth

In the span of a single chapter, I have tried to provide you with a fairly rigorous but selective reading of the state of some resource issues important for humans (land, water, biotic resources). After that I described how the wastes and pollution accumulate in various sinks.

So, what is a fair summary of the earth's "vital signs" in this reading? Evidence exists for both progress and many problems in dealing with specific types of pollution in the MDCs. Although some things are improved in LDCs, much of the world still lives in unsanitary conditions that threaten life and health. Wild biological resources and diversity are threatened globally by human activities and are underappreciated for their usefulness to humans, their role in maintaining ecosystems, and their part in the world's heritage of species and genetic diversity. A severe and rapidly emerging general problem with water supply has to do with (1) the increasing human demand for water and (2) the limited or uneven water supply in regions and the hydrological cycle. Although there are many technical efficiencies to be gained in water use, these problems seem intractable and politically explosive. Similarly, problems of land and food security suggest an upper limit to many of the previously successful techniques of intensive "industrial" agriculture. Human material security requires a great deal of technical innovation *and* institutional change in the way that the nations of the world now operate. In the last five decades, popular and scientific ways of understanding environmental problems have moved from concern with specific environmental problems (such as pollution), with which we have had some success, to a more integrated and holistic view of ecological problems. In that view, they can't really be considered in isolation (Dunlap, 1992; White, 1980).

I end with some other observations. Obviously, the human presence on the earth's resources—the human "footprint" on nature—is so large and intrusive that there is very little untouched "pristine nature" left anywhere in the world. Evidence about this relates to the human use of the earth's net primary production. The *net primary production* (NPP) of the biosphere is the amount of energy captured from sunlight by green plants and fixed into living tissues, which is at the base of all food chains. The NPP is the energy flow that powers all living things. Some years ago, Stanford University's Peter Vitousek and his colleagues calculated how much of the biological product (NPP) of the planet is appropriated for the use of human beings. Their results were astounding: Humans used 25% of the photosynthetic product of the earth as a whole and 40% of the photosynthetic product on land! Humans directly consumed only about 3% of the land-based NPP (through food, animal feed, and firewood). But indirectly another 36% went into crop wastes, forest burning and clearing, desert creation, and the conversion of natural areas into settlements. Furthermore, the impact of pollution on reducing the NPP was not even considered (Vitousek et al., 1986). If the 40% figure were even approximately correct, that would raise an interesting question about the consequences of having significantly larger populations in the future. What would the world be like if humans coopted 80% of the NPP? No one is really sure. At best, it might look like the Netherlands or England, totally manicured and under human control: livable but with no wilderness and no room for expansion or mistakes.

*But wait.* The Netherlands and England import food, feed, wood, and fiber and therefore depend on far more than 100% of the NPP of their national areas. The Netherlands was said to "occupy" somewhere between five and seven times its own territory, largely because of imports of animal fodder from the LDCs. Some countries live like that, but the world as a whole cannot (Meadows et al., 1992: 49–50; Rijksinstituut voor Volksgesondheit en Milieuhygiene, 1991). Environmental scholars sometimes call this the *"Netherlands fallacy,"* when a nation that practices widespread frugality and environmental protection but imports more of its resources, so that its environmental impacts spreads far beyond its borders. Importantly, the more the NPP is appropriated for humans and their protected life forms (corn and cows), the less is left for other species, producing a drastic decline in biodiversity. Is a world totally appropriated and managed by *Homo sapiens* a viable biosphere?

We live mostly in managed or "socialized" nature. In terms of human–environment interaction, it has become an *ecosocial system*—a humanly organized environment. All landscapes, from Los Angeles to Amazonia, are such ecosocial arenas. This doesn't mean that human management of nature has been wholly successful; the boundaries of such control are exposed by the very failures of attempts to extend it indefinitely. Nor does this mean that there are no circumstances from which human beings should attempt to withdraw interventions that affect the environment or try to eliminate side effects. This chapter discussed many such circumstances about use of the earth's resources. But since all landscapes are ecosocial and we can no longer disentangle what is "really" natural from what is social, we must now deal with environmental/ecological problems not only with appeals to "pristine nature." Chapter One ended by arguing that environmental problems are also social issues. Likewise, how far we defer to or try to restore natural processes does not depend only on how complex they are, or to the fact that many are too large for us to encompass—though they undoubtedly are. Trying to improve environmental resource problems depends on to what extent we agree that some natural process we have influenced could best be stabilized or reinstated. That depends on a consensus of human values that form the parameters of protection. In other words, the criteria to address such problems are not given in nature itself, but in the values that guide its management, no matter whether we speak of urban areas or of wildernesses (Giddens, 1995: 210–211).

## Personal Connections

*Questions for Review*

1. What does it mean to speak of the economic and ecosystem services of nature? Illustrate with a real world example.
2. What are the major causes of declining biodiversity? Of deforestation?
3. What are some social issues and political conflicts generated by declining biodiversity and deforestation?
4. What are some ways of addressing the extinction of species, declining biodiversity, and deforestation?
5. What are some of the advantages and disadvantages of different methods of dealing with municipal trash?
6. How has producing more food caused environmental problems? To address these, what social and political issues would have to be dealt with?
7. What does is mean to say that we live in "socialized nature," or that we live in an "ecosocial system"? Illustrate from the community in which you live.

*Questions for Reflection*

Think about these large-scale issues in terms of the material flows in your daily living patterns.

1. You might be interested in calculating about how much water you or your family use during a day. Here are some typical amounts:

| Use | Gallons |
|---|---|
| washing a car with hose running | 180 |
| watering lawn for 10 minutes | 75 |
| washing machine at top level | 60 |
| 10-minute shower | 25–50 |
| average bath | 36 |
| handwashing dishes with water running | 30 |
| automatic dishwasher | 10 |
| toilet flush | 5–7 |
| brushing teeth with water running | 2 |

*Source:* American Water Works Association, cited in Miller, 1992: 356.

   How much water do you think you use in a day? A month? If you live in a college dormitory or apartment setting, how much do you think is used?

2. What is the source of water in the community where you live? Are there conflicts about its costs, or about allocating it to business, agriculture, or consumer use? Has there ever been news about impending water shortages or rationing for particular purposes? What local issues are there about water purity? You might call the local utility company or government regulatory agency about this.

3. As I noted in this chapter, most of the solid waste produced in the United States is from municipalities. It is only 10% of total waste, but that is still a prodigious amount. About 10% of your shopping bills go for packaging costs alone (for highly packaged convenience foods, the proportion is a lot more). The typical family creates two or three large cans of trash each week. Do a two-part mental experiment: (1) Keep track of the trash you create for several days. What is it, mainly? Food wrappers? Newspapers? Pop cans? (2) Suppose that instead of having it hauled off, you just let it pile up in your yard. How long do you think it would take to fill your yard?

4. Do you have or use a computer? If so, do you think it has caused you to use more or less paper? What happens to your "waste" computer paper?

## What You Can Do

Quite a lot, actually, if you want to. It's hard to know how to limit the possibilities of altering your lifestyle to be more environmentally frugal. There are whole books written on this subject, and you can find them in any library or bookstore. Here are a few tips:

## About Water

- Don't leave the tap running while you are doing other things.
- If you buy a new dishwasher, get an energy-efficient one.

- Take showers rather than tub baths (this uses about a third of the water that a bath does, unless you use the shower for relaxation therapy rather than cleanliness). Take shorter showers (sing shorter songs).
- Put some bricks or a quart bottle full of water in your toilet tank to use less water per flush. When you buy a new toilet, buy a water-saving one.
- Install a flow constrictor device on faucets, particularly your showerhead. (I have to tell you that my family hollered a lot when I did this. But they got used to it and now accept it as normal.)
- For your garden, rig a hose for drip irrigation rather than spraying with a hose or sprinkler so that much of the water evaporates. Better yet, connect your gutter downspouts to barrels of some sort and use stored rainwater to water your plants.

## About Trash

- Separate trash into recyclables (aluminum glass, metal, and plastic) and organic wastes (leftover vegetable peelings and so forth).
- If your city or workplace does not have a recycling program, try to find out why not.
- Compost organic wastes: It's easy; just a frame of some sort outside into which go things like vegetable wastes, egg shells, and leaves. (Don't put leftover meat or bones in your compost in the city. You'll attract varmints and maybe the city health department!) After several months, take a shovel and turn the compost, or add water or preparations that make it biodegrade faster. After some months, you will have a nice rich organic humus and fertilizer for somebody's flowers or garden. Some communities have community compost sites.
- When you separate your trash like this, you'll find that most of what you have left is packaging material. That suggests another dimension more important than recycling: Buy things that have less packaging, and if you can, carry them home without a bag from the store.

## Real Goods

- Buy durable or repairable goods rather than disposable goods, including disposable cups, pens, razors, and so forth. Where available, buy beverages in refillable bottles.
- Avoid red or yellow packaging; they are likely to have toxic cadmium or lead.
- Choose items that have less packaging. Store things in your refrigerator in reusable containers rather than wrapping them in plastic.
- Reduce the amount of junk mail you get by writing to Mail Preference Service, Direct Marketing Association, 11 West 42nd Street, P.O. Box 3681, New York, NY, 10163–3861.
- Share, trade, barter, or donate things you no longer need rather than throwing them away.
- Conversely, if you can find used things and they work, buy them. It used to be that thrift stores were only for the destitute. But they now attract a more diverse clientele. A used car will cost much less than a new one. I guess it's cultural heresy among the fashionable affluent to buy it used. But if you can wait a year, you're likely to find it.

As you probably realize, such a list has no logical ending. But you get the idea.

## More Resources

Brown, L. (2004). *Outgrowing the earth: The food security challenge in an age of falling water tables and rising temperatures.* New York: W. W. Norton.

Gleick, P. H. (2003). Global freshwater resources: Soft-path solutions for the 21st century. *Science,* Nov–Dec, *302,* 1524–1527. Also at www.sciencemag.org.

Mock, G. (2001). Domesticating the world: Conversion of natural ecosystems. *World Resources 2000–2001,* September. World Resources Institute.

Olshansky, S. J., Carnes, B., Roberts, R., and Smith. L. (1997). Infectious diseases—New and ancient threats to world health. *Population Bulletin, 52,* 2.

Rudel, T. K. (2002). Path of destruction and regeneration: Globalization and forests in the tropics. *Rural Sociology, 67*(4), 662–636.

Vandermeer, J., and Perfecto, I. (2005). *Breakfast of biodiversity: The Truth about rainforest destruction (2nd ed.).* Oakland CA: Food First.

Williams, M. (2006). *Deforesting the earth.* Chicago, IL: University of Chicago Press.

## Electronic Resources

**www.us-ecosystems.org/**
State of the nation's ecosystems, 2008, from the Heinze center for the study of the environment

**www.nrcs.usda.gov/use/worldsoils/map/index**
Maps of various soil characteristics in the world's regions

**http://soilerosion.net/**
The soil erosion site brings together information on soil erosion from a variety of disciplines and sources.

**http://darwin.defra.gov.uk**
The Darwin initiative assists countries that are rich in biodiversity but poor in financial resources to meet their objectives under a major biodiversity convention.

**http://worldwater.org/conflictIntro.htm**
Water resources and international conflict. Updated 2009.

**http://seawifs.gsfc.nasa.gov/OCEAN_PLANET/ HTML/peril_toxins.html**
Toxic wastes; NASA, Smithsonian Institute, Environmental Protection Agency

**www.scorecard.org**
Environmental Defense Fund environmental "score card." Data-rich about environmental problems and pollution from firms, counties, and regions in the United States.

**http://www.Biodiversityinternational.org/**
Research and information about agricultural diversity

## Endnote

1. In the United States, for example, there are the Clean Air Act (1963), the Solid Waste Disposal Act (1965), the Water Quality Act (1965), and the National Environmental Protection Act (1960), which established the Federal Environmental Protection Agency.

# CHAPTER 3

# Climate Change, Science, and Risk

Flooded homes and street from Hurricane Katrina in New Orleans in 2005.

In the early months of 2006, the weather was bizarre. In January there were floods in Northern California, drought across a wide swath of the Southeast and Midwestern states, visibly melting snow in the Rocky Mountains and glacial ice. At the North Pole, polar ice was melting in January. On the morning of April 18, radio news reported 100-degree weather in Houston, Texas, that was accompanied by "rolling" electrical blackouts, which usually didn't occur there until June or July (National Public Radio News, April 18, 2006). The next year, 2007, tied with 1988 as the second warmest year on record; it was significant because that year cooling influences prevailed (Russell, 2009b). In the United States, National Climatic Data Center researchers found that the 2000–2009 decade was the warmest on record (Associated Press, 2010a) as did the World Meteorological Association for the world, easily surpassing the unusually warm 1990s (Russell, 2009a).

Unlike the weather, the world's climate rarely sends clear signals. *Climate* is determined by the large-scale and long-term interaction of hundreds of variables—sunlight, ocean currents, precipitation, fires, volcanic eruptions, topography, human industrial emissions, and the respiration of living things—that produce a complex system that scientists are just beginning to understand—and which defy precise forecasts. Indeed, feedback relationships between the biosphere and global climate suggest that life and climate *coevolved,* a process in which the close interaction influenced the evolutionary paths of both systems in ways that would not have happened had they not been in each other's presence (Schneider and Londer, 1984; Alexander et al., 1997). But the weather in any given year is so variable that some regions are warmer than normal; some cooler; some wetter; some drier; and many riddled with "severe weather events" like floods, droughts, and hurricanes. Almost all of these can be understood as within the enormous range of climatic variability. Unlike weather, climate is impossible to directly experience, and is detected and measured only in global (or continental) averages.

Global temperature record keeping began in 1867, and since 1900, the world's mean temperature has risen, but since 1976 it has risen three times as much as for the century as a whole. Furthermore, the 10 warmest years on record have all occurred since 1990 (Goddard Center, National Aeronautics and Space Administration, cited in Sawin, 2005a). In fact, Antarctic ice core analysis suggests that the late twentieth century was warmer than at any time since at least 1400 C.E. Geophysical and biological signs of warming are visible in many ways. Mountain snow cover and ice caps are melting around the world, in the Rockies, the Andes, the European Alps, and Mount Kilimanjaro in Africa. Most significantly, Greenland's northern ice cap, which contains so much of the world's water (as ice) that it could raise ocean levels around the world, is melting noticeably. Higher temperatures have effected the migratory and breeding seasons for wild species. In tropical areas, warmer water has "bleached" the earth's coral reefs, which are all under stress. Horticulturalists and gardeners have noticed that growing seasons are becoming longer in Europe and North America. The sea ice around Antarctica has virtually disappeared since the 1950s. The human consequences of climate change are also profound. The shrinking of glaciers

---

## BOX 3.1

### The Summer of 1988

To get some idea of what a generally warmer climate might mean, consider the consequences of a warm summer—the summer of 1988—that represented a dramatic spike in generally increasing global mean temperatures. The North American corn crop was stunted by drought in the grain belt, and corn production fell below consumption (probably for the first time in U.S. history). No grain was added to the nation's reserves. Electricity use skyrocketed as people ran air conditioners around the clock, and public agencies distributed electric fans to the elderly, for whom heat exhaustion was a significant health threat. Water levels in thoroughfares like the Mississippi River dropped so low that barges and their cargoes were stranded for weeks. Forest fires burned uncontrollably in America's great natural parks, a super hurricane threatened the Gulf Coast, and in Asia floods in Bangladesh killed 2,000 and drove millions from their homes.

threatens water supplies, and rising global temperatures are a factor in prolonged drought. The World Health Organization estimated that at least 160,000 people die annually from things related to climate change (Swain, 2005a). In 2010 a special World Meteorological panel predicted fewer but stronger hurricanes (tropical cyclones), and that those with more than 130 mph winds would nearly double by the end of the century (Associated Press, 2010b).

Of course, you *cannot infer* from particular events, or even decades, that a general global climate change is in process. But a warmer climate would increase the probabilities of increasingly severe weather events and for widely disruptive changes in ecosystems and human societies (Silver and DeFries, 1990: 63–64). Evidence consistent with a warming pattern continues to mount.

Climate change is very different than the environmental problems discussed in Chapter Two. Problems with soil, water supplies, deforestation, biodiversity, mineral resources, solid wastes, and water and air pollution do have global ramifications, but they are mainly visible as *ecosystem problems.* There are differences as well as similarities in the type and severity of these problems among ecosystems, but these are still problems that are visible *within* particular ecosystems. By contrast, atmospheric and climate change are *biospheric problems.* As energy and matter circulate in atmosphere around the globe, their consequences affect all individuals, societies, and ecosystems, though certainly not in the same way or with the same intensity. In Chapter One, I noted that the environment has complex sets of limiting factors that determine the success and distribution of living things on earth. The physical and chemical nature of the envelope of gases surrounding the earth—the atmosphere—is among the most important, but also the most taken for granted, of these.

Problems like climate change also have a unique *phenomenology*[1] in that they are not really directly experienced by human senses, or studied very directly. Such *megaproblems* are unique in their vast scope, abstract nature, and the long-time horizon over which they develop. Furthermore, they present high-order risks in terms of their consequences. No one is exempt from their effects, and they exemplify a negative side to the rapidly burgeoning human interdependence in the modern world. Conventional scientific inference related to such megaproblems is always contentious, since it cannot be based on experimental research. A pattern of climate change, for instance, cannot be conclusively demonstrated from any particular measured weather data at a particular time and place. Moreover, such megaproblems are typically remote from the concrete experience of individuals and seemingly unaffected by anything that individuals do. The very existence of such problems and their remedies are so abstract and complex that people are dependent on cadres of experts and their scientific (social) constructions of the problem. That means that such problems and their remedies have a peculiar counterfactual nature: If the remedies work, we will never know whether the original diagnostic claims were right. With or without remedies, the experts who make diagnostic claims are likely to find themselves branded as doomsday merchants (Giddens, 1991: 219). Unless you have been living under a rock, you know that global warming (its reality and appropriate human responses) has certainly been debated frequently and often acrimoniously in contemporary mass media, by citizens, scientists, corporate leaders, and our politicians. (I will have more to say about this throughout this chapter).

This chapter is about climate change as a geophysical problem of the planet, but also about its risks for humans and other species, about alternate strategies to respond to it, and about the difficulty of scientifically studying such problems. The chapter will discuss (1) recent *ozone depletion* in the upper atmosphere and its relationship to increasing levels of solar ultraviolet radiation; (2) the reality and predictions about *climate change;* (3) ethical questions, strategy choices, and policy options about global warming. Since climate change has been such an intense contro-versy, among scientists, the public, and politicians, I end this chapter with (4) a discussion of the sources of scientific uncertainty and the analysis of risk. It seemed particularly pertinent here, but it would be relevant in many places in the book where scientific evidence has implications for social policy.

## OZONE DEPLETION AND ULTRAVIOLET RADIATION

The destruction of significant portions of the stratospheric ozone layer graphically illustrates the unintended long-term consequences of a remarkable human technological achievement. It also illustrates how the nations of the world recognized the overshoot of a particular environmental limit, decided to back off, and gave up a profitable and useful industrial product before there was significant human or ecological damage. In that process, the scientific community and the United Nations effectively communicated to governments evidence of an undeniable international problem and negotiated with them to conclude treaties about the problem. In fact, the resolution of the ozone depletion crisis shows nations, international organizations, and scientific communi-ties at their collective best. We may have resolved the problem in time to prevent drastic damage (O'Meara, 1999).

High up in the stratosphere, twice as high as Mount Everest or as jet planes fly, is a gossamer veil of ozone with a crucial function. Ozone is made of three oxygen atoms stuck together ($O_3$) compared with ordinary atmospheric oxygen, which has two ($O_2$). Ozone is so unstable and reac-tive that it attacks and oxidizes almost anything it contacts. Low in the atmosphere, where it has a lot of things it can react with (including plant tissues and human lungs), ozone is a destructive but short-lived pollutant. High in the atmosphere, where ozone is created by the action of sun-light on ordinary oxygen molecules, there isn't much to react with, so the ozone layer lasts a long time. But there is enough ozone to absorb much of the most harmful ultraviolet wavelength from incoming sunlight (UV-B), which tears apart organic molecules that make up all living things. In humans it can produce corneal damage, reproductive mutations, and skin cancer while suppress-ing the immune system's ability to fight cancer. It damages single-celled organisms and could damage floating micro-organisms (plankton) that are at the base of ocean food chains. Exposure to UV-B light stunts the growth and photosynthesis of green plants; in two-thirds of the crop plants that have been studied, crop yields go down as UV-B goes up. The ozone layer is in fact a stratospheric sunscreen that protects humans and ecosystems from damage in ways that are diffi-cult to predict (Meadows et al., 1992: 141–147).

### Destroying the Ozone Layer

In 1974, two scientific papers published independently stated that chlorine atoms in the strato-sphere could be powerful ozone destroyers and that chlorine atoms could be increasing as chloro-fluorocarbon (CFCs) molecules reach the stratosphere and break up to release them. Their hypothesis was controversial but treated seriously enough by nine countries, which banned the use of CFCs in spray cans in the late 1970s. The first unmistakable sign of the destruction of stratospheric ozone arrived in 1985, when a team of British scientists published findings that stunned the world community of atmospheric scientists. They presented evidence that between 1977 and 1984 the concentration of ozone above Antarctica had plunged more than 40% below the 1960 baseline measurements of the southern hemispheric spring season. Ground-level ozone measurements had not hinted at the decline, but the stratospheric depletion was confirmed by analyzing data from NASA satellites and a 1986–1987 Antarctic scientific expedition of the U.S. National Oceanic and Atmospheric Administration (NOAA).

CFCs, widely used as solvents, refrigerant chemicals, and in the production of plastic "foam," were manufactured mainly in Europe and North America, but they were mixed throughout the lower atmosphere so that there are as many CFCs over Antarctica as over Colorado or Washington, DC. Researchers surmised that upon reaching the stratosphere, CFCs encounter high-energy ultraviolet light, which breaks them down, releasing their chlorine atoms. These then engage with ozone in a catalytic reaction in which each chlorine fragment converts ozone to ordinary oxygen. But through a series of reactions, each chlorine atom can cycle through this process many times, destroying one ozone molecule each time and becoming like the "Pac-Man of the higher atmosphere, gobbling one ozone molecule after another and then being regenerated to gobble again" (Meadows et al., 1992: 148). Each chorine atom can destroy up to 100,000 ozone molecules before it is finally removed from the atmosphere. Chemicals thought most dangerous (CFC-11, CFC-12, and CFC-113) were increasing in the atmosphere by between 5% and 11% annually.

By the late 1980s, there was virtual agreement among the scientific community that CFCs were responsible for Antarctic ozone depletion. The most severe ozone depletion was limited to the Antarctic because the reaction requires the cold temperatures, stratospheric ice crystals, and sunlight characteristic of the early Antarctic spring and also because the circulation of winds (the *polar vortex*) tends to trap the depleted ozone over the Antarctic for several months. Less severe but record ozone losses have also occurred over the populous and agriculturally abundant mid- to high latitudes of both hemispheres. Scientists speculate that increases in sulfurous particles, water vapor, and various pollutants in the stratosphere may provide material surfaces for the ozone-depleting reactions to take place much as ice crystals do in the Arctic and Antarctic (O'Meara, 1999; Silver and DeFries, 1990: 103–112; Stern et al., 1992: 57–59).

## A Cautionary Tale: Technology, Progress, and Environmental Damage

Here's a brief detour from the physical facts of the problem into its social and historical contexts. In the first chapter, I argued that underlying modern environmental problems were the economic, social, cultural, and technological issues. Following is a dramatic example related to ozone depletion. It is also a classic illustration about how undeniable progress can result in unanticipated long-run problems. To really understand the causes of ozone depletion, you need to reach back through a century's history, long before CFCs were invented (the following discussion relies heavily on Stern et al., 1992: 54–59).

Until almost the end of the nineteenth century, refrigerating food and drink depended on ice from natural sources that was chopped from local ponds and stored in warehouses or pits for use in the summer. Households used this ice, but breweries and restaurants were the heaviest users, and stored winter ice was sometimes shipped hundreds of miles to provide refrigeration (Boston ice merchants shipped ice as far as South Carolina and the Caribbean). Because this system of using stored winter ice was difficult and expensive, most food was preserved by chemical additives (most commonly salt, sodium chloride). Pork became the most popular meat because its decay could be easily arrested by salt. Preserved beef was much less popular, and those who ate beef preferred to buy it freshly slaughtered from local butchers. To increase their profits, in the 1870s meatpackers began experimenting with ice-refrigerated railway cars to ship dressed beef, slaughtered and chilled in Chicago, to consumers hundreds of miles away. Soon this new ice storage and delivery technology was used to ship fruits and vegetables from California and Florida and dairy products from urban hinterlands to remote customers. This technology drastically lowered the rate at which food spoiled and made perishable crops available to consumers through much of the year. Eventually refrigeration changed the whole nature of the American diet. But natural ice was unreliable, and in two warm winters (1889 and 1890) the failure of the natural ice crop encouraged the packers to seek more reliable forms of refrigeration.

The principle of mechanical refrigeration—by which compressed gas was allowed to expand rapidly and lower temperature—had been known since the mid-eighteenth century. But mainly urban brewers used the first commercial adaptation of this process in the late nineteenth century. These early refrigerant systems used ammonia, sulfur dioxide, or methyl chloride as refrigerant gases, but they had serious problems. For efficiency, they required high pressures and powerful compressors, which increased the risk of equipment failures and explosions. They were toxic gases that caused a number of deaths. Toxicity and the need for expensive compressors kept mechanical refrigeration from making headway with retail customers, who represented a huge potential market. This led Thomas Midgely, working for General Motors Frigidaire division, in 1931 to develop a new chlorinated fluorocarbon, patented as Freon 12, as a perfect alternative to existing refrigerant gases. Freon was chemically stable, nonflammable, nonexplosive, nontoxic, and required less pressure to produce the cooling effect.

Because smaller compressors were required, American consumers could soon own their own "refrigerators," making it possible to sell chilled foods in retail-sized packages. Frozen foods were marketed in the 1950s, as were the fresh vegetables and dairy products that became rapidly accepted as ordinary parts of the American diet. Europeans followed Americans in adopting these technologies.

Equally important, the properties of Freon made it possible for the refrigeration technology to be applied to space cooling in buildings, thus creating another important market for it. Air-conditioning became common to offices and finally to residences. This development had an enormous impact on the American social pattern. Air-conditioning promoted urban growth in the American Sunbelt—from Florida to California—and in tropical regions around the globe. For many Americans, it would be difficult to envision life in the summer months or warm climates without air-conditioning in their homes, autos, stores, and offices. It shifted the peak use of electricity from the winter (when its use for lighting and space heating peaked) to the summer, when air-conditioning systems use electricity at unprecedented rates. From the 1950s, the sales of CFCs were increased by other uses: as nontoxic propellants in aerosol sprays and as solvents for the manufacture of integrated electrical circuits. Taken together, these technologies had an enormous impact on improving the nutrition, comfort, and physical quality of life for many people. But the very *stability* of CFCs that made them so useful ultimately proved to be their greatest environmental hazard. As they leaked from refrigerators, air conditioners, and spray cans at an ever-increasing rate, they eventually found their way to the stratosphere, where they encountered ozone. The problem with ozone depletion was a direct but long-term consequence of a social pattern—the technical innovations; the search for profitable markets; the residential, consumption, and lifestyle patterns and expectations of people—that evolved in the more developed countries (MDCs).

### A Happy Ending?

Even with the scientific consensus about the relationship between CFCs and ozone deterioration, little would have happened without the United Nations Environmental Program, which hosted and prodded the international political process. Its staff assembled and interpreted evidence, created a neutral forum for high-level discussions, and patiently reminded all nations that no short-term selfish consideration was as important as the integrity of the ozone layer. In consequence, the DuPont Company, which produced 25% of the world's CFCs, declared its intent to phase out CFC production and search for more environmentally benign refrigerant chemicals. In 1987, 49 signatory nations to the *Montreal Protocol* announced their intention to cut CFC production and consumption by 50% by the year 2000. An even more stringent protocol was subsequently signed in London. Firms are producing less damaging chemicals to power air conditioners, act as solvents to clean computer cleaning circuit boards, and make into insulating foam. Only time will tell whether the new compounds are more environmentally benign than CFCs. Hamburgers are being wrapped in paper or cardboard again, and many consumers are returning to washable ceramic coffee cups instead of foam ones. Although CFC production has declined steeply and the ozone hole appears to have stabilized, it will take many years to completely heal, because CFCs take years to reach the upper atmosphere and last for decades, or even centuries, once there (O'Meara, 2002).

In sum, dealing with the ozone problem represents a model for addressing environmental problems involving scientific consensus and its interpretation for policy, international mediation, responsible political and corporate behavior, and public education. Yet, there are many reasons for concern about the broader applicability of this model. Most important, the encouraging resolution of the ozone depletion problem may depend upon special circumstances not applicable to many other environmental problems. There were, for instance, only about two dozen CFC producers worldwide, and banning production threatened few existing firms or long-developed technical infrastructures. So the Montreal Protocol is a risky predictor for how quickly and effectively other international negotiations may turn out. Even if there is scientific consensus, such changes will be much more difficult (1) if the need for change requires greater alterations in social behavior and lifestyle expectations, (2) when there are many millions of responsible actors, or (3) when the costs and benefits of change are less evenly distributed around the planet (Stern et al., 1992: 59). By these criteria, the impending problem of global warming will be *much* more difficult to address.

## TURNING UP THE HEAT: GLOBAL WARMING

Gases in the atmosphere play a critical role in trapping enough infrared solar radiation (heat) to keep the mean temperature of the earth fluctuating within relatively narrow limits that make life possible. The most important of such gases are water vapor, carbon dioxide ($CO_2$), tropospheric (low altitude) ozone, methane ($CH_4$), and nitrogen oxides ($NO_x$). Water vapor and $CO_2$, the most important of these, account for probably 90% of the heat-trapping capacity. Water vapor is controlled by the water cycle discussed earlier, and $CO_2$ is regulated by a similar carbon cycle (discussed in Chapter One). But humans have added $CO_2$ to the atmosphere by burning fossil fuels and deforestation. Forests take in $CO_2$, thereby "sequestering" carbon from the atmosphere.

Such gases were collectively called *greenhouse gases* because the way they warm the atmosphere is analogous to the way that gardeners have long grown plants and germinated seeds in air warmed in glass greenhouses. Remember returning to your car on a sunny day with the windows all rolled up? In principle, the *greenhouse effect* explains the very cold climate of Mars, where water vapor, a highly efficient greenhouse gas, is virtually absent, as well as the hot climate of Venus, where the atmosphere is so thick with $CO_2$ and conditions are so hot that life—as we know it—could not exist (Silver and DeFries, 1990: 64).

After water vapor, $CO_2$ is the most plentiful and effective greenhouse gas. It occurs naturally as a consequence of the respiration of living things. (Remember the carbon cycle discussed in Chapter One?) The atmosphere has so much water vapor that human activity has little effect on it. By contrast, the concentration of $CO_2$ is so small (.036%) that human activity can significantly increase its concentration. $CO_2$ is produced in great quantities by the burning of fossil fuels—natural gas, petroleum, and particularly coal. Atmospheric methane is an important greenhouse gas in addition to $CO_2$. It is produced by bacterial activity in the digestive tracts of ruminant animals (e.g., cows and sheep) and in bogs and swamps, and human garbage dumps. The significance of methane ($CH_4$) produced in large quantities by garbage dumps and the "feedlots" of industrial agriculture has been overlooked (Goodland and Anhang, 2009). When permafrost melts in the Arctic region, detritus will begin the normal decay process, releasing much carbon into the atmosphere. At present rates, 40% of Arctic permafrost will thaw by 2030, releasing more than 200 billion tons of $CH_4$, a more potent greenhouse gas than $CO_2$, and which would greatly accelerate climate warming. We will face this reality, one way or another (Fry, 2010).

Speculations about the implications of anthropogenic increases in greenhouse gases are not really new, and the role of such gases in maintaining the temperature of the earth has been known for more than 150 years. Fourier was the first to discuss the heat-trapping role of $CO_2$ in 1827. At the turn of the twentieth century, Swedish naturalist Arrhenius argued that increasing concentrations of $CO_2$ would raise the global mean temperature. In 1941, Flohn noted that anthropogenic $CO_2$ perturbs the carbon cycle, leading to a continual $CO_2$ accumulation in the atmosphere, and in 1957 Revelle and Suess concluded that "human activities were initiating a global geophysical experiment that would lead to detectable climatic changes in a few decades" (cited in Krause et al., 1992: 11). In 1957, the systematic measurement of $CO_2$ began at the Mauna Loa (Hawaii) observatory and at the South Pole. In 1979, the World Meteorological Organization convened a World Climate Conference in Geneva to discuss the issue. Following this conference were a host of international meetings about climate change issues that led to the first meeting in 1988 of the Intergovernmental Panel on Climate Change (IPCC), sponsored by the United Nations Environmental Program and the World Meteorological Organization. The IPCC, composed of 2,000 leading climatologists, was charged with assessing the weight of evidence from scientific studies of climate change. The IPCC published reports in 1990, 1995, 2001, and 2007. Panels of scientists from the U.S. National Academy of Sciences (NAS) and the American Geophysical Union also examined the weight of evidence from scientific studies of climate change.

To summarize, the greenhouse effect and the possibility of global warming has been known for more than a century, but only since the 1950s has this threat begun to be taken seriously, and only in the 1990s did questions about "preventative" policy measures enter the international political arena.

## General Circulation Models

All of our knowledge about greenhouse gases and climate change are based on *general circulation models* (GCMs) by which climatologists try to construct mathematical models to "represent" or "simulate" the complex workings of the earth–atmosphere interactions. As you might guess, these global interactions are very complex and involve many feedback loops that are only imperfectly understood. So like all models, GCMs represent a vastly simplified version of the real world. Despite this, these computerized mathematical models that predict the ways in which temperature, humidity, wind speed and direction, soil moisture, sea ice, and other climate variables evolve through three dimensions and over time are the only tools available for

---

### BOX 3.2

#### Estimating Global Climate from Long, Long Ago

There are physical signs that make it possible to estimate the planet's climate throughout long geological history. The expansion and contraction of glaciers, for which there are many physical markers, is one fairly good measure of past temperature fluctuations. Other evidence comes from studies of fossilized pollen grains, annual growth rings of trees, and the changing sea levels—as measured by the presence of coral reefs, which live close to the ocean surface because they need light before they die. Cores of sediment extracted from the floor of the deep oceans are particularly important, because of their chemical composition and the presence of warm- or cold-water fossil species. Such sediment samples provide clues to changes in ocean temperature and the volume of polar ice caps. The *most* useful ones comes from analyzing ice cores extracted from ancient glaciers in Greenland and Antarctica for changes in the concentrations of gas bubbles (of $CO_2$ or $CH_4$) over millions of years (Miller and Spoolman, 2009: 497–498; Silver and DeFries, 1990: 25).

---

understanding global climate change. There are five existing GCMs; while their findings generally agree, they are not identical.

With the limitations of simplified mathematical models, how can climatologists use them to simulate the actual dynamics of the earth's climate, with its complex interaction of variable nonlinear feedback loops? In three ways: (1) By starting with existing data, the model can be "run forward" to simulate "today's climate," especially the large temperature swings of the seasonal cycle, (2) by determining whether the model can realistically simulate an individual physical component of the climate system, such as cloudiness, and (3) by running the model backward in time to see whether it can reproduce the long-term changes climate of the ancient earth, about which, surprisingly, a great deal is known. See Box 3.2.

The performance of GCMs has been appraised continuously, and they are getting better at predicting climate change (Schneider, 1990a: 74; Miller, 2005: 470). What do they conclude? In broad strokes, based on the accumulated evidence GCMs and other research, there is a strong and growing consensus within scientific communities about climate change and global warming. Before discussing that a bit, I need to discuss some ambiguity in the evidence about climate change.

### Some Ambiguities in the Evidence

1. While the correlation between greenhouse gas concentration and temperature fluctuation works well for geological history, it works less well for shorter time spans.
2. Climate may not change in a "linear" fashion. The assumed gradualness of linear change underlies the assumption that societies will have time to adjust. Some evidence suggests that climate has changed in abrupt and chaotic fashion in the past (Cunningham et al., 2005: 320).
3. Beyond their role as carbon sinks, the role of the oceans in the warming process is not clearly understood, but it is likely to be large. The oceans store most of the planet's heat and $CO_2$ and have deep circulation patterns that are not well modeled. The enormous oceanic mass will act as a thermal sponge slowing any initial increase in global warming while the oceans themselves heat up, but the magnitude of this increase in temperature will depend on ocean circulation, which may *itself* change as the earth warms (Miller and Spoolman, 2009: 504; Schneider, 1990a: 31).

4. It is difficult for GCMs to factor in effects of vegetation and forests and their impact on ground surface *reflectiveness* (or *albedo*), their function as carbon sinks, or the significance of their release of water vapor and cloud formation.
5. Interactions and feedbacks between temperature change and cloud formation are not clear. Will heating of the atmosphere create more or fewer clouds? If more clouds, would they trap more heat at the earth's surface or reflect more solar radiation into space?

## Evolving Science and Consensus

Systematic observations about climate conditions that began about 1985 produced interesting and curious observations about climate change. Then there was considerable scientific uncertainty about the "global warming" thesis, understood by climatologists to be important but highly speculative. Reflecting this, the earliest edition of this book (in 1996) emphasized the uncertainty and speculative character of the evidence in those years. But that changed, as more physical evidence emerged and a more sophisticated understanding of how "earth systems" work took place.

The uncertainty about global warming of earlier years has been progressively replaced by a strong consensus within the world community of climatologists that global warming is real and a significant threat to human well-being. In the present century as well as longer geological history, there have been *strong positive correlations* between atmospheric concentrations of greenhouse gases and fluctuation in the earth's mean temperatures. Atmospheric concentrations of $CO_2$ have risen from preindustrial levels of 280 parts per million (ppm) by volume to 383.6 ppm today. The Fourth Assessment Report, released by the IPCC in 2007, concluded with 90% certainty that contemporary warming is anthropogenic, and caused by greenhouse gases released by human activities. It is taking place too rapidly to be explained by similar fluctuations throughout the geological history of the planet. It also concludes that while the ocean acts as a vast heat sink, it will continue to warm, adding to the warming that is already taking place (IPCC, 1970). Since the momentum of emissions are inexorable and they persist in the atmosphere for centuries, climate change cannot be avoided, but it might be moderated. See Figures 3.1 and 3.2.

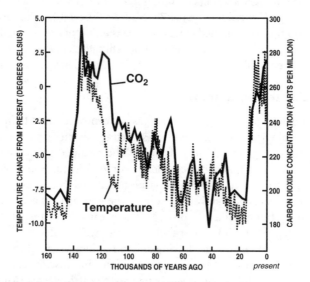

**FIGURE 3.1**   Carbon Dioxide and Temperature: Long-Term Record

*Source:* Adapted from S. H. Schneider, "The Changing Climate," in Editors of Scientific American, *Managing the Planet Earth,* 1990a: 29. New York: W. H. Freeman Co. Used with permission.

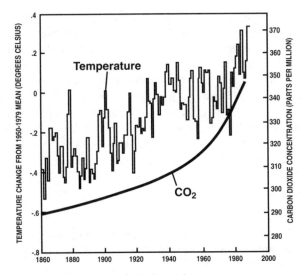

**FIGURE 3.2**   Carbon Dioxide and Temperature, Industrial Era

*Source:* Adapted from S. H. Schneider, "The Changing Climate," in Editors of Scientific American, *Managing the Planet Earth,* 1990a: 29, New York: W. H. Freeman Co. Used with permission.

It is not just that temperature changes threaten us, regardless of the causes, but how rapidly they occur. Past temperature change often took place over 1,000 to 100,000 years. The problem we face is a fairly sharp projected increase of the temperature of the troposphere in this century. In 2002 the NAS issued a study raising the possibility that the temperature could rise drastically in only a decade or two, and in 2006 at the request of Congress, which had requested a broad review of scientific work, the NAS report concluded that "recent warmth is unprecedented for the last several millennia" (Associated Press, 2006).

Polar bears stranded on melting Arctic ice pack.

To grasp the enormity of these probable changes, compare them to the climate history of the earth. A global average warming of 1.5 degrees would represent a climate not experienced since the beginning of agricultural civilization some 6,000 years ago; three to five degrees would represent a climate not experienced since human beings appeared on the earth some 2 million years ago. The last time the earth was this warm was in the Pliocene period (some 3 to 5 million years ago). Furthermore, more than five degrees warming would mean a climate not experienced since 40 million years ago, before the evolution of birds, flowering plants, and mammals, when there were no glaciers in the Antarctic, Iceland, or Greenland (Krause et al., 1992: 28). The projected rate of warming is 15 to 40 times faster than after the major ice ages. Such warming could far outstrip the ability of ecosystems to adapt or migrate (Silver and DeFries, 1990: 71).

## Impacts on Society

A growing body of research is focused on how climate change might affect human societies, although with the uncertainties just mentioned, much of it is speculative. Let me just mention a few issues being addressed in this research:

**1. *Food security:*** Many crop yields are delicately dependent on a particular mix of temperatures, soil conditions, and rainfall patterns that could be disrupted by global warming. According to a senior U.N. official and the Union of Concerned Scientists, by 2025, 70% of the world's land could be suffering from drought. In just a couple of decades in the United States, average summers in the "breadbasket" (Illinois) could be hotter than the 1988 heat wave that wiped out $40 billion worth of food crops (Van Gelder et al., 2010). Heat stress could also severely reduce the productivity of Asian "rice bowl" regions. Reduced yields and less-than-needed yield improvements, combined with growing population and higher food prices, could seriously jeopardize the world's food security (Devereaux and Edwards, 2004).

**2. *Regional impacts:*** Climate change is global, but we may overlook dramatic regional and local weather changes. The World Meteorological Organization reported that by 2009 winter and spring temperatures were four degrees Celsius higher than in 2007. Extreme drought struck North America and China, while massive flood devastated England, South Asia, and many Latin American countries (Russell, 2009a: 56). The impact is likely to increase the price of grain on a worldwide basis, but the impact is likely to be especially severe in the *less developed countries* (LDCs) (largely in the Southern Hemisphere) that have more "unmanaged" ecosystems. While causal links between the weather events in specific regions are not certain, more extreme weather is consistent with a warmer planet.

**3. *Land use and human settlements:*** A modest rise in sea level would threaten the coastal settlements in which *half* of humanity lives. They include Boston, New York, Miami, New Orleans, Los Angeles, Seattle, and Vancouver as well as Tokyo, Osaka, Manila, Shanghai, Guangshou, Calcutta, Lagos, London, Copenhagen, and Amsterdam. The entire Maldives Republic and much of Bangladesh, Indonesia, the Netherlands, and Denmark would be under water. Rich farmland in river deltas would be lost; salinity would move upstream. In the United States, for instance, economic analyses estimated that a *50 cm* rise in sea level by the year 2100 would cost between $20.4 and $138 billion in lost property and damage to economic infrastructures (Alexander et al., 1997: 86). A one meter rise would flood most of New York City, including the entire subway system and all three major airports. A rise of five degrees Fahrenheit in average temperature would melt the Greenland ice cap, the world's largest mass of frozen water. That would raise the sea level enough that most of South Florida (including Miami) would simply disappear into the Atlantic.

**4. *Freshwater supplies:*** Rising global temperatures would be a key factor in threatening water supplies for millions of people and other species. They would reduce stream flows and increase pressure on groundwater while worsening the pollution discharge into smaller flows. This effect could exacerbate the world's existing water problems, which, as Chapter Two noted, are substantial.

**5. *Planning uncertainty:*** In the planning of human resettlement, flood control, and revamping agriculture for changing growing seasons, society might find itself in a constant treadmill, trying to catch up with perpetual change in an environment that is changing rapidly, unpredictably, and differently in different regions.

**6. *Other impacts:*** Global warming could involve increased human health risks as a result of heat stress and more vigorous transmission of tropical diseases over larger areas. Warming could lead to increasing energy consumption for air-conditioning, losses in hydropower availability, and losses in revenue from tourism and fisheries. If ecosystems collapse suddenly, low-lying cities are flooded, forests are consumed in vast fires, grasslands die out and turn into dust bowls, and tropical waterborne and insect-transmitted diseases spread rapidly beyond their current ranges, this would represent a truly a catastrophic "worst-case-scenario." It also represents a significant security threat. A 2003 Defense Department analysis projected widespread rioting and regional conflict in some countries faced with dwindling food, water, and energy supplies, and argued that global warming must "be viewed as a serious threat to global stability and should be elevated beyond a scientific debate to a national security concern" (Miller, 2005: 471– 472).

## Controversy and Conflict

You surely know how contentious and controversial global warming is in the United States, and since it became a widely understood problem in the late 1980s, many people, powerful corporations, and foundations have become powerful forces directed at getting global warming *not* seen as a real problem. One side of the contemporary debate is the massive and growing consensus among scientific communities that global warming is a real and significant problem, and on the other, a tiny minority of scientists—with real credentials—some talented writers and media personalities who are luxuriously supported by large corporations (mainly in mining, lumber, and petroleum industries) to produce and publicize widely the view that global warming is a pseudoproblem—just a "lot of hot air." Noting the real scientific complexity of the climate change, global warming skeptics argued that global warming is not a real problem at all—but one manufactured by networks of radical environmentalists and political liberals for money and political gain. It is a thinly disguised attack on American capitalism and consumerism. To the extent that global warming is real, they argued, it would be beneficial. For instance, in a $CO_2$-enriched atmosphere plants could grow exuberantly and produce more food for the hungry. Warming skeptics, who rarely publish in legitimate scientific journals, work with conservative foundations that seek to influence public opinion and lobby congressmen and conservative administrations not to take global warming seriously (Kennedy, 2005; McCright and Dunlap, 2000, 2003; Pope and Rauber, 2004). Since they have effectively dominated U.S. public opinion and politics about the issues, you can see why the end of this chapter is a good place to discuss sources of scientific uncertainty and risk analysis.

---

### BOX 3.3

### Greenhouse Politics in the United States

A powerful "countermovement" of industry association, private organization, and parts of the national government have worked to portray global warming as "not a problem" (McCright and Dunlap, 2000, 2003). Research documents that prior to 1994, congressional expert testimonies about global warming were dominated by conventional and respected climate scientists, but after 1994 when more conservative Republicans gained control of Congress, prominent "climate change skeptics" were more likely to be asked to testify. That change in congressional testimonials had an effect. After 1994 media articles about climate change were far more likely to give as much attention to the views of the small number of climate change skeptics as those representing the established consensus of the scientific community (McCright and Dunlap, 2003). Others documented that during the 1990s the fossil fuel industry, along with allies in manufacturing and labor unions, mounted a dual campaign of public relations and congressional lobbying to address global warming (Gelbspan, 1997; Newell, 2000). In response to Al Gore's documentary about global warming (*An Inconvenient Truth*), the *Wall Street Journal* ran an editorial entitled "Hockey Stick hokum," citing the same few well-known global warming "nay sayers" (*Wall Street Journal,* 2006: A12). Conservative movement organizations and think tanks with neatly packaged counterclaims flooded the media with press releases and held forums that provided their credentialed climate change skeptics with substantial resources and venues for promoting their ideas (Layzer, 2007). In January 2006, the top scientist at the National Aeronautics and Space Administration (Dr. James Hansen) publicly claimed that the administration of George Bush tried to stop him from speaking out since he called for prompt reductions in the emissions of greenhouse gases (Revkin, 2006).

---

## DO WE KNOW ENOUGH TO ACT?

There are different schools of thought about what (if anything) could or should be done. Let me examine some different assumptions.

**1.** Don't act until you are certain, or *wait and see.* Those holding this view, including some scientists, economists, corporate leaders, and politicians, argue that more research is needed before making far-reaching economic decisions (like phasing out the carbon-based fossil fuel system), and they argue that uncertainties are still too large to warrant costly remedial or preventative measures.

**2.** *Act now to minimize risks.* Those with this view (a growing number of scientists and business and political leaders) believe that uncertainty cuts both ways: If major climate change, for example, should occur, inaction could have catastrophic consequences, and the problem may prove more difficult and costly later. The world's nations should pursue investments and policies now to address the problem (Krause et al., 1992: 3). This is widely known as a "precautionary principle," meaning that when there is a potential threat (even with some uncertainty) to humans or ecosystems, decision makers should take action.

**3.** Act to slow global warming, with *no regrets,* even if the threat of global warming does not materialize. This rationale is widely used in other realms. I insure my house against fire, even though it has never happened, but would prove catastrophic if it did. Similarly, the United States spent billions of dollars during the cold war preparing for a thermonuclear war that never occurred.

I am more persuaded by the last two assumptions. By the time we "wait and see" or scientific knowledge improves, the full brunt of climatic change may be upon us. There are enormous risks and a huge gamble in the wait-and-see-while-collecting-more-data option (Krause et al., 1992: 5). The prudent course is to take some action early in the hopes of forestalling worst possible outcomes. It seems to me that the imprudent course is to do nothing, awaiting a complete confirmation of the models. As a World Bank paper stated: "When confronted with risks which could be menacing, cumulative and irreversible, uncertainty argues strongly in favor of prudent action against complacency" (MacNeill et al., 1991: 17–18). Note that this was written before the scientific consensus was as strong as it is today.

If we act and the threat is real, we win. If we act and the treat is not so real, we lose something, but only the investments and "insurance premiums." If, on the other hand, the threat is real and we don't do anything about it unit it is too late, we risk losing on a catastrophic scale.

*But wait.* Even if the threat of global warming really doesn't materialize, addressing it would not be all cost. Such efforts would have side benefits for human well-being and ecological threats, which make them worth doing on other grounds. They could, for example, improve problems of urban air pollution and acid rain, enhance energy efficiency, and wean us away from the last decades of the carbon-based energy system. They could promote international global cooperation in programs about reforestation, sustainable agriculture, soil conservation, land reform, and probably the alleviation of the most wretched global poverty. In other words, addressing global warming could be a way to unify a basket of separate measures addressing human–environment problems and preserving the "global commons."

## POLICY OPTIONS: WHAT COULD BE DONE ABOUT GLOBAL WARMING?

Human action and responses about global warming fall into three broad categories: *adaptation, mitigation,* and *geoengineering.* They are not mutually exclusive.

Those who urge *adaptation* believe that the large uncertainties in climate projections make it unwise to spend large sums trying to avert outcomes that may never materialize (Schneider, 1990a: 34). They believe that human systems can adapt to climate change much faster than they occur. Those advocating adaptation do not eschew all active policies (such as anticipating flood control or water supply problems), but they generally argue that human individuals, organizations, and communities will quickly adjust to such changes so that much organized governmental response will be superfluous and unnecessary. This is a favorite argument of neoclassical economists. They maintain that while the projected doubling of $CO_2$ will take place over the next century, financial markets adapt in minutes, labor markets in several years, and the planning horizon for significant economic and technological change is at most two or three decades (Stern et al., 1992: 110). So there is plenty of time to adapt to whatever happens.

The real question is not whether climate change will occur, but how rapidly it will occur. If moderate change takes place gradually over several hundred years, adaptation is a perfectly feasible and adequate response. But if global change reaches a threshold where the earth warms suddenly and rapidly, ushering in "large, abrupt, and unwelcome shifts in climate," as hypothesized by a report issued by the NAS in 2004, then the costs of adaptation would be substantial and accompanied by considerable social, economic, and political turmoil (see Haimson, 2002b). Such catastrophic and rapid climate change would also reduce the earth's biodiversity because many species couldn't adapt (Miller, 2005: 471).

*Mitigation* means curtailing the greenhouse gas buildup to prevent, minimize, or at least slow global warming. Advocates of taking action now to mitigate warming argue that because of the time lags in the global environmental system, it may be too late to prevent catastrophe by the time it becomes clear that a response is needed. Even if catastrophe is unlikely, mitigation that slows the rate of change means that successful adaptation would be easier and less costly. They argue that mitigation actions begun now allow for more modifications in process, and even blunders, than if begun at a later time when the situation may be more critical. Mitigation is like insuring against disaster: The costs of the "premiums" are onerous though bearable, but the costs of a world-scale catastrophe may not be. It seeks to avoid the high-risk uncontrolled experiment now taking place with the global environment. Furthermore, the advocates of mitigation believe that the economic arguments against mitigation, citing high costs, are specious in the general case. This is because the costs and benefits of postponing action are not always comparable. If current economic activity destroys the life support systems on which humans depend, what future market adjustments or investments could ever recoup this cost? Neither do economic arguments include some environmental goods (such as biodiversity), which have both economic and intrinsic or spiritual benefits that people value. Furthermore, economic accounting undervalues "common property," which cannot be privately owned (the vast atmosphere is a case in point), and for which prices and property rights are fictitious and only potential (Stern et al., 1992: 111–113).

Mitigation strategies could curtail greenhouse gas buildup by breaking down a large problem into smaller, "bite-sized" pieces, called *wedge analysis*. Thus, a Princeton University ecologist and an engineer proposed using existing technologies—efficiencies in transportation, buildings, power generation—along with some non-technological conservation measures—to mitigate climate change. You can see some of what they proposed in Table 3.1.

| **TABLE 3.1** | Wedge Analysis: Reducing Global $CO_2$ Emissions by 1 Billion Tons Over 50 Years |
| --- | --- |

1. Double the fuel economy or 2 billion cars from 30 to 60 mpg.
2. Cut average annual travel per car from 10,000 to 5,000 miles.
3. Improve efficiency in heating, cooling, lighting, and appliances by 25%.
4. Update all building insulation, windows, and weather stripping to modern standards.
5. Boost efficiency of all coal-fired power plants from 32% today to 60% (through co-generation of steam and electricity).
6. Replace 800 large coal-fired with an equal amount of gas-fired power (four times current capacity).
7. Capture $CO_2$ from 800 large coal-fired or 1,600 gas-fired power plants, and store it securely.
8. Replace 800 large coal-fired power plants with an equal amount of nuclear power (twice the current level).
9. Add 2 million MW windmills (50 times current capacity).
10. Generate enough hydrogen from wind to fuel a billion cars (4 million 1 MW windmills).
11. Install 2,000 GW of photovoltaic energy (700 times current capacity).
12. Expand ethanol production to 2 trillion liters per year (50 times current capacity).
13. Stop all tropical deforestation and replant 300 million hectares of forest.
14. Apply conservation tillage to all cropland (10 times current levels).

*Source:* From National Academy of Sciences, Policy implications of greenhouse warming, pp 54–57. National Academy Press. Copyright 1991. Reprinted with permission from AAAS.

| **TABLE 3.2** | Some Geoengineering Options |
|---|---|
| • *Sunlight screening* | Place 50,000 100 $km^2$ space mirrors in the earth's orbit to reflect incoming sunlight. |
| • *Stratospheric dust* | Use guns or balloons to maintain a dust cloud in the stratosphere to increase sunlight reflection. |
| • *Stratospheric bubbles* | Place billions of aluminized, hydrogen-filled balloons in the stratosphere to provide a reflective screen. |
| • *Low stratospheric dust* | Use aircraft to maintain a cloud of dust in the low stratosphere to reflect sunlight. |
| • *Ocean biomass stimulation* | Place iron in the oceans to stimulate the production of $CO_2$ absorbing plankton. |

*Source:* Adapted from National Academy of Sciences, *Policy implications of greenhouse warming,* p. 58. National Academy Press. Courtesy of the National Academies Press, Washington, D.C. Copyright 1991. Used with permission.

The third type of policy options is *geoengineering strategies,* which use technical measures to counteract climate change. Proposals have included several ways of reducing temperature increases by screening sunlight (e.g., space mirrors, stratospheric dust or soot, reflective stratospheric balloons, stimulating cloud condensation) as well as stimulation plankton growth to increase the uptake of $CO_2$ by the oceans. Reforestation, already mentioned, is really a *sort* of geoengineering. You can see several proposed geoengineering technologies in Table 3.2.

Geoengineering options have a potential to affect global warming on a substantial scale, and some are relatively inexpensive, but all have large unknowns concerning possible environmental side effects (e.g., particles introduced into the atmosphere or the ocean might alter the ocean chemistry—and food chains—in an effort to stimulate plankton growth) (National Academy of Sciences, 1991: 60). If we don't understand planetary dynamics completely, do we really know enough to reengineer the earth on such a scale? Yet, the NAS panel argued that we need to know more about these options, because they may be crucial if global warming occurs, particularly at the upper range of temperature projections. If adaptive efforts fail, and efforts to restrain greenhouse gas production on a global basis fail—for either technical or political reasons—such geoengineering options might be the only effective ones available (National Academy of Sciences, 1991: 62–63).

## Strategies, Social Change, and Inequality

Adaptation and mitigation strategies would both involve significant social change. In terms of mitigation, the IPCC estimated that a reduction in greenhouse gases of between 60% and 80% below 1990 levels would be required to stabilize global mean temperature (Flavin, 1998: 14; Miller, 2002: 464–465). Achieving such results *would not be easy.* Improving energy efficiency would be the fastest, cheapest, and surest way to slash emissions of $CO_2$ and most other air pollutants within two decades. The real energy efficiency of industrial economies is probably less than 5%, which leaves an enormous potential for increased efficiency to meet increased energy demand without new drilling or digging (Ayres, 2001: 34).

But other changes—such as car pooling, shifting to cycling or mass transit, and evolving away from the energy-wasteful low-density residential patterns characteristic of American cities—would involve significant changes in social behavior, consumption patterns, urban growth, and established preferences. Producing the cultural consensus and political mechanisms to develop, market, coordinate, monitor, and control such changes among the multitude of diverse communities, corporations, and households on a societal scale is a *daunting* prospect.

A broad "carbon tax" has been suggested as an elegantly simple solution to this difficult problem. Advocates argue that it would provide the incentives to impel us to adopt energy conservation and efficiency measures, both industrially and at the household level (Amano, 1990; Reddy and Goldemberg, 1990). But the burdens would fall unevenly on different socioeconomic classes. Higher-income households tend to purchase energy-efficient technology and to make building changes, while lower-income households tend to curtail consumption and do without (Dillman et al., 1983; Lutzenhiser and Hackett, 1993). I noted in earlier chapters that environmental problems and their remedies are often related to inequality and social stratification so that their burdens and benefits are not shared equitably. Without programs more evenly to distribute the burden sharing (in housing and transportation, for example), such a carbon tax would have highly inequitable and regressive effects that would burden low-income households much more than more affluent ones.

There is a similar difficulty regarding international inequality between nations. The United States alone produces about 28% of global $CO_2$, China about 23%, Russia and other Eastern European nations produce about 14%, West Europe about 12%, and the remaining 23% is distributed among all other nations (World Resources Institute, 2001, cited in Cunningham, 2005: 324). The richest fifth of the world contributes 63% of total global emissions, while the poorest fifth contributes just 2%. Putting it in individual terms, the average emissions of 1 American equal those of 7 Chinese, 24 Nigerians, 31 Pakistanis, or hundreds of Somalis (Dunn, 1999: 60).

## Greenhouse Diplomacy: Kyoto and Beyond

The 1992 United Nations World Conference on Environment and Development in Rio de Janeiro intended to initiate a global greenhouse treaty, much like the successful Montreal ozone treaty, but as suggested earlier, it proved much more contentious and difficult. In spite of the urgings of the NAS, the U.S. government refused to sign, sabotaging an initial agreement because it had quantitative national targets for emission reduction. What emerged from the Rio meeting was a statement that nations signed pledging "voluntary reductions" in greenhouse emissions, with no quantitative targets or sanctions for noncompliance. As you might guess, not much happened.

As evidence continued to mount, political mobilization around the issue continued in the 1990s. Scientific and environmental organizations, along with insurance liability carriers, urged action. But some industry groups, sensing greater restrictions, regulations, and reduced profits, campaigned against doing anything about global warming. Earlier I noted foundations related to such industries as an *anti-global warming movement*, which started spending millions on "sponsored research" lobbying and advertising to derail effective mitigation treaties and policies. Examples include the American Enterprise Institute, the Cato Institute, The Heritage Foundation, and the George C. Marshall Institute. In addition to depicting global warming as not real, they maintained that policies dealing with global warming would do more harm than good (McCright and Dunlap, 2000). Some labor groups, fearing loss of jobs, joined them.

Responding to global alarm, some 10,000 government officials, lobbyists, representatives of environmental organizations, and industry-related organizations gathered for a high-profile world climate conference at the ancient Japanese city of Kyoto to negotiate a better treaty than the Rio accord. After 10 days of chaotic, complex, redundant, and contentious negotiations, 160 nations formally adopted a *Kyoto Protocol*, legally committing industrial countries to reduce their emissions of greenhouse gases early in the twenty-first century. Why only the industrial nations? Because LDCs objected, noting that their greenhouse emissions are far lower than those of MDCs, even though they are rapidly growing. Led by India and China, they argued that meeting targeted reductions early in the twenty-first century would destroy their fragile developing economies—without financial and technical help from the MDCs. The Kyoto centerpiece was an agreement by all "Annex I" nations (MDCs and former East bloc countries) to cut their output of climate-altering gases collectively by 5.2% below their 1990 levels between 2008 and 2012. While that may not seem significant, it represents emissions levels that were about 29% lower than they would be by 2008–2012 without the treaty (United Nations, 1998a). Most contentious was the target and timetable negotiated for each nation's contribution to the collective goal, which was resolved after many concessions and protracted debate (Dunn, 1998: 33). Again, the United States did not sign the climate accord, partly on the grounds that LDCs were exempted from quantitative goals or timetables. Annual meetings in different cities continued to strengthen and clarify the accord that began in Kyoto, and by 2001 more than 150 nations had ratified it. Ironically, in the summer of 2002, the Bush administration found itself reacting to the weight of scientific evidence and pressure from other nations by recognizing that global warming is a real problem and caused by human impacts, while rejecting the Kyoto accord and proposing a vague "voluntary" approach to the problem. In October 2004, Russia ratified it, enabling it to come into force in February 2005 (Sawin, 2005a). Although an impressive accomplishment, even in the most ideal terms Kyoto only started the global political process, and has several kinds of weaknesses:

1. *Weak commitments:* Its goal of 5.2% reduction in emissions was anemic compared to between 60% and 80% reductions below 1990 levels that the IPCC says are necessary to stop global warming. Little noticed outside climate policy circles was the curious fact that total $CO_2$ emissions by MDCs were already below 1990 levels, due to steep declines in the former Soviet Union. Furthermore, when emissions by the LDCs are added, the global emission total was projected to increase some 30% *above* the 1990 level by 2010. The most hopeful thing that can be said about the Kyoto Protocol echoes Lao Tse's comment that a journey of a thousand miles begins with a single step. Although it will not affect global mean temperatures, it moves the world political process.

2. *Searching for "flexibility":* Some countries, particularly the United States, were anxious to find provisions—critics call them loopholes—that would make it less expensive to meet the protocol's goals and avoid the need to take a big bite out of domestic $CO_2$ emissions. They targeted a "basket" of emissions rather than focusing on each individually, which would arouse a hornet's nest of industry outrage. At the insistence of the United States, Canada, and New Zealand, countries could count—and subtract—carbon absorption by forests and peat bog sinks (Flavin, 1998: 14–16).

3. *Hot air trading:* Another form of flexibility is the concept of emissions trading. It is modeled on the U.S. Clean Air Act, which allows power companies to "trade" their sulfur dioxide reduction obligations for cash, on the theory that this will encourage cuts to be made wherever it is least expensive to do so. Related to global climate change, nations would have the option of buying greenhouse gas emission allowances from other countries that have more than met their own requirements. An emissions trading scheme was viewed as a way of not only trimming emissions costs as efficiently as possible, but also distributing the burden of addressing the problem among various countries. But the idea opens the door for possible loopholes. For example, under the protocol signed, Russia and Ukraine had reduced emissions, given their depressed economies.

Even if their economies rebound robustly, experts do not expect either country to come close to 1990 levels, allowing the United States and Russia to "make a deal," letting the United States purchase its credits for emissions reductions—without reducing U.S. emissions by one molecule (Flavin, 1998: 14–16).

Continuing opposition to ratification by the Congress and both of the Bush administrations reflected the ongoing power, pervasiveness, and media effectiveness of the "anti-global warming movement" of conservatives, U.S. conservative foundations and some corporations noted earlier (McCright and Dunlap, 2000; 2003). Even so, the United Nations Environmental Programme convened other meetings of the world's nations in Kenya, Indonesia, and other places aiming to make the Kyoto accord more effective, with higher targets for reduction of greenhouse gases and more effective monitoring and enforcement. The most widely publicized meeting about the climate problem was in Copenhagen in December 2009 where, after dealing with the problem for about two decades, the world hoped for its resolution. It was widely attended by delegates, the media, and a huge collection of climate activists. But the outcome of the Copenhagen meeting was a great disappointment because after torturous negotiations the major nations pledged voluntarily to reduce greenhouse emissions (the United States pledged a 17% reduction); however, there were no connected international monitoring or enforcement agreements. The meeting was a disappointment both because of the complex geopolitical nature of the megaproblem and growing weaknesses of the media to cover such issues (Block, 2010).

Ironically, while international political processes stagnated, opportunities for economically cutting emissions have blossomed. Some nations did not completely fail in cutting $CO_2$ emissions. The United Kingdom, for instance, had already rolled them back to 1990 levels by 2000, and vowed to reduce them 60% more by 2050. Plans are to "decarbonize" British society and decouple gross national produce growth from $CO_2$ emissions. Germany reduced $CO_2$ emissions at least 10% by switching from coal to natural gas and by encouraging energy efficiency

The 2009 Copenhagen Climate Conference was inconclusive.

throughout society, an illustration of the "no regrets" strategy mentioned earlier (Cunningham et al., 2005: 324). But the biggest surprise was China. Research by the Natural Resources Defense Council found that China reduced its $CO_2$ emissions by 17% between 1997 and 2000, a period when emissions in the United States rose by 14%. The Chinese government did this by reducing U.S. coal subsidies, closing inefficient coal-fired electric plants, accelerating its commitment to increase energy efficiency, and structuring its economy to increase the use of renewable energy resources (Miller, 2005: 482).

Besides nations, some corporations joined the effort to address global warming. In 1998, the Pew Center on Global Climate Change announced that Weyerhaeuser lumber company, one of the world's biggest, formally joined the center's effort to combat the problems of climate change. The "green hybrid" auto, the Toyota Prius, has twice the fuel economy and half the $CO_2$ emissions of conventional autos (Haimson, 2002b: 4). A growing number of transnational corporations, including Alcoa, DuPont, IBM, Toyota, BP Amoco, and Shell, established targets to reduce their greenhouse gas emissions by 10% to 65% from 1990 to 2010 (Miller, 2005: 482). Thus, while many national governments appear to be stalled, efforts by corporations and a surprising number of local and city governments are addressing the problem of global warming.

## Can We Afford the Costs?

Mitigating global warming and shifting to a low carbon economy would be very costly. But doing nothing about the problem would be much more costly over the longer time frame. In October 2006 Nicholas Stern, formerly chief economist for the World Bank, produced a report for the British government that was the first detailed analysis of the impact of climate change and efforts to address it on the global economy. His report has demolished some of the arguments that it is better to adapt to global warming than to mitigate it. The report notes that the damage from climate change in this century alone could be 20 times the costs of solving it for all time.

Stern's report forecasts that the cost of failing to act could approach $4 trillion by 2100. Up to a fifth of the world's wealth could disappear, cutting living standards by 20%, and plunging the world into a recession worse than that of the 1930s. By comparison, the costs of investing in the right technologies would be trivial compared with the potential damage. Investing about 1% of the gross world product (GWP) over the next 50 years could stabilize greenhouse gas concentrations at about 500 to 550 ppm of $CO_2$, 25% above current levels—"high but acceptable"— according to Stern. Although scientists did their best to convince people and governments of the urgency of the problem, they have largely failed. Because most are more attuned to economics than natural science, Stern's report went for the political jugular. More recently Stern warned that because of the seriousness of the problem, the costs of addressing it have doubled (Jowit and Wintour, 2008; Stern, 2006).

But how do we do that? Humanity can afford to emit another 100 billion or so tons of carbon into the atmosphere before the global economy suffers serious damage. Everyone, from the world's richest to the poorest, has to be a part of a global mitigation strategy. This could be based on the size of populations and the average amount emitted per person, and clearly some emit a lot more than others. How should we allocate rights for remaining carbon pollution? The only equitable way to share such entitlements is to share the quota among the global population, and reduce it by about 80% over the coming century. Nations, communities, corporations, and perhaps even individuals should be able to trade their entitlements (Editors, *NewScientist,* 2006a, b; 5–7).

# UNDERSTANDING UNCERTAINTY AND RISK

While there is a scientific consensus that climate change is a significant threat, there is much uncertainty about some basic facts about the magnitude and timing of the threat, and about its social and environmental impacts and costs. As you can see from the foregoing, there is compounded uncertainty about policy options and the feasibility and affordability of creating national and international political policies to address the problem. Public understanding has been blurred by the complexity of the issues, by media miscommunication about them, by political controversies surrounding them, and by debate among scholars themselves.

Uncertainty and risk are not the same thing, but they are connected. *Uncertainty* is related to our knowledge of how true, real, or factual something is (e.g., global warming), while *risk* is a situation or event where something of human value (including humans themselves) has been put at stake and where outcomes are uncertain (Rosa, 1998). In addition to risks from some existing circumstance, both "doing something" and "doing nothing" about it have risks, and it is important to try and understand which is greater (but, as you might guess, this is often very complex!). In this final section of the chapter, let me try to unravel some of the sources of scientific uncertainty as they relate to climate change and other environmental issues.

## Sources of Scientific Uncertainty

I think there are four main sources of uncertainty in scientific understanding. The most obvious one flows from the existing state of theory and evidence. But, there are also uncertainties from paradigms, semantics, and the social context of science itself. What follows explores each.

**UNCERTAINTY FROM THEORY AND DATA**   Scientists are often uncertain about things because they don't have enough or the right kind of facts ("data") or the right theory to explain them. Sometimes there is uncertainty because competing theories are equally plausible. They can't construct a good working model (a vastly simplified theory) of the earth's climate dynamics because the computer capacity does not now exist to handle all the necessary measurements at the same time, and they don't know how some important variables (e.g., clouds, ocean currents) interact with the atmosphere. Taking another example, toxicologists don't know the exact exposure levels at which many pesticides or pollutants cause illness or death, because they have never done well-controlled experiments on human beings to find out (for some pretty obvious ethical reasons!). Some scientists think that genetically engineered species of plants or bacteria could have dangerous and risky consequences when introduced into existing ecosystems in which they have not evolved. Other scientists don't think so. Good evidence about these things is nonexistent. This list could go on and on, but you get the picture.

There is another source of uncertainty built into science that may be less obvious. Contrary to common belief, the core of science is *not* a body of well-ordered facts and findings with a clear meaning, but rather approximations and institutionalized skepticism. The deepest impulse of science is to question accepted truth and the certainty of things that are taken for granted. Scientific inquiry creates points of consensus and reduces (but does not eliminate) uncertainty. In doing so, it normally finds new areas of uncertainty. Some things become understood beyond much doubt, but areas of *current* scientific inquiry are always shrouded in uncertainty. (If they weren't, why would anybody want to study them?) Scientists may challenge not only popular assumptions, but also the "science" of other scientists. My point is that dispute and contention are normal and routine processes that give science life.

Scientists, appropriately, spend a lot of their time arguing about what they *don't* know, and that is true for both natural and the social sciences.

When dispute and contention spills into public visibility and the media, you have the case of "battling scientists." Alas, the "experts" often don't agree. Given the private press's preference for "balanced" news and reporting different sides of the story, a position representing a vast consensus of scientists is pitted against a distinctly minority view—seemingly on a "level playing field." Thus doubts about the seriousness of climate change are expressed much more frequently in the U.S. media than in the media of most other industrial nations. Furthermore, scientific conclusions about things are tentative, conditional, and hedged with "ifs, ands," and "buts." The intrinsic toleration of uncertainty and ambiguity is normal for science but terribly frustrating for people who just want answers, and particularly for those trying to make policy out of science.

**UNCERTAINTY FROM DIFFERENT PARADIGMS**    Chapter One introduced the notion of paradigms as belief structure that organize perceptions about how the world works that people use—often implicitly. A scientific paradigm is an intellectual image containing explicit and implicit assumptions—broader than particular theories—that guide theorizing and research. Scholars and scientists in different fields such as biologists and economists or sociologists and psychologists operate from different "paradigmantic lenses," which often makes communications between them difficult.

Here are some illustrations. Mineral resources issues (e.g., supplies of oil and natural gas) continue to be a point of contention between economists and environmental scientists. Neoclassical economists tend to view the supply of minerals as essentially infinite because of the human ability to develop improved technologies to find and process minerals and to find substitutes. Environmental scientists argue that because of the ultimate finite supply and uneven concentrations of key minerals, there are limits on the grades of ore that can be processed without spending more money than they are worth and causing unacceptable human and environmental damage.

Economists argue that if global warming occurs sometime during this century, well-functioning markets—without the distortions of excessive regulations or subsidies that make thing unrealistically cheap—will address the problems. Markets will work to stimulate investments in increased efficiency, resource substitution, conservation, innovations, and to promote behavior changes by which firms, families, and communities adapt to changing climatic conditions.

Natural and environmental scientists generally argue that effective markets and real-cost pricing will be helpful but are not sufficient, particularly when the full brunt of climate change may be on us. We may not have the options or resources that we possess today. They have proposed a wide variety of adaptive and mitigation measures to reduce greenhouse gas emissions.

Because of these paradigm differences, physical and environmental scientists tend to "frame" problems in terms of the longer-term implications of growth in a finite world. Neoclassical economists tend to frame mineral resource problems in terms of more immediate market failures and resource allocation problems.

Communication across such paradigmatic differences is difficult but, I think, possible. Similar differences in paradigms "taken for granted" operate in the contemporary controversies about energy, population, and growth and sustainability that are explored in later chapters.

**UNCERTAINTY FROM SEMANTICS**    Given that scientist spend much of their time arguing about uncertainties, it is especially important that they clearly communicate to the public and policy makers how much confidence they have in scientific findings. But the translation of complex scientific findings and "probabilities" into ordinary and clear language is fraught with potential for confusion. To illustrate, consider an exchange between noted climatologist Stephen Schneider of the National Committee for Atmospheric Research (cited earlier) and Andrew Solow, a statistician for the Woods Hole Oceanographic Institution. In testimony before a congressional subcommittee, Schneider argued that climate change represented a substantial and unprecedented threat over the twenty-first century. Solow considered the probability low and Schneider's argument irresponsibly alarmist. Here, in some detail is Schneider's account of the conversation after bantering the issue back and forth.

> "I just can't see how you don't think there's at least a 50 percent chance that the next century will see two degrees Celsius or more warming," said Schneider.
> "I never said that," Solow responded.
> "But I thought you said it was a low probability," I replied.
> "Well, that *is* a low probability," said the statistician.
> "What would you consider a moderate probability?" I asked.
> "Oh, 95 percent," he said.
> "Eureka!" I thought to myself, I now understand our "debate." Solow, a statistician, inhabits a culture in which the traditional standard of evidence for accepting any hypothesis is the 95 percent or 99 percent confidence level. (Schneider, 1990b: 33)

Schneider argued that such criteria for evidence might be appropriate for accepting or rejecting scientific hypotheses but are unrealistic guides for understanding risks or policy making.

> What business, individual, or government leader ever has the luxury of having 95 percent certainty about the facts underlying any major decision? Do Pentagon officials know what the probability is that a terrorist event will occur? Of course not; yet they run hundreds of alternative conflict scenarios . . . whose probability . . . are probably by a factor of 10 less than that for unprecedented global warming over the next 50 years. (Schneider, 1990b: 33–34)

In other words, the disagreement between Schneider and Solow was largely semantic. One expert said a probability was high, while another said it was low, even though scientific consensus put the probability at 50% or better. This is a slippery issue as experts attempt to communicate complete findings to the media and policy makers. They are, at minimum, required to clearly interpret what words like *high*, *medium*, and *low* mean.

**UNCERTAINTY FROM SOCIAL CONTEXTS**    Uncertainty deriving from inadequate theory and data, from paradigm differences, and semantics is difficult, but still a straightforward intellectual disagreement—potentially resolvable by argumentation, evidence, and debate. But some uncertainty and dispute also derive from the social settings—organizational, economic, and political—in which scientists work. About environmental issues, scientists are likely to differ in relation to their sector of employment. Academic institutions, government agencies, industries, and private environmental organizations provide different political climates and research agendas. The media are likely to give more attention to those scientists whose work suggests serious problems and have implications that affect large numbers of people. This means that those affiliated with academic and private institutions are likely to have high media profiles.

Certainly, those affiliated with environmental movement organizations (e.g., The Sierra Club or the Environmental Defense Fund) are most likely to dramatize environmental threats. Somewhat less likely to emphasize environmental threats are academic and government scientists, although this is highly variable. At the very least, government scientists work under pressure to represent that interests of the agencies in which they work. Scientists working for the Corps of Engineers or the Environmental Protection Agency are under extreme pressure not to emphasize the regulatory "failures" of their employers.

Least likely to emphasize environmental threats are industry scientists, whose work is shaped by corporate needs for profits, as well as by the more restricted range of issues that concern them. Indeed, scientists ranging from the chemical and pesticide industries to the tobacco industry have normally been busy defending the "benign" character of their products. Scientists working for the fossil fuel industry have been less likely to emphasize the dangers of global warming. Indeed, I noted earlier the powerful "countermovement" of industry associations—and their scientists—working to portray global warming and "over-use" of public lands as "non-problems" (McCright and Dunlap, 2000). Aside from this, industry scientists are likely to have a relatively low media profile except during time of intense political controversy surrounding issues related to a particular industrial practice (Schnaiberg and Gould, 1994: 146).

I don't mean to suggest that scientists are nothing more than hired guns, dressed up in white coats and armed with charts and statistics. In fact, scientists are prominent among organizational *whistleblowers*, who report organizational malfeasance to the press and public. They do so often at considerable personal and career costs, a fact that made whistleblowers interesting subjects of study (Tsoukalas, 1994). The point is that scientists work in agencies that are rarely fully objective about research outcomes, and they experience varying degrees of organizational and political pressure to represent the interest of those organizations. In addition to organizational pressures, other social factors limit the objectivity of science, such as (1) methodological specialization between scientific disciplines, (2) the dominance within scientific disciplines of established theories, sometimes independent of compelling evidence, and (3) research driven by the goals of a policy system for "correct answers" in the face of uncertainty.

Such considerations left many scholars to argue that scientific knowledge claims, like other knowledge claims, are ultimately *socially constructed and therefore subjective* (Knorr-Cetina, 1981). Some sociologists have adopted social constructionist approaches to the study of risks (Dietz et al., 1989; Buttel and Taylor, 1992). In truth, social interaction, organization interests, and cultural transmission shape all knowledge claims. They are therefore socially constructed and fallible. *But not all claims are equally fallible,* and many facts of science, including environmental risks, have a basis in reality that is more than a simple social construction. For example, the health effects of lead exposure have many subjective features, which is why they were ignored until the 1950s. But sufficient doses of lead are toxic in all societies, whatever the shared beliefs of people or scientists. It is just as clear that science, particularly "policy science," is deeply intertwined with vested interests and politics (Dietz et al., 1989). Having discussed the sources of uncertainty in science, I turn the coin: How *do* science and society assess risks, dangers, and hazards?

## Assessing Risks: Analytic Modeling

Risk analysis can be traced back to ancient Babylon, where it is mentioned in the code of Hammurabi. But using risk as an analytic and management tool is really a twentieth-century phenomenon (Rosa, 1998). Early research about risk assessment focused on the individual perceptions of risk. These studies, conducted mainly by psychologists, assume that individual members of the public are the final judges of acceptable risk. They concluded that (1) people take mental shortcuts in making sense of risk information, (2) perceptions of risk vary with the social location of the persons, and (3) people are more tolerant of risks where exposure is thought to be voluntary. An important conclusion was that the public's sources of information (primarily TV and newspapers) systematically distort data about risk, because people need cognitive heuristics (simplified pictures of complex realities), shortcuts, and stereotypes to make sense of complex information about hazards (Clarke, 1998: 23). Because people are often ignorant of the details about environmental and technological hazards and do not think in terms of complex probabilities, many believe that only experts are best qualified to make decisions about the risks society faces. This is at best a half-truth.

**ANALYTIC RISK MODELS**    Environmental movements of the 1950s increased public concern and growing pressures for the state to rationalize and regulate technological and environmental risks. They stimulated concerns with measuring risks like the hazards of pesticide exposure, toxic waste dumps, ocean oil spills, space exploration, and the commercial production of nuclear energy (Rosa, 1998). This led to attempts to quantify risks and produced a *risk establishment* by which I mean networks of scholar-specialists who conduct risk analysis, translate them for policy makers, and weigh them for policy making. Many formal models were developed to measure and quantify risks. It is beyond the scope of this book to discuss these in much depth, but I will briefly note three of them to give you a sense of what they are like.

**Fault Tree Analysis.**    Contemporary formal risk modeling began when the nuclear power industry attempted to add objectivity—or at least its appearance—to traditional engineering judgments about the safety of nuclear reactors (Mazur, 1981). The basic logic of this method is to specify the combinations of separate breakdowns that would have to occur to produce a failure of the total system. Then, if the probabilities of the separate component failures are known, they are combined (multiplied) to get the probability of a total system disaster. When the probabilities of a total system breakdown are calculated for complex technical systems with many fail-safe features (e.g., the likelihood of the crash of a jet liner, an ocean tanker oil spill, or a nuclear meltdown), they are very small. The likelihood of a nuclear power reactor disaster was calculated as being minuscule.

**Social Impact Assessment (SIA).**    The goal of SIA is to predict the social effect of policies and programs on communities, and to use these predictions to aid public decision making and debate. Early SIAs used computer simulations about "primary jobs," the labor required for new projects like dams or power plants, and "secondary jobs," like teachers, cooks, and police. SIA measured to what extent these required migration from outside the community. Finally, it measured the stresses on government services and budgets (Freudenberg, 1984; Stern et al., 1992: 187–188). The risks and hazards assessed are not technological ones, or necessarily even monetary ones, but those associated with rapid change, growth, and the potential for the disruption of community life.

**Cost-Benefit Analysis (CBA).**    CBA is the premiere technique among economic thinkers for *valuing,* or attempting to assess the risks (costs) and benefits of various impacts and options. CBA assigns market values to impacts, either directly or by imputation. Future values are discounted. Then, having assigned a value to all costs and benefits in current dollars, the ratio of benefits to costs can be calculated. While the practitioners of CBA typically caution against taking the final calculations too seriously as decision criteria, it does provide an explicit framework for valuing otherwise incommensurable options or impact and may provide a basis for preferring one option over others (Stern et al., 1992: 193).

**LIMITATIONS AND CRITICISMS OF RISK RESEARCH AND MODELING**    The appeal of these risk assessment models is great, but you need to know some of their limitations. When projecting the probabilities of nuclear accidents in the longer-term future, fault tree analysis has proven notoriously unreliable (Fischoff et al., 1980; Flavin, 1988). The measurement of impacts by SIA is often in error. That is because many of the key measures assumed to be constant (such as the ratio between primary and secondary employment, and the generation of crime or traffic problems) are themselves highly variable over time. CBA has been similarly criticized. Many of the costs and benefits are not real market price values at all, particularly future use values and social costs, which people care about very much but for which it is hard to assign price tags. It is also fair to ask about the *distribution* of costs and benefits. Whose costs? Whose benefits?

A problem with all of these models for risk assessment is that such concrete-looking quantitative analyses often come, in the heat of policy debates, to be taken as objectively factual when in reality they are heuristic ("as if") models. Research communities understand their limitations, but they are often abused in the policy-making process by being interpreted as what *will* happen, or given an undue aura of scientific objectivity. At best, they may stimulate or clarify assumptions about decisions related to risks. But the lessons of the last two decades illustrate the limited uses of such formal models to aid scientific knowledge or serious discourse on policy (Stern et al., 1992).

## Social Contexts of Risk: Organizations and Society

Beyond methodological problems in the work of experts, deeper questions exist about the role of experts in such questions relative to the broader social process and tradeoffs with a political system. As mentioned earlier, scientific and technical analysis is shaped by the social context in which it takes place. While scientific methods can never replace the political process in assigning values to impacts, it is equally naïve, I think, to believe that science cannot inform the public and political decision process. Many scholars believe that laypersons should play a more central role in assessing, evaluating, and managing environmental and technological risks (Fischoff, 1990).

**ORGANIZATIONS, RISKS, AND BOUNDED RATIONALITY**    Many of the problems investigated by psychologists about risks have a large role for individual choice. Examples include using seatbelts or dietary choices, but the role of organizations in shaping policy is often neglected (Freudenburg, 1992: 2). I noted earlier the powerful role of big organizations in shaping the outcomes of global greenhouse treaty negotiations and the contexts within which scientific research is conducted. In fact, what drives democratic political systems more clearly and directly than individual preferences are the interactions between community organizations, interest group organizations, regulatory agencies, and scientific communities—in other words, interest-groups politics at its finest. As sociologist Lee Clarke argued with considerable force, organizations, not the public, are the crucial actors in dramas of risk assessment, and what shapes policy outcomes is *organizational power* as much as *objective risk* (Clarke, 1988). Furthermore, there is evidence that organizations often misperceive risks or define an environmental threat in terms of the threat of any action to their organization's interests (which is a kind of rationality about the organization, but not pure scientific rationality about the wider problem). Regulatory agencies and organizations are often "captured" by the industries they are supposed to regulate and often do not effectively enforce existing regulatory laws for a variety of reasons (Clarke, 1993; Freudenburg, 1993)

In short, the real process of assessing risks is a complex interaction among big organizations, political and institutional actors, scientific communities, environmental movements, the media, and the public. In this complex social process, various actors strive to frame controversies and to legitimate different definitions of environmental risks. Participants enter this process with different values, interests, and capacities to mobilize "expert knowledge" on their own behalf. One study of conflict and controversy about environmental risk found the leaders of environmental organizations attributed conflict largely to different organizational interests and value differences. It found that risk experts attributed conflicting opinions to public ignorance, while congressional staffs were more distrustful of expert opinion, particularly when connected with private industry (Dietz et al., 1989).

That said, I think it is still true that a kind of *bounded rationality* sometimes works to shape risk assessments and policy, even for big issues. Bounded rationality was a notion introduced by economist Herbert Simon to recognize the limits on human rationality, and point to the unreasonableness of the search for "pure" rationality. Bounded rationality means that while there are always limits, the outcomes of social processes are not therefore completely irrational, and may, under some conditions approximate rational outcomes (Simon, 1982). In the Unites States, the profile of bounded rationality in terms of outcomes that effectively address environment problems has, I think, six components:

1. A rough scientific consensus about a problems (not empirical certainty)
2. A generally knowledgeable public
3. Effective advocacy and social movement organizations
4. Receptive media and political leaders
5. Corporations willing to find profits in more benign ways
6. Pressure from international organizations

Those were at least present in the social process that led to the mitigation of the ozone hole problem and some other environmental problems (water and air pollution) as well as some public health problems like cigarette smoking. Even with the strong limitations on rational policy noted earlier, I argue that under *some* conditions that democratic interest groups jockeying and politics can be bounded by broader problem-solving rationality. Will these elements be sufficiently present to produce a rational international policy about climate change? Who knows?

**CONTEMPORARY SOCIETIES AND RISK**    Looking at the big societal picture, European sociologists added new dimensions about understanding risk (Beck, 1986; Giddens, 1991). They observed that people in earlier societies were mainly threatened by external and objective dangers, like floods, disease, droughts, storms, and famines. By contrast, life in modern technological societies is often safer because a host of special experts have constructed defenses and plans for dealing with dangers of all kinds. But to be an expert in one or two small corners of modern knowledge systems is all that anyone can achieve, which means that such obstruct knowledge systems are opaque to the majority (Giddens, 1991). Thus in the vastly expanded scope and scale of modern life, with greater awareness of problems of many kinds, we do not feel safer. The reflectivity of modern life means that by our very power to control ourselves and environments, we wind up with extremely complex sets of contingencies and must think in terms of probabilities and risks rather than certainties. German theorist Ulrich Beck termed modern societies as *risk societies* (1986)—this important development connects risk to the fundamental nature of modern societies.

## Conclusion

I think that climate policy should be developed in terms of three main assumptions. First, the nature of the threat obviously requires a cooperative arrangement among nations that recognizes the different resources and capacities to address the problem. Second, that many mitigative carbon-cutting measures—beyond those specified by the Kyoto treaty—do pass accepted cost-benefit tests, and ought to be taken quickly. Some adaptive measures (e.g., protecting ocean flood plains, reconstructing human habitats, and adapting agriculture to new climate realities) have substantial costs that will be necessary to phase in as circumstances require. Third, there are good reasons for addressing the problem aside from global warming itself, which make them worth doing on other grounds.

They could, for instance, help stabilize biodiversity, improve problems of urban air pollution and acid rain, enhance energy efficiency, and promote international cooperation in programs about reforestation and land reform and probably the alleviation of the most wretched global poverty. In other words, addressing global warming could be a way to unify a basket of separate measures addressing human–environment problems and preserving the "global commons."

## Personal Connections

*Questions for Review*

1. What are some kinds of evidence about how much and how fast climate change is taking place?
2. What are some important "greenhouse gases"? How are they being produced and concentrated in the atmosphere?
3. What is the IPCC? How does it operate? How have its major conclusions changed over the decades of its existence?
4. Why have the IPCC's conclusions produced major controversy on a national and international scale?

5. What are some of the ways that climate change could change the earth and human societies over the next century?
6. How are the three major proposed ways of addressing climate change different?
7. What were the conclusions of famous British economist Nicolas Stern about the costs of addressing climate change over the next century, compared to the costs of "business as usual" (doing nothing and letting nature take its course)?
8. Given that are there uncertainties in science, what is the importance of Herbert Simon's concept of "bounded rationality?"

*Questions for Reflection*

1. Ask some of your acquaintances of different ages, education, or circumstances what they think about climate change. The diversity of opinions may surprise you. You also have read about the scientific consensus. Who do you trust the most?
2. Assume that projections about climate change are right, and that a general and significant rise in mean global temperatures will happen during the next 40 to 50 years. You would probably experience some consequences during your lifetime. You can't predict them specifically, but can make informed guesses about their probable consequences. Think about how you will bear a share of the costs of coping with these consequences of global warming.
3. In 1990, the federal government estimated costs of mitigating greenhouse gases at about $10 billion a year. What are some ways the costs or taxes of doing this might show up for you as a typical consumer or taxpayer?
4. A huge number of North Americans live in coastal regions. Look at the location of the really big American cities and metropolitan areas in this light. If ocean levels rise because of climate warming, you will be affected. If ocean levels rise modestly, dense human settlements will have to be protected and people relocated or evacuated inland. Think about the costs and chaos of doing this, particularly for America's large coastal cities like New York, Los Angeles, Seattle, and Miami. Increasing sea levels would flood scores of estuaries, freshwater aquifers, and other resources on which societies depend. You will bear a share of those costs that cannot be precisely calculated, but they are enormous! Some of them will be shifted to you even if you don't live in a coastal region, like higher costs for goods and services, higher property insurance premiums, and taxes for state and federal disaster relief programs. Think how people bore such costs due to Hurricane Katrina.
5. Climate zones and vegetation may shift unpredictably. Global warming would increase both evaporation and precipitation, and atmospheric models suggest that regional effects would be extremely uneven. In 2006, the Midwestern and Great Plains states were plagued by a severe and prolonged drought. Soil moisture was deficient and crop production was down. If this becomes chronic, how might it affect food prices, world grain markets, and food security? How do you think you would change your lifestyle to adapt to these circumstances? What kinds of adaptive measures could be taken?
6. *You may already be beginning to absorb such costs.* One likely consequence of global warming is rapid weather changes and more frequent severe weather patterns. A warmer atmosphere and warmer seas may result in greater exchange of energy and momentum to the vertical change processes important to the development of cyclones, tornados, thunderstorms, and hailstorms. Certainly, you absorbed such costs in 2005 if you lived

in New Orleans area during Katrina, or in Florida, when the state was crisscrossed by five hurricanes in one season. *How?*

The insurance industry has not exhibited the same skepticism about global warming as have some others, when paying losses for flooded farmlands, crops, hurricanes, tornados, and other disaster losses. Indeed, in its own long-term interest, the insurance industry is joining efforts to find ways of mitigating or adapting to global warming.

## What You Can Do
## Real Goods

**1. *Ceiling fans.*** Eco-friendly technology's answer to air-conditioning, ceiling fans, cool tens of millions of people in LDCs. Air-conditioning, found in about two-thirds of U.S. homes, is a real electrical "juice hog" of electrical energy. Ceiling fans, on the other hand, are simple, durable, repairable, and take little energy to run. They run at very low speeds (summer and winter) and help even out the "layers" of room temperature. A fan over your bed circulates enough air that you may not have to run your air conditioner as much.

**2. *The reel-type push lawnmower (without a gas engine).*** They're back! And, they cost about one-fourth of the cost of a self-propelled power mower, and probably a sixth of the cost of a riding mower. They are made with lighter metal alloys that are easier to push than historic versions. It is easy to push up a 45-degree incline on my front yard (where my previous power mower would stall because it drained oil into the engine, and where I always feared that it would tip over and slice my foot off). No gas, tune-ups, smoke, pollution, or noise. There is only a quiet clik, clik, clik as it moves, which brings back nostalgic childhood memories. The kids in the neighborhood had never seen one before, and came over to ask, "What is that thing?"

**3. *Compact fluorescent light bulbs.*** They are three or four times as efficient as regular incandescent bulbs. One 18-watt compact fluorescent light bulb provides the light of a 75-watt incandescent bulb and lasts 10 times as long. Currently they are pretty pricey but should get cheaper as more people use them. Even so, over the life of its use, an 18-watt compact bulb can keep more than 80 pounds of coal in the ground and about 250 pounds of $CO_2$ out of the atmosphere.

## More Resources

Bryson, R. (1977). *The climates of hunger: Mankind and the world's changing weather.* Madison, WI: University of Wisconsin Press.

Devereux, S., and Edwards, J. (2004). Climate change and food security. *IDS Bulletin, 35*(3), 22–30.

Firor, J., and Jacobsen, E. (2002). *The crowded greenhouse.* New Haven and London: Yale University Press.

Moore, T. G. (1998). *Climate of fear: Why we shouldn't worry about global warming.* Washington, DC: Cato Institute.

National Assessment Synthesis Team (2000). *Climate impacts on the United States: The potential consequences of climate variability and change.* New York: Cambridge University Press.

Schneider, S. H., et al. (Eds.) (2002). *Climate change policy.* Washington, DC: Island Press.

Speth, J. G. (2004). *Red sky at morning: America and the crisis of the global environment.* New Haven, CT: Yale Nota Bene, Yale University Press.

## Electronic Resources

**www.epa.gov/globalwarming/news/**
EPA site about global warming

**www.tellusinstitute.org/**
Web site of The Stockholm Environment Institute. Material and reports about large-scale social and environmental change, and sustainability.

**www.mountwashington.org/climatechange**
Links about regional, national, and global climate change to NASA, NOAA, IPCC, and others; links about the human impacts of global warming; and to Web sites of global warming skeptics.

**www.climatecrisis.net**
The Web site that goes with Al Gore's movie about climate change (*An Inconvenient Truth*). It has an interesting "carbon counter" to compute how much carbon you put in the atmosphere that is fun to play with.

**www.eldis.org/go/topics/resource-guides/climate-change**
1,088 links to information about climate change

## Endnote

1. Phenomenology is a philosophical term that means how humans experience something.

# CHAPTER 4

# Energy and Society

A coal-fired power plant emitting steam and greenhouse gases.

Chapter One noted the ideas of the famous Austrian biophysicist Alfred Lotka, who proposed in the 1920s that the evolution of ecosystems is shaped by how efficiently various species of life appropriate the energy in the environment. In fact, general increases in human living standards have been possible only because of substantial increases in the amount of energy consumed. But growth in energy consumption is not only connected with human progress. The modern carbon-based energy system is connected with air pollution, oil spills, and, as Chapter Three noted, scientists are convinced that it is one of the primary human drivers of global warming. By 1990, the total energy consumption by humans around the world was 14 times larger than it was in 1890, early in the industrial era. Growth in energy consumption vastly outstripped population growth, which doubled during the same time period. But the human use of energy—its mining, refining, transportation, consumption, and polluting by-products— accounts for much of the human impact on the environment (Holdren, 1990: 159). Earlier chapters argued that human societies are "embedded" in the biophysical environment. Most fundamentally, in fact, they are embedded in systems of energy production and consumption. In other words, energy mediates between ecosystems and social systems and is a key to understanding much about the interaction between humans and environmental systems.

Energy is basically a physical variable—measured variously as calories, kilowatt-hours, horsepower, British Thermal Units, joules, and so forth. But energy is also a social variable, because it permeates and conditions almost all facets of our lives. Driving a car, buying a hamburger, turning on your computer, or going to a movie could all be described in terms of the amount of energy it took to make it possible for you to do those things. A kilowatt-hour of electricity, for instance, can light your 100-watt lamp for 10 hours, smelt enough aluminum for your six-pack of soda or beer, or heat enough water for your shower for a few minutes (Fickett et al., 1990: 65). All of social life, from the broad and profound things to the minutiae of everyday life, can be described in terms of energy.

It may well be that energy mediates between ecosystems and human systems, but that's a very abstract way of putting the human-energy–environment relationship, and its implications may not be clear to you. So before I clarify the agenda of this chapter, let me provide a concrete illustration of this statement by taking you on a historical detour, back to the 1970s.

## A HISTORICAL DETOUR: RECENT ENERGY CRISES

In most of the industrial world, the winter of 1973 was an awful one, and not because of the weather. The reason was a sudden change in the availability and price of energy supplies. The world market for oil, which had become the industrial world's premier source of commercial energy, was very tight, meaning that in previous decades the global consumption of petroleum products had almost outgrown the world's capacity to produce, refine, and distribute them. The U.S. domestic oil production was declining. The more developed countries (MDCs) were increasingly dependent on the oil reserves of the less developed countries (LDCs), such as Nigeria, Venezuela, and particularly the nations around the Persian Gulf, which possessed most of the world's known reserves. In September 1973, Japan's prime minister predicted that an oil crisis would come within 10 years. It came in more like 10 days, with the surprise attack that launched a war between Israel and her Arab neighbors that was later called the Yom Kippur War. In retaliation for the Western support of Israel, the cartel of oil-producing nations (OPEC), led by the Arab nations, declared an embargo on the export of oil to the MDCs. Nations and oil companies scrambled to buy, control, and ration existing supplies in storage and in the pipelines around the world. Oil prices zoomed from $2.50 to $10.00 a barrel, and the world economy went into rapid downturn—with price increases of almost everything, rapid inflation, plant closings, and layoffs. Rationing of energy supplies meant sudden uncertainty about the supplies of industrial, heating, and transportation fuels that Westerners had taken for granted as cheap and plentiful (Stanislaw and Yergin, 1993: 82–83). American President Richard Nixon left it to the energy departments of each state government to figure out how to allocate existing fuel. As increased costs of energy percolated through the whole economy, every facet of the American economy and lifestyle seemed threatened.

---

## BOX 4.1

### Winter in Omaha, 1973

In the winter of 1973, Christmas displays were turned off. The Salvation Army "Tree of Lights," a holiday tradition at the county courthouse, burned for only one hour a day. Lights in urban office buildings were turned off. Everyone worried about keeping enough gas in their cars as gas stations periodically ran out of gas. Nebraska gas stations were closed on Sundays, and every Saturday night there were long lines. The days of supercharged V-8 muscle cars were numbered, as was the 75-mph interstate speed limit. Thermostat settings in offices and homes were turned down. In the state of Iowa, individual coffeepots were banned in the statehouse, and all high school basketball games were banned after December 22 (Kotok, 1993: 1). The latter was *serious* business, if you were a high school student in the rural Midwest!

---

The crisis continued in 1979, when a revolution in Iran disrupted world supplies and created a panic that drove oil prices from $13 to $33 a barrel. All this seemed to foretell permanent shortage and continued turmoil. Adding to the mood of crisis, a prestigious group of scholars and computer modelers (the Club of Rome) produced studies to show that among other things, the world would be visibly "running out of gas" in the future (Meadows et al., 1972). But none of the worst fears caused by the "oil shocks" of the 1970s really came true. The ability of the OPEC nations to control the world's oil supply declined as non-OPEC production increased at a rapid pace. OPEC's share of the world oil market fell from 63% in 1972 to 38% by 1985 (Stanislaw and Yergin, 1993: 82–83). People responded by changing the way they lived and worked. They insulated homes and bought more fuel efficient autos and appliances. All over the world, utility companies began switching from oil to other fuels. By 1992, the people in my home state (Nebraska) consumed 100 million fewer gallons of gasoline than they did in 1973 (Kotok, 1993: 1). Energy conservation, a consequence of both technological and behavioral changes, proved more powerful than expected, so that by the 1990s the combination of reduced demand for oil and increased supplies made its real price cheaper in 1993 than in 1973. Around the world, MDCs tried to establish security measures that would help moderate future crises. These included the creation of the International Energy Agency, an international sharing system, increased communication, the creation of a global oil futures commodity market, and the establishment of prepositioned supply reserves.[1]

Even with these positive responses to the oil shocks of the 1970s, they were a great historical wake-up call that forever changed our understanding of energy. The 1970s marked a transition in coming to grips with the environmental and sociopolitical costs of energy. Problems of air and water pollution, many of them associated with energy consumption, came to be recognized as pervasive threats to human health, economic well-being, and environmental stability (Holdren, 1990: 158). Indeed, energy problems came—perhaps for the first time in history—to be widely recognized as an integral part of environmental concerns. In addition, consciousness of growing dependence on imported oil graphically demonstrated the growing economic and geopolitical interdependence among nations and continues to shape our foreign policy problems in, for instance, the 1992 Gulf War, and in 2006 the war in Iraq and America's tensions with Venezuela.

After about a decade of "moderate" energy prices, in mid-1990 a rapid and significant increase in oil prices began that continued in the first decade of the twenty-first century. This led to the familiar—though episodic—process of hand-wringing by politicians and the media about rising oil prices, dependency on Middle Eastern oil, and the absence of a sustained and coherent federal energy policy (Lutzenhiser et al., 2002: 222). Whatever public complacency there was ended quickly after 1999 as oil, gasoline, and natural gas prices increased significantly. When George W. Bush was inaugurated in 2001, he proclaimed another "energy crisis." The new Bush administration proposed another "supply side" policy to open up public lands, including the Arctic National Wildlife Refuge (ANWR) for drilling and exploitation. This policy proposal contained large subsidies for the fossil fuel and mining industries, with precious little to develop alternative energy sources. After 9/11, energy fears became enmeshed with the expensive, unpopular War in Iraq, which lasted longer than World War II. Even with Republican congressional majorities, the controversial energy bill failed regularly in Congress, faced with opposition for many reasons. Energy was again a contentious and highly visible part of America's political controversies, now connected with the nation's balance of payments problems, and with climate change. In 2005, a version of the energy bill became law (but without drilling rights in ANWR or funds for alternative energy development). After dominating the auto market for a decade, the sales of large autos (particularly sport utility vehicles [SUVs]) slumped, and smaller, fuel-efficient autos were again becoming popular—though not a significant part of America's vehicle fleet. After about 35 years of price hikes and dollar inflation, the price of a barrel of oil on world markets fluctuated at between 50 and 100 dollars per barrel, which translated into a pump price of between 2 and 3 dollars, occasionally spiking to near 4 dollars per gallon (in the United States).

This historical detour frames some of the ways that energy mediates between human societies and the environment. As you can see, energy "crisis" moods come and go, as do political and media attention to energy problems. If there is no energy crisis, there certainly is an *energy predicament*. A *crisis* is a rapidly deteriorating situation that, if left unattended, can lead to disaster in the near future. But there is an energy *predicament*, that is, an ongoing chronic problem that, if left unattended, can result in a crisis (Rosa et al., 1988: 168). This predicament has a number of dimensions to which this chapter turns, including (1) sources of energy problems; (2) studies about the relationship between energy and society, or what some scholars have termed *energetics;* (3) the current energy system and some possibilities for alternative methods of producing energy; and (4) some policy issues about transforming existing energy systems.

## ENERGY PROBLEMS: ENVIRONMENTAL AND SOCIAL

Our energy predicament has four interacting dimensions, or problems: (1) source problems, having to do with energy resource supplies; (2) problems related to population growth and economic growth and development; (3) global policy and geopolitical problems; and (4) sink problems, having to do with energy by-products, health hazards, and greenhouse gas emissions.

### Source Problems: Energy Resource Supplies

As the twenty-first century began, three nonrenewable fossil fuels (oil, natural gas, and coal) supplied about 75% of the world's commercial energy needs. Nuclear power supplied 6%, and renewable sources, such as hydropower and wind, solar, and geothermal power, together supplied another 7%. In the LDCs, an important source of renewable energy is *biomass* (mostly fuelwood and charcoal made from wood). It is still the main source of heating and cooking for about half of the world's population (U.S. Department of Energy, British Petroleum Institute, Worldwatch Institute, and the International Energy Association, cited in Miller, 2005: 351–352).

Since the pessimistic estimates of world oil reserves in the 1970s, estimates of known reserves doubled (Stanislaw and Yergin, 1993: 88), and energy analysts agree that in the near term the earth's supply of fossil fuels will not be a problem. At present consumption rates, known reserves of crude oil and natural gas will last many years, and there is an awful lot of coal in the world, but its use carries extraordinary risks compared to those of oil and natural gas.

Consider oil. There is a rough consensus among energy analysts that at current rates of consumption, about 80% of known oil reserves will last for between 40 and 90 years (Miller, 2005: 353). But world oil discovery peaked in the 1960s and has been declining ever since, and experts currently estimate that world oil production will peak sometime between 2010 and 2020 and will decline thereafter (Aleklett, 2006; Podobnik, 1999; Prugh, 2006). The discovery, production, and consumption of energy resources are said to "peak" because they follow a bell-shaped curve, beginning small, rising steadily, and declining unexpectedly to near exhaustion, a pattern first described by Shell Oil geologist oil expert M. King Hubbert in 1956. Like global warming, the concept of an "oil peak" is accepted, but the particulars of timing are controversial (Motavalli, 2006; Roberts, 2004: 171–173; Yeomans, 2004: 106–108). But if you think that new oil discoveries will forever push back resource depletion, consider some stubborn facts. At present (not future) rates of consumption, (1) the estimated crude oil reserves under Alaska's North Slope—the largest ever found in North America—would meet world demand for only six months, or the U.S. demand for three years. (2) With the world's largest oil reserves, Saudi Arabia alone could supply the world's oil needs for only 10 years (Miller, 2005: 229). Hardly anyone thinks that in the future, this much oil will be discovered every 10 years. Oil company executives have known this for some time. Two decades ago, Robert Hirsch, then vice president and manager of research services for Atlantic Richfield Oil Company, urged beginning an orderly transition to alternate energy technologies in the early to middle twenty-first century (Hirsch, 1987: 1471).

Like projections about other scientific questions like global warming, how long it will take to deplete fuel and mineral reserves are expert guesstimates, notoriously dependent on assumptions and contingencies. To mention a few in particular, if trends toward greater MDC energy efficiency resumes with full force, declining demand could stretch out supplies many years beyond current estimates. On the other hand, depletion–time estimates could shorten because of the lack of success in exploring likely geological sources, or unexpected growth in either the world market economy or the economic development in the LDCs. My point is that even if constraints are not as strong as thought in the 1970s, supply concerns continue.

## Population Growth, Economic Development, and Distribution Problems

In 2000, the world's 6 billion people consumed almost 14 terawatts of energy (a terawatt is a trillion watts, and equal to the energy in 5 billion barrels of oil). But that world consumption statistic hid very unequal consumption among nations. MDCs have about one-fifth of the world's people but consume almost three-fourths of the world's energy. Even among MDCs, North Americans consume more energy per capita or per dollar of GDP than do other MDC people. Americans drive bigger cars and drive them farther; live in bigger houses and heat, cool, and light them more; and work in buildings that use substantially more energy per square meter than do Europeans (Joskow, 2002: 107). Comparisons with LDCs are more stark: One American consumes as much per capita energy as do 3 Japanese, 6 Mexicans, 14 Chinese, 38 Indians, 168 Bangladeshis, 280 Nepalis, or 531 Ethiopians (Goodland et al., 1993: 5).

If projections for future energy demands and population growth hold true—and we keep our current disregard for energy efficiency—by the year 2100, by most estimates the world's

10 billion people will need about 50 terawatts of electricity, or around four times what we produce today. That is a staggering amount of power. Generating it would require an energy infrastructure far larger and costlier than any that exists today (Roberts, 2004: 223). Furthermore, if the large numbers of Chinese, Indians, and others in LDCs were to become energy consumers living even remotely close to the present living standards of MDC people, that would place enormous strains on the supply of global energy resources, and the resulting environmental degradation, toxic wastes, and heat-trapping greenhouse gases would be intolerable.

## Policy and Geopolitical Problems

As noted earlier, the momentum toward greater energy efficiency stalled by 1990. Even though some of it lasted, there were disturbing signs of increasing per capita energy consumption (Klare, 2002: 101). The rebound in energy consumption was partly a consequence of the marketing of gas-guzzling SUVs and pickup trucks that made up about half of all U.S. new car sales. At a deeper level, the rebound in consumption was a consequence of public policy. Recent U.S. energy policy has been *supply-side policies* promoting an increased supply of energy resources and ensuring a low price for energy. Such policies undercut much of the potential for conservation to have an effect on energy markets. Chapter One discussed that "economic externalities," and energy markets have some significant costs—ones not directly paid for by either energy producers or consumers. Here are some important ones, emphasizing oil markets:

- Government subsidies and tax breaks for oil companies and road builders
- Pollution cleanup
- Military protection of oil supplies in the Middle East (at least $30 billion a year not including the Iraq war)
- Environmental, health, and social costs such as increased medical bills and insurance premiums, time wasted in traffic jams, noise pollution, increased mortality from air and water pollution, urban sprawl, and harmful effects on wildlife species and habitats (Miller, 2005: 384)
- Various costs in U.S. deficit balance of payments between exports and imports (more than one-third of which are due to energy imports) (Kingsley, 1992: 119)

If you really want to get a sense of some of these, imagine factoring into the price of each gallon of gasoline you buy *a share* of other costs. Think about your share of the total and cumulative costs of U.S. military and foreign aid in the Middle East to maintain relations with oil suppliers—including the wars in Iraq and Afghanistan. Indeed, if all of the health, geopolitical, and environmental costs of oil were internalized in its market price and if government subsidies from production were removed, oil would be so expensive that much of it would quickly be replaced by improved efficiency or other fuels.

Demand-side policies that evolved during the 1990s had similar problems. Although by eschewing price controls, rationing, and energy-allocation policies of the 1970s, it viewed the proper role of government to respond to market imperfections and breaking down regulatory barriers. They did moderate prices, which fell steadily by about 20% during the decade even though they were very volatile. But energy consumption grew steadily—17% from 1991 to 2000—and net imports grew by more than 50% during the 1990s. Canada became the major supplier of U.S. natural gas, while the Persian Gulf continued to provide about 30% of world oil production. Although the United States imports only about 18% of its oil from the Gulf, it has a significant strategic interest in the region because its major allies (Japan and Western Europe) rely mainly on the Middle East (Stanislaw and Yergin, 1993: 86–87).

The International Energy Agency, in its *World Energy Outlook 2000*, expects fossil fuel consumption to grow by 57% (2% annually) between 1997 and 2020 (Dunn, 2001: 40). In the world economy, geopolitical conflicts of interest are likely between the commodity-producing nations and the consuming nations for both fuel and nonfuel minerals. Most disadvantaged will be nations that have neither the money to buy much fuel nor the resources to sell. Abstractly, energy is an important part of the patterns of world trade and politics that will determine who is poor and who is affluent, and who is well fed and who is hungry. It is unthinkable to try to understand either current world tensions or environmental problems without considering the importance of the production and distribution of energy around the world.

The important point is not that fossil fuels are becoming absolutely exhausted, but that the era of relatively cheap fuels is coming to an end. It is easily available oil that is scarce, not all oil. Meeting energy needs in the future will require much greater investments than in the recent past. It means extracting fuels from increasingly difficult and marginal sources, accommodating the needs of a growing human population, and paying the geopolitical overhead costs of an orderly energy market in a world system of nations. These costs don't even include the costs of increased environmental damage (Hirsch, 1987; Holdren, 1990: 158; Klare, 2002; Mazur, 1991: 156; Motavalli, 2006: 29).

## Sink Problems: Energy and Environment

Although energy supplies are thought to be less constraining now than in the 1970s, environmental problems caused by the present energy system are more severe and getting worse (Flavin and Dunn, 1999: 24; Motavalli, 2006; Roberts, 2004; Stanislaw and Yergin, 1993: 88). Stated abstractly, the most pressing problems may not be source problems, but sink problems.

Burning fossil fuels is a major source of anthropogenic $CO_2$, a major heat-trapping greenhouse gas. Burning oil products also produces nitrous and sulfur oxides that damage people, crops, trees, fish, and other species. Urban vehicles that run almost exclusively on petroleum products cause much urban pollution and smog. *Oil spills* and leakage from pipelines, storage, transportation, and drilling sites leave the world literally splattered with toxic petroleum wastes and by-products. The ecosystem disruption from oil spills can last many years, and spread widely by ocean currents. Oil slicks coat the feathers and fur of marine animals, causing them to lose their natural insulation and buoyancy, and many die. Heavy oil components sink to the ocean's floor or wash into estuaries and can kill bottom-dwelling organisms (e.g., crabs, oysters, and clams), making them unfit for human consumption. Such accidents have serious economic costs for coastal property and industries (such as tourism and fishing).

In 1989, the large tanker *Exxon Valdez* went off course, hit rocks, and spilled 11 million gallons of oil in Alaska's Prince William sound, resulting in unthinkable damage to ecosystems and local human communities. It wound up costing $7 billion (including cleanup costs and fines for damage).

By 1998, virtually all merchant marine ships had double hulls, but only 15% of oil supertankers did, even though in theory the Oil Protection Act of 1990 regulated supertankers to reduce the danger of such oil spills. To get around the law, many oil carriers shifted their oil transport operations to lightly regulated barges pulled by tugboats, a reduction in oil-spill safety that led to several barge spills. In 2002, the oil tanker *Prestige* sank off the coast of Spain and leaked twice as much oil as did the *Exxon Valdez*.

But the gargantuan environmental disaster was not oil spilled from tankers, but about 100 miles off the coast of Florida in the Gulf of Mexico, where in 2010 a British Petroleum deep sea drill rig was drilling for oil on the floor of the Gulf of Mexico. When the drill pipe broke apart

An oil-soaked pelican being cleaned after the Gulf oil spill in 2010.

about a mile deep in the ocean, as much as 50 million of barrels of oil (a barrel of oil is about 40 gallons) began spewing into the Gulf. It continued for weeks after repeated efforts to stop the flow failed, and released more oil per week into the Gulf than total spill from the Exxon Valdez. A *vast* oil slick spread throughout the Gulf both on the surface and in deeper water. It is measurably reaching the U.S. gulf coastal regions from Louisiana to Florida, and Gulf "loop currents" may spread it to the east around the tip of Florida and up the Atlantic coast. It will produce damage to wildlife, coastal wetlands, fishing and shrimping industries, beach property, and tourism, as well as the U.S. economy. It will eventually result in many billions of dollars of economic damage, as much as $20 billion in liability claims by human establishments (National Public Radio News, 2010a). Damage to ecosystems is conveniently "externalized." Though British Petroleum and two of its contractors said that they would be responsible for compensation, the legal limit of their liability is $75 million—a subject of fierce debate by American lawmakers. Gulf deep sea drilling is not likely to be stopped suddenly because the United States gets 30% of its oil from the Gulf (National Public Radio News, 2010b). Though government regulators require disaster "contingency plans," one risk assessment expert, sociologist Lee Clark, termed them "fantasy documents" when it comes to big oil spills (Bruno, 2010).

Because they are such graphic media topics, oil tanker accidents, pipeline accidents, and drilling blowouts get the most publicity. But experts estimate that between 50% and 90% of the oil reaching the oceans comes from the land, when waste oil dumped on the land by cities, individuals, and industries ends up in streams that flow into the ocean (Miller and Spoolman, 2009: 549–550).

*Coal* is hazardous to mine and the dirtiest, most toxic fuel to burn. Mining often devastates the land, soil, and water tables, whether by digging tunnels or by stripping the land (soil, trees, etc.) to get at seams of coal. Mountaintop removal, the most environmentally devastating form of strip mining, triggers a cascade of eroded mountains and polluted rivers that is impossible to repair. Miners work in hazardous conditions, and often die from black lung disease. Burning coal produces larger amounts of particulate matter and $CO_2$ than burning other fossil fuels, and electric power generation (mostly from coal) is the second largest producer of toxic emissions in the United States. Burning coal alone accounts for more than 80% of the $SO_2$ and $NO_x$ injected into the atmosphere by human activity. In the United States alone, air pollutants from coal burning kill thousands of people each year (estimates range from 65,000 to 200,000), contribute to at least 50,000 cases of respiratory disease, and result in several billion dollars in property damage. The most threatening product of coal-burning power plants are particles of toxic mercury.

In 2000, the National Academy of Science estimated that 60,000 babies a year might be born with neurological damage from mercury exposure in pregnant women who have consumed mercury-laden fish. Also, burning coal releases thousands of times more radioactive particles into the atmosphere per unit of energy produced than does a normally operating nuclear power plant. Damage to the forests of Appalachia, the northeast United States, eastern Canada, and Eastern Europe can largely be attributed to coal-fired industrial plants. Reclaiming the land damaged by coal mining and installing state-of-the-art pollution control equipment in plants substantially increase the costs of using coal. As with petroleum, if all of coal's health and environmental costs were internalized in its market cost and if government subsidies from mining were removed, coal would be so expensive that it would be replaced by other fuels (Fulkerson et al., 1990: 129; Miller, 2005: 365).

*Summarizing,* our energy predicament includes future source constraints and the ways in which the present energy system is intimately connected with environmental degradation, population and economic growth, climate change, and the global equity and geopolitical tensions that plague the world. Later in this chapter, I will turn to some of the possibilities and options for transforming the present system to address our energy predicament. But there are some clues about these from the relationship between energy and society, and studies of that relationship by scholars, to which I now turn.

## THE ENERGETICS OF HUMAN SOCIETIES

The ultimate source of *all* the world's energy is radiant energy from the sun. Fundamental to understanding the energy flows of both ecosystems and human social systems, autotrophic (green) plants transform solar radiant energy into stored complex carbohydrates by the process of photosynthesis. These are then consumed and converted into kinetic energy through the respiration processes of other species. Energy filters through the ecosystem as a second species consumes the first, a third the second, and so on. Unlike matter, energy is not recycled but tends to degenerate through the process of *entropy* to disorganized forms such as heat, which cannot be used as fuel for further production of kinetic energy or to sustain respiration. Such inefficiency means that only a portion of stored potential energy becomes actual kinetic energy.

Of course, this inefficiency is a great benefit, because we are now living off the stored energy capital of millions of years ago, but it is also true that the second law of thermodynamics (entropy) means that the relatively plentiful supplies of these fuels are ultimately exhaustible. More precisely, we will never absolutely use them up, but they can become so scarce and low grade that the costs of the energy and investment necessary to extract, refine, and transport them exceed the value of their use. We will have to squeeze the sponge harder and harder to get the same amount of energy, and the damage to the environment will increase as we do so.

| TABLE 4.1 | Per Capita Energy Consumption in Different Types of Societies |
|---|---|

| Society | Kilocalories per Day per Person |
|---|---|
| MDC (U.S.A.) | 260,000 |
| MDC (other nations) | 130,000 |
| Early industrial | 60,000 |
| Advanced agricultural | 20,000 |
| Early agricultural | 12,000 |
| Hunter-gatherer | 5,000 |
| Prehistoric | 2,000 |

*Source:* Adapted from Miller, 2002: 333.

## Low- and High-Energy Societies

All human societies modify natural ecosystems and their energy flows, but they vary greatly in the extent to which they do so. Human respiration alone requires enough food to produce about 2,000–2,500 calories a day, but people in all human societies use vastly more energy than this minimum biological requirement to provide energy necessary for their shelter, clothing, tools, and other needs.[2]

Table 4.1 illustrates the prodigious growth of world energy consumption since the beginning of the industrial era and the increasing human dependence on petrochemicals. By contrast, the traditional fuels of preindustrial societies (e.g., wood, dung, plant wastes, and charcoal) are still the energy mainstays of many people in poorer LDCs. While the aggregate energy consumption of the world has grown, it is also important to note that most of that growth is accounted for by the MDCs as high-energy societies. Indeed, a typical suburban household of an upper-middle-class American family consumes as much energy as does a whole village in many LDCs!

**INDUSTRIALIZATION AND ENERGY**   Industrialization was possible because new technologies of energy conversion were more efficient than traditional fuels. During the first phase in the early nineteenth century, the dominant technology depended upon coal mining, the smelting and casting of iron, and steam-driven rail and marine transport. The system's components were closely intertwined, and the creation of integrated mining, smelting, manufacturing, and transportation infrastructures made industrialization possible. By the beginning of the twentieth century, the system was being radically transformed again—by electric power, internal-combustion engines, automobiles, airplanes, and the chemical and metallurgical industries. Petroleum emerged as the dominant fuel and "feedstock" for the petrochemical industry. See Figure 4.1.

Withdrawals of so much energy from nature in the United States and other MDCs required substantial modifications of natural energy flows. Industrial cities alter ecosystems radically, requiring enormous amounts of energy from remote reserves of fossil fuels to power industry, heating, lighting, cooling, commerce, transportation, waste disposal, and other services. Cities become inert and relatively abiotic. Wastes are no longer naturally absorbed but must be transported to waste

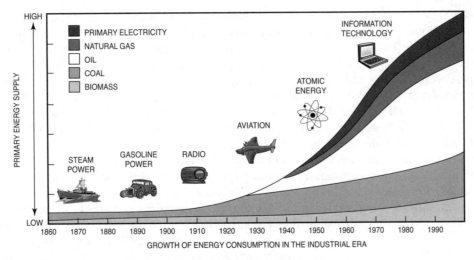

**FIGURE 4.1** Growth in Energy Consumption in the Industrial Era

*Source:* Based on G.B. Davis, *Energy for Planet Earth,* 1990. Copyright by Scientific American Inc.

treatment plants (Humphrey and Buttel, 1982: 139). In addition, industrial farmers use machinery, fertilizer, and fuel manufactured by urban industries, and food is no longer consumed mainly on farms. MDCs thus have integrated agricultural-industrial consumption systems that use enormous amounts of fossil fuels and vastly modify natural ecosystems and energy flows. Since energy plays such a powerful role in connecting and modifying both ecosystems and social systems, it is therefore an important topic for the social science understanding of human–environment relationships.

## Social Science and Energetics

Remarkably, in spite of how obvious the last sentence in the preceding paragraph is, in early social science there were only fragmentary attempts to understand the energy–society relationship (Carver, 1924; Geddes, 1890; Ostwald, 1909; Soddy, 1926; Spencer, 1896).[3] Beyond the notion that energy is the crucial linkage between societies and their biophysical environments, about the only generalization that remains from these early analyses is that increases in energy production and efficiency are related to increases in the structural complexity and the scale of human societies (Lutzenhiser et al., 2002: 223). That represents very little in terms of cumulative development of understanding the environment–energy–society relationship!

After World War II, prominent anthropologist Leslie White (1949) rekindled interest in energetics by describing the resource and technological bases for social evolution, and sociologist Fred Cottrell developed the notion that available energy limits the range of human activity. He tried to demonstrate the pervasive social, economic, political, and even psychological change that accompanied the transition from a low-energy society (preindustrial) to a high-energy society (industrial), and argued that the vast social change to modernity could ultimately be traced to energy conversion (Cottrell, 1955; Rosa et al., 1988: 153).

**MACROLEVEL STUDIES OF LOW-ENERGY SOCIETIES**    In the 1960s, anthropologists conducted meticulous empirical studies about environment–energy–society interactions in diverse ecological settings among such cultures as the Tsembaga Maring people of the central New

Guinea highlands (Rappaport, 1968), the Eskimos of Baffin Island north of Canada (Kemp, 1971), the !Kung Bushmen of the Kalahari Desert in Southwest Africa (Lee, 1969), and the rural Western Bengali (Parrick, 1969). For a summary, see Kormondy and Brown (1998: Chap.14). Armed with such detailed empirical evidence, scholars for the first time could compare energy flows between societies and look for orderly patterns. Anthropologist Marvin Harris made the most significant attempt to do so and to recast older ethnographic evidence in energetic terms (1971, 1979). Application of this formula to societies with diverse food production technologies—hunter-gatherers, hoe agriculture, slash-and-burn agriculture, irrigation agriculture, and modern industrial agriculture—revealed several patterns.

*First,* while confirming the central insight of historic energetic theories (about the relationship between energy efficiency and societal size and social complexity), these studies cast doubt on the argument of early analysts that increased technological efficiency led to increased available energy, which in turn led to larger populations and greater social complexity. The newer anthropological evidence suggested that population pressure was often the driving force of this process, promoting increased technological efficiency of energy conversion to meet rising demands (for a recent confirmation of this, see Boserup, 1981). *Second,* anthropological studies suggested that high-energy societies would typically replace or assimilate low-energy societies whenever they came into contact. The most obvious example for Americans is the outcome of contact between Europeans and Native Americans, but evidence of this replacement around the world is compelling.[4] *Third,* these studies questioned the long-term outcomes of the process of energy intensification. The recurrent response to population pressures was an upgrading of consumption, and preindustrial societies often overburdened their environments, depleting essential resources faster than they could be regenerated, and disrupting ecological cycles—and their own long-term sustainability. Anthropological literature is replete with evidence in preindustrial societies about ecological collapse (Diamond, 2004). Importantly, this evidence provides a historical context for our contemporary energy predicament: problems with growing energy/resource consumption and social and environmental sustainability (Rosa et al., 1988: 157).

**MACROLEVEL STUDIES OF HIGH-ENERGY SOCIETIES**    Analysis of energy flows in complex MDCs is no easy matter. Economists dominated energetic research after the oil shocks of the 1970s, and they emphasized the importance of energy to the economic performance of societies. Longitudinal research within societies and comparative analyses all suggested a strong relationship between the growth of energy production and the increase in measures of economic growth, such as the gross national product (GNP) (Cook, 1971). See Figure 4.2.

These studies interpreted economic indicators such as the GNP as indicative of social well-being, and since economic growth represented improvements in societal well-being, it was but a short step to infer that energy growth was essential to societal well-being (Mazur and Rosa, 1974). The implication was that constraints placed on energy consumption would lead to a decline in wealth, although much room remained for increased efficiency of energy use.

*But note:* When MDC market economies were separated from the LDCs and nonmarket socialist economies, this relationship virtually disappeared. Many studies supported this finding. These included cross-national longitudinal studies; studies examining the energy use of countries with similar living standards; case study comparisons (such as between the United States and Sweden); and cross-national studies of the relationship between energy intensity, social structure, and social welfare (Rosa et al., 1981, 1988; Schipper and Lichtenberg, 1976). You

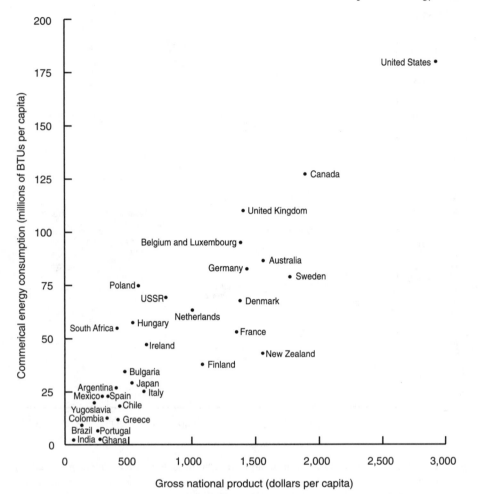

**FIGURE 4.2** The Relationship between Per Capita Energy Consumption and Gross National Product, 1971
*Source:* Based on E. Cook, 1971.

can see the "looseness" of this relationship between energy consumption and GNP measures in Figures 4.2 and 4.3, and particularly in the area marked off with an elliptical field in Figure 4.3.

Macrolevel studies and historical data point to the same conclusion: that economic development in the MDCs went through two phases, from (1) rapid industrialization and consumption being highly dependent on increased use of energy from fossil fuels to (2) economic growth becoming less energy-intensive. In the latter phase, economic growth and social well-being can increase with decreasing energy intensity because of shifts in production from industrial to service sectors and because of the adoption of more efficient technologies. In other words, a threshold level of high-energy consumption is probably necessary for a society to achieve industrialization and modernity, but once achieved, there is a wide latitude in the amount of energy needed to sustain a high standard of living. Given that latitude, industrial societies could choose slow-growth energy policies without great fear of negative, long-term consequences to overall welfare (Reddy and Goldemberg, 1990: 113; Roberts, 2004: 215).

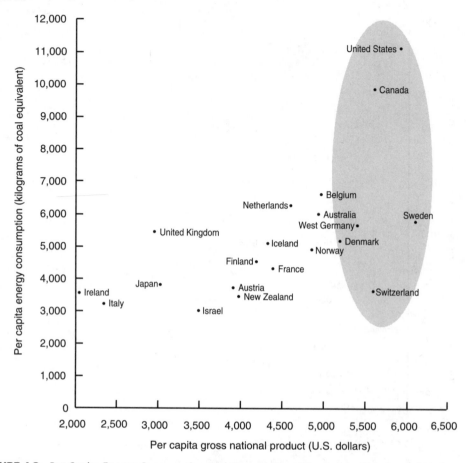

**FIGURE 4.3** Per Capita Energy Consumption and Gross National Product in 20 Industrial Nations

*Source:* From Humphrey/Buttel. Environment, Energy, and Society, 1e. © 1982 Wadsworth, a part of Cengage Learning, Inc. Reproduced by permission. www.cengage.com/permissions.

This evidence has profound implications for understanding and addressing the current world energy predicament, but it has not had much impact on political debates and discourse about energy. For instance, Amory Lovins, cited earlier, had a significant impact by popularizing energy frugality through his prolific publications and media appearances (1977). He emphasized different energy "paths" that could be pursued: A "hard path" organized highly around fossil fuels produced in very centralized ways, and a "soft path" organized around alternative energy sources (such as renewables like wind power, solar, and increasing efficiency) produced in more decentralized ways.

Public opinion surveys have shown support for "soft path" alternatives (Farhar, 1994). To the extent that we have moved somewhat away from a "hard path" trajectory (in small incre-ments)—it is due partly to Lovins' considerable persuasive abilities—resulting in what some have called a "mostly hard" hybrid system (Lutzenhiser et al., 2002: 238). But for social scientists, the most interesting elements of the soft path are the claims made for its sociopolitical impacts. These include an increased viability of society, economic self-sufficiency, better satisfaction of basic human needs, public health benefits, the growth of human values, environmental protec-tion, and an end to the chronic "crisis mentality" and fears about resource wars. These claims, of course, need empirical confirmation. There is, however, an empirical social science research literature about energy, to which I now turn.

**MICROLEVEL STUDIES: PERSONAL AND HOUSEHOLD ENERGY CONSUMPTION**   The oil shocks of the 1970s stimulated microlevel studies of energy consumption as well as macrolevel studies. The main goal of these studies was to develop a scientific understanding of whether people could significantly reduce their energy consumption without deterioration in their quality of life. Technical experts concluded that they could, saving half the nation's energy consumption (Ayres, 2001: 31; Ross and Williams, 1981). Since individuals and households consumed about a third of the nation's energy—roughly evenly divided between transportation and home needs— they were viewed as a vast untapped potential source for energy conservation that would be responsive to social policy.

Engineering perspectives guided early microlevel studies, assuming that energy consumption could be easily explained by physical variables such as climate, housing design, and the efficiency and stock of appliances and vehicles (Rosa et al., 1988: 161). As applied to vehicles and transportation, the design of more efficient vehicles caused effective energy savings in the 1980s and early 1990s. The fuel efficiency of American cars and trucks doubled as the cumulative result of many engineering changes significantly contributed to increasing the nation's energy efficiency. Changes such as installing catalytic converters to reduce urban air pollution also addressed other environmental concerns (Bleviss and Walzer, 1990: 103, 106). These were engineering modifications that over time changed the machines driven and the composite fleet of cars and trucks, but not alternations or curtailments in the driving behavior of Americans. The only successful behavior change of the era was the one mandated by law, lowering the federal interstate speed limit from 75 to 55 mph (later, as you know, it was raised back to 65 mph, and 75 mph in some states). Attempts to encourage *voluntary* behavior change and curtailment, such as driving less, car pooling, bicycling, walking, or making greater use of mass transit, were dismal failures—at least on a scale large enough to make much difference.

As with transportation, energy conservation in housing was dominated by energy engineering perspectives emphasizing physical variables like climate, housing design, and the number and efficiency of household appliances. Unlike transportation, however, the assumption that reengineering homes and appliances would significantly reduce energy use was not confirmed. For instance, the Princeton University Twin Rivers Project, a massive and detailed five-year field research effort, found that townhouses in similar housing tracts with similar square footage, number of rooms, and appliance packages varied enormously in energy consumption, when occupied by families of similar size. The energy use of new occupants could not be predicted from that of the previous occupants, and the impacts of lifestyle on household energy consumption was dramatic (Rosa et al., 1988: 161; Socolow, 1978). Furthermore, other studies of nearly identical units occupied by demographically similar families have reported 200% to 300% variations in energy use, and in particular end-use levels. Vastly different amounts of energy were used for appliances, household heating and cooling, hot water, and so on. The "average consumer" in energy analysis is somewhat mythical (Lutzenhiser et al., 2002: 240).

Much of this research was not guided by a particular concept or theory and sought commonsense ways of asking people to reduce household energy consumption, such as turning down their thermostats, closing off unused rooms, or taking shorter showers. As policy-oriented research, early post-oil shock studies provided information and education programs about conserving energy, including home energy audits. They were consistently unsuccessful, and their only successes focused on giving consumers better feedback information about their consumption.

They did, however, recognize a particularly difficult barrier to the self-monitoring of energy use in households: that energy is largely invisible.

Unlike early studies, later studies of household energy consumption were guided by two conceptual models: an *economic-rationality model,* favored mainly by economists and engineers, and an *attitude-behavior consistency model,* favored by social psychologists. The economic model emphasized that humans "rationally" respond to changing energy prices, given the presence of more efficient technologies. While escalating energy prices and efficient technologies played an important role in energy conservation, a large body of research suggested that economic analyses exaggerate their importance, while underestimating the effects of noneconomic behavior in shaping energy flows (Lutzenhiser, 1993). Partly because of the relatively constant (or "inelastic") nature of energy demand, behavior is slow to respond to price changes, and many energy-use behaviors remain unexplained by price changes.

Furthermore, the acquisition of accurate and reliable *information* about energy use, prices, investment costs, expected savings, and other nonprice factors are assumed, but ignored by a simple economic-rationality approach (Gardner and Stern, 1996: 100–124; Rosa et al., 1988: 162–163). Even when consumers claim to be well informed about energy and believe they are acting in an economically rational way, they may be mistaken. Since energy use is invisible and intrinsically difficult to quantify and analyze (even for experts), people are forced to develop ad hoc ways of accounting that—quite reasonably—overestimate the cost of conservation investments. Because people must pay attention to larger goals and tasks, many routine energy-related actions simply go unnoticed. For example, studies about household energy-related behavior that asked people to keep diary records reported that people were surprised at how often they "caught themselves in the act" of doing things like opening doors, peering into the refrigerator, or running hot water (Lutzenhiser et al., 2002: 246–247).

In contrast, attitude-behavior approaches seek to discover the effect of attitudes on energy problems and consumption. Researchers understood attitudes broadly as having cognitive, affective, and evaluative dimensions and focused on how education and information could change energy-use behavior. But studies often found discrepancies between attitudes and behavior. Attitudes may not overcome barriers to change, price and affordability, lack of knowledge, or energy-use conditions that are found in society rather than personal choices (such as the kinds of homes and autos being marketed). One study of household energy-use curtailment analyzed the interaction of price and attitudinal factors. It found that as the kind of energy-saving activity went from easy and inexpensive (such as changing temperature settings) to difficult and expensive (such as insulation and major furnace repairs), attitudes became less powerful as predictors of energy use (Black et al., 1985, cited in Gardner and Stern, 2002: 77). The conclusion reached by many studies is that while prices and other economic factors play a significant role in household energy behavior and decisions, they can be limited by social, psychological, and marketing factors, such as the vividness, accuracy, and specificity of information; the trustworthiness of sources of information; institutional barriers to investment; and other noneconomic factors (Stern and Aronson, 1984).

Other studies about values and attitudes that more carefully controlled for differences in information found powerful effects of personal values—moral obligations to change—that often outweighed the power of price incentives (Heberlein and Warriner, 1983). Still others suggested the importance of involvement in civic and neighborhood organizations as predictive of energy conservation behavior by households, particularly in the contexts of community conservation programs (Olsen and Cluett, 1979; Dietz and Vine, 1982). Importantly, studies found that socioeconomic status shapes the modes of energy conservation behavior. More affluent households invest in energy efficiency, while poorer households cope with energy problems by lifestyle modifications and curtailments (Dillman et al., 1983; Lutzenhiser and Hackett, 1993).

Taking together the macrolevel and microlevel studies of energetics, one thing is obvious: Energy behavior and consumption are far too complex to be accounted for by either a simple economic-rational or an attitude-behavior model. Scholars need an integrated conceptual framework that combines economic, social, and attitudinal factors (Stern and Oskamp, 1987). One does not now exist, but summaries of research literatures provide some clues. Economic incentives for energy conservation are likely to be effective when

1. They are directed at specific external barriers, such as costs, access to credit, tax relief, or "inconvenience."
2. Significant barriers are not located in the larger social system. These might include urban sprawl with large distances between work, home, and shopping, the "inconvenience" factor, or the unavailability of super-insulated houses or efficient autos if they are not on the market.
3. They are not counterproductive, such as raising energy prices (without compensatory policies) that force low-income or elderly people to choose between heating homes and buying food in the winter.
4. They are combined with other influence techniques, such as information, public campaigns, curbside recycling programs, and moral and ethical arguments (Gardner and Stern, 2002: 120–122).

Similarly, information and attitude change programs are more effective when they provide

1. *Accurate feedback* that ties information directly to people's behavior. One of the successes of early household energy conservation programs was to provide people with information about current energy use.
2. *Modeling* that provides illustrations about effective energy-use curtailments (rather than simply discussing the problem). Studies have, for instance, shown people videotapes about effective methods of energy-use curtailment rather than resorting simply to moral persuasion.
3. "*Framing*" messages to be consistent with people's worldviews and values. North Americans, for instance, are more receptive to arguments about improving "energy efficiency" than to those framed in terms of energy conservation. (Gardner and Stern, 2002: 83–88)

Despite the different approaches to understanding energy consumption, there seems to be a consensus that better ones must be more directly concerned with the *social contexts of individual action*—a recognition that behavior is inherently social and collective. Individual consumers often pursue social (and often noneconomic) ends when making energy-related decisions. This means that factors such as status display, ethical consumption, and pollution reduction influence how consumers assess incentives. Furthermore, various groups of consumers evaluate incentives differently (Stern et al., 1986: 162). A better approach to understanding energy consumption will require understanding how economic, attitudinal, and social processes interact to represent the complexity of real-world energy consumption. It will also require analysts to understand how technologies diffuse, as well as social networks and organizations. This becomes obvious when you think about it. Energy consumers get goods, services, information, housing, automobiles, and so forth through social networks and organizations that affect energy demand, use, and the environment. These include networks and organizations of architects, builders, subcontractors, code officials, automobile dealers, utility company representatives, appliance salesmen, and so on. They regulate and mediate the structure of relationships between consumers and manufacturers, and usually such intermediaries have few incentives to pursue energy efficiency (Lutzenhiser et al.,

2002: 248, 255; Stern and Aronson, 1984). Taken together, research about energy consumption (going as far back as the Princeton University Twin Rivers research) reaffirms what was noted in Chapter One, that social and cultural factors (e.g., lifestyles, family traditions, group affiliations, marketing, social networks and institutions) are powerful conditioners of energy consumption, in comparison to economic incentives or physical factors alone. There are more clues about dealing with the present energy predicament in the world's present energy system, to which I now turn.

## THE PRESENT ENERGY SYSTEM AND ITS ALTERNATIVES

I noted earlier that most (84%) of the world's present energy needs are supplied by finite or non-renewable resources, and that most of that comes from three fossil fuels: oil, coal, and natural gas. Renewables such as hydropower, solar, wind, and biomass supply the remainder. Traditional biomass fuels such as wood, crop refuse, and dung are important fuels in poorer LDCs, where they may be commercially traded or obtained by foraging outside commercial markets.

See Table 4.2 for the percentages of the commercial energy flows in 1999 for the world and the United States. These proportions have not changed much in the recent decades. But they do change slowly, because of changing availability, costs, and technologies. In fact, there have been significant changes in the proportion of different fuels in the world's energy flows in the twentieth century. Coal declined from 55% to 22%, oil increased from 2% to 33%, natural gas rose from 1% to 22%, nuclear energy increased from 0% to 6%, and renewables (mainly wood and flowing water) decreased from 42% to 18% (Miller and Spoolman, 2009: 373). Other renewables, such as wind power, solar energy, geothermal, and hydrogen, together make up only a small fraction of U.S. and world energy flows, but some are growing at a rapid rate and have great future potentials.

### Fossil Fuels

This chapter discussed supply issues and other problems with most of the fossil fuels earlier, so I won't repeat that here. I should, however, note some of their advantages. *Oil* is relatively cheap

| TABLE 4.2    Commercial Energy by Source for the World and the United States, 1999 | | |
|---|---|---|
| | **World (%)** | **U.S. (%)** |
| *Nonrenewable* | *82* | *93* |
| Oil | 33 | 39 |
| Coal | 22 | 23 |
| Natural gas | 21 | 23 |
| Nuclear | 6 | 8 |
| *Renewable* | *18* | *7* |
| Hydropower, solar, wind | 7 | 4 |
| Biomass | 11 | 3 |

*Source:* U.S. Department of Energy, British Petroleum, Worldwatch Institute, and the International Energy Agency. Cited in Miller and Spoolman, 2009: 373.

and easily transported, and it has a high yield of *net useful energy*. Net useful energy is the total useful energy left from the resource after subtracting the amount of energy used and wasted in finding, processing, concentrating, and transporting it to users. Oil is a versatile fuel that can be burned to propel vehicles, heat buildings and water, and supply high-temperature heat for industrial and electricity production.

*Coal* is everybody's least favorite fuel. But, there's an awful lot of it. Known and probable coal deposits could last the world between 200 and 1,125 years, depending on the rate of usage (Miller, 2005: 364). Burning coal produces a high useful net energy yield, and because its mining and use is highly subsidized and many costs are externalized, it is the cheapest way to produce intense heat for industry and to generate electricity.

*Natural gas*, which I did not say much about earlier, is a naturally occurring geological mixture of methane, butane, and propane. In contrast to coal, it is clean burning, efficient, and flexible enough for use in industry, transportation, and power generation. It generates fewer pollutants, particulates, and $CO_2$ than any other fossil fuel: Natural gas releases 14 kilograms (kg) of $CO_2$ for every billion joules of energy produced, while oil and coal release 20 and 24 kg, respectively. But

---

## BOX 4.2

### Dirty Coal and Clean Energy?

Coal is dangerous to mine, toxic to miners and consumers, destructive of the land, and the greatest producer of greenhouse gases of all fossil fuels. Experiments to capture (or "sequester") the carbon emissions from goal plants by injecting them into porous layers of rock or shale have not been encouraging. But experiments are underway between China and the United States, which together produce 40% of the world's greenhouse gases to produce energy from coal without the emissions. Coal *can* be used in less dangerous ways, and *must* be since there is really no substitute, in spite of the progress in developing wind, solar, and other alternative sources noted below. Coal-fired plants produce about half of the electricity in the United States and the world. Experiments with "clean coal" could use postcombustion technologies that inject emissions in rock after it is burned, or precombustion technologies that chemically treat coal to produce a flammable gas with lower carbon content than untreated coal. Needless to say, the scientific and technical means to do this are daunting. Yet the Chinese were working on just such plants, with American assistance.

A large-scale partnership is emerging between China and the United States. Why China and the United States? Partly because they are two different societies, and neither could do this on the necessary scale alone. The United States is more of a "bottom up" capitalist system with many different companies and government agencies that are not always focused on a few most hopeful strategies. China, by contrast, is a "top down" centrally controlled society, in which stable policy can flow from the central government to energy producers throughout the nation. While there are many virtues of the American system, it takes years for a single innovative new energy plant to be licensed, while the Chinese can build a new energy plant in 21 months. There is no way that the United States could transform its energy system with the speed, the scale, or the policy stability as could the Chinese. The cooperative effort would use the Chinese ability for the rapid construction of a different national energy system, and the American scientific and knowledge of energy technologies and infrastructure. By 2010 that joint effort was visible, and the U.S. DOE created a consortium that included three universities, three national science laboratories, two nongovernmental energy agencies, and six companies, including General Electric and Duke Energy corporation, one of the largest in the United States (Fallows, 2010).

methane emission from leakage and incomplete combustion is a heat-trapping greenhouse gas 25 times more potent than $CO_2$. Like oil, natural gas is concentrated in a few parts of the world. Conventional supplies of natural gas and unconventional supplies (at higher prices) are expected to last from 62 to 125 years, depending on how rapidly its use grows. The Middle East, Russia, and Canada contain more than 70% of the world's known reserves, and production from Canadian wells, from which the United States imports the most, is expected to peak between 2020 and 2030. While natural gas can be shipped by pipeline cheaply on the same continent, it must be converted into *liquid natural gas* and shipped in refrigerated tankers to move it across the oceans—at present a difficult, dangerous, and expensive undertaking (Miller and Spoolman, 2009:381–382). Incidentally, coal can be used to produce synthetic natural gas by gasification or liquidification, resulting in what is called "syngas." But its production and use produces about 50% more greenhouse emissions. Without huge government subsidies, most analysts believe that syngas has a limited future (Miller and Spoolman, 2009: 386). Because of the advantages of natural gas over oil, coal, and nuclear energy, many analysts see it as the best fuel to help make the transition to improved energy efficiency and greater use of renewable energy in the next 50 years.

Besides their technical advantages, other advantages of fossil fuels are economic, political, and institutional. Quite simply, even with their problems, we have an enormous *sunk investment in infrastructures* to produce, process, and use them. To develop new energy technologies that are economical and practical on a wide basis requires large investments and decades of experimentation. Not surprisingly, the rules of the present energy economies were established to favor the systems now in place, not new possibilities, whatever their advantages. To illustrate, between 2002 and 2008 federal subsidies for fossil fuels were $72 billion, compared with $1 billion for solar energy and similar small subsidies for other kinds of renewable fuels (Resch, 2009). Maintaining the fossil fuel system has short-term but very real advantages for both individuals and the powerful corporate interest groups that profit from them. Historically, a set of tax biases and subsidies encourage the use of fossil fuels and favor present operating costs rather than long-term investment in alternatives.

Even though fossil fuel consumption will need to grow by 57% (2% annually) until 2020 to maintain their 84% share of current world energy, the "fossil fuel age" is probably coming to an end sometime in the next century. We cannot see its end, but its decline is already visible (Flavin, 2005: 30; Goodstein, 2004; Roberts, 2004). What could replace fossil fuels? Fifteen years ago, most experts would have said, with little hesitation, nuclear energy.

## Nuclear Energy

Nonmilitary uses of nuclear energy produce electricity. In a nuclear fission reactor, neutrons split Uranium 235 and Plutonium 239 to release a lot of high-temperature heat energy, which in turn powers steam turbines that generate electricity. In principle, nuclear fission reactions are the same kind used in the atom bombs of World War II. The complicated systems required to regulate, modulate, contain, and cool such reactions make nuclear plants much more complex to operate than coal plants. I'm sure you know this is a very controversial way of producing energy.

In the 1950s, researchers predicted that nuclear energy would supply 21% of the world's commercial energy. But by 2000, after almost 50 years of development and enormous government subsidies, and $2 trillion in private investment around the world, the commercial reactors in 32 countries were producing only 6% of the world's commercial energy and 19% of its electricity. Only China plans to build more than 50 new plants by 2020 to reduce its dependence on coal (Flavin, 2006). In the United States, no new nuclear power plants have been ordered since

1978, and all of the 120 plants ordered since 1973 were canceled. Forty-three out of 104 operating plants have been shut down more than a year to restore safety features. The Nuclear Regulatory Commission (NRC) has not been asked to license a (real) new plant in many years (Miller, 2002: 347). Given the original expectations for nuclear energy, it has been a disappointment. Why?

National security reasons are well known. Nations that have the technical capacity for nuclear power can also build nuclear weapons. So the diffusion of nuclear energy contributes to the potential proliferation of nuclear weapons and geopolitical tensions. Several international rogue nations, such as Iran and North Korea, have not been open to international inspection, and are widely suspected of using the development of nuclear electricity as a cover for developing a covert nuclear weapons capability. In 2010, the tensions between the MDCs and these nations continued to be intense and politically destabilizing.

*Second* and equally well known are the risks of nuclear meltdowns and accidents that tarnished the public image of the nuclear option. Some became household words: Three Mile Island (TMI), a U.S. nuclear plant in Pennsylvania that allowed radioactive gases to escape, and Chernobyl, a plant in the former U.S.S.R. (now Ukraine) that experienced a complete meltdown. At TMI, partial cleanup, lawsuits, and damage claims cost $1.2 billion, almost twice the reactor's $700 million construction cost. The Chernobyl meltdown burned uncontrollably for 10 days, releasing more radiation into the atmosphere than the Hiroshima and Nagasaki bombs combined. Prevailing winds and rain sent radioactive fallout over much of Europe, and was measured as far away as Alaska (Charman, 2006:12). These are dramatic but isolated events. To be fair, you should know that because of built-in safety features, the risk of exposure to radioactivity from nuclear power plants in the United States and most other developed nations is said to be very low.

*Third,* unlike coal or natural gas-fuelled plants, nuclear plants do not produce $CO_2$ or other greenhouse gas emissions. But they *do* produce long-lived, low-level radioactive waste, which is now accumulating in storage facilities on nuclear plant sites. The federal government has defaulted on its commitment to take back nuclear waste and store it safely in permanent waste repositories. They would need to be secure from corrosion, leakage, earthquakes, or sabotage for a *long* time. Close to where you live, perhaps?

*Fourth,* and less widely appreciated, the planning, construction, and regulation of nuclear plants make them a very uneconomic investment. This has been the greatest barrier to the expansion of nuclear energy. A state-of-the-art coal-fired plant is a much less costly way of generating electricity. Economics may be a more potent barrier to the expansion of nuclear energy than negative public opinion or antinuclear activists. Furthermore, dismantling and securing the world's aging stock of spent reactors and the disposing of nuclear wastes pose safety hazards, political problems, and economic costs that may exceed those of the development and operation of plants (Gibbons et al., 1990: 88). Banks and lending institutions in the United States are leery of financing new nuclear plants, and utility investors have largely abandoned them.

Nuclear energy thus has enormous costs, demonstrated potential for serious accidents, destabilizing geopolitical qualities, and unresolved problems in disposing of wastes. Even with these imposing problems, research continues about—yet to be perfected—"breeder reactors" that generate their own fuel. Excitement is building about a different nuclear option, using thorium, a safe, and "green" fuel so abundant that it could power the United States for 1,000 years (Martin, 2010). With all its difficulties, electricity demand, improved reactor designs, and climate change fears have meant a revival of hope for nuclear energy. Continuing to promote a variety of energy alternatives, in 2010 President Obama declared more than $8 billion in federal loan guarantees to build two nuclear reactors, and the nuclear industry is poised to start at least a half dozen plants over the next decade (Associated Press, 2010c). Even though it has no greenhouse gas emissions and is a "ready" technology, nuclear energy has many unresolved problems as a way to weakening our dependence on fossil fuels. What are other options that deserve pursuing? Renewable power sources, for instance, now supply about three times as much electricity as does nuclear, and in 2006 new nuclear plants equaled only about one-tenth of capacity of new wind power installations (Flavin, 2006).

## Renewable Energy Sources

Renewable energy sources are both the oldest energy sources used by humans and those with the greatest potential to address the many problems created by the present system. Today renewable energy sources collectively constitute only 18% of the world and 7% of the U.S. energy sources. With investment and technological development, renewable energy from water, biofuels, wind, and the sun *could* produce half of the world's energy within the next 50 years, and maybe sooner if combined with comparable investments in energy efficiency. The principles of generating energy by each source are well established, even though some are not now practical or affordable for commercial energy on a large scale (Jacobson and Delucchi, 2009).

**HYDROPOWER**    Hydropower uses water from dammed reservoirs to turn turbine engines that generate electricity. In 2004, hydropower generated about 20% of the world's electricity and 6 % of the total energy flow. Hydropower dams themselves produce no greenhouse emissions or other pollutants, and they have an operating life span of two to three times that of coal or nuclear plants. *Large dams* can be used to regulate irrigation and to provide recreation and flood control, but they are not cost free, either for humans or for the environment. They rot plants on flooded land producing greenhouse gas emissions and methane, decrease the natural fertilization (the re-silting) of prime agricultural land, destroy wildlife habitats and uproot many people, and reduce fish harvests below dams (Li, 2006). These problems make large-scale hydro systems inappropriate in many parts of the world, particularly in the LDCs.

**BIOFUELS**    Most of the world's people and about 80% of LDC residents burn *traditional fuels,* such as wood, charcoal, dung, or plant residues. These account for about 10% of world energy flows. Such fuels have a low net energy yield and are dirty to burn, producing a lot of carbon particulate, carbon dioxide, and carbon monoxide as by-products. Heating a house with a wood or charcoal stove produces as much particulate matter as heating 300 homes with natural gas. While people in LDC cities may buy wood or charcoal, the great human virtue of traditional fuels is that most people who use them do not purchase them. In rural areas, women and children usually gather twigs and branches or animal dung for cooking fuel instead of buying wood. In principle, biomass fuels are renewable and environmentally benign. But often the pressure of growing populations has stripped the land of trees and vegetation in the search for fuel wood, contributing to deforestation and desertification. The forests of China have been cut down for centuries, and the search for fuel wood today exacerbates desertification, soil erosion, and environmental degradation in much of sub-Saharan Africa, Nepal, and Tibet. Biomass can be used to produce other fuels. In many LDCs, *biogas digesters* use anaerobic bacteria to convert plant wastes, dung, sewage, and other biomass fuels to methane gas that can be used for lighting or cooking. After the generation of methane, the solid residue can be recycled for fertilizer for food crops or trees. The supply of biomass fuelstock often varies seasonally, and if used in biogas generators, it reduces its availability for its usual use as crop fertilizer (Reddy and Goldemberg, 1990).

*Ethanol* is now being produced from corn and plant residues, and in the United States is, as you know, being added to gasoline to "stretch" petroleum supplies and lower greenhouse emissions. Not surprisingly, Midwestern corn farmers see this as a bonanza for the sluggish farm economy. Ethanol can also be refined from sugarcane, and Brazil and the United States control most of the world ethanol market, even though far less of this fuel is internationally traded than fossil fuels (Hunt and Stair, 2006). Other methods can produce ethanol more efficiently from shrubs, sycamores, and prairie grasses like switchgrass. It can even be produced from green algae, with an astonishing productivity given the technology to do so. At any rate, corn ethanol is not a panacea for our fuel problems. If you consider the energy it takes to clear land, grow corn, and to refine it to ethanol is not that much better for the environment than gasoline. Furthermore, if you used the whole U.S. corn crop to produce ethanol, it would satisfy the U.S. need for gasoline for about six months! Even so, existing technologies and vested economic interests will make it difficult for the United States to shift to other ways of producing ethanol.

An important problem with ethanol fuel (as now produced) is an *ethical one*. In a world where many lack food, do we use agricultural resources to produce fuel? The growth of ethanol distilleries in corn-belt states has been an economic bonanza for farmers, who need to make a living. But, the more corn we use for fuels means driving up the price of meat and anything that has fructose (corn sugar) such as most canned goods and beverages. As we use agricultural resources for fuel, we consequently make the problem of human nutrition more difficult and "pricy" where many have difficulty affording enough food. The U.N. Food and Agricultural Organization reported that the rising demand for biofuels alone increased the price of food between 8% and 13% in various nations around the world (Monfort, 2009). You can approach the food-fuel trade-off ethically ("What is the most defensible compromise for how we such our resources?") or politically ("Which interest groups, agribusiness, or transportation will "win" in the market and policy debate?"). If not a "zero sum game," who will benefit how much? This issue is being widely discussed, but as an eater or energy consumer, you will probably never get to vote!

---

## BOX 4.3

### Biodiesel?

Diesel fuel is an old idea. Rudolf Diesel, who invented the diesel engine, ran his demonstration model on peanut oil. Diesel engine fuel can be made from a variety of vegetable oils, including soy, palm, rapeseed (canola), and sunflower oil. Such biodiesel is cheaper and more environmentally friendly than petroleum diesel. Biodiesel fuels (from all sources) produce net greenhouse gas reductions like ethanol made from sugarcane and corn. By one estimate, biodiesel typically reduces $CO_2$ by 41%, more than three times the reduction from corn ethanol. But, there are problems. For instance, Brazil's production of biomass ethanol requires just 3% of its agricultural land. But to supply 10% of the U.S. needs from biomass and biodiesel fuels would require 30% of its agricultural land. To supply palm oil, for instance, Malaysia plans to convert 3 million hectares of its tropic forest (about the size of Massachusetts) into a palm plantation. Opponents say producing biodiesel on a large scale would trash rainforests, deplete water reserves, reduce biodiversity, and raise food prices. While the small-scale production of biodiesel from waste oil and low-level conversion of oil crops could deliver a modest reduction in greenhouse emissions, the environmental benefits don't scale up. (*New Scientist,* 2006: 38–40)

**WIND POWER**    *Wind generators* basically hook modern windmills to electric generators to produce power directly. Such power can be produced only in areas with enough wind. When the wind dies down, you need backup electricity from a utility company or some kind of energy storage system. Furthermore, unlike coal or oil, which pack a lot of energy in a small amount of fuel, the amount of wind that blows across each square meter carries only a little bit of power. It takes the combined effort of *many* wind generators installed across large areas of land to produce as much energy as a single fuel-burning power plant. Even with these limitations, wind power has a *vast* potential. In 2004, Stanford University engineers mapped the global potential for wind energy, and their data indicate that capturing only one-fifth of the wind energy at the world's best sites could generate more than seven times the amount of electricity now used in the world and thus help phase out energy-wasting coal and nuclear plants (Miller and Spoolman, 2009: 419–420).

In some areas the wind blows continuously, such as in the 12 contiguous U.S. Rocky Mountain and Great Plains states from the Canadian border to Texas. This region contains 90% of the wind power potential in the United States, which the U.S. Department of energy (DOE) has dubbed the "Saudi Arabia of wind." Similar windswept areas around the world could produce a substantial proportion of world electricity needs. Wind generators produce no $CO_2$ or other air pollutants during operation, they need no water for cooling, and their manufacture and use produce little pollution. Modern wind turbines are complex and sophisticated machines, with some 8,000 components, including gear boxes that require exotic and scarce metals (e.g., Neodymium). As a result, engineers are now developing "gearless" turbines (Sawin, 2009a). Some critics have charged that wind turbines suck birds and migratory birds into their blades. But, as long as wind farms are not located along bird migratory routes (which are mapped by very sophisticated studies), most birds learn to fly around them. Studies demonstrate that larger numbers of birds die when they are sucked into jet engines, killed by domestic and feral cats, and crash into skyscrapers, plate glass windows, communication towers, or auto windows (Miller and Spoolman, 2009: 421). The land occupied by wind farms can be used for grazing and other agricultural purposes.

Wind energy is no longer a research project: It works cheaply and reliably enough to compete with other energy sources. Since the 1980s, the price of a kilowatt hour (kWh) of U.S. wind electricity dropped dramatically, making it competitive with electric power from coal, natural gas, or hydropower, and three times cheaper that electricity from nuclear power. With the same government subsidies as those sources, its price could drop to 1–2 cents per kWh, making it the cheapest way to produce power. Recognizing these economic advantages, several large corporations have begun to invest in wind power (General Electric, Royal Dutch Shell), signaling a transition underway (Miller, 2005: 396–397; Sawin, 2005b). Despite the fact that it now only produces a small proportion of the world's energy, it is a fast growing source (between 25% and 31% per year). It accounts for twice as much electricity as produced by nuclear plants, and may produce 10% to 25% of the world's energy budget by 2050 (Sawin, 2005b).

**SOLAR ENERGY**    The direct use of energy from the sun has the greatest potential as an alternative energy sustainable source. An enormous amount of radiant energy falls on the earth's surface, which—if trapped and converted into usable forms—could supply the energy needs of the world. The total potential of *solar power* is enormous but, like wind power, it is variable, only possible where and when the sun shines, needing storage and backup systems. Solar radiation intensity varies by latitude and with the weather, but still, solar energy is available 60% to 70% of the days in the northern tier of American states, and 80% to 100% in the southern half of the country (U.S. Department of Energy, 1989). In the sunny regions closer to the equator that include many LDCs, the potential for solar energy is enormous and could supply much of the world.

Solar energy is now practical for space and water heating. The technology of using solar collectors for these purposes is relatively simple. For an investment of a few thousand dollars, using skills possessed by the average carpenter, it is possible to *retrofit* an older home to reduce the use of fossil fuels for heating water or rooms. A *passive solar heating system* captures sunlight directly within a structure through windows or sunspaces that face the sun and converts it into low-temperature heat. The heat can be stored in walls and floors of concrete, adobe brick, stone, or tile and released slowly during the day and night. *Active solar heating systems* have specially designed collectors, usually mounted on a roof with unobstructed exposure to the sun. They concentrate solar energy, heat a medium, and have fans or pump systems that transmit space heat or hot water to other parts of a building. The potential is very large for reducing America's combined heat bill this way. On a lifetime-cost basis, solar space and water heating is inexpensive in many parts of the United States. But since subsidies of fossil fuel prices make them artificially low in the United States, active or passive solar investments have been lower since the 1990s than after the oil shocks of the 1970s—when energy prices were higher and a number of tax incentives (briefly) existed. In many warm, sunny nations, such as Jordan, Israel, and Australia, solar energy supplies much of the hot water now, as it does for new housing in Arizona and Florida.

*Photovoltaic electricity* (PVE) is produced directly when semiconductor cells that create an electric current absorb solar radiation. You are probably familiar with PVE cells that energize small calculators and wristwatches. In many ways, PVE is *the* superb energy source to create electricity: It creates no pollution, has no moving parts, and requires minimal maintenance and no water. It can operate on any scale, from small portable modules in remote places to multimegawatt power plants with PVE panels covering millions of square meters. Furthermore, most PVE cells are made of silicon, the second most plentiful mineral on the earth's surface. But unlike solar space heating, producing wafer-thin silicon semiconductor solar cells is a high-tech enterprise with considerable costs, and unlike land around wind generators, land occupied by solar panels *cannot* be used for grazing or agriculture. But solar panels can sit on rooftops, along highways, and in sun-rich but otherwise empty deserts. Furthermore, the use of land would not be excessive. Hydropower reservoirs use enormous amounts of land, and coal mining needs more land than solar generators if you include the area devoted to mining.

The main obstacles to the spread of PVE technology are its high cost (per megawatt), and the significant costs of building an infrastructure of solar panels. Presently PVE accounts for a small portion of world energy flows. Even so, like wind power, PVE is growing rapidly, 51% in 2007 alone, and since 1996 enough to meet the electricity demand for 3 million homes in Europe (Sawin, 2009b). There are several reasons why. PVE generators found niche markets in the world economy, where they are the cheapest way of delivering electricity to 2 billion rural villagers without having to extend centralized power grids from cities or big regional plants. By the late 1990s, PVE electricity was growing rapidly in places like Vietnam and Jamaica, where sunlight is plentiful. Increasingly, PVE cells are used to switch railroad tracks; supply power for rural health clinics; operate water wells and irrigation pumps; charge batteries; operate portable laptop computers; and power ocean buoys, lighthouses, and offshore oil-drilling platforms. In the United States, PVE cells did not have access to a single acre of public land in 2009, while oil and natural gas companies operated on 45 million acres (Resch, 2009: 20). Furthermore, several European nations are also in the process of removing the traditional subsidies for coal and oil and transferring them to wind power and PVE.

Thanks to economies of scale, rising energy conversion efficiencies, and more efficient use of silicon use in solar cells, PVE prices continue to decline. Solar electricity is likely to become cost-competitive with the retail price of electricity in many parts of the world in the next several years. According to a stock broker with New York's Piper Jaffray, "whether it's 2010, 2012, or 2015, I think everyone can read the writing on the wall." When solar becomes competitive with conventional power "solar power demand is infinite" (cited in Sawin, 2009b: 40).

**HYDROGEN FUEL**    If you took high school chemistry and conducted *water electrolysis*, running electricity through water and splitting water molecules into oxygen and hydrogen atoms, you can understand the potential of using *hydrogen gas* as a fuel. An alternative method, often more practical, is to use a reformer (or converter) device that strips hydrogen molecules from other fuels such as natural gas, methanol, ammonia, gasoline, ethanol, or even vegetable oil (W. Cunningham and M. Cunningham, 2010: 456). You could make hydrogen using solar, wind, or conventionally produced electricity. It is a clean-burning fuel with about 2.5 times more energy by weight than gasoline. When burned, it produces no heat-trapping greenhouse gases, but combines with oxygen in the air to produce ordinary water vapor. Hydrogen can be collected and stored in tanks like propane is today, or it can be transported by pipeline. It is easier to store than electricity, but as a gas, hydrogen is bulky and explosive. Liquid hydrogen takes up less space than gas, but must be kept below −250 degrees centigrade, not a trivial task for most applications. Hydrogen will combine with reactive metals to form solid compounds called *hydrides*, which could be stored to be heated releasing hydrogen as needed. Combining hydrogen and oxygen gas in what are called *fuel cells* could produce electricity to power vehicles or produce heat and light for buildings.

Fuel cells are ideal for many applications: They are highly reliable, have no moving parts, are highly efficient, produce only water as a byproduct, and are small. They may be connected or "stacked" in huge arrays that multiply their output, but such a "stack" providing almost all the electricity needed by a typical home (including water and space heating) would be about the size of a refrigerator. They could be scaled up to huge applications. For example, a 45-story office building at 4 Times Square in New York City has two 200-kilowatt fuel cells on its fourth floor that provide both electricity and heat, along with other conservation measures. Such applications exist but are not common because of their imposing technological requirements (W. Cunningham and M. Cunningham, 2010: 456).

Gradually switching to hydrogen and away from fossil fuels as our primary fuel resources would mean a far-reaching *hydrogen revolution* on a profound scale. Technical and social transformations required over the next 50 years could change the world as much as did the agricultural and industrial revolutions. A solar-hydrogen economy would be based on resources that are more abundant and evenly distributed than fossil fuels and could reduce the geopolitical tensions and costs produced by dependence among nations.

What's the catch? Well, there are some big ones. *First,* hydrogen ($H_2$) is locked up in water and organic compounds like the fossil fuels. *Second,* it takes energy and money to produce $H_2$ from water and organic compounds. Although I have written about $H_2$ as a fuel, it is not directly a source of energy, but a way of storing energy by using energy from other fuels. *Third,* while fuel cells are the best way to use hydrogen to produce electricity, current versions are expensive. We can use heat and chemical processes to separate $H_2$ from the complex carbon-based molecules of coal, natural gas, ethanol, or gasoline, but at present, doing so is more expensive and produces as much $CO_2$ as does using these fossil fuels directly (Miller and Spoolman, 2009: 428–430). In sum, hydrogen power has only theoretical potential, but it is an enormously attractive one.

**EFFICIENCY AS A RESOURCE**    Even with such an impressive menu of alternatives to fossil fuels, it is important to emphasize that efficiency is the cheapest, easiest, and fastest way to address our present energy predicament. We often forget just how effective energy efficiency is, and how it makes economic sense. The U.S. power sector alone could reduce electricity rates by 40% and cut $CO_2$ emissions in half by upgrading power plants and transmission systems (Roberts, 2004: 220). As Amory Lovins, an outspoken efficiency advocate, pointed out, "Just a 2.7 miles-per-gallon gain in fuel economy of this country's light-vehicle fleet could displace Persian Gulf import entirely" (cited in Roberts, 2004: 215).

Efficiency also makes corporate sense. "Anywhere companies have pursued energy efficiency, they have ended up making money, even if making money wasn't their initial goal" (Goldstein, cited in Roberts, 2004: 225). America has many ways of increasing energy efficiency; and in order of increasing price, they include:

1. Converting to efficient lighting equipment, which would save the United States electricity equal to the output of 120 large power plants, plus
2. $30 billion a year in maintenance costs. Using more efficient electric motors, saving half the energy used by such
3. Motor systems, which would save the output of 150 large power plants and repay conversion costs in about a year
4. Eliminating pure waste electricity, such as lighting empty offices
5. Displacing electricity now used with better architecture, weatherization, insulation, and solar energy for water and space heating
6. Making appliances, smelters, and the like cost-effectively efficient

Amazingly, these six measures could quadruple U.S. electrical efficiency, making it possible to run the economy with no changes in lifestyles and using no power plants, whether old or new (Lovins, 1998). This assessment does not include the energy efficiencies that would result from *cogeneration* (combined heat and power systems). See Box 4.4.

Possibilities for "mining" efficiency are producing a profound shift in thinking. Economists traditionally viewed conservation and environmental protection as involving only economic restraint, higher costs, and curtailment of consumption. But some now envision a vast future market for efficiency as profitable for investors, and the basis for a virtual "second industrial revolution." Nations that fail to develop "greener" economies are likely to lose out economically as well as environmentally (Brown, 2001; Flavin and Dunn, 1999; Hawken et al., 2000; McDonough and Braungart, 2002). I will return to this theme, particularly in Chapter Seven.

---

### BOX 4.4

#### Mining Efficiency: Combined Heat and Power Systems

Combined heat and power (CHP), a kind of cogeneration, captures waste heat as electricity is produced, and recycles it to provide another energy service (like space or water heating). Conventionally heat is simply dumped into the environment, and more fuel must be provided for that service. There are great efficiency advantages. The average coal-fired power plant had a conversion efficiency of 33%, and the most efficient natural gas-fired plant has efficiencies of 60% to 64%, but CHP systems have efficiencies of between 75% and 90%, with lower transmission losses because the two processes are spatially close. CHP systems are found in energy-intensive sectors (including paper and printing, chemicals, metal refining, and food production) that account for 80% of the world's CHP capacity. In addition to large-scale industrial applications, CHP and power systems can provide both electricity and heat to individual or dense groups of residential buildings. In North America, such systems are most often found in universities and hospitals.

CHP systems are more common in Western and Eastern Europe, where publicly owned facilities are connected to residential districts for heating and cooling. Denmark is the global leader, producing 52% of its electricity needs with CHP systems. In Eastern Europe, it produces almost 19%, an odd legacy of Soviet-era central planning, which called for widespread cogeneration technology. In the United States, CHP systems presently account for a modest 8% of power production. According to the International Energy Agency, CHP could reduce greenhouse emissions by at least 4% in 2015, and 10% by 2030. With post-Kyoto climate negotiations still on the world's agenda, cogeneration is an energy efficiency "tool of choice" to address climate issues (Chiu, 2009: 50–52).

---

## BARRIERS, TRANSITIONS, AND ENERGY POLICY

Our energy *predicament* has intrinsic links to other social and environmental problems. These include pollution, loss of biodiversity, environmental degradation, health problems, urban sprawl/congestion, a large national debt and balance of payments problem, geopolitical costs of maintaining access to oil and gas fields, and a volatile economic dependency that amplifies international instability and sometimes war. In LDCs, the energy predicament is related to deforestation, desertification, barriers to development, poverty, and hunger. Most ominously, our present energy system is thought to be a chief culprit in the most serious macrothreat to the future of humanity: anthropogenic climate change.

A 2009 assessment of the potential of a new "mix" of energy sources (including renewables) to provide a way out of this predicament is optimistic. An environmental/civil engineer and a specialist in the economic analysis of sustainable transportation and fuels from Stanford University and the University of California at Davis argue that

> A large-scale wind, water, and solar energy system can reliably supply the world's needs, significantly benefiting climate, air quality, water quality, ecology, and energy security. [The] . . . obstacles are primarily political, not technical. A combination of feed in tariffs plus incentives for providers to reduce costs, elimination of fossil fuel subsidies, and an intelligently expanded grid could ensure rapid deployment. [With modest and likely policies] . . . full replacement of the fossil fuel system may take 40 to 50 years. (Jacobson and Delucchi, 2009: 65)

Needless to say, such a transformation would require heavy investments over decades, and overcoming the economic advantages of the "sunk investments" of the existing energy regime. But such investments are not "handed out" by governments or consumers, but paid back through the sale of electricity and energy. A decade ago, it was not clear that a global water, wind, and solar system would be technically or economically feasible. Given their analysis, the energy and economic experts Jacobson and Delucchi now think that it is.

## Barriers to Change

We have a rich menu of technical possibilities that could, in combination, move the world toward more efficient, affordable, and environmentally friendly energy systems. With these possibilities why, for instance, if renewable energy is so great, does it produce only 18% of world energy and 7% of energy in the United States? There obviously have been some powerful barriers to change.

*First,* efficient and renewable energy receives much lower tax breaks, subsidies, and research and development funding that do fossil fuels or nuclear. Public policy makes it a very uneven playing field. If it was leveled, alternative energy would develop rapidly and that would effect economic performance. Economic performance is directly correlated with energy prices. But, *contrary to intuition,* the more costly and highly taxed the energy resources, the more technological innovation and economic growth. For instance, between 1976 and 1990 researchers found that among industrial nations where energy prices were subsidized and below world market value, both innovation and economic growth lagged significantly behind (Hawken, 1993: 180). By 2009 the world's major industrial nations (G-20) agreed to start a phaseout of fossil fuel subsidies, not suddenly but in the "medium term," and the Waxman-Markey energy/climate bill passed by the U.S. House of Representatives (but not the Senate) would shift some subsidies and investment incentives from fossil fuels to renewables (Mason and Ennis, 2009; Sheppard, 2009).

*Second,* like many other social problems, the salience of energy problems follows an *issue-attention cycle,* a cycle of rising and falling concern due to energy-related national events and the volume of media coverage they attract (Downs, 1972; Rosa, 1998; Mazur, 1991). When supplies increase and prices moderate, the combination of public concern and media attention that would impel political action is at a low ebb (Joskow, 2002: 105). That was the fate of global warming, a premier social problem after the long hot summer of 1989, but which "cooled" in the 1990s, only to return slowly to public debate and discourse (Ungar, 1992, 1998). Safe to say that after mild winters, devastating hurricanes, and $3.00 a gallon gasoline, by 2010 both energy and global warming are high-definition social problems that have our attention again!

*Third,* energy policies have been fragmented, contradictory, and often paralyzed. In the United States, energy policy has been separated by fuel type, with different institutional associations, interests, and regulatory bureaus for each, with few attempts at broader coalition building. The Bureau of Mines deals with coal problems and interests, the Department of Interior with gas and oil, and the Nuclear Regulatory Commission with nuclear energy. Electricity is regulated differently in each of the 50 states. The net result is that government energy policies have intervened in markets with supply-side policies that subsidize costs and increase consumption rather than promote efficiency and alternative fuels (Switzer, 1994: 138).

A *fourth* barrier to effective energy policies is that they need to be articulated on a global basis. Even dramatic improvements in energy efficiency will not be sufficient to protect the global environment if they are confined to the MDCs. Pleas from MDCs to address global environmental and climate problems through energy restraint will fall on deaf ears in the LDCs, unless the

MDCs can find ways to help them achieve increased economic well-being and environmental protection at the same time.

## Transitions and Policy

Even with such powerful barriers to changes in policy, it is important to underscore that the world changes, including the web of connections between energy and societies. This means that, as always, *some kind of energy transition is underway.* Consider two previous world energy transformations.

Before the industrial revolution, people depended for energy on a combination of traditional biomass fuels (like wood and dung), animal power, and water power. Beginning in the 1800s, a new energy regime evolved around coal, which was the foundation for a steam-powered industrial system. (The term *energy regime* means the network of industrial sectors that evolve around a particular energy resource, as well as the consequent political, commercial, and social interactions.) The coal regime diffused around the world in the late nineteenth century; between 1850 and 1913, this single energy resource went from providing 20% to more than 60% of the world's total commercial energy. Until 1915, petroleum had a niche market for kerosene to light lamps and was between 3 and 12 times as expensive as coal in Europe and North America. But under the stimulus of converting naval ships and military vehicles, a petroleum-based energy regime was established more rapidly than it could have been by private enterprise alone. The share of world energy provided by oil grew from 5% in 1910 to over 50% by 1973, and after World War II it was the key resource for transportation, electricity generation, and heating in most of the industrialized world (Podobnik, 1999).

**THE PRESENT AND THE FORESEEABLE FUTURE**    What kind of world energy transition are we in the midst of now? I rely on global appraisals by the International Energy Agency (IEA), formed in the wake of the 1970s oil shocks and represents mainly MDCs: 26 countries such as the European Union, the United States, Australia, Japan, Turkey, and Japan. The IEA does not see significant changes in the present mix of commercial fossil fuels, but does project a significant growth in the world commercial energy consumption, close to 50% by 2020.

Energy scenarios of the future offer a wide range of estimates of how much renewable sources can contribute and how fast. (Remember, scenarios are not a projection of what *will* happen, but speculations about more or less likely futures.) The IEA recently projected that the share of primary world energy from renewables will remain at 13% between 2005 and 2030. But if national policies under consideration are implemented, that share could rise to 17%, and renewables could be generating 29% of global electricity by then (IEA, 2007). The Intergovernmental Panel on Climate Change (IPCC) projected that, with a $CO_2$-equivalent price of up to $50 per ton, renewables could generate 29% of global electricity by then (IPCC, 2007). The IEA estimates that $45 trillion in investments, or an average of 1% of annual global economic output between now and 2050 would be needed to wean the world off oil and cut $CO_2$ emissions in half. The vast majority of these investments would be in efficiency improvements and renewable energy (IEA, 2008). In 2007, a review of global energy scenarios noted, the "energy future we ultimately experience is the result of choice; it is not fate" (Hamlin et al., 2007: 1).

In the energy transition of the twenty-first century, oil, like coal in the late nineteenth century, is entering a state of slow growth and relative stagnation. Experts estimate that production will peak sometime between 2010 and 2020 and thereafter begin to decline. Sometime in the twenty-first century, a new and more diverse world energy regime will emerge. In this new regime, a more diverse mix will continue to rely on oil and coal when possible, but also on more natural gas and a rapidly growing decentralized mix of nonrenewables like wind, solar, and solar-hydrogen energy. This new regime would be a "bridge" economy—a transitional phase arresting the worst of the current energy trends while giving us more time and flexibility eventually to create a radically different energy system. The United States could encourage this transitional stage by (1) immediate moves to expand natural gas imports, (2) the rapid deployment of a carbon tax, and (3) dramatically improved automotive fuel efficiency. The gas bridge economy might last for two or three decades, and the emissions growth rate would begin to slow. Fuel cells would be slowly but steadily penetrating both the automotive and stationary power markets and laying the groundwork for the eventual emergence of a hydrogen economy, once technology makes hydrogen from renewables cost competitive (Roberts, 2004: 313, 315).

## Conclusion: Energy and the Risks We Take

Let me return to the future scenarios of the world energy system projected by the IEA for the first several decades of the twenty-first century. It projects around 50% increases in the consumption of commercial energy, primarily met with carbon-based fossil fuels like oil, coal, and natural gas.

Wow! What risks are involved in such enormous increases? There are two kinds. The *first* is global and long-range, but nonetheless powerful. How would the increased carbon emissions from such increases contribute to an already warming global climate? The *second* kind of risk is social and political. What will be the global consequences of the growing energy dependence among nations, of MDCs on LDC resources, and the aspirations of people everywhere? What kinds of social and political instabilities will result within and between nations, partly driven by the energetic base of social life and the world network of nations (Humphrey et al., 2002: 171)?

## Personal Connections

*Questions for Review*

1. What are different kinds of interacting concerns about present energy systems, and which is thought to be relatively more serious than it was a few decades ago?
2. What do the following concepts mean, and how are they important to understand our energy concerns? Useful net energy, energy intensity, energy infrastructure, sunk investment, cogeneration, Hubbard's "peak oil."
3. Even though we have many technological alternatives to the present "fossil fuel based" energy system, what are some of the reasons it is difficult to change?
4. What is the cheapest and most technologically ready of the newer renewable energy technologies?
5. Nuclear energy is efficient and nonpolluting. What are the biggest obstacles to its development?
6. What are some difficulties with large-scale hydropower projects (dams)?
7. How are present lifestyles in cities and suburbs founded on certain forms and costs of energy (particularly for transportation)?
8. What are the cheapest and easiest ways of increasing the energy supply for heating and cooling?
9. What are the important long- and short-term risks that we take by staying with our present energy systems?

*Questions for Reflection*

Here are some questions to help you think about your personal relation to energy consumption and a variety of social and environmental issues.

1. Chapter Three argued that our carbon-based energy system is one of the primary drivers of global warming. The average human sends the equivalent of his or her body weight of carbon into the atmosphere for about every $200 spent. That figure is based on a world average: As North Americans, you and I probably contribute much more. Do the math: How much do you think you, or you and your family, contribute? Multiply by 300 million Americans (deduct some for children when you do).

2. This chapter noted that as nations move from LDCs to MDCs and from early to late industrial (more service-based) economies, they become more energy efficient per unit of economic output. Yet the data displayed in Figure 4.3 demonstrated considerable variation among developed market economies in the relationship between energy input and economic output, with Americans leading the pack in terms of energy inefficiency. Given what you know about conditions and lifestyles in America and other nations, why do you think that is so?

3. Since transportation is such an important part of our energy budget, here's a pointed question: If you drive a car, how much would gasoline have to cost per gallon to induce you to cut your driving by a meaningful amount? How might people with different occupations answer that question differently? What other changes in community life would make it easier for you to do this?

## What You Can Do

Small lifestyle changes that relate to possibilities for greater energy frugality are well known:

- Drive less, keep your car tuned; when possible walk, bicycle, or ride the bus or commuter train; car-pool.
- Insulate your house and turn the thermostat down in winter; adjust to changing temperatures by changes of clothing rather than heating or cooling your house; run appliances frugally, and replace them with more energy-efficient appliances when you can.
- Buy "green goods" that have less stored energy used in their production by the time they get to you. Etc., etc. . . . (You know the litany of small things you can do. If *many* people did them, they would add up.)

The larger and more meaningful lifestyle changes are more difficult and challenging. They require more planning, investment, and working toward integrated lifestyles. What do I mean?

- Plan to live close to where you work, reducing both transportation time and costs. Perhaps you can find an appropriate job close to where you live, or move closer to where you now work. Either is likely to be a challenge, and there are some important barriers for most of us.
- Choose a career that enables you to "walk lightly" regarding energy and other impacts on the environment—in other words, one that rewards frugality. Exactly what kinds of careers would those be? I'm not sure I know, but I think it's meaningful to pose the question. Buddhism emphasizes the notion of "right livelihood" as an ethical imperative. What would right livelihood mean in an ecological sense?
- In general, try to simplify your life in ways that still support your sense of well-being. Doing this is not easy. It raises issues about how you could do this (if you wanted to—and many don't!). It also forces you to examine the exact sources of your sense of well-being.

## Real Goods

*The bicycle.* The bicycle is the most thermodynamic and efficient transportation device ever created, and the most widely used private vehicle in the world. The bicycle lets you travel three times as far on a plateful of calories as you could walking. And it's 53 times more energy efficient—comparing food calories with gasoline calories—than the typical automobile. Nor do bicycles pollute the air, lead to oil spills and oil wars, change the climate, send cities sprawling over the countryside, lock up half of urban space in roads and parking lots, or kill a quarter million people in traffic accidents each year. The world doesn't yet have enough bikes for everybody, but it's getting there quickly: Best estimates put the world's booming fleet of two-wheelers at 850 million—double the number of autos, and growing more rapidly than the auto fleet. We Americans have no excuses on this count. We have about as many bikes per person as do the Chinese. We just don't ride them as much.

I admit to being a bike enthusiast (some of my friends have different words for it!). Like many American kids, I grew up riding a bike (a big heavy Schwinn is the one I remember) and didn't discover lightweight bikes with gears until midlife. I found cycling a life-saving form of exercise and a mood enhancer. For many years I enjoyed weekend rides through the green fields of the urban hinterlands and discovering the diversity of urban neighborhoods in a more intimate way than I ever could by driving around in my car. I'm fortunate to live close to my work (about 20 minutes away by bike). Until I had some knee injuries (not from biking!), my car often sat at home in the driveway. Many Americans are connected to work by a nerve-racking four-lane auto umbilical cord.

## More Resources

Campbell, Colin C. (2002). Petroleum and people. *Population and Environment, 24*(2), 193–207.

Deffeyes, K. (2001). *Hubbert's peak: The impending world oil shortage.* Princeton, NJ: Princeton University Press.

Flavin, C., and Lessen N. (1994). *Power surge: A guide to the coming energy revolution.* New York: W. W. Norton.

Freudenburg, W. R., and Gramling R. (1994). *Oil in troubled waters: Perceptions, politics, and the battle over offshore drilling.* Albany, NY: State University of New York Press.

Geller, H. (2003). *Energy revolution: Policies for a sustainable future.* Washington, DC: Island Press.

Humphrey, C. R., Lewis, T. L., and Buttel F. (2002). *Environment, energy, and society: A new synthesis.* Belmont, CA: Wadsworth/Thompson Learning.

Jacobson, M. Z. (2009). Review of solution to global warming, air pollution, and energy security. *Energy and Environmental Science, 2,* 148–173.

## Electronic Resources

**www.energy.gov/**
U.S. Department of Energy

**www.eia.doe.gov/**
Energy Information Administration; sources, environment, forecasts

**www.em.doe.gov/index4.html**
U.S. DOE; Office of Environmental Management organizations

**www.worldenergy.org/wec-geis/**
The World Energy Council represents 90 nations and is accredited by the U.N.

**www.iea.org/envissu**
The International Energy Agency; about energy, environment, climate change, sustainable development

**www.awea.org**
American Wind Association

## Endnotes

1. A futures market for commodities is one that attempts to avoid large, unpredictable price swings by allowing investors to commit to buy the commodity at a specified future date for a particular price. They gamble their profits on being right about future prices.
2. A *calorie* is the amount of energy needed to raise 1 gram of water 1 degree centigrade.
3. Sir Patrick Geddes was a Scottish biologist, sociologist, city planner, and cofounder of the British Sociological Society in 1909. Unlike Spencer, he sought a unified calculus of energy flows to study social life (1890/1979). Wilhelm Ostwald and Frederick Soddy were both Nobel Prize-winning chemists in the early twentieth century. T. N. Carver was an American economist, who gave energetic theory an ideological coloration. He argued that capitalism was superior because it was the system most capable of maximizing energy surpluses and transforming them into "vital uses" (Rosa et al., 1988: 150–151).
4. The most meticulous study of contact between high- and low-energy societies is Pelto's 12-year study of the consequences of the introduction of snowmobiles among the Sami people (Lapps) of northern Finland. The introduction of snowmobiles and repeating rifles were the energy and technological means of the gradual absorption of the Samis into Scandinavian societies. They readily adopted these material culture items, and it transformed their life. It vastly increased the geographic mobility of hunters and the amount of game that could be killed. It shortened the workweek of hunters and trappers, increased their leisure time, increased their earnings, and established a new basis for stratification in their communities (based on who owns and who does not own a snowmobile). It also generated a serious ecological imbalance, as populations of snowbound game animals were wiped out. And it increased their dependence on the Finns, Swedes, and Norwegians for gasoline, consumer goods, and so forth (see Pelto, 1973; Pelto and Muller-Willie, 1972: 95).

# CHAPTER 5

# Population, Environment, and Food

The earth's rapidly growing population makes more demands on all kinds of natural resources and increases the amount of waste and pollution.

Imagine a human community with 100 people, 50 women and 50 men. Imagine further that during the next 25 years, each of the women had four children (two boys and two girls) and that each of the girls grew up and also had four children. Thus, the original 50 mothers had 200 children ($50 \times 4 = 200$). Of these, 100 became mothers, giving birth to 400 grandchildren ($100 \times 4$). Our hypothetical community has now grown from 100 to 700 ($100 + 200 + 400$), a sevenfold increase. This imaginary scenario illustrates *exponential growth*, and, like all living populations, human populations have the capacity to

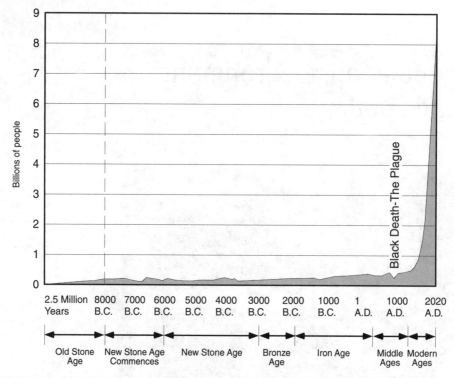

**FIGURE 5.1** World Population Growth Throughout History

*Source:* M. Kent (1984), *World Population: Fundamentals of Growth.* Population Reference Bureau.

grow at exponential rates. In fact, the human population of the world has grown at a dramatically exponential rate.

For thousands of years, the human population grew at a snail's pace. It took over a million years to reach about 1 billion people by the beginning of the nineteenth century. But then the pace of population growth quickened: A second billion was added in the next 130 years, a third in the next 30 years, and the fourth billion in just 15 years (McNamara, 1992). By the 1990s, there were more than 5 billion people on the planet. In early October 1999 human baby number 6 billion was born, most likely in a poor nation, and by 2009 there were 6.8+ billion people in the world (Gelbard et al., 1999; Population Reference Bureau, 2009). See Figure 5.1.

Another way of expressing the rate of exponential growth is by computing the *doubling time*—the number of years it takes for population size to double. From 1750 to about 1950, the doubling time for the world population was about 122 years. But by 2010, the doubling time was only about 61 years.[1] World average growth rates mask lots of variation between nations: For the more developed countries (MDCs), the doubling times are 60 to 70 years, and for less developed countries (LDCs) with higher birth rates, they may be as low as 20–30 years. Think about that: About every 25 years poor nations like Mexico must double its supplies of food, water, housing, and social services just to maintain living standards (Weeks, 2008: 33, 52). In the world's poorest nations such as Haiti, Bangladesh, and Rwanda, the doubling time is even shorter. The global growth rate was 1.2% per year in 2009, and with such a large base of women in their prime childrearing years, the world is expected to have 7 billion people by late 2011. The U.N. Population

Division projects standardized world future growth outcomes using different scenarios for fertility and mortality. In the most likely scenario, the world will have 8.1 billion people in 2025 and 9.4 billion in 2050 (Population Reference Bureau, 2010).

These numbers are truly staggering, and the popular term "population explosion" is indeed a proper description for the demographic history of recent times. If 6.8 billion humans have visibly stressed the environmental carrying systems (as demonstrated in earlier chapters), what impact will 8 to 10 billion have? This chapter will discuss (1) the dynamics of human population change; (2) the controversy about the role of population growth related to environmental and human problems; (3) the relationship among population growth, food supply, and the prospects of feeding a much larger population; and (4) some contentious policy questions about stabilizing the growth and size of the world's population.

## THE DYNAMICS OF POPULATION CHANGE

Concern with exponential population growth is not new. Contemporary concerns about population growth are still framed by questions raised by Thomas Malthus (1766–1834) in his *Essay on Population,* first published in 1798. His book went through seven editions and has undoubtedly been the world's single most influential work on the social consequences of population growth. Malthus and other classical economic thinkers wrote at the start of the nineteenth century, when accelerating population and industrial growth were raising demands for food faster than English agriculture could respond. They saw real wages falling and food imports rising. Most classical economic thought emphasized the limits that scarce farmland imposed on agricultural expansion, arguing that applying ever more labor and other inputs to a fixed land base would inevitably encounter diminishing returns (you might want to review the discussion of the classical economists in Chapter One). Their argument was that limited productive land as well as limits of the supply of capital and labor would determine how many people could be supported by a nation.

Malthus turned these arguments upside down. He argued that since "sexual passion was a constant," human population would increase exponentially (in his words, "geometrically"), while the supply of land, food, and material resources would increase arithmetically. Thus instead of limited natural resources (land) and labor causing limits to population growth, Malthus believed that population growth caused resources to be overused and the market value of labor to decline. Population growth rather than lack of resources and labor produced poverty and human misery. "Overpopulation" (as measured by the level of unemployment) would force wages down to the point where people could not afford to marry and raise a family. With such low wages, landowners and business owners would employ more labor, thus increasing the "means of subsistence." But this would only allow more people to live and reproduce, living in poverty. Malthus argued that this cycle was a "natural law" of population: Each increase in the food supply only meant that eventually more people could live in poverty.

Malthus was aware that starvation rarely operates directly to kill people, and he thought that war, disease, and poverty were *positive checks* on population growth (the term "positive" in this context has always puzzled me!). Although he held out the possibility of deliberate population controls (*preventative checks*) on population growth, he was not very optimistic about their effectiveness. Rejecting both contraception and abortion as morally unacceptable, he believed that only moral restraint (such as sexual abstinence and late marriage) was acceptable.

In sum, Malthus argued that poverty is an eventual consequence of population growth. Such poverty, he argued, is a stimulus that *could* lift people out of misery if they tried to do something about it. So, he argued, if people remain poor, it is their own fault. He opposed the English Poor Laws (that provided benefits to the poor) because he felt they would actually serve to perpetuate misery by enabling poor people to be supported by others (Weeks, 2008: 80–82). Many in our day criticize the government "safety net" and welfare systems on just such grounds. Malthus's ideas were attacked from all sides. I will save these criticisms for later, because they foreshadow many contemporary objections to demographic explanations of environmental problems. Certainly, in the short run, events have not supported the Malthusian view. He did not foresee

> [the] expansion of world cropland to more than double its 1850 acreage; development of agricultural technologies capable of quadrupling yields achieved by traditional farming methods . . . the diffusion of health services and improved hygiene, lowering death rates and then birth rates. He would never have predicted, for instance, farmers being paid not to plant, in order to cut surpluses and to reverse erosion. . . . And he would be amazed at the growth in world population. (Hendry, 1988: 3)

Whether Malthus will continue to be seen in serious error is another matter, as world population and related problems continue to grow dramatically. As you can see from the questions raised here and in earlier chapters, there are plenty of grounds for concern, and indeed, *neo-Malthusians* today are alarmed about population growth as a cause of environmental and human social problems. But before returning to these issues, I'll examine the outlines of the way demographers understand population dynamics and change.

## The Demographic Transition Model

One of the most universally observed but still not clearly explained patterns of population growth is termed the *demographic transition*. By the 1960s, George Stolnitz reported that "demographic transitions rank among the most sweeping and best documented trends of modern times . . . based upon hundreds of investigations, covering a host of specific places, periods, and events" (1964: 20). This model of population change has three stages: (1) primitive social organization, where mortality and fertility are relatively high; (2) transitional social organization, where mortality declines, fertility remains high, and population shows a high rate of natural increase; and (3) modern social organization, where mortality and fertility stabilize at relatively low levels, and near stationary population is possible (Humphrey and Buttel, 1982: 65). See this Figure 5.2.

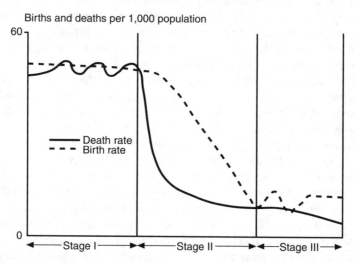

**FIGURE 5.2** Demographic Transition Model

Explanations of this transition vary and are pasted together from somewhat disparate elements, but in general they flow from assumptions about the demographic consequences of modernization and industrialization. First, industrialization upgraded both manufacturing and agricultural productivity so that the economic base could support much larger populations. Second, medical advances in the control of epidemic disease and improvements in public services like urban sewerage, water systems, and garbage disposal contributed to improved health and reduced mortality rates. Third, as populations became increasingly urbanized, family changes occurred. The children of rural peasants are generally an economic asset: They eat little and from an early age contribute substantially to the family farm and household. But urban children—their education and rearing—become more of an economic burden than an asset (Weeks, 2008: 89–91).

Industrialization was also coupled with opportunities for women to work outside the family and eventually improved the status of women. Birth rates are high where the status of women remains low and they are economically dependent on men (Keyfitz, 1990: 66). Industrialization also produced societies that established national social security programs apart from kinship, which meant that parents were less dependent on the support of their children in old age. Industrial modernization had, in other words, a variety of incentives that promoted smaller families. As social and economic incentives changed, cultural norms promoting large families began to weaken. Finally, research demonstrated that while industrialization was inversely related to fertility, it also changed the level of economic equality. In the European nations, "the demographic and economic transitions led to a general improvement in living standards for all persons and a gradual reduction in income inequalities" (Birdsall, 1980). There is good reason to doubt the unique impact of family planning programs as a cause of fertility decline apart from deeper socioeconomic causes, but abundant evidence exists that information about birth control and access to contraceptives have been important factors in fertility declines in all countries (Keyfitz, 1990: 66).

However it happened, the demographic transition process has meant that beginning with social and economic modernization, death rates declined, followed after a time interval by declining birth rates. But between these events was a period of *transitional growth* when birth rates remained high but death rates rapidly declined. That transitional growth period is what the population explosion since the beginning of the industrial era is all about. As you can see, when applied at a global level, the demographic transition model provides reasons for expecting world population growth to eventually stabilize. It is a broad abstraction that fits the facts of long-term population change in the MDCs, but the variety of causes suggested do not form a very coherent theory about it.

There are at least two other limitations of the demographic transition model. It is *ethnocentric* in assuming that historic processes of demographic change in MDCs are being repeated in the LDCs, when in fact the historical, political, and economic circumstances in which they entered the modern world differ importantly. Related to this criticism is another— that the model has not been capable of precisely predicting levels of mortality, or fertility, or the timing of fertility declines at national, much less at global, levels. This is both because the causes of demographic transition are not well understood, and also because historical events (such as wars or economic collapse) cause unpredictable changes in the stability of demographic projections. Small differences in projected numbers stretched over long periods of time can add up to big differences. That is why agencies that make population projections typically make high, medium, and low ones, letting the user decide which is most reasonable. This means that some really important questions such as "How rapidly will global stabilization occur?" and "At what equilibrium number?" cannot be answered with much certainty. These uncertainties are much like those discussed about climate change in Chapter Three.

## The Demographic Divide: MDCs and LDCs

As MDC populations went through the period of transitional growth, they expanded into less densely populated frontier areas, rich with land and resources to be developed. This process of European expansion and colonization began in the 1500s, before the industrial revolution. Until 1930, European and North American countries grew more rapidly than the rest of the world. But since then, population growth has slowed and geographic outward expansion has virtually ceased. Today most MDCs are far along the path toward population stabilization, well into stage III of the demographic transition. They exhibit declining birth rates and slow rates of growth. Many are coming close to the equilibrium or replacement rate of fertility, which would result in zero population growth (2.1 children per female). By 2000 in Western Europe, population growth was almost zero or even declining, even with the impact of immigrants from other parts of the world. Germany and Italy were declining by 1% each year. In France and the United Kingdom, populations grew slowly, and the United States had the highest MDC growth rate (0.9% per year). In these, population growth is almost entirely due to the influx of immigrants. In much of postcommunist Eastern Europe, including Russia, Romania, Lithuania, and Ukraine, economic and social conditions were so bad that birth rates were below replacement levels and population size declined slightly each year (Population Reference Bureau, 1999: 8; Weeks, 2005: 5).

In LDCs, the story is very different. Their rapid transitional growth came later in the twentieth century without the benefit of territorial expansion—that is, without the relatively unpopulated land or colonies to absorb the pressure of population growth. In addition, they have birth rates and levels of mortality much higher than European MDCs. As a result, LDC populations are growing rapidly, especially in the poorest of the poor nations. In the MDCs, demographic transition proceeded apace with internal economic development. But the decline of death rates in LDCs was more related to the rapid introduction of effective techniques of disease control by outsider agencies like the World Health Organization. Babies born in the poor nations today have a historically unprecedented chance of surviving to adulthood, and the average life spans of nations have converged. Most babies born in the world today live in the LDCs. At the turn of the year 2000, the world was adding about 86 million people per year, and at least 90% of this growth was happening in the LDCs.

Even so, economic development—with its widespread improvement in living standards, improved education and opportunities for women, incentives for smaller families, and the establishment of national social security systems—has not kept pace in the poorest LDCs. Cultural and religious norms favoring large families are still powerful. Even when the world economy was growing, people in the poorest nations experienced little economic growth, while population growth continued vigorously. Often economic growth has been literally "eaten up" by exploding populations. The continuation of this demographic divergence between MDCs and LDCs into the next century may increase geopolitical tensions, pressure on migration and refugee flows, and a corresponding social and environmental duality among rich and poor nations. In LDCs both rural and urban populations are growing rapidly, pressures on natural resources are increasing, and economic and technical resources are often overwhelmed as local and national governments try to provide employment for increasing labor forces and infrastructure for expanding cities, like electricity, clean water, and waste disposal. The divide between the MDCs and LDCs is demographic, but there are many other kinds of forces in operation.

## Population Redistribution: Urbanization and Migration

So far, I have focused on population growth in terms of the dynamics of demographic transition. Another type of population change is *population redistribution,* meaning the net spatial changes in population as individuals and families move from place to place. The two most important forms of population redistribution are urbanization and migration. Both are related to the pressures of population growth.

**URBANIZATION**  Most North Americans now live in—and were born in—cities. While we may be attracted to the amenities of cities or curse their problems, we recognize that urban life is the cultural, economic, and political center of modern society. Urbanization, or the redistribution of people from the countryside, is not new but has dramatically accelerated with the explosive transitional growth just described. Compared to rural dwellers, urban dwellers made up only about 11% of the world's population in 1850, but 30% in 1950, and 48% in 2000. Among the MDCs, at least 75% did so by the turn of the twentieth century, and by 2008 half of the people in the world were urban dwellers (United Nations Population Division, 2006).

Cities are, of course, nothing new. They emerged with the agricultural revolution, but those cities were not very large by today's standards. Ancient Babylon might have had 50,000 people, Athens maybe 80,000, and Rome as many as 500,000 (2008: 356). To put this in perspective, Rome, the premiere imperial capital of much of the Mediterranean world and hinterlands beyond, was at its peak a bit smaller than my hometown of Omaha, Nebraska. Ancient cities were unusually dense settlements that were the political, ceremonial, and administrative centers in a diffuse "sea" of rural villagers. Villagers made up perhaps 95% of the total population of such societies, and their crops and livestock were the real sources of wealth, on which urban elites lived by imposing taxes. Ancient (and medieval) cities were neither economically nor demographically self-sustaining. Poor sanitation and the rapid spread of epidemic disease (the plagues of ancient and medieval worlds) meant that they had higher death rates and lower birth rates than the countryside. They often had an annual excess of deaths over births, which meant that they had to be replenished by migrants from the countryside. They were not demographically self-sustaining.

**Urbanization of the MDCs.**  Industrial era urbanization was fueled not only by expanding urban opportunities, but also by the push of rural overpopulation, poverty, consolidation of land holdings, and declining farm labor markets resulting from the industrializing of agriculture (noted in Chapter Two). As economic development proceeded in Europe and North America, cities grew because they were more efficient. They brought more raw materials, workers and factories, financiers, and buyers and sellers together in one location than did dispersed rural production. Furthermore, as industrial societies developed, evolving modes of production continually reshaped the economic base of cities from the commerce and trading centers of the 1600s and 1700s (e.g., Amsterdam, London, Boston) to those centered on factories and industrial production in the late 1800s (e.g., Birmingham, Pittsburgh, Chicago). Since World War II, improvements in technology and the growth of an economy based on "services and information" have meant that the economic base of many cities is no longer manufacturing but, more often, the corporate headquarter locations of far-flung multidivisional and multinational firms and banks (e.g., Minneapolis, Dallas–Fort Worth). Now the largest MDC cities, such as Tokyo, New York, and Los Angeles, are really "world cities" that produce wealth by organizing and controlling international trade, commerce, and finance.

After the year 2008, the world passed something of a milestone when over half of its population was classified as urban. In 2015, the LDCs will be more than 50% urban (in 1950 only one-fourth were).

**Urbanization of the LDCs.**    Consider the world's 10 largest cities. In 1950, only 2 of the 10 largest urban conglomerations in the world (Shanghai and Calcutta) were located in the LDCs. But by 2025, United Nations demographers project that 9 of the top 10 will be in the LDCs. In order, they are Mexico City, Shanghai and Beijing (China), Saõ Paulo (Brazil), Greater Mumbai and Calcutta (India), Jakarta (Indonesia), Dacca (Bangladesh), and Chennai (India). New York, Chicago, London, and Paris, all on the 1950 list, will be nowhere in sight. While Tokyo–Yokohama will still be the largest urban area in the world, it will be followed in 2025 by the demographic giants of the third world, Mexico City and Saõ Paulo (Brazil) (United Nations Population Division, 2006).

As in the MDCs in an earlier era, the explosive urbanization in the contemporary LDCs is fueled by the poverty, hunger, and destitution of peasants pushed off the land and also by the less visible but powerful forces of high birth rates and population pressure. But there is a fundamental difference between the two eras. MDC urbanization was also accompanied by the pull of exploding economic opportunities in the industrializing cities. Urbanization in the LDCs today is largely a matter of the push of rural poverty without the simultaneous pull of dynamic urban economic growth. In other words, the LDCs have developed very rapidly in the post–World War II period, but they have skipped the prolonged period of industrial and manufacturing economic growth the MDCs experienced. Although less developed, many LDC cities have come to represent service economies without passing through the transitional stage of industrial growth (Walton, 1993: 289–302).

A service economy, as we have discovered in the United States, often produces less employment and comparatively lower wages for many people than do industrial and manufacturing economies. Thus, cities such as Calcutta, Cairo, Dakar, Jakarta, and Rio de Janeiro are becoming awash with displaced peasants with grim prospects for fruitful urban employment.

> To escape deepening rural poverty . . . [millions] of "environmental refugees" are on the move in Latin America, Africa, and parts of Asia, mostly from rural to urban areas. City services are collapsing under the weight of urban population growth, and unmanageable levels of pollution are creating a variety of threats to human health . . . solid waste could quadruple . . . [many] rivers are virtual open sewers, and many waterways flowing through metropolitan areas are biologically dead. (Camp, 1993: 130–131)

Such urban masses live in shantytowns and typically scrape out a meager existence as street vendors of petty goods and services. According to the United Nations, more than 1 billion people now live in the slums of the cities of "the South"(in what I have termed LDCs). As depicted by Davis in *Planet of Slums,* the exponential growth of such slums is driven by population growth, in combination with corrupt leadership, the failure of institutions, and the imposition of the "structural adjustment policies" of the International Monetary Fund—which pressures poor nations to use their precious money to pay international debts rather than to invest in urban infrastructures and human well-being. The resulting world urban proletariat—disconnected from industrialization and significant economic growth—is a new development not foreseen by by classical Marxism or capitalist (neo-liberal) economic theory. It has resulted in a massive transfer of wealth from the poor to the rich, and urban futures that look radically unequal and explosively unstable (2007).

**MIGRATION**    Urbanization is really a special form of *migration,* which means the relatively long-term movement of an individual, household, or group to a new location outside their community of origin (de Blij, 1993: 114–115). Being cultural foreigners and new claimants for existing jobs and services, their presence in new host communities is usually contentious and difficult. They may send money and information to their nonmigrant kinfolk back somewhere. Indeed, you need to understand migration as not only the numerical redistribution of people, but also a slow but pervasive *social interaction process* that diffuses and reshapes human cultures—and the distributions of power and wealth.

Migration may be *forced,* as in the case of prisoners that the British shipped to penal colonies in Georgia and Australia. It was also the case of the African slaves brought to the New World, and the 50,000 Asians forcibly expelled from the African nation of Uganda in the 1970s—with only the belongings that they could carry on their backs. But migration may also be *voluntary,* as in the case of most Europeans who came to North America in the late nineteenth and early twentieth centuries seeking material improvement and greater opportunities. While they were attracted by better opportunities, they were also often fleeing from rotten conditions in their homelands. Some, such as the Irish immigrants to Boston and New York, came fleeing from famine, poverty, and unemployment in their homelands (Remember the Irish potato blight and subsequent famine mentioned in Chapter One?). Others fled from wars or political and sometimes religious oppression.

High-volume waves of internal migration weaken but do not destroy extended kinship networks. The phenomenon requires that host institutions adjust to shifts in the numbers and characteristics of people served. It alters, for example, the availability of labor, the demands for geriatric medicine, and the numbers and characteristics of students to be served by educational systems. Since migrants always insert themselves into or remove themselves from community status hierarchies, they always change the stratification system of communities: In-migrants tend to improve their status by moving into communities, while out-migrants improve it by moving out. In sum, adjustments, often difficult ones, are required in both the communities that migrants leave as well as in their new host communities. *Internal migration* is usually "free," in the sense that people are choosing to move in relation to their perception of better living conditions elsewhere. *International migration* is sometimes free, but it usually means that the migrant has met fairly stringent entrance requirements, is entering illegally, or is being granted refugee status.

**Explaining Migration.**    The most common theory about the causes of migration is what demographers and geographers have called the *push-pull theory,* which says that some people move because they are pushed out of their homelands, while others move because they have been pulled or attracted to a new place. In reality, a complicated mix of both push and pull factors operates jointly to impel migratory behavior. Pushes can include poverty and lack of economic opportunity; fears for personal safety; political, cultural, or ethnic oppression; war, including civil war; and natural disasters such as droughts and floods. Often underlying the push of these concrete factors is population pressure from rapid growth. The pulls are the mirror image of these and are likewise complex: the perception of better economic opportunities, greater social stability, and affiliation (desire to join relatives and friends). At any rate, social science conjures up the migrant as a rational decision maker who calculates the costs and benefits of either pulling up stakes and moving or staying put. This thesis was posed as long ago as 1885 by British demographer Ernest Ravenstein, who studied internal migration in the British Isles (1889).

Ravenstein found, as have many investigators since, that migrants have some common characteristics: They are younger than nonmigrants; they are less likely to have families, or if they do, they have fewer and younger children; and they are likely to be better educated (Weeks, 2008: 285). In fact, voluntary migrants are a select population, usually more talented, capable, adaptable, and ambitious than nonmigrants. In addition to personal characteristics such as these, the push-pull causes of migratory behavior are also conditioned by intervening factors or barriers. These include the costs of moving, lack of knowledge about migration options or managing complicated moves, broad themes of the sociocultural environment like established values about the importance of geographic "roots," risk taking, and openness to change. As you can see, in spite of the simple attractiveness of the push-pull thesis, the actual situation is quite complicated and not simple to predict. (See De Jong, 2000, for an ambitious effort to conceptualize the complex causes of migratory behavior.)

**Old and New Patterns of Global Migration.**    We do not know exactly how many persons have migrated around the world at any given time, but beginning with the modern era (in the 1500s) there were discrete waves of immigration involving particular locations that accounted for the greatest volume of immigrants. One such stream, as I'm sure you are aware, virtually *constituted* the nations of North America. Except for Native Americans, the citizens of the United States, Canada, and Mexico are *all* descendants of immigrants from somewhere else. In the United States, immigrants from Europe (and particularly Britain) were always more welcome, and by the 1920s the United States was so concerned about the flow of "unsuitable" non–Anglo-Saxon immigrants that it passed laws establishing quotas by nations that severely restricted non-European immigration.

Before World War II, the main currents of migration were out of the more densely settled regions in Europe and Asia and into North and South America and Oceania. Since the 1960s, that changed so that the net migration flows were back into Europe, out of South America and Asia, and (still) into North America, but increasingly from non-European nations. About half of all international migration is from one LDC to another, but the net flow of international migration is now from the LDCs to the MDCs (Gelbard et al., 1999: 16). The pressure of rapidly growing LDC populations since World War II enormously increased the pressure on natural resources and the demands for employment and social services, while in the MDCs a slowly growing population and buoyant economic growth often created a demand for lower-cost workers from the LDCs. Thus "guest" workers flowed into northern Europe from nearby Algeria, Egypt, Turkey, and the Middle East as well as from comparatively less developed southern and Mediterranean Europe and—more recently, as the communist world collapsed—from Eastern Europe. War, including civil war, often creates the social chaos that stimulates a flood of immigrants and refugees. Immigrants are considered refugees or asylum seekers if they can demonstrate that they left their home countries to avoid persecution.

Refugees and asylum seekers to Europe and America are both legal and illegal. They arrive on foot and by rail, air, and sea from diverse origins. Some are smuggled in trucks and ships jammed together under terrible conditions. As always, floods of immigrants create conflict and controversy as they seek employment and raise questions about the political and cultural coherence of nations. By 2006, immigration had triggered a significant and volatile political controversy in the United States and many European nations. Germany in particular was busy revising its generous asylum laws. As LDC populations rapidly grow, it becomes harder and harder to find a niche in the domestic labor force, and people are often compelled to move. And as the United States and Europe are learning, it is very difficult and costly to stem the tide of immigrants who want to move and find ways.

## BOX 5.1

### Immigration to the United States

About a million foreigners enter the United States each year. Most are not immigrants planning to settle permanently, but tourists, businesspeople, students, and temporary workers from other countries who are in the United States for a few days or months. About 2,600 daily become legal U.S. residents, and another 1,400 are added to the population of unauthorized immigrants. Before the 1960s most immigrants were from Europe, but later waves of immigration have brought greater diversity to the U.S. population:

- 41% from Latin America and the Caribbean (about half from Mexico)
- 32% from Asia
- 18% from Europe and Canada
- 9% from other countries

In 2005, there were 37 million foreign-born residents in the United States, of which 39% were legal foreign residents (both permanent and temporary), 31% were naturalized citizens, and 30% were unauthorized (Martin and Midgley, 2006).

Whether we like it or not, a significant portion of people from the LDCs are coming to be our neighbors. And they will change the demography, culture, and eventually the politics of the nation. The U.S. Census Bureau, for instance, predicts radical shifts in the racial and ethnic composition of the nation, fueled by both immigration and the higher birth rate of ethnic minorities. Immigration accounted for at least one-third of recent U.S. population growth. The proportion of whites is expected to diminish from about 67% in 2000 to a tenuous majority of 52% by 2050, and Hispanics may well replace African Americans as the largest minority group (Martin and Midgley, 2006). The prime immigrant entry ports, such as Los Angeles, Miami, and New York, may in fact become "global" as well as American cities.

**Population, Environment, and Social Stability.**    I have discussed types of population change—growth, urbanization, and migration—in some detail. Now I would like to summarize their relevance as hypothetical causes of environmental problems. It has been argued since the time of Malthus that the tremendous population growth of modern times has damaged the environment. It has done so by increasing demands for food, water, energy, and natural resources; most think that this problem will become increasingly acute as the world population increases to 9 or 10 billion in the next century. Recall the discussion of soil erosion and water problems in Chapter Two. Population pressure contributes to both migration and urbanization so that the environmental impact of population growth is not evenly distributed. Problems are particularly acute in urban areas where the air, water, and land cannot absorb the wastes and toxic by-products of industry and dense populations. Other than problems of population density, the very *location* of cities causes environmental hazards. Because urban populations and industries need lots of water, they tend to be located along lakes, rivers, and bays. As a consequence, rivers like the Missouri, Mississippi, and Ohio; lakes like Erie and Michigan; and bays like the Chesapeake and New York Harbor become badly polluted (Eitzen and Baca Zinn, 1992: 101). Finally, by creating chaos and hardship in the LDCs, population growth will further accelerate the streams of internal and international immigration. However enriching immigration is in the long term, at a given time host nations and communities will find it a socially and politically disruptive burden.

Evidence suggests that large flows of refugees are associated with social disruption and civil vio-lence (Homer-Dixon, 1996). This is particularly so when the world economy is sluggish. It is a fantasy to think that because of the demographic divide just noted, the problems associated with population growth will be "contained" in the LDCs. Like it or not, much of the Third World is coming to live with us!

In sum, many demographers and ecologists argue that population growth threatens global social stability, human material well-being, and environmental integrity. In the next century, population growth may effectively overwhelm the carrying capacity of the planet. That, at least, is the *demographic* and *neo-Malthusian* interpretation of things. But, as I noted earlier, it has been a controversial and contentious point of view since the time of Malthus. Many scholars, then and now, have found it fundamentally flawed. How so?

## HOW SERIOUS IS THE PROBLEM OF WORLD POPULATION GROWTH?

Most contemporary objections to Malthusian theory were raised 150 years ago. One of his con-temporaries, French political economist Condorcet, foreshadowed contemporary technological optimists by arguing that scientific advance would offset diminishing returns. Condorcet said: "New instruments, machines, and looms can add to man's strength . . . [and] improve at once the quality and accuracy of man's productions, and can diminish the time and labor that has to be expended on them. . . . A very small amount of ground will be able to produce a great quantity of supplies . . . with less wastage of raw materials" (Condorcet, 1795). Fifty years later, Marx in par-ticular fulminated against Malthus's theory. He dismissed it as nothing more than a rationale for class exploitation and argued that the real cause of human misery and deprivation was the increasing concentration of wealth in the hands of the few capitalist owners. It was they, who exploited workers to the point of misery and exhaustion—rather than population pressure—who were the cause of human poverty and misery. Then as now, the dominant currents of eco-nomic thought discounted natural resource constraints (including population size) to emphasize the adaptability of market-induced substitution and innovation. In another classical objection to Malthusian views that foreshadowed modern objections, Nassau Senior asserted that improved living standards for the poor would not lead them blindly to expand their numbers but to restrict their fertility in order to preserve the gains they had realized (Hutchinson, 1967). So you can see that even though his book was a bestseller for decades, then as now Malthus got it from all sides (Poor Tom!). Even so, scholars have been unable to dismiss completely his haunting forecast of an impending demographic apocalypse.

Few debates in the social and natural sciences have been so heated or protracted as this one about the consequences of population growth. In contemporary discourse, there are three broad positions (the same paradigms I have been talking about since Chapter One!). *One* argues that population growth is a severe threat, perhaps *the* most significant underlying cause of environ-mental degradation and human misery. The *second* argues that population growth is not an important threat because markets will allocate scarce resources and stimulate efficient innova-tions. A more recent variant of this position, termed *supply-side demography*, argues that popula-tion growth may in fact be a benefit because the historical record demonstrates that as world population has grown, human welfare has improved: The more people, the better. The *third posi-tion* argues that human misery and environmental problems are caused by maldistribution that results from the operation of social institutions and economic arrangements (global or national inequality, poverty, trade policies, high prices, wars) rather than population growth per se. This argument, in effect, turns the table on Malthus, arguing that structurally induced misery causes both population growth and environmental deterioration, rather than the other way around. Let me elaborate each of these perspectives.

## Neo-Malthusian Arguments

The standard ecological neo-Malthusian perspective is that population growth causes human misery and environmental degradation. This has been the position of many demographers, but particularly of biologists, ecologists, and natural scientists (Ehrlich and Holdren, 1974; P. Ehrlich and A. Ehrlich, 1992). Some predictions of global demise have been concrete and dramatic. In 1968, Stanford University zoologist Paul Ehrlich wrote, "The battle to feed humanity is over. In the 1970s the world will undergo famines—hundreds of millions are going to starve to death" (cited in Stark, 1994: 558). There were indeed famines and widespread malnourishment in the 1970s in particular parts of the world, such as sub-Saharan Africa. But nothing on the magnitude predicted, and global food production continued to outstrip population growth.

Modern history has not been kind to the neo-Malthusians, who have been arguing that "the wolf is at the door" routinely since the 1940s. But the wolf has—so far—failed to materialize. *Or has he?* Neo-Malthusians don't believe that one actually dies from overpopulation, but from other, more concrete causes (disease, war, malnutrition, or famine). They argue that the doubling of the world's population in about one generation is the broad underlying cause of the stress placed on the global environment and human well-being, even though it is manifest in more concrete causes. For example, population growth helps widen income disparities among nations. In the past 20 years, the LDCs as a group have actually raised total economic output more rapidly than have the MDCs. But many of these gains have been offset by higher population growth rates. In per capita terms, the relative gap has narrowed negligibly, while the absolute gap has widened substantially. Compare India and the United States from 1965 to the mid-1980s. Total GNP grew significantly faster in India, but because population grew twice as fast, India's average annual per capita income growth was 1.6%, slightly less than that of the United States, 1.7% (Repetto, 1987: 13). As population has mushroomed, so have wars. The number of armed conflicts around the world has grown from 12 in 1950 to an all-time high of 50 in 1991, and declined to 25 in 2005 (Renner, 2007: 112). Most were intrastate conflicts, but often having international dimensions and involvement, such as in Somalia, Rwanda, and Sudan.

Neo-Malthusians do not think that other factors (drought, poverty, wars) are unimportant sources of environmental or social stress, only that population growth must be considered primary. If, they think, all other factors could be made environmentally neutral, population growth of this magnitude would still spur resource social stress and environmental degradation (Stern et al., 1992: 76–77). Indeed, they argue that once population has reached a level in excess of the earth's long-term capacity to sustain it, even stability and zero growth at that level will lead to future environmental degradation (P. Ehrlich and A. Ehrlich, 1992). These scholars believe that, indeed, there is a carrying capacity and that in the long run, it applies to humans as it does to the bacteria in a petri dish. At some point, there are limits to the physical capacity of the planet to sustain growth.

## Economistic Arguments

Neoclassical economic theory maintained that population growth is not a problem, and may be a source of progress (Boserup, 1981; Simon, 1990). It argues that population growth—and other resource problems—stimulates investment in increased efficiency, resource substitution, conservation, and innovation. When resources become scarce, well-functioning markets encourage people to allocate them in the most efficient ways and protect them by raising the price. It is a fact that in the long sweep of human history, population growth has been correlated with growing, rather than declining, resources—as well as with improvements in human health, longevity, and well-being. Today more people live longer and better than when the human population was much smaller. Even in the rapid post–World War II population explosion, global food production always outstripped population growth. Contrary to neo-Malthusian expectations, shortages—whether the result of population growth, increased consumption, or environmental problems—have left us better off than if shortages had not arisen.

The reason is that the accumulating benefit of intellectual inventiveness (human capital) met and overcame the challenge of shortages. We have found human-made substitutes for natural resources and more abundant natural resources for scarce ones, and we have invented technologies that allow more efficient use of the resources available. Neoclassical economists argue that finding substitutes for scarce natural resources is likely, and they rely on the ability of markets to respond effectively to resource scarcities. In this view, the cause of problems is not growth, but policies and market failures that do not price things realistically and that subsidize waste, inefficiency, and resource depletion. You get what you pay for, and you lose what you don't pay for. Neoclassical economists argue that the neo-Malthusians ignore the role of markets in generating adjustments that bring population, resources, and the environment back into balance (Simon, 1998).

A newer variety of this argument, termed *supply-side demography*, maintains that population growth is not a problem, but a positive benefit (Camp, 1993). In contrast to the Malthusian view of diminishing per capita resources over time, the holders of this view argue that the ultimate resource is human inventiveness, which itself accumulates over time as populations grow, and has multiplied resources as they are available to people. A wide range of illustrations can support this view. When a shortage of elephant tusks for ivory threatened in the last century, celluloid was invented, followed by the rest of our plastics. When whales were almost hunted to extinction in the nineteenth century to produce oil for lamps, petroleum distillates such as kerosene were substituted to fuel lamps and thus created the first petroleum industry. Englishmen learned to use coal when trees became scarce in the sixteenth century. Satellites and fiber optics (derived from sand) replaced expensive copper for telephone transmission. Importantly, the new resources wind up cheaper and more plentiful than the old ones were. Such, it is argued, has been the entire course of civilization (Simon, 1990). To neoclassical economists, the notion of a human carrying capacity is a static population-resource equation that conceals more than it reveals and has no empirical validity. It ignores technical inventiveness and market allocation. Counterintuitive as it may seem, as populations grow, resources multiply rather than become scarce. Rather than stressing a finite resource base, it is more correct to recognize that 10,000 years ago only 4 million humans could keep themselves alive, but by the nineteenth century the earth could support 1 billion people and today it can support 6 billion (Simon, 1998). In this view the unique potentials of humans make them almost *exempt* from the physical limits of the earth.

## Inequality Arguments

The inequality (or stratification) argument maintains that human misery and environmental degradation, as well as population growth, are caused by vastly unequal social structural arrangements. This is a more complex and nuanced argument. It is favored by neo-Marxians, but also by a wide variety of other social scientists, economists, agronomists, and some biologists. Unlike the neoclassical economists, they argue that population size *is* a problem. It's just that Malthusians have always gotten the causation wrong. The operation of global political and economic structures and inequality cause population growth, human misery, and environmental problems rather than the other way around. They argue, for example, that instead of rapid population growth stalling economic development, economic stagnation in the LDCs is caused by poverty, inequitable trade policies, and ongoing dependencies. In other words, continued LDC poverty is maintained by the operation of the global economy, and in a condition of deep poverty and stalled development there are few incentives to have smaller families. Although I have noted this before, Indian scholar M. Mamdani provided a clear explanation of why the poor in LDCs have large families:

> Children provide a form of support for the elderly in nations that provide no retirement security. Children provide economic support through their labor on the farm or the sale of their labor to others, and they add little to household expenses in a condition of deep poverty. Living in chronic poverty provides no incentives for reduced fertility, and population control policies are likely to fail (1972).

The final act of the world demographic transition, so the argument runs, is delayed by stalled economic development in the LDCs, not overpopulation.

Strongly objecting to the neo-Malthusian arguments of Paul Ehrlich and others, biologist Barry Commoner argued that plans to limit population that focus on birth control, abortion, or sterilization of people in LDCs ignore the principal cause of rapid population growth—poverty. Furthermore, Commoner argued that on the whole, advanced technology and affluent lifestyles are more environmentally damaging than growing numbers of people (1992). He and others argued that the reality of global environmental deterioration is that large multinational corporations, not the growing masses of the poor in the LDCs, are responsible for most environmental destruction. It is not, for instance, the indigenous people and subsistence farmers who are destroying the world's rainforests. It is the lumber companies, large cash crop estates, and mining companies.

Similarly, others argue that neither the malnutrition that now routinely afflicts at least one-fifth of humanity nor the periodic famines in which people actually starve are produced by population growth. The most direct cause of hunger is not too many people, but the lack of money and high food prices. At the *system level* of analysis, hunger and malnutrition are most directly caused by the political-economy of agriculture, here meaning patterns of investment and land holding, and the structure of trade in the world economy (Norse, 1992). Consider some evidence for the view provided at the end of the 1990s:

- The 22 most food-deficient African countries could meet their food needs with just 11% of the food *surplus* held by neighboring countries.
- China has only half the cropland per capita as India, yet Indians suffer widespread and severe malnutrition, while the Chinese do not.
- In Thailand, rice production increased 30%, but with exports of rice increasing nine times faster, per-person availability of rice has fallen.
- In Chile, farm exports have increased over 30% since the early 1970s. However, 40% of Chileans consume only 75% of the calories necessary for survival.
- In the 1970s, when India had more than 300 million malnourished people, the Indian government, working with large corporations, ensured that India ranked as one of the biggest exporters of food among the LDCs (Lappé et al., 1998).

Globally, the LDCs now export more agricultural products *to* the MDCs than they receive in food aid or agricultural subsidies. Consequently, the majority of the world's population remains poor and often hungry. The problem, then, is not with the lack of food but its global distribution patterns (Buttel, 2000a).

Another variety of the inequality argument finds causes of human misery and environmental degradation not in the operation of world markets or structures of inequality, but in authoritarianism and the absence of responsive governments or free markets. Nations with democratic regimes, free markets, and a free press can deal with droughts and fluctuations in prices and food supplies to prevent famine, whereas authoritarian regimes do not. It is no accident that the worst starvation happened in one-party states, dictatorships, or colonies: Maoist China, British India, or Stalin's USSR. The last great Chinese famine, in which perhaps 30 million starved, was in the 1960s during Mao's Great Leap Forward, which forcibly confiscated and collectivized the landholdings of villagers. Famine vanished when the Chinese reprivatized agriculture during the reforms of the 1970s. With these and other illustrations, Sen argues convincingly that corruption, the absence of democracy and a free press, and government reluctance to admit problems let droughts grow in to mass starvation (Sen, 1993). Perhaps more familiar to Americans were the gruesome pictures of starving Somali children that dominated the media in 1992–1993. But that starvation was not caused—most directly, anyway—by too many people or even too little food, but rather by civil war, chaos, and the looting of the nation's food supplies by warring clan factions.

The inequality perspective maintains that poverty is not only the more direct cause of high fertility and human misery, but is also connected to environmental destruction. Notwithstanding the larger role of multinational mining, agribusiness, and lumber companies on the environment, it is still true that poverty adds considerably to the resource pressures in the LDCs. Poor households are often virtually forced to overuse natural resources daily for subsistence. Thus, desperate farmers grow cassava and maize on highly erodible hillsides. Rural households in fuel-wood-deficit countries strip foliage and burn crop and animal residues for fuel rather than using them for fertilizer. This practice also contributes to desertification, since land stripped of trees and plant residues is less likely to hold moisture. Underemployed men in coastal villages overexploit already depleted fisheries (Repetto, 1987: 13).

Controversy about the significance of population growth is not, and never has been, just an academic one. Population issues are so important that in recent decades, the U.N. has organized three international population conferences: in Bucharest in 1974, Mexico City in 1984, and Cairo in 1994. Particularly in the United States, dealing with population problems was *very* contentious. Under different presidential administrations, the U.S. government has alternately funded, withdrawn, and reauthorized funds from such U.N. efforts, primarily because population and family planning were connected with the contentious cultural controversy about abortion. The Cairo meeting, the International Conference on Population and Development, was the most widely attended gathering of government officials and representative of many nongovernmental organizations (NGOs). It finally agreed on an ambitious agenda to promote population stabilization.

## MAKING SENSE OUT OF THIS CONTROVERSY

If you are a bit confused about the complexity of these issues, you are in good company. They begin to come clearer by recognizing that, like some of the controversies previously discussed, they are not only about facts, but different paradigms.

Physical scientists and ecologists—and many demographers—see the world in terms of problems of growing scale in a world with ultimately physical limits. In contrast, neoclassical economists see the world as a largely mutable system of possibilities, because of human technical inventiveness and also because of the capacity of market allocation to adjust to scarcities and stimulate resource substitution. They argue that ecologists simply fail to appreciate the magic of the market.

Ecologists retort that the reason that economists believe this is that they miss entirely the environmental "debts" that growth incurs which results in a delayed form of deficit financing. Those who fail to recognize the ultimate physical limits of the planet, says environmental economist Herman Daly, are "treating the earth as if it were a business in liquidation" (in Brown, 1991: 9).

Inequality and stratification arguments are similar to economic ones because they emphasize the importance of human social factors rather than natural limits as causes. But proponents of this view are like the ecologists in seeing both exponential population growth and environmental degradation as real problems. Briefly, in understanding the relationships between population growth and human and environmental problems, neo-Malthusian arguments emphasize *scale issues,* neoclassical economic arguments emphasize *market allocation issues,* and inequality arguments emphasize *distribution issues.* Although these paradigms have very different views of the way the world works, they are each partial—and not necessarily mutually exclusive. I think it is possible to reconcile some of their differences.

Considering the broad sweep of human history, the neoclassical economists and technological optimists have a better factual argument. There were, to be sure, particular times and cases where population growth contributed to environmental and social disasters, particularly in the preindustrial world. But, in the industrial world as a whole, technological progress has always outrun the pressure of population growth. In sum, the neo-Malthusians have always been wrong about a global demographic disaster: The wolf never *was* really at the door.

In its own way, however, the neoclassical economic paradigm is as static and ahistoric as the physical science notion of fixed limits. It posits an unchanging linear relationship between population size and the ability of technological innovation and markets to overcome problems. It fails to recognize that the enormous *growth in scale* of the human population since World War II has put us much closer to absolute physical planetary limits than ever before in human history. To put it in economic terms, the elasticities of substitution between natural and human-made resources are historically quite variable and are now declining. *Elasticities of substitution* simply ask how much human technical capacities can stretch (are "elastic" enough) to surmount natural limits. If it is high, there is no problem; but if elasticity is low, then beyond a certain point, human inventiveness is not enough to overcome resource limits. I have argued that it is higher in industrial than in preindustrial societies, but is now declining because of absolute population growth and accumulated environmental damage.

Furthermore, there are physical limits beyond which *no* substitution is viable. Wheat, for example, cannot be grown with only labor, or without water. I think that the enormously large world population—which may reach 10 billion in the next 50 years—means we will have fewer options, less maneuvering room, a more degraded resource base, and less ability to absorb and recover from environmental damage than ever before in history. We may face an "ingenuity gap." I believe that the dependability of economic and technological capabilities diminishes relative to the threats of scale posed by the present and future population size. Ecological neo-Malthusian theory should be taken more seriously because the population–environment equation is historically dynamic. The wolf is not yet at the door, but he's certainly in the neighborhood, and a lot closer than he was as recently as 100 years ago!

The conflict between neo-Malthusian and inequality arguments is, I think, more apparent than real. Neo-Malthusian arguments are more persuasive in the abstract and on the long-term horizon. But stratification arguments are more convincing explanations of human misery and environmental degradation in the concrete here and now. In other words, things like hunger, poverty, and water pollution are more directly and concretely caused by social, political, and economic arrangements than by the underlying specter of overpopulation. Whether you prefer a demographic or a stratification argument depends upon whether you prefer more direct and concrete or more distant and underlying causes. It also depends on whether you emphasize short- or long-term time spans. But as you can see from the foregoing, they do have very different policy implications for how human and environmental problems are addressed.

Finally, contrary to the arguments of the new "supply-side demography," most responsible scholars now believe that in general more people is not necessarily better and quite probably worse. The most damaging evidence comes from a review of existing evidence from a panel of experts of the National Research Council (within the National Academy of Sciences), who found little evidence that "lower population densities lead to lower per capita incomes via a reduced stimulus to technological innovation, efficiency, and economies of scale." Regarding the LDCs, the panel concluded that "slower population growth would be beneficial to economic development for most of the developing world, but . . . a rigorous quantitative assessment of these benefits is context-dependent and difficult" (National Research Council, 1986: 90). In sum, there is a large consensus that virtually all current and future problems with resource supplies, human material security, and environmental integrity would be easier to deal with if world population growth gets slowed more rapidly and stabilized at a lower "equilibrium number" (Repetto, 1987; National Research Council, 1986).

The emerging consensus among demographers and environmental scientists argues that population growth is one among many causes of human misery and environmental deterioration, but not the only one. Here is how two demographers described this consensus as it applies to problems in the LDCs:

> The most important lesson learned from continued study of the relationships between population and development is the key role of institutions in mediating these relationships. . . . Institutional obstacles . . . [include] the unequal distribution of wealth and political power, poor management and organization, and waste of resources on military activities. Rapid population growth exacerbates many of the resulting problems but slowing population growth will not remedy the situation without positive steps toward change. Some . . . characterize rapid population growth as the "accomplice" rather than the "villain" in this story. (King and Kelly, 1985, cited in Merrick, 1986: 29).

This is a more complex and nuanced consensus than any of the broad paradigms described earlier.

## POPULATION, FOOD, AND HUNGER

Perhaps population growth is only one aggravating cause of human misery and environmental degradation, but what about food and hunger, the elementary human need about which Reverend Malthus speculated 200 years ago? Surely, many argue, there is reason for concern, with booming world population growth and evidence that most agricultural resources (soil, water) are under visible stress. Hunger agencies estimate that about 30 million Americans are malnourished, and the

| TABLE 5.1 | Water to Produce Food |
|---|---|
| Potatoes | 500 |
| Wheat | 900 |
| Maize (corn) | 1,400 |
| Rice | 1,910 |
| Soy beans | 2,000 |
| Chicken | 3,500 |
| Beef | 100,000 |

*Source:* Pimentel (1997)

U.S. Department of Agriculture reported in 1999 that at least 10% of all American households did not have access to enough food for a healthy diet (Charles, 1999). Malnutrition is indeed a real presence in America and around the world.

You can think of global food consumers as being on three levels or tiers. *At the bottom* are about 1.1 billion people (about 20% of the world's people) who are unable to provide themselves with a healthy diet. These people are classified as *food-energy deficient,* and at least 60% of them are children. Chronic malnutrition may not be as grotesquely visible as massive famine, but its consequences are nonetheless devastating. In children it delays physical maturity, impairs brain development, and reduces intelligence, even if replaced by an adequate diet later on. Malnourished adults are unable to work hard or long and have lower resistance to diseases. The danger of epidemics is always high in overpopulated and underfed areas. *On the middle level* are about 4 billion grain eaters, who get enough calories and plenty of plant-based protein, giving them the healthiest basic diet among the world's people. They typically receive less than 20% of their calories from fat, a level low enough to protect them from the consequences of excessive dietary fat. *At the top* are the world's billion meat eaters, mainly in Europe and North America, who obtain close to 40% of their calories from fat (three times that of the rest of the world's people). As people in the middle level (in China, for instance) become more affluent, they tend to "move up the food chain" to emulate people at the top (Brown, 1994). The high meat diet of those at the top is not only unhealthy, but creates a demand for meat production that causes a substantial share of the global inequity of food resources and environmental abuse. See Table 5.1. To illustrate, ignore the high inputs of fuel and chemicals it takes to produce meat, and consider only how many liters of water it takes to produce 1 kilogram of various foods.

At least a third of the world's grain is fed to animals to produce meat. Hence, the simple act of eating less meat could "stretch" the world's grain supplies, making it possible to feed a much larger population and significantly to reduce the current global food inequity.

## Change and the Contours of World Hunger

Importantly, since the 1950s, as population has grown the prevalence of world hunger has declined. It is equally important to note that the steepest declines were in the earlier decades, from about 30% to 20% from the 1960s to the 1980s. In the 1990s, the decline in alleviating hunger lost momentum, declining only slightly from 20% to 19% (Buttel, 2000a). While declining hunger rates may be cause for optimism, it is also true that in terms of absolute numbers there are more hungry people in the world and in America than ever before, because of the continued momentum of population growth. Of the world's 6 billion plus people in 2009, 1.02 billion were hungry, representing nearly one in seven. FAO agronomists and development experts agreed that the resources and technical knowledge are available to increase food production by 50% in 2030 and 70% in 2050—the amounts needed to feed a population expected to grow to 9.1 billion in 40 years. But whether the food can be grown in the LDCs where the hungry can actually get it, at prices they can afford, is another matter (New York Times, 2009).

Hunger is highly concentrated in different regions. Sub-Saharan Africa has the highest rate of undernourishment, while North Africa and the Near East have the lowest rate among developing regions. Latin America, the Caribbean, Southeast Asia, and South Asia, particularly the Indian subcontinent, have intermediate levels. But because East Asia and Southeast Asia, especially China, have much larger populations than does sub-Saharan Africa, the vast numbers of the world's hungry people are found in these regions (Buttel, 2000a; DeRose et al., 1998).

Getting a handle on the factual contours of chronic hunger is relatively easy. Trying to explain why it persists in America and the world is more complex and contentious. Some things related to the causes of hunger are matters agreed on by all observers, regardless of political and ideological differences about food issues. *First,* for the present at least, chronic hunger is not caused by too many people or too little food. The world's farmers produce enough cereals, meat, and other food products to adequately feed the world's population. Taken all together, there is enough to provide 2,800 calories per day per person, well over the minimum daily calorie requirement, even for those whose jobs involve physical labor (2,200–2,800 calories) (Halweil, 2006). *Second,* problems of hunger are caused by the way food is distributed—put another way, because people lack access to the food that exists (Field, 1993). Beyond this consensus, the causes of the perpetuation of chronic hunger are controversial and contentious. In addition to citing biophysical factors, explanations of hunger allude to things like inequality and income distribution, population density and growth, agricultural research agendas, social disruptions like wars, social welfare and insurance policies, and agricultural trade and commodity prices. In other words, explanations of hunger and how to address it are controversial and contentious because they take us into the heart of the dominant social institutions in societies around the world in the twentieth century.

## Explaining World Hunger

Within academic and food policy circles, there are several styles of thinking to explain why hunger exists, each with different emphases, some supportive evidence, and very different policy implications (Buttel, 2000a). They illustrate and specify the sociological perspectives about environmental problems discussed in Chapter One. *Agricultural modernization* argues that the world hunger problem is caused by not enough food and the poor productivity of traditional agriculture, particularly as it is practiced in the LDCs. This approach, which has great intuitive and popular appeal, is the favorite of Western agribusiness firms and agencies like the USDA. However appealing, it is misleading, since everyone admits that the problem is not that there isn't enough food, but how it is distributed. Furthermore, there is reason to think that if such "modernization" of traditional agriculture were to take place under the aegis of large multinational agribusiness firms, the world would have more total food, but still there would exist the hunger of those who are malnourished because they are poor. *Ecological neo-Malthusianism* is the second way of theorizing about the causes of hunger. Its logic seems straightforward: The more people there are, or the faster the rate of population growth, the less food and other materials will be available to other people. But as all food analysts agree, even as rapidly as population has grown, it has been outstripped by total food production increases. Old-fashioned Malthusianism, which viewed population growth as a simple and direct cause of human problems, is very much out of fashion. Neo-Malthusianism, however, which views population as an important underlying condition related to many problems, is very much alive. Population size or growth may not directly cause people to be hungry or die, but it may be a distant and pervasive factor related to more direct causes. Ecological neo-Malthusianism sees population growth in conjunction with the progressive degradation of food-producing environmental resource bases like soil and water.

In its most sophisticated forms, ecological neo-Malthusianism sees environmental sustainability as being more important than population size or growth alone in explaining hunger. This is particularly the case in terms of future threats to food security. Scholars have documented how many gains of the second agricultural revolution in the twentieth century were achieved by environmentally threatening practices and techniques. Earlier we discussed many of these, like soil erosion, waste and degradation of water resources, oversalinization from continual irrigation, declining biodiversity, overuse of petroleum resources, and pervasive pollution from confined animals and agrochemicals. Although agricultural environmental degradation affects farmers in the United States, analysts recognize that it is particularly threatening to the food status of the poorest rural farmers around the world (Halweil, 2000). Moreover, even though there is enough food to go around, *per capita* production—not total production—leveled off in the 1980s and 1990s. Agricultural resources (fertile soil, water for irrigation, soil, rangeland) are under stress everywhere. See Figures 5.3–5.5.

Ecological neo-Malthusianism is a well-established academic viewpoint that has only modest influence in food and agricultural policy circles. Cross-national research, for instance, finds population size and growth rates to be less strongly related to hunger than other factors, and the significance of population as a driver of hunger is very regionally specific. But there are other reasons why its influence in policy circles is modest. It does not bolster the legitimacy of prevailing institutions by providing reasons to extend Western-dominated world food trade, to "modernize" the world, or to provide technological substitutes for social reform (e.g., as with genetically engineered crops). By contrast, ecological neo-Malthusianism views the limits of the global resource base as constraining consumption and requiring more sustainable forms of agriculture. It would require shifts in agricultural technology and practices away from those that have been successful

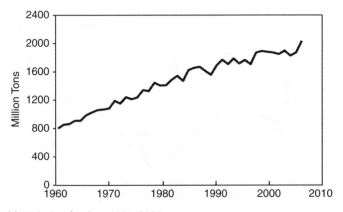

**FIGURE 5.3**  World Grain Production, 1961–2004
*Source:* Food and Agricultural Organization and Halweil, 2005.

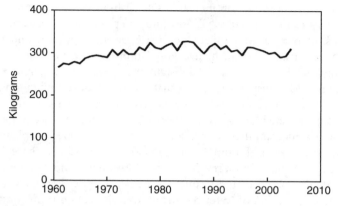

**FIGURE 5.4** World Grain Production Per Person, 1961–2004
*Source:* Food and Agricultural Organization and Halweil, 2005.

and profitable but environmentally damaging. And it would limit food consumption by the afflu-ent. You can see why it is not a dominant perspective explaining hunger.

Given its lack of appeal for policy makers and venture capitalists, ecological neo-Malthusianism is a compelling perspective. Hunger is concentrated in nations and regions where poverty and population growth reinforce each other. The South Asian subcontinent, for instance, is adding 21 million people a year, the equivalent of another Australia. According to U.N. projec-tions, India alone will add 515 million more people by 2050, in effect adding about twice the cur-rent U.S. population. The subcontinent, already the hungriest region on earth, is thus expected to add another 787 million people by mid-century (Buttel, 2000a: 156–217).

Ideas about *inequality and political-economy* (I & PE) represent a third style of explaining hunger, which particularly illustrates sociological conflict theory, as discussed in Chapter One. It assumes that social inequality and poverty produced in the United States and developing nations—both locally and globally—cause hunger. In a globalizing era, inequality and poverty are perpetuated, and perhaps amplified, by growing world markets for food and other traded goods. Such world markets are organized by large corporations with the support of government

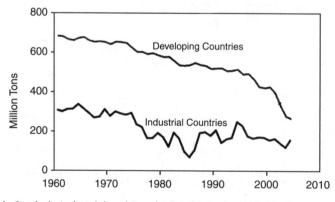

**FIGURE 5.5** Grain Stocks in Industrial and Developing Countries, 1961–2005
*Source:* Food and Agricultural Organization and Halweil, 2005.

subsidies and international regimes like the World Trade Organization. World markets concentrate economic assets and increase the total volume of goods to be sold, but displace and disadvantage small producers and workers in many nations. Such huge markets work very well for the people with money, but not well at all for those who have little money, or who are pushed out of jobs or off their land in the process.

I have noted things that lend credibility to I & PE explanations. For instance, chronic hunger is more directly related to the distribution of food rather than to the total supply, and hunger is a problem of access to food in nations where others eat and are overnourished. Furthermore, many of the difficulties with agricultural modernization ideas explaining hunger support I & PE styles of explanation:

- When self-provisioning peasants and farmers are driven off the land by modernization and consolidation of land
- When modernization produces more food for markets but not for displaced and poor people
- When investing in more productive technology amplifies hunger by putting people out of work
- When affluence encourages meat-rich diets, requiring much grain to feed animals that could support the diets of many hungry people

These different styles of theorizing about the causes of hunger all have virtues and limitations. The agricultural modernization approach rightly points to lack of capital investment in agriculture and agricultural research and development as related to both poverty and hunger. But while investing in agricultural modernization, attempts to produce food security must take into account environmental sustainability. Ecological neo-Malthusianism reminds us that solutions must be developed within the limits of the biosphere and must be understood from a long-term perspective, but it overemphasizes population and environmental resources as independent causes of hunger rather than in context with the social and political factors that shape hunger. I agree with Frederick Buttel that the I & PE approach is best able to incorporate insights of the other three perspectives, while pointing to dynamics that the other three downplay—that the taproots of hunger lie most fundamentally in social relations.

While going a long way toward explaining hunger, these three perspectives gloss over several explanatory factors found related to the persistence of malnutrition. For instance, research demonstrates that *social disruptions* like wars and civil unrest are the main antecedents of famine, particularly in areas where "entitlements to food" are low. Even people in very poor countries can usually manage to avoid famine where there are no social disruptions (Messer, 1998). Second, *natural disasters* such as severe storms, hurricanes, floods, and droughts are related to famine. Although natural disasters and famine are of some importance, researchers and policy circles have overemphasized them. Famines and natural disasters are estimated to cause only about 10% of all hunger deaths, and they are in many respects made by people. Third, *local social relations* like rural landholding structures, ethnic stratification, class and caste relations, regional inequalities, and community power structures shape hunger (Buttel, 2000a). Fourth, *gender relations,* gender inequality, and household power dynamics are not dealt with directly by the four perspectives. But all perspectives and scholars recognize that access to food is strongly gendered. Finally, Nobel prize-winning economist Amartya K. Sen emphasized that hunger is related to food *entitlements,* or the ability of individuals and groups to "command food." Entitlements defined by custom, social status, and law shape who eats and who doesn't because they reflect access to social power. They reflect power relations at international, national, local, and household levels (1993).

## FEEDING NINE BILLION PEOPLE IN THE NEXT FIFTY YEARS?

Clearly, dealing with inequality, poverty, and social circumstances such as those noted that surround food is the key to addressing world malnutrition in the short term. Though there is theoretically enough food to feed everybody adequately, per capita production has declined and the world's margin of safety regarding food has declined. (Look at Figure 5.5 again.) Key measures of food security are the "carryover stocks" measured in days of consumption, as the amount of grain left in the bins when the new yearly harvest begins. When the carryover stock falls below 60 days, as it did in the early 1970s, grain prices become highly volatile, sometimes doubling (U.S. Department of Agriculture, 1993). Even though the "more food" and "population growth as the singular cause" arguments about hunger are flawed, it is still true that we will need more food in the longer term. Accommodating the larger population that will appear by the end of the century will require a greater increase of current food output levels on stressed global food resource bases. This feat will challenge the ingenuity of the world's policy makers and farmers under *any* circumstances, and particularly if it is done in a sustainable way. We will need to simultaneously produce more food and halt the destruction of the agricultural resource base. How?

The most obvious way of increasing food supplies is to extend the technologies that have served us so well since the 1950s: Bring more land into cultivation; use more fertilizer, pesticides, and herbicides; irrigate more; and so on. Yet continuing these techniques produces little significant increase in crop yields. The J-shaped curve of early rapid growth slows down, reaches its limits, and levels off, becoming an S-shaped curve. Grain yields per hectare still increase in most nations, but at a slower rate. But not only do the intensive agricultural techniques from the 1950s no longer produce increasing per capita yields, they measurably degrade the resource bases for agriculture (Bender and Smith, 1997: 25–40). It is doubtful whether even current yields of such intensive agriculture as practiced in Europe and the United States are environmentally sustainable throughout this century without considerable modification. It is even more doubtful that temperate zone monoculture agriculture could be successfully exported wholesale to the tropics and subtropics—even if companies and governments were willing to *give it away* or the LDCs had the money to *buy it*. On the scale required, we won't and they don't.

### Biotechnology?

Some view new biotechnology (or genetic engineering) as a technological panacea of the coming decades that will give an enormous boost to agricultural productivity, becoming a gene revolution like the green revolution seed hybrids of the 1960s. The *green revolution* refers to a massive global effort to crossbreed species producing crop seeds that were much more productive per unit of cultivated land, thereby increasing total food production. The global diffusion of green revolution hybrids significantly decreased the genetic diversity of crops around the world. By gene splicing and injection, new genetic engineering techniques could produce new varieties that "Mother Nature never knew"; potentially more pest resistant, earlier maturing, drought resistant, salt resistant, and more efficient users of solar energy during photosynthesis. Because of such potential benefits and their profitability, genetically modified (GM) crops were rapidly entering the American farming/food system by the year 2000, when about two-thirds of soybeans were grown from engineered seed species. Globally, four crops accounted for most GM crops by 2007: 51% soybeans, 31% corn, 13% cotton, and 5% canola. The vast majority were grown in just three nations: the United States (the global leader, which accounts for half of the world's GM crop area), Argentina, and Brazil. GM crops are mainly engineered for two traits, herbicide tolerance and pesticide resistance, sometimes combined ("stacked") in the same plant (McKeown, 2009). Not by accident, GM seeds are patented and sold by the same corporations that market herbicides. It is important to note that, in spite of the publicity and hoopla about the "global biotechnology revolution," it has mostly been a few crops with two engineered traits (herbicide and pesticide resistance). So far, the diffusion of GM crops has been deep but very narrow. Outside of these few crops in three countries, very little of the world's crop acres are planted in GM crops. Given that the world's three major food crops are rice, wheat, and maize (corn), there is scarcely a real beginning of such a revolution in the staple crop sectors (Buttel, 2002: 7).

There are ecological reasons for caution about GM crops. Without huge amounts of fertilizer and water, most green revolution crop varieties (of the 1960s) produced yields that were no higher (and sometimes lower) than traditional varieties. Similarly, if genetically engineered crops increase productivity by accelerating photosynthesis, they could also accelerate the loss of soil nutrients, requiring more fertilizer and water. Without ample water, good soil, and favorable weather, new genetically engineered crops could fail. Furthermore, new species would be inserted into natural food chains, predator systems, and mineral cycles with unpredictable results. Weeds might acquire the special defenses or enhanced photosynthetic capacity of a GM crop plant, and crop plants with built-in pesticides might harm many insects other than target pests. Furthermore, new organisms introduced into an environment can themselves become pests. Please don't think this an unimportant issue: In the United States, nonnative plant invaders have caused an estimated $138 billion in damage, including the costs of controlling them (Pimentel, 1999). Historically, more than 120 intentionally introduced crop plants *have* become such weed pests in the United States. Unlike people in the United States, Europeans have demonstrated strong skepticism about the biotechnology industry's claims that no adverse health effects are associated with consuming GM food. Europeans are also wary of the unintentional—and damaging—introduction of genes or substances into the environment. At the turn of the twenty-first century, a serious food trade war between the United States and Europe was brewing about this issue (Halweil, 1999, 2000).

Other reasons why biotechnology is a questionable panacea for malnutrition around the world have to do with economics and institutional contexts. Genetic engineering requires heavy capital and technical investments and is being conducted by large private companies that will hold patents on "their organisms," available to buyers at the right price—rather than cheaply to those most in need of food. So far, biotechnology research has been more driven by the desire for agribusiness sales and profits rather than for food for the hungry or agricultural sustainability. Priorities have been, for example, to develop herbicide-resistant crops producing higher sales and profits for herbicide companies. In the most widely known illustration, the Monsanto Company was developing a high-yield seed with a *terminator* gene, meaning that after the crop was grown, harvested seeds could not be regrown. Rather than being saved by farmers, each year's seed had to be purchased anew from the company. Reactions were so negative that the company has abandoned the project, but in corporate circles the race is on. Because of risky but extraordinarily high profit potentials, agribusiness firms now compete vigorously to develop and patent engineered species. The prospect of producing more food cheaply for the world's poor and hungry has so far eluded researchers and—more important—attracted little interest by investors.

None of this means that genetically engineered crop species should be rejected out of hand, particularly if the research agenda could be redirected toward more food and fewer ecological impacts rather than more profits. Doing this would mean shifting some control of research and development agendas to the world's food consumers and farmers. Like many new

---

### BOX 5.2

#### Golden Rice

Thus far there is only one GM crop that would address the needs of the world's hungry. In 2000, a Swiss research institute was developing a strain of rice that would supply vitamin A (beta carotene) and not block the absorption of iron, both problems among rice-eating populations. The so-called "golden rice" strain was not patented or sold by a multinational corporation, but given to the International Rice Research Institute for distribution in LDCs. Even so, many food experts believe that golden rice has such miniscule amount of beta carotene that it would not make a meaningful difference. Multinational corporations would use it for public relations to promote GM-based food in poor nations. (Millerand and Spoolman, 2009: 277–278)

---

scientific technologies, genetic engineering has impressive promises mixed with serious and sometimes sinister possibilities—environmental but also economic and political.

### Sustainable Agriculture: Agroecology and Low-Input Farming?

As the limitations of modern intensive agriculture and the hazards of biotechnology become apparent, agronomists and ecologists are rediscovering some of the virtues of more labor-intensive traditional agricultural practices. These are most obvious for increasing food in tropical LDCs, where rural labor is plentiful but capital and technology are scarce. Though often less profitable in the world market economy, many traditional methods were superior in productivity per hectare when energy inputs and long-term sustainability were considered (Armillas, 1971). Now a newer agricultural paradigm of *agroecology* recognizes that a farm is also an ecosystem and uses the ecological principles of diversity, interdependence, and synergy to improve productivity as well as sustainability (Altieri, 1995). The tools of industrial intensive agriculture are powerful and simple and mean using products like insecticides bought off the shelf. By contrast, agroecology is complex and its tools are subtle. It involves intercropping (growing several crops simultaneously in the same field), multiple cropping (planting more than one crop a year on the same land), crop rotation, and the mixing of plant and animal production—all time-honored practices of farmers around the world (Lappé et al., 1998: 77–78). Agroecology can be combined with *organic* and *low-input* techniques. Farmers can, for instance, recycle animal manures and "green manure" (plant residues) for fertilizer, and they can practice low-tillage plowing that leaves plant residues to prevent erosion and improve soil productivity.

Consider an example. In 1999 on a 300-acre farm near Boone, Iowa, farmer Dick Thompson rotated corn, soybeans, oats, and wheat inter-planted with clover and a hay combination that includes an assortment of grasses and legumes. The pests that plagued neighboring monoculture farms were less of a problem because insect pests usually "specialize" in one particular crop. In a diverse setting, no single pest is likely to get the upper hand. Diversity tends to reduce weed problems because complex cropping uses nutrient resources more efficiently than monocultures, so there is less leftover for weeds to consume. Thompson also keeps weeds in check by grazing a herd of cattle, a rarity on Midwestern corn farms. Most cattle are now raised in feedlots. Cattle, hogs, and nitrogen-fixing legumes maintain nutrient-healthy soil. Moreover, Thompson is making money. He profits from his healthy soil and crops and the fact that his "input" costs—for chemical fertilizer, pesticides, and the like—are almost nothing (Halweil, 1999: 29).

Such techniques can be highly productive, *but only when human labor is carefully and patiently applied.* Evidence from developing nations is impressive. The agriculture of China, Taiwan, Korea, Sri Lanka, and Egypt is now close to this mode—with high yields to show for it. But it was in Cuba that such alternative agriculture was put to its greatest test. Before the collapse of the communist world, Cuba was a model green revolution–style farm economy, based on enormous production units using vast quantities of imported chemicals and machinery to produce export crops while over half the island's food was imported. When, around 1990, Cuba lost trade and subsidies from socialist bloc nations, Cuba was plunged into the worst food crisis in history, with per capita calories dropping by as much as 30%. Faced with the impossibility of importing either food or agrochemical inputs, Cuba turned inward to create more self-reliant agriculture based on higher crop prices to farmers, smaller production units, and urban agriculture. By 1997, Cubans were eating almost as well as they had before 1990 (Rosset, 1997).

Urban agriculture is based on the idea of getting urban dwellers to grow vegetable crops in empty lots, backyards, and other spaces in and around cities. In 1996 such gardeners in Havana supplied 5% to 20% of the city's food. Urban gardening is not a new idea. For instance, during World War II such "victory gardens" produced 40% to 50% of the fresh vegetables in the United States. Urban gardening is now a major source of food in the large cities of the LDCs, such as Shanghai and Calcutta, where food security is often a matter of survival. In the United States, organizations have been formed in many cities to support urban gardeners, which meet regularly to sell and swap their produce. Advocates see urban agriculture as one means of helping urbanites to reclaim neighborhoods from crime and pollution; training low-income residents in business skills; and teaching young people about nutritional, environmental, and food security issues (Nelson, 1996). The movement toward community-supported agriculture (CSA) that started in the 1970s included 1,500 farms by 2008 (W. Cunningham and M. Cunningham, 2010: 219–220).

*Is organic agriculture economically viable?* Organic farming is a small but rapidly growing part of a sustainable agroecology. Many Americans identify organic food with delusional hippies, hysterical moms, and self-righteous farmers, and many scientists don't think organic food production could address world food problems. As a Cambridge University chemist bluntly put it: "The greatest catastrophe . . . is not global warming, but a global conversion to organic farming—an estimated two billion people would perish" (Halweil, 2006: 18). But a number of agribusiness executives, agricultural and ecological scientists, and international agriculture experts believe that a large-scale shift to organic farming would not only increase the world's food supply, but might be the only way to eradicate hunger and lower the impacts of agriculture on the environment. The "external costs" of organic agriculture are lower than conventional production—in terms of soil erosion, chemical pollution of drinking water, the death of birds and wildlife, and toxic agrochemical residues on food.

Many studies from around the world show that organic farming can produce about as much, and in some settings more, food than conventional farms. Where there is a gap, it is largest in MDCs, where lots of agrochemicals and pesticides are used. Looking at data from more than 200 studies in Europe and North America, a Cornell University study found that organic yields were about 80% of conventional yields. Reviewing 154 growing seasons' worth of data on U.S. rain-fed and irrigated land, University of California–Davis scientists found that organic corn yields were 94% of conventional yields, organic wheat were 97%, and organic tomatoes showed no yield difference. Importantly, British researchers at the University of Essex found that in

An organic orange grove has a "Do not spray" sign.

poorer nations where most of the hungry live, the yield gaps completely disappeared, and were sometimes higher on organic farms (Halweil, 2006).

Whether a complete conversion to a sort of organic utopia could address the world's hunger and environmental problems is the wrong question. Roland Bunch, an agricultural extension agent with decades of experience in Africa and the Americas, points instead to "a middle path" of agroecology, or

> low input agriculture that uses many of the principles of organic farming and depends on a small fraction of the chemicals. Such systems can immediately produce two or three times what small farmers are presently producing, and is less costly per unit of production. More small farmers in LDCs will adopt it rather than going completely organic, because they aren't taking food from their children's mouths. If five farmers eliminate half their use of chemicals, the effect on the environment will be two and a half times as great as if one farmer goes totally organic. (Bunch, cited in Halweil, 2006:23–24)

After noting this compelling evidence and possibilities for change, I note that, ironically, U.S. agriculture is *not* presently evolving toward such smaller alternative farming systems, but rather toward larger, chemically intensive monoculture farms owned or controlled by large agribusiness firms. This is true for both grain crops and animals, as illustrated by the huge cattle feedlots and confined animal feeding operations (CAFOs) that raise hogs and chickens. Agricultural research, state and Federal subsidies, and pricing policies have favored such operations. There is, however an organization, The Sustainable Agriculture Initiative, formed by more than 30 of the world's largest corporate food industries that promote sustainable agriculture. In 2010, their global conference was in Belgium (www.saiplatform.org). Altieri, the agricultural scientist who coined the term *agroecology,* observed that "it is clear that the future of agriculture will be determined by power relations, and there is no reason why farmers and the public in general, if sufficiently empowered, could not influence the direction of agriculture toward goals of sustainability" (1998: 71).

## STABILIZING WORLD POPULATION: POLICY OPTIONS

The rate of population growth has been falling around the world for about a decade as fertility rates fall around the world. Several causes contribute to the world decline in the rate of growth, which are enormously variable among nations and regions: (1) the socioeconomic development and falling birth rates that complete the demographic transition in some LDCs; (2) the successes of family planning programs; (3) the global diffusion of feminism and women's rights movements; and (4) the increasing malnutrition, misery, and HIV/AIDS that increase the death rates.

During the 1980s, women around the world began forming small NGOs to lobby for improvements in their social, economic, and political circumstances. By the 1990s, women in LDCs were advocating improvements in family planning programs in order to improve information and access, and encouraging service providers to treat clients with greater respect. Opposition by women's groups to existing family planning programs as well as ethical, scientific, and religious debates about population growth formed the backdrop for the fifth U.N. conference on population. The International Conference on Population and Development (ICPD) was unique in directly linking population problems with development issues. When the ICPD met in Cairo in 1994, the level of participation by NGOs was unprecedented; more than 1,200 NGOs participated as observers or delegates and worked with government officials to craft the ICPD program of action. Directly linking population and development issues was unique among population conferences (Gelbard et al., 1999: 34).

By an overwhelming consensus, ICPD delegates argued that population growth *is* a serious problem that exacerbates core social and environmental problems, while they rejected the notion that population growth is *the* cause of all human problems. They emphasized the necessity of creating conditions under which couples willingly lower the number of children they have, and that three different policies be employed in combination to create those conditions. Those are (1) making the traditional strategies of family planning/contraception available to all people, (2) addressing the worst poverty and destitution that amplify population growth, and, something new, (3) empowering women. Many women—particularly in LDCs, where 90% of the world's population growth will happen—have large families simply because they have no other way to achieve social and economic security for themselves. Women in strongly patriarchal (male-dominated) societies are often forced to marry young. They get paid much less than men when they are allowed to work, have little access to land or bank credit, and have few opportunities to participate in civic life. A pervasive consensus, among women's organizations as well as scholars of development and population policy, maintains that the policies that improve the well-being and social choices of women would go far to limit population growth, to address environmental problems, and to promote human development. Where women have low status and are financially dependent on their husbands, fertility remains high. There are no known exceptions to this generalization (Camp, 1993: 134–135; Sachs, 1995: 94). But you can understand why those in power in patriarchal societies may strongly resist such changes. Powerful evidence suggests that these three policies have made a difference everywhere.

What is the "scorecard" for demographic change a decade after the ICPD? "Mixed," I think. Global decline in fertility rates continued in the 1990s, and progress in improving the status and social choices of women has been measurable in many nations. But confronting volatile demographic pressures on societies and the environment requires tackling population growth head on. Extending population and family planning programs requires international cooperation and resources. The world is facing critical shortages in supplies needed for contraception, HIV/AIDS prevention, and other reproductive services. For instance, the annual cost of supplying enough free and affordable condoms worldwide is expected to double to about $557 million by 2015 (Mastny and Cincotta, 2005: 36).

Unfortunately, just when the need is most urgent, international support decreases. The U.S. pledge to support population issues was $1.9 billion, of which about one-third was actually contributed. In 2004, the U.S. government withheld the $35 million it owes the United Nations Population Fund, which represented about 10% of the budget of that agency (Mastny and Cincotta, 2005: 36–37).

## Conclusion

While the signs that the demographic transition is working in some fashion on a global basis provide the basis for some optimism, world population is an enormous problem because of the built-in momentum of absolute growth. Using a metaphor of a semi truck speeding toward us for population growth, the optimist would note that it has slowed from 80 to 60 miles an hour. The pessimist would note that while we were looking the other way, someone just doubled the weight of the cargo!

## Personal Connections

*Questions for Review*

1. What was Thomas Malthus's major prediction about population growth and the human future? In studying this, what was his distinction between linear and exponential growth?
2. What are some of the main causes of the "demographic transition" that nations go through as they develop?
3. What does it mean to speak of the "demographic divide" between more and less developed nations?
4. How has the ongoing interaction between population change and environmental quality been a major controversy? How has this been changed and nuanced by scholars who emphasized matters of scale, allocation, or distribution—related to different paradigms?
5. How has the proportion of hungry people in world changed since the 1950s? What about the *number* of hungry people? How have these changes continued since the 1990s?
6. The green revolution changed the production of food, as does the current biotechnology revolution. How were they different, with differing consequences?
7. How do experts assess the potentials of low input farming and agroecology to address the world's food needs?
8. What major policies did recent United Nations conferences endorse to stabilize world population growth?

*Questions for Reflection*

Large-scale population change is so abstract and pervasive that you probably don't think much about your everyday life circumstances, problems, and opportunities as related to it. Here are some leading questions to help you explore the demographic contexts of life:

1. High population density means that people live more closely together, interact more frequently, and compete with each other more intensely for living space and all resources

for which supplies are limited. Think of the times when you have lived in a smaller, dense environment with others (in a shared apartment, college dormitory, boarding school, or military base, for instance). How would you describe the experience? What kinds of problems did you and others experience? What kinds of things became important that weren't important in a less densely populated living environment? What kinds of special rules or regulations evolved to deal with problems of increased population density? You might think of all the special rules that college dorm systems and military bases need to deal with problems of living in such facilities. Not all such rules deal with crowding and density problems, but many do.

2. The stabilization of population growth has been on the world's political agenda for some years, and most notably from the ICPD conference at Cairo. That conference defined strategies for slowing population growth that involved the continuation of established family planning programs, social development in LDCs, with assistance from international agencies, and enhancements in the status of women around the world. How much of a priority do you think this should be, compared to other issues? How urgent should it be for the politicians who collect your tax money? How do your age, family status, education, political attitudes, or religious background shape answers to these questions?

## What You Can Do

This chapter's twin concerns were population and food. Food security may be an alien concern to you, unless you're among the minority of Americans whose food supply is chronically in jeopardy. But food security is a problem for an estimated 30 million Americans, in addition to people in many other nations. In the midst of a seeming surfeit of food in America, what contribution could you make to increase the food security in the world?

1. You could buy food in bulk, uncooked, with fewer layers of packaging. That makes food cheaper per unit of production, likely to be healthier, involves less energy to produce, and creates less trash. More of your food costs go directly to producers and to corporate intermediaries who process it. And by selective buying, you can support natural or organic food production, and local or regional producers. These may be very difficult to do among busy dual-income families, and in food systems increasingly dominated by fast foods, supermarkets, and prepared meals. They are for my family!

2. As to hunger and food security itself: The most obvious way of helping is to give generously to food banks and international food relief agencies. That does help feed people who are desperate, but it does not contribute in any way to increase their ongoing food self-sufficiency. Most food relief agencies, such as Oxfam International, now emphasize contributing to the development of food-producing capacity. You can contribute to both public and private food development programs. If you or your friends want a really challenging but important project, try to organize on behalf of the world's hungry people. Try to get food agricultural development programs to those who directly produce food rather than state ministries or firms. While you're at it, you might try to redefine domestic political priorities at any level—city, state, federal—more toward enhancing the food for the hungry. As you can see, addressing food security issues is not easy, and can be as much political as personal.

3. Among the important personal things you can do is to grow some of your own food in a backyard plot, a window planter, a rooftop garden, or a cooperative community garden.

Spending $31 to plant a living room-size garden can give you vegetables worth about $250. Try getting a return like that in the stock market! (Miller, 1992: 386)

**4.** Even more important is eating "lower on the food chain," meaning eating less meat and more grains, fruits, and vegetables. If this lifestyle change became common, the benefits for environmental problems, dietary health, and food security would be enormous. It would save money and energy and reduce your intake of fats that contribute to obesity, heart disease, and other disorders. It also would reduce air and water pollution, water use, reforestation, soil erosion, overgrazing, species extinction, and emissions of greenhouse gases (methane) produced by cattle. In the United States, animal agriculture pollutes more fresh water than all municipal and industrial uses combined. If Americans reduced their meat intake by only 10%, the savings in grain and soybeans could adequately feed 60 million people. More than half of U.S. cropland is devoted to growing livestock feed. Livestock also consume more than half of the water used in the United States, either by direct consumption or by irrigating to grow their feed or processing their manure. Each time a single American becomes a vegetarian, 1 acre of trees and 1.1 million gallons of water are saved each year, and that individual pollutes half as much water. Currently only about 3% of Americans are vegetarian (Miller, 1992: 368).

**5.** The beef about beef: I hate to mention this. Particularly since I live in Omaha, which comes close to being the beef capital of the nation. Its hinterlands are loaded with cattle ranches, feedlots, and packinghouses, and the beef industry is terribly important to the local economy. (Have you seen those ads for "luscious" Omaha steaks that could be shipped to you?). In fact, in Nebraska nothing comes closer to sacrilege than encouraging people to eat less beef. But you should. Why? Most obvious are health reasons, because it is high in saturated fat. Beef requires more inputs of feed and other agricultural inputs per pound than any other livestock. It takes about 9 calories of energy input to get 1 calorie of food output from beef. So, you can see that in energy terms, it's a net loss. Most rangeland degradation in the United States is from cattle, not hogs or chickens. Not all the beef we eat comes from the United States. The most ecologically damaging beef is from cattle raised on tropical soils of Latin America.

After all this, I have to be honest. My family and I still eat meat, including beef, but we often buy "naturally raised" beef from smaller regional farmers. I'd feel a lot better about eating beef if more of it were raised grass fed on ecologically managed rangeland rather than in crowded feedlots where cattle are usually fattened up with processed food, pumped full of growth hormones and antibiotics, and produce concentrated waste disposal problems. But little American beef is currently produced on open rangeland.

## Real Goods

The Chinese Diet. It consists overwhelmingly of rice or noodles; vegetables like onions, peppers, and tomatoes; and locally produced pork—sometimes with chicken, beef, fish, or shellfish for variety. The Chinese eat one-fifth as much meat as Americans, making them paragons of low-on-the-food-chain ecological correctness. It also reduces their saturated fat and cholesterol consumption to levels the National Cancer Institute and the American Heart Association don't let themselves dream of in America. Consequently, the Chinese suffer fewer heart attacks, strokes, and cases of breast cancer. They also have lower levels of anemia and osteoporosis in spite of their lower calcium intake (Durning, 1994: 98). As China develops, many Chinese are giving up their traditionally healthy diet and learning to eat more like affluent Americans.

My family likes Chinese food and we cook some of it, both with meat and without. But watch it. Chinese-American restaurant food often comes with fried rice, which loads the fat and cholesterol back in. Most restaurants are happy to substitute the fried rice with ordinary steamed rice.

## More Resources

Birdsall, N., Kelley, A., and Sinding, S. (Eds.) (2001). *Population patterns: Demographic change, economic growth, and poverty in the developed world.* New York: Oxford University Press.

Blockstein, D., and Weigman, L. (2009). *The climate solutions consensus: What we know and what to do about it.* Washington DC: Island Press.

DeSouza, R., Williams, J., and Meyerson, F. (2003). Critical links: Population, health, and the environment. *Population Bulletin, 58, 3.*

Entwisle, B., and Stern, P. (2005). *Population, land use, and environment: Research directions.* Washington DC:

National Research Council of the National Academy of Sciences.

Kent, M., and Haub, C. (2005). Global demographic divide. *Population Bulletin, 60, 4.*

Livernash, R., and Rodenburg E. (1998), Population, resources, and environment. *Population Bulletin, 53, 1.*

Mcfalls, J. (2003). Population: A lively introduction. *Population Bulletin, 58, 4.*

Weeks, J. (2008). *Population: An introduction to concepts and issues* (11th ed.). Belmont, CA: Wadsworth.

## Electronic Resources

**http://www.census.gov/main/www/cen2000.html**
Gateway to the 2000 U.S. Census

**http://popenvironment.org**
Links to a variety of topics about population and environment

**http://www.populationenvironmentresearch.org**

**http://www.jhuccp.org/popenviro/**
Johns Hopkins University, information program, population and environment

**http://worldwatch.org/alerts/000304.html**
National Wildlife Federation population pages

**http://www.fao.org**
United Nations Food and Agriculture Organization home page.

**http://www.saiplatform.org/**
The sustainable agriculture initiative, formed by more than 30 large food corporations that promote sustainable agriculture.

**http://www.ucsusa.org/resources/index.html**
The Union of Concerned Scientists. There are many resources in this website, but click on "global resources" and "population growth" and go from there.

## Endnote

1. The doubling time can be computed by the *rule of 69*—that is, 69 divided by the growth rate per year (expressed in percentage). So at the world growth rate in 2008 of 1.2% per year, the doubling time was 58 years. Exponential growth is expressed in logarithms. So to find the doubling time, you must find the natural logarithm (or $\log_e$) of 2 (for doubling), which turns out to be 0.69, which is multiplied by 100 to get rid of the decimal point.

# CHAPTER 6

## Globalization, Inequality, and Sustainability

A famous composite photo from the National Aeronautics and Space Administration taken from orbiting satellite shows the geographical basis for global environmental problems.

When historians write about our times, they will surely describe the last half of the twentieth century and the beginnings of the twenty-first century as eras of an intensification of *prodigious growth* and *globalization* in practically every dimension of human activity. It is easy to find "markers" for both of these processes in our everyday lives. Check out where the clothes in your closet were made, eat out in any modest-sized American city, and you have quite an international choice of eateries (Chinese, Japanese, Italian, Greek, Korean, Mexican, Vietnamese, and much more). The reverse is also true: You can get a Big Mac in Beijing, Moscow, Guatemala, and more than 100 other countries. We live in an era of unparalleled electronic connectivity and information technology. We fear tropical diseases and the effects of nonnative species from around the world. Then, there are our anxieties about trade deficits, jobs, terrorism, and wars. We recognize a growing world market economy, and a loosely integrated but extremely volatile global system that both intrigues and frightens us. Contact between nations around the world is certainly not new, but more so than in the past, the world is becoming one integrated but volatile system. Differences between people in various regions and nations continue, but increasingly in the last 100 years we have come to share similar ideas, material goods, and problems.

In the previous few chapters, one theme worth reiterating is that of *continual growth:* in population, forests cut, water used, food produced, mineral and fuels consumed, chemical pollutants generated, air pollution, greenhouse gas emissions, depleted ocean fisheries, and urban sprawl. During the last half century, the world economy expanded sevenfold. "Most striking of all, the growth in the world economy during the single year of 2000 exceeded that of the entire nineteenth century. . . . Stability is considered a departure from the norm" (Brown, 2004: 4). The planet has indeed been transformed by the human footprint.

The major concerns of this chapter are the connections between globalization, sustainability, and the prospects of transformations to achieve sustainability. I raise what is certainly *the* big environmental question, about global sustainability, and explore it in various ways in the rest of the book. *First,* this chapter will discuss the causes and processes of globalization. *Second,* it will discuss the notion of sustainability itself. *Third,* it will examine two major perspectives about sustainability and some research and criticisms about each. *Fourth,* the chapter will examine what the characteristics of more sustainable societies would be. *Fifth,* I will examine the prospects for large-scale social change toward greater sustainability.

## SOCIAL SCIENCE PESPECTIVES AND GLOBALIZATION

How and why did the process of global integration accelerate in the last 100 years? What were some of its driving forces? Three perspectives will get to the heart of these questions, and they can be framed with social science perspectives, discussed mainly in Chapter One.

### Globalization Perspective I: Neoliberalism

One perspective from classic sociology (*functional theory*) maintains that society and change are shaped by the activities and processes required for the viability and survival of society itself. These processes are termed *functions*, and there are also *dysfunctions,* which have the opposite effect. Early functional thinkers were concerned with the evolution from traditional to industrial societies (Durkheim, 1893/1964; Spencer, 1896). But, by the 1950s functional theorizing was dominated by thinking that depicted societies as "equilibrium-seeking structures" that avoided change (Parsons, 1951). More recent functionalist thinking attempts to understand social change by assuming that whenever stresses or strains seriously threaten a society or system, it will initiate "compensatory actions" to counter these disruptions in an attempt to preserve its key features. These may succeed or fail, but in either case they are likely to produce considerable change throughout the system. From this perspective, social survival is a perpetual process of social reorganization (Alexander, 1985; Olsen, 1968: 150–151). Since its beginnings, functionalist thought has been concerned with modernization and the spread of Western culture and institutions. It is particularly consistent with neoliberal economic thinking about globalization.

The neoliberal perspective embodies the thinking of economists about markets and politics. It is rooted in a simple and dramatic assumption that will sound familiar to you—that the best human system results from individuals being free to pursue their own interests, under restraint of law. Until fairly recent times, people and governments assumed that it was right for governments to promote the society's well-being by special export subsidies for national industries and to protect them from foreign competition by import tariffs—just as armies protect from foreign invaders. That policy beginning in the seventeenth century was known as *mercantilism*, when European kings attempted to control commerce and trade to benefit their nations. Today, this is known as *economic nationalism*. It is by no means dead today, in spite of the global market system, as when struggling businesses seek government protection from "unfair" foreign competition (as many do).

But economic nationalism was questioned when two world wars with a world depression between them produced prolonged, devastating, worldwide chaos, conflict, and misery. Toward the end of World War II, the world's bankers and economic ministers met at Bretton Woods (a resort in New Hampshire) to consider how to prevent similar events in the future. They thought that those troubles were caused by excessive economic nationalism that stifled trade, produced economic and political instability and unemployment, and raised consumer prices. They agreed to embark on policies of international free trade. The *Bretton Woods system* envisioned a free system of international trade in open markets without barriers. States should continue to have important roles for economic regulation *within* nations, but free markets were intended to dominate relations *between* nations (Balaam and Veseth, 1996: 16, 42, 50).

The growth of the world market system and this understanding of it are not only consistent with functionalist thinking about the sources of social viability, but they also reinforced the goals of investors and corporations to expand their markets and profitability through international trade. New technologies in agriculture, manufacturing, and transportation, and *particularly* the development of the new information technologies since the 1970s (computers and the Internet) decreased the costs of doing business at widely scattered locations around the globe (Castells, 2000). Corporations, especially transnational corporations (TNCs), prospered and the aggregated growth rates of world goods and services mushroomed. *World aggregate economic output more than quintupled since the 1950s—vastly exceeding population growth rates.*

This *neoliberal* economic understanding of world trading shaped negotiations between nations. It was, for example, the dominant thinking that spawned international institutions like the World Bank (WB), the International Monetary Fund (IMF), the World Trade Organization (WTO), and the North American Free Trade Agreement (NAFTA). These organizations became so powerful that today they often control global markets, policy, and often the fates of nations and regions. See Table 6.1. There are many similar trade and tariff alliances that have been formed throughout the world.

Although the world market economy has dramatically increased trade and production and was thus compatible with the needs of TNCs, it was certainly not free of serious problems and contradictions. Growing global integration led by huge TNCs meant the scope and assets of the largest corporate players made a very unlevel field for negotiation, even between many nations and TNCs. The neoliberal global integration was much less compatible with the concrete interests of governments, since TNCs often evaded national taxes and regulations by investing in tax and regulatory havens and by shipping products and profits back to consumers and investors where they were headquartered.

The growing "world economic integration" was also less compatible with the interests of workers, who were often displaced by the new economic technologies and the search for

| TABLE 6.1 | International Trade Organizations |
|---|---|
| Organization or treaty | Function, what it does? |
| World Bank | Founded in the 1940s to rebuild war-torn Europe. It has become a large bank to provide financial and development aid to poor nations. |
| International Monetary Fund | Established by donor nations to regulate the world's currency system so that inflation or recessions in particular countries don't spread throughout the world. |
| World Trade Organization | Evolved over decades from trade talks ("rounds") that did away with international tariffs, and has become the organization that provides rules about free trade and adjudicates disputes between nations. |
| North American Free Trade Association | Established in the 1970s by treaties between Canada, the United States, and Mexico that established North America as a tariff-free trade zone. |

cheap labor around the world. Human labor was often marginalized, and the resulting tensions of unemployment or substandard employment produced social burdens assumed by nations and local communities. "Free trade" neoliberal organizations and treaties have magnified such problems—as well as the equitable provision of health care, education, food, shelter, and environmental protection. Some now have "side agreements" purporting to deal with these issues. Thus, the neoliberal world market economy had a deep contradiction: growing aggregate production and affluence alongside mushrooming inequality and poverty both within and among nations. Such problems and tensions associated with the emerging world-system spawned a plethora of social movements, nongovernmental organizations (NGOs), and international nongovernmental organizations (INGOs), collectively known as the "civil society," which attempts to address the gaps left by corporations and governments in meeting social needs.

## Globalization Perspective II: World-System Theory

Besides functionalism, another social science perspective (*conflict theory*) suggests that society and change are shaped by conflict and power relationships among groups, organizations, and social classes (the "parts" of society) as they compete to control the distribution of limited values and resources. As most people understand, social conflict can be destructive, but it may also reinforce social stability, or at least an ongoing relationship between the dominant and contending parts of human systems. Furthermore, it can produce a "new deal" of power relationships that bring with them new social arrangements, which benefit a broader—or at least a different—spectrum of people. Conflict between social groups and classes produced parliamentary democracy, for example, when English nobles forced King John to sign the Magna Carta (the earliest democratic constitutional document), giving them certain rights not to be ruled by royal decrees (Collins, 1975; Dahrendorf, 1959). Conflict thinking originated from the ideas of Karl Marx, and one major perspective on globalization (world-system theory) is virtually the extension of Marxist thought to encompass the world.

Conflict perspectives in the social sciences provide a frame for a very different understanding of globalization than neoliberalism. They begin not with assumptions about states and markets, but with the political and economic history of the modern world, beginning in the 1500s. Most of the world has been in contact with modernizing European nations since about 1500, and by 1800 the scope of that contact had increased so that through colonial empires Europeans controlled most world trade. The global diffusion of Western technologies, culture, and values accelerated during this period. Colonial nations imported cheap raw materials from their colonies and re-exported more expensive manufactured goods in markets controlled by colonial administrations. But by 1900, the colonial empires (of the British, Dutch, French, and Germans) began to break up, and political control was replaced with economic control through a system of trade. The world market system mentioned earlier is, in this view, a global economic exchange network divided among competing national entities (corporations as well as governments). But it is a very unequal and stratified exchange system in which the industrially more developed countries (MDCs) provided investment capital and technology, while the less developed countries (LDCs) were the providers of raw material and, increasingly, of cheap labor.

A global hierarchy of the evolving world-system and its division of labor was driven by a highly unequal system of trade between the MDCs (largely in the northern hemisphere) and the LDCs (largely in the southern hemisphere). MDCs retain decisive control of the world-system because they control finance capital and the terms of trade. LDCs became increasingly enmeshed in the world-system in dependent status as debtor nations, which is precisely how they continued to be "less developed." Thus, MDCs and LDCs evolved together. The policies of the Bretton Woods institutions (the World Bank and the IMF) operate to amplify inequalities and power-dependent relations, and their policies and loans. Advice by the world's bankers and financial leaders has had a decided "tilt" largely to benefit the already wealthy MDCs—a fact that is now widely recognized around the world. They encourage LDCs to borrow money for development, to open their economies to domination by TNCs, and to find money to pay external debts by cutting budgets that weaken education and health care (IMF's term for this is "structural adjustment," mentioned in Chapter Five).

Such trade inequality was called *dependency theory* by economists (Frank, 1997), but the whole global system of inequality was increasingly known as *world-system theory*. Its theoretical reasoning extended Marxian thought about economic class, conflict, and inequality within societies to understand the world economic and political structure. Hence it is sometimes understood as a "new historical materialism." Wallerstein, its most articulate advocate, envisioned the structure of the emerging world-system in three tiers. *Core nations,* powerful and affluent MDCs (e.g., the United States, Germany, and Japan), have diversified industrial economies and exercise political, economic, and fiscal control over the world-system. *Peripheral nations,* the most powerless, have narrow economic bases of agricultural products or minerals and often provide cheap labor for TNCs (e.g., Bangladesh, Rwanda, Indonesia, Ecuador). Somewhere in between are *semiperipheral nations,* intermediate in terms of their wealth, political autonomy, and degree of economic diversification (e.g., Mexico, Malaysia, Brazil, Venezuela) (Wallerstein, 1980; see also Chase-Dunn, 1989).

The most obvious difficulties with world-systems theory is that it depicts MDCs as acting too coherently in a complicated world, and it provides wealthy elites in LDCs with a ready set of ideas to blame the MDCs for their plight. Such leaders and elite classes in LDCs are very much involved in the problems of developing nations, from which they often benefit. For more information and critiques of this perspective, see Harper and Leicht (2007), Lenski and Nolan (1999), Sanderson (1995), and Wolf (1982).

## Globalization Perspective III: Landscapes and Global Flows

A perspective from cultural anthropology that can frame a third view of globalization begins with the spread (diffusion) of culture items, both material and non material. It emphasizes *processes* or global "flows," rather than structures or systems, as do the functional and conflict perspectives. Put another way, people, ideas, money, technologies, products, and labor flow across national borders, and the boundaries between "us" and "them" in structures often seem confused and compromised. These flows or "-scapes," (to use a common suffix, as in "landscapes") are fluid and irregular, and may operate somewhat independently or even in conflict. They are thus more in tune with those who emphasize that globalization continues to involve heterogeneity, diversity, and hybrids, rather than producing an increasingly homogenous system. Cultural anthropologist Appadurai argued that there are five important global flows, or "-scapes" (1996):

1. *Ethnoscapes* are mobile, moving groups and individuals such as tourists, refugees, and guest workers who play such an important role in the shifting world (think about migration, the spread of infectious diseases, and anthropogenic invasive species).
2. *Technoscapes*, including all the technologies (e.g., the Internet and all its cousins), which now move so freely around the world. Think also about the diffusion of Western economic and agricultural technology.
3. *Financescapes* are the processes by which huge sums of money move around the world through markets, currency exchanges, stock exchanges, etc.
4. *Mediascapes* involve both the electronic capability to produce and transmit information as well as the images of the world that are created and disseminated (Magazines, videos, CNN, and Al-Jazeera are examples).
5. *Ideoscapes* are like mediascapes, but are largely images about political and cultural ideologies produced by nations or social movements that seek to gain power or displace current powerholders (1996).

It is important to note two things about such flows. They operate through similar "-scapes," but there are often glaring disjunctures among them. For example, the Japanese are very much open to ideas and technologies (ideoscapes and technoscapes) but notoriously closed to immigration (at least one of the ethnoscapes) (Ritzer, 2010: 289). Second, while such social and cultural flows use a variety of mechanisms that may produce homogeneity (for instance, advertising and technology), the result is often considerable diversity and heterogeneity. For an environmentally relevant illustration, most people in the world know about climate change problems, but there are great differences in judgments about how severe such problems are, and what (if anything) ought to be done. Think about the inconclusive results of the Copenhagen negotiations in 2010, even when there was considerable scientific consensus about the stakes.

## Globalization and Social Inequality

I mentioned social inequality (or stratification) in many places, but now need to address it in more depth, particularly as it relates to environmental conditions. Relevant dimensions of *stratification* around the world are economic, racial, and ethnic inequality. All have steadily increased in recent decades. Consider that by 2006, the richest 20% of U.S. households had more than half the income generated in the United States, and the chasm continues to widen (U.S. Bureau of the Census, 2007). Income is different from *wealth*, which is even more unequally distributed. In the late 1990s, just 10% of the population owned half of all house-hold wealth, and the top 30% owned more than 80% of it (U.S. Bureau of the Census, 2001b, tables 4 and 5).

Clearly, income and wealth differences are very large within the United States, existing in layers that social scientists call socioeconomic classes. The pattern of such class stratification didn't change much for a long time in the United States, but began to become significantly more unequal starting in the mid-1970s, when the gap between the rich and the poor grew larger than ever. One statistical analysis found that the United States had the most unequal distribution of household income among all 21 industrial countries studied (Sweden had the most equal) (Smeeding, 2000).

Economic inequality is strongly connected to racial and ethnic inequality. In the United States, the racial wealth gap has persisted, growing even larger within the last 30 years. According to the Federal Reserve Board, in 2007 for every dollar that a median white family owned, the median Latino family owned 12 cents and the median black family owned a dime (Martin, 2009). The various forms of racial and ethnic inequality in the United States are so familiar that they require little comment here. Like different social classes, various racial and ethnic groups are con-nected to their biophysical environments in different ways. A groundbreaking 1987 study spon-sored by the United Church of Christ concluded that African Americans and other people of color were two to three times as likely as other Americans to live in communities with commer-cial hazardous waste landfills. For example, in Detroit 3% of all whites but 11% of all minority people lived within a mile of hazardous waste facilities, a difference by a factor of nearly four (Bryant, 1995).

Later studies found that the distribution of air pollution, solid waste dumps, and toxic chemicals and the location of hazardous waste facilities correspond to residence patterns by race, socioeconomic class, and often both. An enormous body of research demonstrates that both lower socioeconomic classes and racial minorities bear more than their share of the costs of envi-ronmental problems and change (Bryant, 1995; Bullard, 1990, 1993). However, some studies that use different units of analysis in research challenge this finding about race, but they always demonstrate a strong relationship between environmental hazards and social class. Whether related to race or class, such conditions facilitated the idea that *environment is a social justice issue,* and they helped galvanize environmental justice movements and grassroots movements for change. I will return to them in Chapter Eight.

*Global inequality* stands out in similar sharp relief between nations around the world as well as within societies. At the beginning of the industrial revolution in 1879, people living in the fifth of the world's wealthiest nations received nearly seven times the income as the fifth of peo-ple living in the world's poorest ones. By 1960, people living in the wealthiest countries com-manded 30 times as much as people living in the poorest countries. But, as if that concentration of world income is not bad enough, more recently the richest fifth of the world's nations com-mand 68 times as much income as do the poorest fifth (United Nations, 1998a; Bell, 2004: 19). Interestingly, as inequality grew within nations, the degree of inequality between nations may have stabilized and perhaps even contracted slightly in the 1980s and 1990s (for evidence, see Goesling, 2001). If you measure income inequality by persons around the world, instead of nations, the income inequality is even more striking: The richest fifth of the world's people com-mand 150 times the world's income as do the poorest fifth.

You might put these inequalities differently to soften their human implications a bit, because the percentage of the world's people living in poverty is about the same now as it was in 1960—about 20%. But the absolute number (not percent) of poor people has doubled since

Manila, squalor in the foreground, skyscrapers in the background.

1960, keeping pace with the growing world population. Other comparisons are even more strik-ing. During the world economic expansion of the 1990s, the world's 200 richest people con-trolled $1 trillion, "a cool $5 billion each, about double what they had in 1994" (Bell, 2004: 19). In contrast the poorest 40% of the world's population live on less than $2 a day and account for only 5% of global income (United Nations Development Programme, 2005). Global inequality is graphically illustrated in Figure 6.1 by what has come to be termed the "champagne glass of world wealth distribution."

This global income gap is an equally severe *consumption gap,* with significant implica-tions for differences in lifestyles and well-being. In the 1990s, compared to an average LDC person, an average MDC person consumed 3 times as much grain, fish, and fresh water; 6 times as much meat; 10 times as much energy and timber; 13 times as much iron and steel; 14 times as much paper; and 18 times as many chemicals (Durning, 1992: 50). Along with the spread of affluent lifestyles, others live in physical deprivation. In the LDCs, nearly 800 million people were malnourished (about 18% of the world's population). One billion of the world's 6.2 billion did not have adequate shelter to protect them from rain, snow, heat, cold, filth, and rats and other pests. One hundred million had no shelter at all. More than a billion lacked access to safe drinking water.

## Inequality and Environmental Impact

It might be obvious to you how social and political sustainability is jeopardized by such gaping domestic and global inequality, but not how growing inequality is *itself* a potent and proximate cause of environmental degradation. Let me explain.

By now ample evidence shows that people at either end of the income spectrum are more likely than those in the middle to damage the earth's ecological health—the rich because their affluent lifestyles are likely to lead them to consume a huge and disproportionate share of the earth's food, energy, raw materials, and manufactured goods, and the poor because their poverty

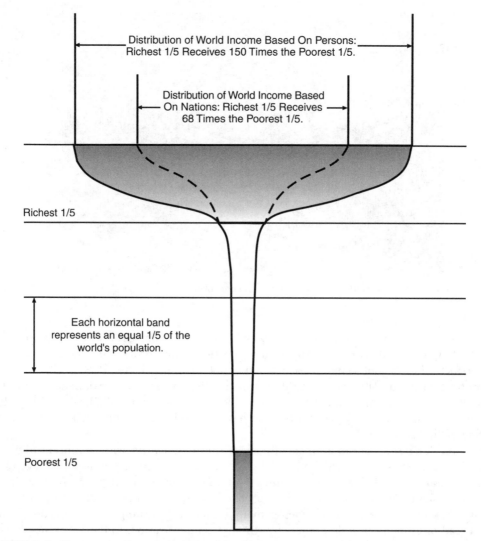

**FIGURE 6.1**    Champagne Glass of World Wealth Distribution
*Sources:* United Nations (1998a: 219); Bell, (2004:20).

drives them to damage and abuse the environment. The poorer classes in MDCs damage the environment not because they consume so much, but because they are able to afford mainly older, cheaper, less durable, less efficient, and more environmentally damaging products—autos, appliances, homes, and so forth. Thus such savage inequality means that people not only have greatly different levels of material consumption and security, but also impact and experience environmental problems in different ways. The affluent are able to respond to environmental problems with minimal consequences for modifying their lifestyles. They are, for instance, the best able to afford higher prices or energy taxes or to purchase more efficient homes, autos, or appliances. Poor people are less able to do so. Their poverty may pressure them to modify behavior or curtail consumption even more. In other words, the affluent—who can afford the newest and most efficient of everything—damage the environment because of the sheer volume of energy and material they consume. The poor do so because whatever they consume is likely to have a greater per unit environmental impact (Dillman et al., 1983; Lutzenhiser and Hackett, 1993). It is important to note that it is not the *poorest* among the poor—who have no autos, apartments, or appliances of any kind—who are environmentally most damaging. It is rather the most marginal segment of unskilled workers (working class, or lower middle class) who still have sufficient amenities to have an impact on the environment rather than, for instance, transient or homeless persons, or the destitute, who have virtually nothing.

In LDCs, population pressure and inequitable income distribution push many of the poor onto fragile lands where they overexploit local resource bases, sacrificing the future to salvage the present. Short-term practices such as abbreviated fallow periods, harvests exceeding regeneration rates, depletion of topsoil, and deforestation all permit survival in the present but place an enormous burden upon environmental sustainability and future generations (Goodland et al., 1993: 7). In fact, with uncanny regularity, the world's most impoverished regions also suffer the worst ecological damage; maps of the two are almost interchangeable. In China, India, Pakistan, and Afghanistan, for instance, the impoverished live in degraded semi-arid and arid regions or in the crowded hill country surrounding the Himalayas; Chinese poverty is particularly concentrated on the Loess Plateau, where soil is eroding on a legendary scale (Durning, 1989: 45).

Often, the environmentally destructive behavior of the world's poor is connected with highly skewed land ownership patterns. Rural small landholders whose land tenure is secure rarely overburden their land, even if they are poor. But dispossessed and insecure rural households often have no choice but to do so. Hired workers, hired managers, and tenant farmers are not likely to care for land as well as owners do (which is also evident in the United States!). Being landless is in fact a common condition among rural households in many LDCs. In the 1990s, between 40% and 90% of rural households were landless or near landless among Africans, Indians, Filipinos, Ecuadorians, Brazilians, and Dominicans. While such poverty impacts the environment, the causality is not one way. Even before it is degraded, a marginal area by nature does not usually produce enough surplus to lift its inhabitants out of poverty. Poor areas and poor people destroy each other. A reformed land tenure system that gives secure ownership of land, even in small parcels, to the landless peasants of the world would go some distance toward moderating the high birth rates and staunching the destruction of ecosystems by the world's poor.

Illegal and unregulated resource extraction often comes with this highly skewed land ownership pattern. Illegal resource extraction—oil, timber, diamonds, copper—is closely linked to arms trafficking, paramilitary violent conflict, human rights violations, humanitarian disasters (e.g., famine), and *environmental destruction*. The beneficiaries of such illegal resource extraction are the MDCs, but the burdens of sociopolitical conditions and environmental devastation are shouldered by LDCs and the world's poor (Renner, 2002: 149–172).

The affluent classes of the MDCs also threaten the global ecosystem, but not because they are desperate with few alternatives. MDCs have consumerist cultures, purchasing powers, and economic arrangements through the world market economy to consume a disproportionate share of the world's resources. They account for a disproportionate share of resource depletion, environmental pollution (including greenhouse gas emissions), and habitat degradation. A world full of affluent societies that consume at such levels is an ecological impossibility (Durning, 1994: 12).

In sum, affluence *and* poverty both threaten the environment, and they do so increasingly as the chasm of social inequality widens, driven partly by contemporary globalization processes. Reducing social inequality both within and between nations, more feasible that trying to eliminate it, would reduce pressure on the environment. It could do so by reducing the huge resource consumption of the affluent *and* the poor's need to overharvest, overgraze, or overfish to meet their subsistence needs. Furthermore, it is unlikely that the world's poor or poor nations would willingly agree to environmental agreements to preserve or restore the natural environment (usually by lowering their consumption in the near time horizon) unless questions of *equity* are addressed. To those who live in misery, talk of "saving the environment" by the world's wealthy often sounds like a new form of imperialism: *green imperialism.* Some argue that poverty reduction must come before environmental sustainability, while others argue that environmental sustainability is a prerequisite for social sustainability. This is a classic chicken-or-egg question, but how we answer it has important policy implications (Passarini, 1998: 64).

## SUSTAINABILITY

Ideas about sustainable societies and development have long and mixed histories. In the last decades, these notions transcended the specialized concerns of scholars to become common goals, or at least irresistible slogans, in public discourse and debate about the environmental issues. What is sustainable development? Conceptually and abstractly, the matter is quite simple: *Sustainable* means that the change process or activity can be maintained without exhaustion or collapse; *development* means that change and improvement can occur as a dynamic process (Southwick, 1996: 96). It does not mean profligate use of the natural world without regard to the future, but neither does it imply a static condition. In human terms, it means inventing ways of meeting human needs while preserving the capacity of the biophysical environment to do so. A sustainable society "can persist over generations without undermining either its physical or its social systems of support" (Meadows et al., 1992: 209). In more human terms, a sustainable society is one that "meets the needs of the present without compromising the ability of future generations to meet their own needs" (World Commission on Environment and Development, 1987).

Historically, the notion of sustainable development probably seemed like a utopian idea, but not very practical. Nor was it necessary to think about it much. After all, human populations were smaller, economic technologies less powerful, and nature's bounty seemed infinite. But now coming to some approximation of sustainability is not just a nice idea; it is imperative to consider it for the future of the world's people—certainly for a future that is materially secure, reasonably equitable, and democratic. Who could really oppose sustainability or development? As an old saying has it "No one wants to dance with the devil."

Sustainability is often spoken of in terms of the *three E's*—economics, ecology, and (social) equity. It invokes a vision of human welfare that takes into consideration both *inter* and *intra*generational equity. It neither borrows from future generations nor lives at the expense of current generations. But lurking just under the surface of these abstractions are substantial conflicts between actors and institutions (Passarini, 1998: 60–63). Consider the conflicts of interest generated by public debate about whether to encourage or discourage material consumption of particular products (like gasoline or inorganic fertilizers). People who sell the products, who immediately benefit from their use, or who see them as dangers to human health or ecological well-being have *very* different outlooks and interests. Similarly, what needs justify the generation of environmental toxins and pollutants? Who should pay the costs of their abatement, or what resources (physical or biotic) should be kept free of human impact, or left for future generations (like virgin forests or wetlands)?

In public discourse, *sustainable development* and associated notions like the *carrying capacity* turn out to be universally acknowledged but inherently politicized concepts. The resulting controversy generates different advocacy organizations and movements with different objectives, resources, and political influence. In the United States, for example, the Sierra Club, a large environmentalist organization that has existed for decades, and the Sahara Club have similar names. The Sahara Club was formed in the late twentieth century by American interest groups fed up with "pious environmentalists" trying to take away individual freedoms, and eliminate jobs and the nation's economic strength. In its view, humans are masters of the earth, and its resources should be exploited for human use, pure and simple (Southwick, 1996: xix).

Scholarly controversy about sustainability goes to the very heart of the paradigm conflicts that I have discussed. Think again about potential conflicts integrating the three E's (economy, ecology, equity). For policy, do we start with developing an economy that is less damaging to nature while maintaining rapacious consumption? Do we begin by preserving ecosystems, even if it means sequestering them from human exploitation and restraining consumption? Do we begin with equity, addressing poverty and social inequality to produce the cohesion and social sustainability that make agreements about environmental sustainability even possible (Gould, 1998; Passarini, 1998; Redclift, 1987)? Does this have a familiar sound? It should. Paradigms: resource allocation? growth in finite systems? maldistribution and social stratification?

Similarly, the concept of carrying capacity, so useful for population ecologists, is controversial when extended to human systems and the planetary scale. Chapter One discussed the idea that the environment has three functions for humans: as living space, as supply depot, and as waste depository. Dunlap and Catton, as well as others, think that the exponential growth of the human population and their uses of the earth means that we have already exceeded its long-term carrying capacity (2002). See Figure 1.5 in Chapter One.

In fact, Catton has argued that there is no such thing as sustainable development. It is a rhetorical and ideological term for those who wish to continue destructive growth and "feel good about it" (1997: 175–178). Environmentalists Lester Brown and Donella Meadows believe that we have already probably exceeded the earth's carrying capacity, but continue to hedge their bets (Brown and Flavin, 1999; Meadows et al., 2004). Economist Julian Simon was a tireless advocate of the idea that there is no finite carrying capacity and that development and growth in material consumption should be vigorously promoted to proceed as it has for the last 50 years (1998).

Exhaustively reviewing the history of such ideas, theoretical biologist Joel Cohen argues that concepts like sustainable development or the earth's carrying capacity are important, but not very useful for scientific research (1995). He argues that questions like "How many people can the earth support?" are inherently *normative* and value laden. How many and at what levels of material well-being? With what technologies? Living in what kinds of biophysical environments? With what kinds of cultural values or political and legal institutions? Rather than a benign and participatory sustainability, one could imagine a sustainability of managed scarcity coercively administered by powerful authoritarian elites—resembling a virtual societal slave labor camp (see Heilbroner, 1974; Schnaiberg and Gould, 1994; or rent a video—now a DVD—from the early 1970s, *Soylent Green,* for a powerful malevolent portrayal of unsustainability based on a science fiction novel by Harlan Ellison).

It may surprise you to learn that I think Cohen is right. Sustainability and carrying capacity are not objectively quantifiable concepts. *But please don't misunderstand.* They are critical as normative social facts and helpful to envision worlds we would like, or wish to avoid. In the larger picture, they embody the only policy questions that really matter, but which require citizens, scientists, and policy makers to address difficult normative and value questions. Natural scientists and neoclassical economists are not accustomed to dealing with normative social facts or policies involving complex normative solutions—but those are sociological specialties. Passarini suggested several sociological contexts for research that contribute to understanding sustainability: time horizons, risk analysis, differences between public and private realms, and social change (1998). I will return to some of these issues (time horizons and social change) toward the end of this chapter.

## GROWTH AND SUSTAINABILITY: TWO PERSPECTIVES

Since 1950, the world's human population has doubled and is now between 6 and 7 billion. It will undoubtedly continue to rise. Since then, global economic output has quintupled. The cultural ethos of consumerism that favors high growth and ever-expanding consumption is rapidly diffusing around the world. At the same time, the chasm of inequality grows and poverty proliferates, while the prospects for greater global equity seem increasingly remote. There are signs that most ecosystems and biospheric environmental systems are becoming degraded, coupled with a very real prospect for altering the climate of the planet.

*Suppose these trends continue.* Can they do so without devastating the planet? Even if humans could use their ingenuity to survive, would it be in terms of such conditions that many would freely choose? Will humans replicate on a global scale the *outbreak-crash* familiar to ecologists and population biologists, as illustrated by the bacteria in a petri dish, the reindeer on Matthew Island, the Mayans, or the humans on Easter Island—where prosperous and complex human communities collapsed when they finally exhausted natural resources? Or, will none of this occur? Are we ingenious enough to invent and "grow" our way into a sustainable high-consumption world for *very* large numbers of people on the planet? These questions were emerging in the last half of the twentieth century. There are different ways of thinking about the trajectory of humans on the planet, and within scientific and intellectual circles diverse and conflicting theories have their defenders, supporting evidence, and strong critics. I examine two of them.

### Limits to Growth: Outbreak-Crash

*Limits to growth* (LG) is a human ecology perspective articulated in the 1970s as a result of the growing popularity of neo-Malthusian ideas about the longer-term global consequences of exponential growth in population, industrial production, and material consumption. The term LG was invented by the *Club of Rome* (a nonprofit research foundation), which commissioned computer simulations of global data about growth over time, stretching from past and projected into the future. Reports based on these studies have been continually updated (Meadows et al., 1972, 1992, 2004). They have suggested that the combination of population growth, exponentially growing per capita economic productivity and consumption, and the resultant pollution would eventually overburden the subsistence base for human societies. This would mean a decline in human population, development, and well-being for people around the world. They hypothesized an "outbreak-crash" model of the human–environment future, a model well known to population ecologists. See Figure 6.2.

Related perspectives arrive at the LG prognosis by different assumptions. Conflict and neo-Marxist perspectives, as applied to the environment, argue that environmental exploitation is driven by the structure of market economies, the institutions of modernity, and the relentless commitment to growth in modern, particularly capitalist, production systems (Benton, 1989; Bookchin, 1982; Roberts and Grimes, 2002; Schnaiberg, 1980). For Schnaiberg and Gould (1994),

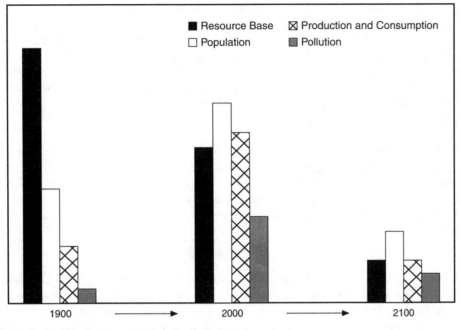

**FIGURE 6.2**   The Limits Scenario "Standard Run"
*Source:* Based on Meadows, Randers, and Meadows, 2004, *Limits to Growth: The 30 Year Update,* p. 169.

a "treadmill of production" (mentioned in Chapter One) is the driving force behind modern economies, as well as environmental degradation. To maintain profits, producers must constantly seek to expand production, creating an "enduring conflict" between society and the environment. Expansion is, however, limited because of ultimately finite natural resources. O'Connor described this as the "second contradiction of capitalism," whereby escalating production depletes the natural resources required to sustain production, which escalates costs, resulting in shrinking profits (Connor, 1994; York et al., 2003: 286).

To deal with an eventual apocalypse, LG analysts recommended reforms that slowed or halted growth of the increase in natural resource consumption (but provided few clues about what policies or reforms would produce this result). World-system theorists opined that there had to be a radical restructuring of the world-system to limit the hegemony of core industrial nations, or to break up the existing world market system.

Not surprisingly, such recommendations provoked outrage and vigorous criticism from many quarters, since they struck at the heart of dominant ideologies about human progress (as well as profits) in the industrial world as well as prospects for effective development in third world nations. Such calls for reform resulted in the proliferation of environmental organizations (NGOs), government departments for the environment, and environmental regulations, or what some have called the "environmental state" (Fisher and Freudenburg, 2004; Frank et al., 2000). In the 1970s, such a configuration of state and NGOs emerged almost simultaneously in North America, Japan, and Europe, and now exists everywhere—even in "peripheral" nations (Mol, 2003: 50). Such reform efforts of the 1970s and 1980s produced greater awareness of environmental problems and cultural change, but only marginal improvements (if any) in the actual reduction of the environmental impacts of modern economies or rapaciously growing consumption patterns. Neo-Malthusian and environmental concerns continued, but social institutions remained largely unchanged and failed to deliver reforms in any meaningful way. In fact, in June 2004, an update of *The Limits to Growth* was published by the same authors with new data and a new sense of urgency after the passage of 30 years (Meadows et al., 2004). Indeed, the LG ecological model, often combined with neo-Marxian political economy assumptions, was the soil from which environmental sociology grew, and continues to inform its dominant modes of theorizing and empirical analysis (Dunlap and VanLiere, 1984; Schnaiberg, 1980).

**LIMITS OF GROWTH: MEASURES, EVIDENCE, AND CRITICISMS**    In a famous attempt to capture the relationship between growing population, consumption, and environmental impacts, biologist Paul Ehrlich and energy scientist John Holdren created the $I = PAT$ equation. They argued that the impact ($I$) of any population or nation upon its environment is a product of its population ($P$), its level of affluence ($A$), and the damage done by particular technologies ($T$) (Holdren and Ehrlich, 1974). Thus:

$$I = P \times A \times T$$

This is an elegantly simple way of illustrating different dimensions of environmental impact as functions of the number of people, the amount of goods (resources) they consume, and the technologies they use to produce those goods. The relative weights of these are subject to debate, but it is methodologically useful for scientific research because it is possible to develop quantitative summary measures for each term of the formula (Dunlap, 1992: 464).

Population size and growth rates are obvious indicators for $P$. For $A$, you could use measures of per capita gross domestic product, or per capita consumption of selected goods (copper, meat, steel, timber, cars, plastics, etc.), and for $T$, per capita kWh of electricity, or some other energy measure of economic productivity. $A$ models inequality more broadly, and $T$ models a measurable item of material culture, but implies nonmaterial culture (including beliefs, world views, and values) more broadly considered. $I$ can be measured as hectares of eroded lands or deforestation, depleted ocean fish, pollution, $CO_2$ emissions, etc. Tom Dietz emphasized that it is $PA$ that matters, not just growth in population alone. Considering the human environmental impact, it is useful to think of *biospheric equivalent persons* (*BEP*) who account for the per capita impact rather than just growing numbers of people ($BEP = AT/P$). While India or China will contribute much more to future world population growth, every American, Canadian, or German baby will have a vastly greater per capita environmental impact over a lifetime. If we worry about soil erosion, declining biodiversity, greenhouse emissions, and the like, we should worry more about the per capita impact of North Americans and Europeans, rather than only the numbers of Indians or Chinese (Dietz, 1996/1997).

Although useful as a heuristic notion, the IPAT (and its derivatives noted above) is of limited use in hypothesis testing, since it is an accounting equation that must balance by definition. So balanced, it assumes *a priori* that the effects of P, A, and T on I are completely proportional. To address this limitation, York, Dietz, and Rosa reformulated the IPAT equation in a stochastic form, and studied the interaction of these variables on a sample of nations. They termed this STIRPAT for <u>ST</u>ochastic estimate of <u>I</u>mpacts by <u>R</u>egression on <u>P</u>opulation, <u>A</u>ffluence, and <u>T</u>echnology (2004). Empirical analyses using STIRPAT focused on cross-national analyses of the driving forces of environmental degradation, particularly demographic and economic factors (Dietz and Rosa, 1994). The most striking finding from their research program that spanned more than a decade was that population size is a persistent major factor influencing the scale of national environmental impacts of all kinds. It is not, however, merely a reaffirmation of neo-Malthusian thinking. After controlling for population size, they found dramatic inequality among nations, with wealthy core nations consuming the bulk of the world's resources and emitting the bulk of the world's wastes. National impacts increased proportionately with affluence, providing little support for the "environmental Kuznets curve" hypothesis or Ecological Modernization theory (discussed subsequently) (Rosa and Dietz, 2004; York et al., 2003a, b).

Ecological economist Mathis Wackernagel and his colleagues developed more widely known evidence supporting LG by measuring what they called the human *ecological footprint*—at both the household and national levels (Wackernagel et al., 1996, 1999, 2000, 2002; ecological footprint Web sites). The ecological footprint is the biologically productive land and water required to produce the resources consumed and to assimilate the wastes generated by a given human population. It is an aggregate measure that reflects the fact that land is a basis for the three functional benefits provided to humans by the biophysical environment: living space, source of resources, and sink for wastes (York et al., 2003a: 282). An advantage of this method is that it does not require researchers to know specifically what each consumed resource is used for, and can capture indirect effects of consumption that are difficult to measure. In mathematical terms, *consumption* = [production + imports] − exports (Wackernagel et al., 2000).

The earth's total biocapacity per capita for humans was calculated at about 2.1 hectares—not accounting for the other animals on the planet. That is, nations with ecological footprints at or below 2.1 hectares per capita could be replicated by all nations without threatening long-term sustainability (if there were no further population growth). Remarkably, national-level footprints range from 0.35 hectares to 16 hectares per capita, indicating significant overuse of natural resources—or overshoot (Wackernagel et al., 2000, 2002). Examples of recent per capita ecological footprints are 12.2 for the United States, 6.3 for Germany, 1.8 for China, and 0.6 (among the lowest) for Bangladesh (Wackernagel et al., 2000). The total global footprint can temporarily exceed the available productive land areas because some resources are being extracted faster than they are being replenished (e.g., forest products). Furthermore, the footprint includes the amount of land necessary to absorb $CO_2$ emissions, which is accumulating in the atmosphere (York et al., 2003a: 282).

Jorgenson framed the "ecological footprint" issue in a cross-national way, arguing that a nation's position in the world-system shapes the size of its per capita ecological footprint. He hypothesized that the ecological footprints of core nations would be highest and peripheral nations would be lowest, and his study of a sample of 208 nations confirmed that. The position of a nation in the world-system, when combined with the indirect effects of other variables hypothesized to increase consumption (domestic inequality, urbanization, and the literacy rate), explained 77% of the variation in a nation's per capita ecological footprint (2003). Note the importance of the other variables considered: Both urbanization and high literacy rates signify higher consumption and the "cultural ideology of consumerism/consumption"; thus as with the STIRPAT research, the size of the ecological footprint is not a simple function of population or gross national product (GNP) (Clapp, 2002).

Besides IPAT, STIRPAT, and Ecological Footprint measures, there is a fourth empirical research tradition supporting the LG model that needs brief mention. That is materials flow analysis (MFA) first developed by Ayres and Kneese (1968). While the policy implications in Meadows et al. in the Club of Rome report amounted to the claim that economic growth would have to be stalled so as not to exceed the earth's carrying capacity, Ayres and Kneese's diagnosis was more subtle. According to them, it was not economic growth as such that mattered but the growth in human societies' *material throughput* that mattered. In other words, if one could find a way to reduce the amount of material input, economic growth could continue. Their conclusion using MFA to study "society's metabolism"concludes that population and technology seem to dominate over affluence as far as environmental impact is concerned, and that both the IPAT and Kuznets models fail to take into account the intricate interdependencies *among* different socio-economic systems, and create a too optimistic image of "dematerialization" in affluent industrial countries (I will return to the notion of dematerialization and its limitations in the next chapter) (Fischer-Kowalski and Weiz, 1999; Fischer-Kowalski and Amann, 2001).

Critics of the LG perspective note that it depends on the notion of a fixed and finite biospheric carrying capacity that humans risk "overshooting," and that it minimizes "elasticities of substitution" produced by technological innovation. As previously noted, rigorous examination of the notion of a finite carrying capacity suggests that it may have important rhetorical uses, but is less useful as an analytic tool for science (Cohen, 1995). Critics, both popular and scholarly, never tire of pointing out that the environmental apocalypse never arrived on schedule. For instance, neo-Malthusian Paul Ehrlich predicted that most of mankind would be starving by 1975. In fact, while about 30% of humans around the world suffered from traditional malnutrition in the 1960s, by the late 1990s that figure had dropped worldwide to about 19% (Buttel, 2000b).

## Ecological Modernization: Prosperity While Protecting the Environment

There is a radically different point of view, suggested by neoclassical economists, environmental economists, and some (mainly European) sociologists. They acknowledged that growth and modernity has produced environmental problems, but that further economic development could solve such problems rather than add to them. Environmental quality is assumed to be a "luxury good," affordable and of interest mainly to affluent societies. When requisite affluent levels are reached, public concern, pressure from NGOs, and environmental state policies will make the mitigation of environmental problems cost-effective, and lead businesses to invest in environmental protection (e.g., "green technologies"). This hypothesized relationship, known as the environmental Kuznets curve, was named after economist Simon Kuznets (1955), who demonstrated a similar relationship between economic development and income inequality—that economic inequality grows in early phases of economic growth but shrinks in later phases as economies "mature." See Nordstrom and Vaughan (1999) for a summary of Kuznets theory and research.

By the late 1980s, environmental sociologist Fred Buttel and colleagues noted that the focus of environmental debates was shifting from "limits to growth" to "global change" (1990), in other words, the "environmental dimensions of globalization processes" (Mol, 2003: 55). In 1987, the World Commission on Environment and Development advocated a global ethic and reforms directed at sustainable development. Indeed, *sustainable development* became the rhetorical unifying slogan of the times. Even having many critics, the language of sustainable development has entered contemporary discourses and retains currency across a remarkably broad swath of the political spectrum. This new emphasis was stimulated by accumulating evidence of a slowdown of environmental disruptions, and a decline in energy intensity in many of the most developed nations, such as Germany, the Netherlands, Japan, the United States, and Scandinavian nations. Some saw this as signaling the beginnings of delinking or decoupling material flows from economic flows, and diverse signs of the reform of modern institutions to be less destructive of the human subsistence base.

Called *ecological modernization* (EM), it was theorized first in West Europe, particularly in Germany, the Netherlands, and the United Kingdom. It can be described as a less deterministic sociological rendition of the ideas of neoclassical economists, and is similar but not identical to other strands of sociological theory about the evolution of modern societies, such as post materialism (Ingelhart, 1990), reflexive modernization (Beck, 1995; Giddens, 1991), and the emergence of a "world civil society" (Frank et al., 2000). EM is more popularly known by a variety of names, including ecoefficiency, clean production, industrial ecology, natural capitalism, restorative technology, the natural step, design for the environment, and the next industrial revolution (Brown, 2001; Collins and Porras, 2002; Daily and Ellison, 2002; Daly and Cobb, 1989; Hawken et al., 2000; McDonough and Braungart, 2002; Prugh et al., 2000).

**ECOLOGICAL MODERNIZATION PROCESSES**    Let me be more specific. Some processes by which EM works would include:

- *Biomimicry,* restructuring an industrial economy to resemble an ecosystem with recycling and feedback loops—and minimizing linear processes of production and consumption that connect extractive sources and waste sinks.
- *Cogeneration,* or using the waste material of one industrial process as the "feedstock" of another (like using the heat generated by a factory to produce electricity for many uses). Industrial engineers are experimenting with "low emissions" industrial parks, whose tenants constitute an industrial ecosystem in which one company will feed upon the nontoxic and useful wastes of another.
- *Radically increased resource productivity,* which slows the depletion of natural resources and lowers pollution, toxicity, and—often—produces more jobs. Nearly all environmental and much social harm flows from wasteful use of natural and human resources. It means that for each unit of output, there will be progressively fewer environmental resources required. Consumer appliances, for instance, use far less material than they did in the 1970s, but it is worth noting that such "dematerialization" is often cancelled by increased consumption or growth by investment in other infrastructures.
- *A service and flow economy* is emerging, where instead of being made and sold, goods are leased to consumers, serviced, and recycled (or remanufactured) by producers. A service and flow economy is being tried for industrial equipment, office copy machines, commercial carpets, and even automobiles. Corporations committed to EM (by any of its names) include big names, like Monsanto, 3M, DuPont, Duracell, and Johnson & Johnson. By practicing the three R's—reduce, reuse, recycle—they have reduced their environmental impacts, saved money, and received welcome publicity (Cunningham et al., 2005: 514).
- *Incentive shifting* like changes in taxes, markets, or government subsidies can counter many of the "perverse subsidies" that create ecological damage. Such incentive shifts do not increase taxes, but reduce some taxes (like income taxes) while increasing others (such as taxes on fossil fuel burning, the generation of garbage and toxic wastes, or the use of pesticides). Virtually every European Union nation is experimenting with such tax and subsidy shifts, with some real gains to show for it (Roodman, 2000: 138–139).

EM does not imply a diminution of human well-being, as many allege about proposed LG reforms. Rather, EM means "re-rationalizing the division of labor of modern industrialism" to be less ecologically destructive, and to internalize costs and impacts that are currently externalized (Mol and Sonnenfeld, 2000). Illustrations of EM come from diverse places, and are manifest at different levels. Some involve political policy change (as in the case of European incentive shifting), others involve subpolitical institutional (e.g., corporate) change, and other examples involve cultural and behavioral change through the operation of collective action and social movements (Mol, 2003).

**ECOLOGICAL MODERNIZATION: EVIDENCE AND CRITICISMS**   Most rigorous contemporary social science empirical research has supported the LG and ecological footprint notions discussed earlier. Yet research supportive of EM has emerged—several dozen studies, predominantly case studies on the energy and related economic sectors in industrialized nations, but also in Southeast Asia (Mol, 2003: 57). While important for an in-depth understanding of particular cases, critics argued that this is a weakness, since most EM research is not based on systematic measures of probability samples of nations, and that they demonstrate more about institutional change and symbols of hope rather than measurable environmental damage (Buttel, 2000a: 118; York et al., 2003b). But several studies partly address these problems. Fisher (2004) and Fisher and Freudenburg (2004) examined predictors of $CO_2$ as an indicator of global warming. They studied a sample (N = 30) of industrial (OECD) nations for whom such data were available. Like other researchers, they used population growth and GDP as causal variables that might predict greenhouse emission production, but applied a more finely grained set of control variables in their multivariate regression equations, while other studies used mainly summary control measures.

In Fisher and Freudenburg's research, the variables most predictive of $CO_2$ production included industrial waste in 1998, percent change in energy consumption 1980–1997, and motor vehicle travel per capita 1997 ($R^2$ = .722). All of these declined in recent years, and were obviously the kinds of energy efficiency variables specified by EM. Significantly, when they were introduced as control variables, GDP per capita—a major LG variable— "did not prove to have significant effects on $CO_2$ in *any* of the multivariate analyses" [emphasis in the original] (Fisher and Freudenburg, 2004: 177). This is a case of EM having an effect on ecological conditions (not just institutional change); and since the variables in question were related to state policy, the researchers understood this as an instance where the environmental state has *substantive* rather than merely *symbolic* consequences.

Subsequent research suggests possibilities for efficiencies of the sort that the EM perspective envisions by examining the notion of the "treadmill of production" (Freudenburg, 2005, 2006). It does not question that economic growth in the United States is broadly connected with environmental degradation, but asks whether such degradation is inherent in capitalist (even "late capitalist") modes of production for all firms proportionately across the American economy. If so, environmental damage would be broadly evident across most sectors and firms in the U.S. economy. Freudenburg examined toxic wastes from the 2,039 firms in 1993 that reported handling toxic wastes on their Toxic Release Inventory (TRI), required by the government. He found that 60% of all industrial emissions can be traced to just two industrial sectors—chemicals and primary metals. Within that small sector, which accounted for about 4% of the GNP, just two firms (DuPont and Freeport-McMoran) accounted for 14% of the all toxic releases in the nation, and one facility (Freeport McMoran's IMC-Agrico of St. James, Louisiana) alone accounted for 4.55% of the nation's over 2.8 billion pounds of toxic emissions in 1993 (2005: 20–21). The treadmill of production may be intrinsic to capitalist firms, but that generalization cloaks the enormous differences among them and the *disproportionality* of their impacts on the environment. While certainly not definitive proof of the validity of EM, it suggests that much of the economy has a potential for the greater efficiencies and lower environmental impact as envisioned by EM theorists. For similar research analyzing the impact of urban recycling in North America, see Scheinberg (2003).

You can also find support for both LG and EM in other sectors of contemporary economies, such as agriculture and food. Making a case for LG would emphasize the overuse of water and soil erosion; agricultural disruption of natural habitats that destroys biodiversity; monoculture production of highly "technified" crops with agrichemicals, nitrates, and organic endocrine disrupters that find their way into water tables and the human body; and the growing depletion of ocean fisheries. Most of these topics were discussed in Chapters Two and Five. But other observations could support EM. Efficiencies are apparent in water use, and have reduced per-acre water use in the United States. Surprisingly, the total amount of water used has remained virtually unchanged since the 1970s, but during the same period irrigated acreage increased by 20% (Perry, 2004: 2A). Soil erosion slowed in its biggest historical drop ever, protected by the Conservation Reserve Program (CRP) and its successors in the 1985 Farm Bill, which encouraged the conversion of fragile farmland into grassland or trees. While industrialized agriculture captures headlines, Chapter Five noted the spread of "agroecological" practices among America's farmers as well as the proliferation of natural foods, and outdoor "farmers' markets" where people buy fresh foods from local producers. Vegetarian menus are a menu choice available everywhere now, quite different from earlier decades. At retail stores, "natural" or organic foods are now the fastest-growing shelf space (even though still relatively small markets at high prices!). Chapter Five also mentioned similar cases of growing agroecology in other nations, including some LDCs like Cuba, China, Korea, and Sri Lanka (Halweil, 2000; Harper, 2005).

## Understanding the Controversy

Having described two different views of human–environmental futures with very different implications for sustainability, let me examine them in tandem. I think that the weight of the best evidence so far suggests that LG does indeed capture the dominant trend in human–environment relations, which is moving slowly and inexorably in an unsustainable direction. Or, paraphrasing York and his colleagues, total environmental impacts generally increase steadily with economic development, but not quite proportionally due to improvements in efficiency (2003a: 281). Understandably, social scientists have always depended more on evidence about "measures of central tendency" than variance and outliers. I think the most serious criticism of EM is that it has not adequately distinguished between *efficiency* and *total resource consumption*. This problem has been termed the "Jevons paradox," after the nineteenth-century British engineer Jevons, who observed that increases in the efficiency of coal use did not lead to decreases in total coal consumption, because greater efficiency made coal more attractive to investors ([1865], cited in York et al., 2003a). Thus, the dematerialization due to greater efficiencies envisioned by EM is something of an illusion. Critics are right when they suggest that, so far, EM illustrates more about the possibilities of institutional and cultural change than about change in the human impact on the earth's biophysical resources.

That said, it is important to note that there are obvious signs of EM processes in many places and many dimensions of modernization, particularly in "late modernity," that illustrate "reflexive modernization" as understood by Giddens (1991). For the sake of argument, suppose that EM succeeds significantly in MDCs, the main source of its supportive evidence so far. That still leaves most of the world's people in LDCs replicating the kind of modernization and consumption growth that produces environmental overshoot. In spite of some evidence of EM from LDCs, in such countries where modernization has been even modestly successful (e.g., China and India) newly affluent classes are rapaciously adopting Western-style consumerism. But one could also envision a very mixed situation, where EM succeeds in places and at times in both MDCs and

LDCs. LDCs, in fact, are often closer to preindustrial traditions and economies, making it easier for them to create adaptations that approximate EM.

Despite the tenuous state of evidence for EM, when compared with that for the LG, I think the theory deserves more examination and testing around the world but particularly in the United States where some local governments, corporations, and agricultural producers have taken steps in accordance with EM theory, with little support or sympathy from the U.S. federal government (more about this in Chapter Eight). EM theory is rife with possibilities for environmental reforms in the direction of greater sustainability (Dunlap and Marshall, 2006: 31).

So far, however, processes of modernization, growth, and globalization illustrating LG and its pessimistic implications are the "main show," while EM processes are a distinctly visible "sideshow." Analysts use a homely metaphor, familiar to almost everyone, to illustrate—the tortoise and the hare. The hare can run very fast, but does so sporadically, often wasting time and going nowhere, while the tortoise plods along slowly but at a steady pace. Of course, the race is won by the tortoise. As York et al. note, the central question is "whether the hare of institutional and technological transformation can outpace the tortoise of relentless growth" (2003a: 280).

This is not only the opinion of a handful of academic researchers. In the 1990s, a broad consensus among the organized scientific bodies of the world about the importance of attending to the issues of limits and sustainability emerged (Science Advisory Board, U.S. Environmental Protection Agency, 1990: 17; Union of Concerned Scientists, 1992). *Most remarkably,* in 1992 the Royal Society of London and the U.S. National Academy of Sciences, two of the world's most prestigious scientific organizations—neither known for taking extreme stands—issued an unprecedented *joint statement* that "advances in science and technology no longer could be counted on to avoid either irreversible environmental degradation or continued poverty for much of humanity" (1992).

## Promoting More Sustainable Consumption

The LG perspective is not a doomsday scenario, pure and simple; it should be taken as a future we would wish to avoid by more positive possibilities. At this point, you may be wondering exactly how, particularly when consuming "more" is always preferable to stopping growth of consumption. It is so deeply embedded in American culture that the question "How much is enough?" appears unnatural.

EM provides many possibilities for reducing human impact per unit of natural resources, but they need to mean more than the justification for continued consumption on a massive scale (even if done efficiently). Positive change would mean productive efficiencies coupled with real reductions in material consumption. It would involve reining in what environmental sociologist Michael Bell called the *treadmill of consumption,* by which people consume more material without any real gains in human satisfaction or well-being (Bell, 2004: 49).

The idea of reducing consumption and living more gently on the earth is not new. In fact it embodies the teachings of the world's religious traditions that emerged in pre-industrial agrarian societies. See Box 6.1.

Ideas about not desiring wealth recently became a visible social and cultural movement that urged people to adopt lifestyles of *voluntary simplicity* (Elgin, 1982). Similar ideas were popularized in the widely read book, *Small Is Beautiful* by maverick English economist and philosopher E. F. Schumacher (1973). In the 1980s, millions of Americans and Europeans were undertaking voluntary simplicity (Durning, 1992: 137). However, simple living *is* less convenient by many of today's standards. It means simpler habits and appliances (e.g., cooking from scratch

| BOX 6.1 |
| --- |

### Religious Teachings About Desires, Wealth, and Poverty

- **Christian:** "It is easier for a camel to go through the eye of a needle than for a rich man to enter the kingdom of God." (Matthew 19: 23–24)
- **Jewish:** "Give me neither poverty nor riches." (Proverbs: 30: 8)
- **Islamic:** "Poverty is my pride." (Muhammad)
- **Hindu:** "That person who lives completely free from desires, with longing . . . attains peace." (Bhagavad Gita, 11.71)
- **Buddhist:** "Whoever in the world overcomes his selfish cravings, his sorrows fall away from him, like drops of water from a lotus flower." (Dhammapada, 336)
- **Confucian:** "Excess and deficiency are equally at fault." (Confucius, XI. 15)

*Source:* Durning (1992: 144)

rather than eating frozen manufactured convenience or fast foods, clotheslines rather than drying machines, walking, using mass transit, and bicycling more and certainly driving less). Voluntary simplicity would require more forethought and attention to how life is grounded in the seasons and nature. Lowering consumption need not deprive people of goods and services which *they say* really matter, and it may free them to pursue some—conversation, family and community gatherings, theater, music, and spirituality (Durning, 1992: 140–141). Note that voluntary simplicity has little relevance for the poor—they already live in an "involuntary simplicity" of a more malevolent kind.

In fact, relatively few people were willing to *voluntarily* give up the pleasures of "life in the fast lane" for a simpler lifestyle. Such efforts are opposed by powerful and well-financed marketing and media promotions that seek, rather successfully, to increase material consumption—or at least the desire for it. Often people find it hard to integrate simpler lifestyles with the realities of work and hectic family schedules. Many in the MDCs spend more time and energy figuring out how to increase consumption rather than practice material frugality and voluntary simplicity! Yet the idea is more than a passing fad—and much evidence exists that advocacy of the idea of voluntary simplicity was growing again in the late 1990s, and not only (or even mainly) from ecological concerns (Bell, 2004; Cohen, 1995). It is a social (or in this case, cultural) movement of some significance. I will return to this in Chapter Eight.

## Growth, Well-Being, and Happiness

As you read this, you may be thinking, "Voluntary simplicity might help, if enough people adopted that lifestyle, but would I (or we) really be happy if I were more frugal and refrained from consuming all the things and having the conveniences I want?"

*Is there, in fact, a positive relationship between continual economic growth, affluence, and well-being or happiness?* World Bank data show that life expectancy and other objective indicators of a population's health no longer increase once income growth passes a moderate $7,000 to $8,000 per year (in international dollars) per capita. Even more surprising, beyond a certain income level, there is little evidence of improved subjective assessments of well-being or "happiness" (Frey and Stutzer, 2002; Rees, 2002: 258). Between 1957 and 1993, U.S. real per capita

---

**BOX 6.2**

### Why Are Costa Ricans Happy?

A Happy Planet Index (HPI), created in 2008, multiplies years of life expectancy by life satisfaction (as measured by the Gallup Poll and World Values Survey) to obtain "Happy Life Years," which are then divided by pressure on ecosystems as measured by the ecological footprint (Garrigues, 2010). In total 143 countries were ranked. Costa Rica ranked number 1, and the United States ranked number 114.

    Why was Costa Rica at the top? It enjoys a privileged position as a mid-income nation where people have sufficient spare time and abundant interpersonal relations. The country abolished its military in 1948, allowing it to spend more on health and education. There is little difference in life expectancy across income levels, unlike the United States, which has vast differences depending on income, location, race, and other factors. The Costa Rican government's promotion of health and peace extends to its relationship with the planet. In the 1970s, the country began to respond to deforestation by setting aside rainforests in national parks that prohibited some logging. Even so, by 1986 illegal logging, cattle ranching, and development had reduced the country's rainforest from 73% to 21% of the landscape. In 1996, Costa Rica introduced a Payment for Environmental Services Program (PES) for some industries such as oil importers and water bottlers to do business in the other countries, while other businesses contribute via a voluntary carbon offset fee. Such programs have had mixed results, but in connection with a U.N. sponsored tree planting program begun in 2007, the country is once again more than half covered with rainforests. According to the HPI, the average Costa Rican has an ecological footprint one-fourth that of the average person in the United States (Garrigues, 2010:12–15).

---

income doubled. In 1957, 35% of American respondents to a poll by the National Opinion Research Center said they were "very happy." With doubled affluence in 1993, only 32% said the same. Americans are richer, and no happier (Myers and Diener, 1995: 14). Other studies in the United States and elsewhere report the same thing (Schor, 1992). For a comprehensive review, see Lane (2000), whose book is interestingly entitled *The Loss of Happiness in Market Democracies*. Except for the very poor and utterly destitute, the link between increasing wealth and happiness is not at all clear.

    What does seem to affect subjective well-being is *relative* income. Among MDCs, it is not the richest societies that have the best individual and population health or subjective happiness, but rather those within countries with the smaller income gaps between the rich and the poor (Wilkinson, 1996). Another important factor is a sense of control over decisions affecting daily life. Frey and Stutzer (2002) found that the more local autonomy, the more developed local democratic institutions that involve people in politics increase happiness more than does rising income. *Ironically*, growing inequity and greater alienation of people from decision processes affecting their lives are major trends connected with globalization (Rees, 2002: 259).

## MORE SUSTAINABLE SOCIETIES?

Even if we are not living now or moving in the direction of greater sustainability, it is a vision of a desirable future, and it is important to consider what kinds of characteristics more sustainable human sociocultural systems have. What would such sociocultural systems be like? No one can say by what policies such transformations might come about, but such policies should consider

Even though municipal waste is a small fraction of total solid wastes in industrial societies recycling may begin to raise consciousness about a more sustainable world.

their potential to result in political tyranny and to reduce inequality within and among nations. Seeking to avert large-scale social-environmental collapse is supremely important, but the choice of methods is probably as important for many humans as averting the collapse itself. Completely sustainable societies have rarely (ever?) existed since the neolithic revolution, but their broad characteristics are relatively clear as hypothetical or "ideal" types. These would relate to their (1) biological base, (2) population, (3) energy, (4) economic efficiency, (5) social forms, (6) culture, (7) resilience, and (8) inclusion in a world order.

**1.** A more sustainable society would work to conserve and restore its biological base, including fertile soil, grasslands, fisheries, forests, wetlands, freshwater bodies, and water tables. Insofar as possible, a more sustainable society would design agriculture to mimic nature in its diversity and mineral recycling rather than degrading nature with monoculture cultivation and industrial agrochemicals.

**2.** A more sustainable society would dampen population growth and work to stabilize its size. Slowing growth and a more stable population size implies that people have access to contraception and family health care, control resources to alleviate extreme material insecurity, and reduce gender inequality.

**3.** A more sustainable society would gradually minimize or phase out the use of fossil fuels. It would shift to less polluting carbon fuels (like natural gas), but would eventually depend more on energy from a diversity of more renewable energy sources—as feasible by local conditions (Roodman, 1999: 172–173).

**4.** A more sustainable society would work to become economically and environmentally efficient in all senses. It would greatly increase investments in efficient equipment and buildings, and maximize the recycling of materials and wastes. More fundamentally, it would reduce waste in processes of production, packaging, and distribution of goods and services. It would reduce waste by decreasing the material component of goods and services (Frosch and Gallopoulos, 1990; Hawken et al., 2000).

**5.** A more sustainable society would have social forms compatible with these natural, technical, and economic characteristics. Coordinated decentralization and flexible centralization would exist, including entrepreneurialism, small-scale networks, large organizations, and urban life. People would come to understand that small is not always beautiful and large is not always ugly (Lewis, 1994: 254). Sustainable societies would continue to have social restraints on behavior, but tolerance of diversity, social justice, and democratic politics would be valued as necessary to elicit the required responsiveness, cooperation, and coordination of people (Roodman, 1999: 182–185). A more sustainable society would have policies aimed at inhibiting both grinding poverty and redundant material wealth.

**6.** A more sustainable society would require a culture of beliefs, values, and social paradigms that define and legitimize these natural, economic, and social characteristics. Dominant social paradigms that underlie belief and action would change appropriately. The virtues of material sufficiency and frugality would replace the culture of materialism. Western (particularly American!) free-wheeling consumerism could not survive the transition to sustainable societies (Brown et al., 1990: 190). Much of the energy now devoted to consuming goods and accumulating material possessions could be directed at forming richer human relationships, stronger human communities, and greater outlets for artistic and cultural expression.

**7.** A more sustainable society would be *resilient*, meaning the ability of systems to absorb change and still persist (Holling, 1973). Resiliency requires (1) persistence, or the capacity to maintain structure and function when faced with shocks and change (e.g., for a forest to withstand a storm), (2) adaptability, or the collective capacity to learn and adapt to changing conditions to stay within a desired state (e.g., safeguarding water supplies in a dry climate), and (3) transformability, meaning the capacity to innovate and transform in periods of crisis when conditions make the existing system untenable (e.g., turning a financial crisis into opportunities to revitalize local economies) (Pearson, 2008). Resilience is such an important component of sustainability that I will return to it in concluding the next chapter about markets and politics.

**8.** In a world where societies are connected with each other and to a shared global environment, more sustainable societies would be required to cooperate in the negotiation of sustainability—in terms of their different circumstances. A more sustainable society would participate in multinational accords, treaties, and regulatory agencies, and would work to promote a *world of sustainable societies* rather than one of growing inequality and environmental destruction. In a finite world, it would work to balance the requirements for some sort of global regulatory system with desires of national autonomy (Roodman, 1999: 176).

As you can see, I have described the characteristics of more sustainable societies in stark (some would say utopian) terms. But I think that real sustainability may require some approximations of them. Are today's societies anywhere close to being such more sustainable ones? *Obviously not.* Surely sustainability is relative, and may involve change in small, incremental stages. But to be effective over time, they would need to result in dramatic social transformations. Given the difficulties of such social transformations, is it reasonable to think that they have even a chance of happening? That depends on how we think about social change.

### Integrating Perspectives: Agency, Structure, and Time Horizons

Many social scientists are uncomfortable with the lack of coherence among the ensemble of classical perspectives, noted in Chapter One and continuing near the beginning of this chapter. Analysts of historical change have been especially critical of the macrostructural theories—inherited from the nineteenth century—like functionalism and conflict theories, which assumed that social change and the evolution of societies is law-like and predictable. Such perspectives, from which the actions of real people were strangely absent, could not in fact give a very good account of the particulars of actual historical change. Charles Tilly suggested some general features of social change that get beyond some "pernicious assumptions" that entrapped classical theories and still retain a broad focus:

1. Society is a process and undergoes constant change.
2. Change is mostly endogenous (from within), taking the form of self-transformation.
3. The ultimate motor of change is the human agency power of human individuals and collectivities.
4. The direction, goals, and speed of change are contestable among multiple agents and become the arena of conflicts and struggles.
5. Action occurs in the context of encountered structures, which it shapes . . . [and results in] a "dual quality" for both structures and actors.
6. Human interchange of action and structure occurs in time, by means of alternating phases of human agency creativeness and structural determination. (Tilly, 1984; cited in Sztompka, 1993: 200)

This is helpful, but it is still important to sort out the relationship between the forces that drive change and change that actually happens. *First*, there are *actors* or *agents*, meaning individuals, perhaps as members of groups or social movements, who behave and have impulses to behave—intentionally or not—that promote change. Such actors or agents are active within the structures that limit, constrain, or facilitate their impulses and efforts. Smaller groups themselves may become agents for change within larger systems that constrain them. *Second*, there are *systems* or *structures*, composed of abstract "wholes" such as societies, social systems, communities, organizations, cultures, and social institutions. Such systems exhibit repeated patterns or dynamics in the way that they operate or function. For instance, General Motors, the Roman Catholic Church, and the U.S. Congress, all large organizations, have repetitive and somewhat predictable patterns in the ways that they operate that differentiate them from other systems.

Agents and systems are the drivers of change, and carry potentials for change, but *actual change results from the interaction of agents and systems.* That is a reciprocal process: Agents work within systems, sometimes to transform them, and systems constrain or facilitate the efforts of actors. For instance, citizens may work to promote or prevent change, and in doing so, they encounter systems that define the limits of what is possible. You might think that the power is on the side of systems, but there are times and circumstances in which the passions, efforts, and ingenuity of actors succeed in dramatically transforming systems. After World War II, for instance, environmental activists and organizations produced a genuine transformation of the relationship between U.S. society and its natural environment (e.g., soil, air, water, and species diversity). But by 2000, they discovered the necessity of revisiting such arrangements. The actual change outcomes that result from encounters between change agents and systems or established structures are sometimes called *praxis*. That term, which may be strange to you, comes from the Greek root word from which we get the words *practical* and *practice*. It is a dialectical synthesis of what is going on in society and what people are doing. Praxis is the confluence of operating structures and purposely acting agents. It is doubly conditioned, from above by functioning of the wider society and from below by the conduct of individuals and their groups. But, it is not reducible to either. It is the "really real changing reality of the social world" (Sztompka, 1993: 217).

### Time Horizons

Large-scale change outcomes that would result in sustainability are strongly shaped by time horizons from which actors and systems operate. How far into the future they are willing to think and plan depends on their willingness to forgo present benefits for future ones. If actors and collections of people have short time horizons and an orientation toward individuals, they will find it rational to defer the costs of unsustainability (for example) to others and to future generations. If, on the other hand, they have long time horizons and a more social orientation, the most rational action may delay immediate gains by contributing to the collective good, in expectation that both they (or their children) and their communities will benefit in the long run. You can see how important this is: At present, corporations have time horizons from one business quarter to three years, and governments may plan four years in advance, or maybe until the next election. Some individuals and groups may think in terms of 25 to 50 years, or their grandchildren's lives (Passarini, 1998: 64–65). "Anticipations of the future become part of the present, thereby rebounding upon how the future actually develops" (Giddens, 1991: 177–178).

## Conclusion: A Transformation to Sustainability?

*The whole point* of this detour about social change is to consider the likelihood of a transformation to a more sustainable world. Social science perspectives are not useless but have large areas of contingency ("it all depends") in knowing outcomes. Let me address the likelihood of moving toward sustainability by posing a series of rhetorical questions. Is a major transformation on this scale possible? *Quite simply, yes.* Is it probable? *Who knows? Educated guesses vary widely.* Can the purposive actions of humans based on current knowledge shape that process? *Yes.* Are the longer-term outcomes of that process concretely knowable or predictable? *No.* Outcomes of change may be mostly negative, mostly positive, or mixed, *but* (and I think this is important) we are not really trapped in a particular set of societal structures, institutional arrangements, structures of power and domination, consumption dynamics, and so forth, unless we choose to be.

There are, in fact, examples of such massive and purposive social transformations that have taken place rather quickly. In the nineteenth century, feudalism was abandoned in Japan, and slavery was legally outlawed around the world (though extralegal human trafficking continues to exist in various places). The twentieth century saw the

retreat of imperialism and the creation of a United Europe. War provides obvious examples. Given the belief that national survival was at stake during World War II, the U.S. population mobilized and transformed itself in remarkable ways. Equally impressive was the Marshall Plan for reconstructing Europe after the war, and starting in 1947 America spent nearly 3% of its GNP on this huge set of projects for about a decade (Ruckelshaus, 1990: 131–132). More recently the Soviet system collapsed, largely through the action of agents internal to that huge system. Most remarkably, by 1993 the Union of South Africa had transformed itself *peacefully and democratically* from an outrageously brutal and authoritarian racial caste system to a multiparty and multiethnic society with a native African as the popularly elected prime minister. Along with the accelerated economic and technological integration in the world market, we have witnessed the emergence of a whole panoply of multilateral institutions, which attempt to deal with war and peace; international monetary instability (like the IMF, for all of its problems); as well as the growth of scholarly, scientific, cultural, and humanitarian networks on a heretofore unprecedented scale. We have witnessed the emergence of a truly global culture emphasizing democracy, universal human rights, and ecological concern that is quite unprecedented.

While these transformations are unprecedented, they are tentative, and some are embryonic and emerging. None turned out exactly "as intended" and none brought a problem-free world into being. Such illustrations certainly don't of course prove that transformations to greater sustainability will happen. But before these illustrative transitions had occurred, many people, including experts, would have found them highly unlikely or impossible. In the 1980s, there were few articles in political science that said, "Hey, keep an eye on Eastern Europe and the Soviet Union, big change is coming" (Diamond, 2002). In addition, there were many forecasting a probable racial bloodbath in the Union of South Africa. But in the 1990s one morning people woke up and realized that the great socialist experiment was over, and there was a democracy in place in South Africa. These illustrations demonstrate, I think, that such large-scale transformations are possible and often unforeseen.

Not only are massive social transformations possible, but some societies have existed sustainably for thousands of years without collapse. Jared Diamond mentions Java, Tonga, and Tikopia (the latter two are contrary cases to the kind of collapse that happened on Easter Island), and (until 1945) Japan. Today both Germany and Japan have successful reforestation programs, and their forests are expanding rather than shrinking. The Alaskan salmon fishery and the Australian lobster fishery are being sustainably managed. The Dominican Republic, a poor country with an authoritarian history, nevertheless set aside a comprehensive system of protected areas encompassing most of the nation's habitats, making it a rarity in Latin America and the Caribbean (Diamond, 2003: 51; see also Diamond, 2004).

The last part of this book focuses on barriers to and possibilities for greater sustainability. It examines more closely the drivers of change noted in this chapter—the joint operation of (1) systems and structures, with (2) the actions of people as they interact with such systems and structures. That can produce large-scale transformations (praxis). Chapter Seven is about economic markets, politics, and public policy. Chapter Eight examines human agency about the environment, meaning activism, ideology, and the various forms of environmentalism that have emerged.

## Personal Connections

*Questions for Review*

1. Why is "free trade" an important idea and basis for laws in contemporary globalization? How has it been strongly defended and criticized?
2. Large multinational organizations play an important role in globalization. Be able to describe the roles of the World Bank, the International Monetary Fund, and the World Trade Organization. What are some social and environmental reasons why their critics think they are in need of reform?
3. Why do minorities and poor people bear a disproportionate share of the costs of environmental damage? What social justice issues are raised by this fact?
4. What is "green imperialism" and why do some charge that it is being practiced today? Do you agree? How do green imperialism and traditional imperialism differ?
5. What does it mean to say that environmental sustainability involves the "three E's"? What difference does it make for policy to improve sustainability? Which of these would you start with?

6. As formulas for studying environmental impact, what do IPAT and STIRPAT mean? Using these, what factors has research found related to understanding the environmental impact of nations?

7. What is ecological modernization? What are some of its dimensions?

8. What has contemporary research concluded about the relationship between a growing economy, money, and happiness (or well-being)? Why are Costa Ricans so happy?

9. How are the operation of structures and human agency two connected aspects of social change? What would illustrate each?

*Questions for Reflection*

Chapter One raised questions about consumerism in the Personal Connections section as an attempt to help you concretize the very rarefied abstraction of the dominant social paradigm. Here are some questions to help you think about some personal implications of affluence and the consumerist culture that supports it.

1. Consumption in itself is not a problem. Consumption sustains life itself and provides the goods and services that make human life meaningful beyond elementary physical survival. *Consumerism* as a cultural complex is something quite different. It suggests that buying and consuming an ever-increasing supply of things and services will provide security as well as personal happiness and satisfaction. Affluence is an indicator of social power and status. And having the right things (the right makeup, deodorant, or fashionable clothes or autos) is linked to personal and sexual attractiveness. None of the world religions teach that happiness and fulfillment can be achieved through material acquisition and consumption. In fact, most go to pains vehemently to deny this idea. How, then, did we come to buy the consumerist ethos? There are many forces that impel us to do so: our early socialization, wanting to be liked and accepted, our ability to have burning wants in addition to needs, and—oh yes—a multimillion dollar advertising industry that gets us to consume on a grand scale. You might think about how some of these factors have worked in your own life.

2. Here's a quote from Gandhi, leader of the Indian independence movement, and inspirer of much of the thinking embodied in the small-is-beautiful movement: "Civilization, in the real sense of the term, consists not in the multiplication, but in the deliberate and voluntary reduction, of wants." Do you agree with him? Why or why not?

3. Calculate your "ecological footprint." Simple ways of doing that are available. Go to a Web browser and search for **www.myfootprint.org**. That should take you to the Web site developed by Redefining Progress (an organization), and by answering a few elementary questions, it will calculate an ecological footprint for your household. How many worlds would it take to support the world's people if they all lived like you do? Even if there are large error factors built into such calculations (say, 50%), it is a real eye-opener!

## What You Can Do

Here are some hints about living more sustainably ("Greener") for college and university students.

1. Practice the three R's: Reduce, Reuse, and Recycle.

2. Printer and paper use: If possible, print on both sides of the page. Think twice about whether you need a hard copy of a Web page or document—could you bookmark a page or save a file on your computer?

3. Limit your use of disposable products, including cups, plates, and paper napkins. The next time you grab a handful of napkins at your dining hall or in a restaurant, ask yourself whether you really need that many. One might be enough.
4. Use compact fluorescent light bulbs in your dorm room or apartment. They may cost more, but will last longer and save you money.
5. Walk, bike, and limit your car use.
6. Carry a refillable water bottle. No more bottled water.
7. Buy recycled products if you can. This includes paper for printing.
8. Use refillable binders instead of notebooks. Or, go electronic and take notes on your laptop.
9. Buy used clothing and furniture. It is a great way to save money, and good for the environment too.
10. Share your message—get others to "live greener" on campus.

Some of the United States's greenest campuses in 2009 were Arizona State University; Bates College in Lewiston, Maine; College of the Atlantic in Bar Harbor, Maine; Georgia Tech.; and Emory University, Georgia. (Adapted from Rockler-Gladen, 2009).

## Real Goods

There are two "real goods" I want to mention here. Neither are products nor things.

**1.** A healthy skepticism about "green goods." Producers and advertisers got the message about environmentally sophisticated consumers. Not everything that is labeled "green," or environmentally benign, natural, or organic, is. In the United States, about one-fourth of all new products are labeled "ozone friendly, biodegradable, recyclable, compostable, lite, natural, local," or something similar. Sometimes these claims are real, and sometimes they are misleading, a fact recognized by consumers as well as environmental scientists. There has been pressure to label the contents of products and display warnings on labels, but reading the labels of products is usually a confusing experience for consumers who don't have the knowledge to evaluate them as truth claims. Such green deceptions generated counterpressures. In the 1990s, the U.S. Pure Food and Drug Administration required that food producers use standardized labels to make them easier to understand, detailing the additives, caloric, fat, and mineral content of their products (over howls of protest from some industry groups). Environmentalists in the Netherlands and France have attempted to cut away misinformation by introducing a 12-point environmental advertising code in their national legislatures (Durning, 1993: 17–18).

**2.** Public interest groups: Such groups monitor marketing campaigns and advocate advertising and media reforms. You can recognize these groups because they are not connected to a particular industry and usually not to a professional community. They are organizations of civic activation. By no means are all concerned with environmental or health matters; some are animated by social justice, religious, family, or political reform issues. For instance, Action for Children's Television is a Boston-based group that won a victory in late 1990s by getting the U.S. Congress to limit commercials aimed at children. The Australian Consumers' Association attacked junk food ads, calling for a ban or restriction on ads selling unhealthy food to children. In Europe, public interest organizations have been doing the same thing, as has the American Academy of Pediatrics in America. These are optimistic signs, but their effects are often overwhelmed by large, powerful lobbies.

## More Resources

Cohen, J. (1995). *How many people can the earth support?* New York: W. W. Norton.

Edwards, A. (2005). *The sustainability revolution: Portrait of a paradigm shift.* Gabriola Island, British Columbia: New Society Publishers.

Olson, M., and Landsberg, H. (Eds.) (1973). *The no-growth society.* New York: W. W. Norton.

Wackernagel, M., and Rees, W. E. (1996). *Our ecological footprint: Reducing the human impact on earth.* Philadelphia: New Society Publishers.

## Electronic Resources

**http://dir.yahoo.com/society_and_culture/ environment_and_nature/sustainable_development**
Many links related to sustainability and similar topics

**http://www.iied.org/enveco/**
Homepage: International Institute for Environmental Economics, UK; features downloadable papers about poverty, inequality, and environment

**http://www.fordham.edu/halsall/mod/wallerstein. html**
Emanuel Wallerstein on world-systems theory

**http://www.unep.org/unep/products/eeu/eeupub. htm**
European Union, papers about environmental resource accounting and impact assessment

**http://www.sristi.org/**
A nongovernmental organization about sustainable technologies, products, and entrepreneurial opportunities; many links

**http://www.webdirectory.com/sustainable_ development**
Largest Web directory on environmental issues

**http://dmoz.org/society/issues/environment/sustainable_development/**
Open directory project; 234 links about sustainable development

# CHAPTER 7

# Transforming Structures: Markets and Politics

Economic markets shape the environmental impacts of all human activities. They are as diverse as village markets and global markets coordinated by brokers in stock exchanges, like the New York Stock Exchange.

In 1973, when architect Jaime Lerner was appointed mayor of Curitiba, Brazil, it was a sprawling town of 500,000, half full of festering less developed country (LDC) slums (favelas). The *favelas* had many problems, not the least of which was garbage that could not be collected because of narrow or nonexisting streets. Because trucks could not get in, and because the garbage was attracting rodents and disease, Lerner had to come up with a way to get the garbage out. The solution was to pay people for their garbage by placing recycling bags around the *favelas* and by giving tokens to the city's transport system for the separated and therefore recyclable trash. The mayor gave tokens that could be exchanged for food for organic waste, which was taken by farmers and made into fertilizer for their fields. It worked spectacularly. Kids scoured the *favelas* for trash and learned to spot the difference between low-density and high-density polyethylene bottles. The tokens gave poorer citizens the means to get out of the *favelas* to where the jobs were while promoting cleanliness, frugality, and the reclaiming and recycling of waste. The plan was innovative but simple: The money gained from recycling combined with the money saved by not having to take trucks into the narrow streets paid for the tokens. It was a cyclical, waste-equals-food system implemented at the grass roots level (Hawken, 1993: 213–214).

Curitiba is now considered a world landmark in urban development that is ecologically sustainable and socially equitable. It is not a futuristic dream, and has grown into a vibrant Brazilian city of 2.5 million people with a prosperous corporate economy in Brazil and the world market. Bike paths run throughout most of the city, and cars are banned from about 50 blocks in the downtown area. The city uses less energy per person, has less air pollution, greenhouse gas emissions, and traffic congestion than most comparable cities. It recycles 70% of its paper and 60% of its glass, metal, and plastic, which is sorted by households for collection three times a week. Some old buses are used as roving classrooms to teach basic skills to unemployed people, while others operate as daycare centers, free to low-income families. The poor receive free medical, dental, and childcare. In Curitiba almost all households have electricity, drinking water, and trash collection. About 95% of its citizens can read and write, and 83% of adults have at least a high school education. Polls show that 99% of the city's inhabitants would not want to live anywhere else (Cunningham et al., 2005: 494; Miller, 2005: 563). Though not typical of cities in LDCs, or most cities in the United States for that matter, Curitiba demonstrates what is possible. There are numerous U.S. cities attempting to move toward sustainability; the most successful are probably Portland, Oregon, and Chattanooga, Tennessee (the case of Portland is relatively well known; regarding Chattanooga, see Cunningham et al., 2005: 478).

These "city stories" can frame part of the perspective from Chapter Six about agency and structure. This chapter focuses on the transformation of structures, and the next chapter discusses human agency—environmentalism and environmental movements. Both are essential components of a dialectic of social change. More concretely, in this chapter I will examine (1) markets, (2) politics and policy, (3) the potential for structural change, and (4) the global political economy.

## MARKETS

Humans have obvious needs for an incredible variety of goods and services ultimately provided by the resources of the earth. The systems through which such goods and services are distributed that bring investors, producers, sellers, and buyers together are economic *markets*. Think of a city farmers' market or traditional markets in villages around the world in ancient times or in contemporary LDCs. In such markets, people compare quickly and see what the competition is; you can taste a wedge of pear, smell a bunch of roses, or drop an olive on your tongue. You can haggle about prices, compare the quality of goods in different stalls, and, if they are not to your liking, you can walk away. Such pleasures are deeply embedded, richly satisfying, and universally observed (Hawken, 1993: 76). In the longer term, such markets have built-in protections against fraud and misrepresentation. (How many times will you be cheated by the same seller?)

In contemporary society, markets are often not concrete places like traditional markets, but rather abstractions to represent the interaction among the costs of production, the asking price, and the price consumers are willing to pay for goods and services. More simply put, real economic values (prices) are determined by the interplay of supply and demand. Markets are important because they can send realistic signals about the actual economic value of goods and services, the work that you do, and the prices that people are willing to pay for a particular product or service in specific circumstances. So there are specific markets for compact discs, Fords, bushels of wheat, books about environmental issues, and the development of more environmentally benign products. All of these products have prices attached that must be paid (by someone), and they have amounts or levels of benefits that you can get for particular prices. To think otherwise is to be either uninformed or naive.

Because neoclassical economic theory views such markets primarily as structures to allocate values, it emphasizes that many human problems (social and environmental) can be understood as market problems and failures. As noted in earlier chapters, neoclassical economic theory is embedded in a *resource allocation paradigm* of the human world and its problems. The theory argues that producers and consumers respond to changing relative incomes, prices, and external constraints, so that—*if* the market signals are allowed to reach individuals *and* market prices include all the social costs and benefits of individual actions—responses to problems will be rapid and efficient (Stern et al., 1992: 136). It is important to note that the global recession that began in 2008 reduced damage to the environment because it reduced human economic activity that produces environmental impacts. It may have had positive environmental effects, but the human costs of a sudden and dramatic world recession had devastating human consequences, in terms of lost income, jobs, and human well-being!

But it is important to note that the theory of the "perfect market" is a tidy abstraction that is useful as an approximation device and a policy tool. Its conditions are often *not* met in the real world. Economic growth and profits "unbalance" the market, and many human social and environmental problems result from *market failures* (Casten, 2009).

## Market Failures

One reason that markets don't always work is because all resources are not owned or used in the same manner. In some types of resource arenas, markets do not work efficiently to send the kinds of real signals just mentioned. Such resource arenas fall into three categories: (1) there are *private-property resources,* which can be owned and used by an individual (or organization). Others can be excluded from using such resources, and since individuals (or organizations) can own them, they are normally more willing to use them frugally and to invest in their upkeep and maintenance. In short, we are more likely to use private property resources sustainably. Private-property resources not only include things like clothing and automobiles, but also privately owned farmland, business equipment, and financial investments. There are (2) *common-property resources,* to which people have virtually free and unrestricted access. They are not owned by individuals; therefore, few real economic costs exist for individuals (or organizations) overusing them, and few incentives exist to manage them or pay for their upkeep. Many resources illustrate common-property resources: air, rivers, groundwater, international waters, and all the chemical and biological resources that they contain. Somewhere in between private- and common-property resources are (3) *public-property resources.* These are jointly owned by all people of a country, state, or local community, and are managed by a government or public agency. National and state forests, wildlife refuges, beaches, coastal waters, parks, and rangelands are examples of public-property resources restricted from private ownership. Social institutions can also be understood as public property resources, and in the United States they include such things as fire protection, public education, military security, highway systems, and prisons. Obviously people use (or participate in) all these public-property resources, but governments have the exclusive rights to regulate their use. Precisely how much and what needs are met through private-property and public-property resource pools change among societies in terms of different cultural, legal, and political traditions.

This distinction among kinds of resources is an important one for understanding the environmental consequences of economic processes because there are problems particular to common-property and public-property resource arenas. Air and rivers have been polluted, water tables drawn down, international fishing grounds depleted. Because they are controlled by the governments or international agencies and subject to pressures from powerful interest groups, rights of access to timber, grazing land, minerals, and energy resources are often "priced" far below what they would be if they were private-property resources. Individuals following their "rational" best interests often results in a social and collective disaster, and a powerful commons social dilemma. Zoologist Garret Hardin popularized the notion of environmental commons problems as the *tragedy of the commons* (1968). Because social traditions and laws often allow free access, he observed that pastureland owned in common was often overgrazed, compared to private land. The same principle applies to polluting the atmosphere or overfishing the oceans. In short, commons problems produce market failures because of the lack of clearly defined private property rights that leaves no one with any incentives to prevent environmental degradation. Some analysts understand the tragedy of the commons as so powerful and pervasive that it is like a "law" of the natural world. I think this is misleading, and will return to this notion.

**OTHER SOURCES OF MARKET FAILURE**    Commons problems represent a generic source of market failure. But others exist. *First,* I mentioned the problem of *externalities* in earlier chapters, meaning that someone must pay the "full costs of production and consumption," but they are not calculated into the existing market price. Individuals not involved in buying or selling a good or service may nevertheless be affected. Pollution affects people and other species generally as it flows downstream or drifts in the wind, not just the industries that produce it, or the consumers of products. As noted in Chapter Four, the full diplomatic, foreign aid, and military costs of keeping crude oil flowing "through the pipelines" are not calculated into the costs of each gallon of gasoline in the United States. The costs of decommissioning a nuclear power plant (which has about a 40-year life span or less) could be prorated into your electric rates but probably aren't. Externalities may be a substantial hidden "tax" on you or others in the future. *Second,* for understandable reasons, governments often impede or supersede the market by providing price regulations, subsidies, or by creating a *quasicommon* (public-property resource) from what *could* be privately owned. Examples include the oil depletion allowances and artificially cheap access given to public lands to ranchers and lumber industries. In Western parts of the United States, water rights are defined in a way that precludes the emergence of realistic water markets. *Third, cost accounting problems* exist. Markets may not send real signals about complete values/costs because of the difficulty and costs of collecting information about the net value of something that considers its costs to all impacted producers, consumers, and nonconsumers. The accounting problem is particularly intense when we face a dilemma of consuming something now or saving for the future. Because of constant price inflation, neoclassical economists usually "discount" future values and argue that consuming it now is of greater economic value (Gardner and Stern, 2002: 100; Roodman, 1999; Rubenstein, 1995).

## Market Incentives: Environmentally Perverse or Not?

You need to understand the powerful and pervasive ways that government interventions distort markets. They actively encourage public and private decisions that stimulate unsustainable resource use and environmental degradation. Evidence for this is overwhelming. Such interventions flow from the understandable efforts of powerful economic groups and firms to get government leaders to provide protection from the unalloyed discipline of the market and from the desire of politicians to keep people working and prices low. For instance, virtually the entire food cycle in North America, Western Europe, and Japan attracts huge subsidies, amounting to about 30% of farm income, as well as others for irrigation water, and agrochemicals (Halweil, 2003:96). They encourage farmers to occupy marginal lands; clear forests; and encourage profligate use of pesticides, fertilizers, and aquifer water. Such perverse subsidies now total about $850 billion, or about 2.5% of the global economy and create a huge economic incentive for environmental destruction (Myers and Kent, 2001: 188).

But, economic subsidies are not always environmentally "perverse." Some countries have begun reducing environmentally harmful subsidies. Japan, France, and Belgium have phased out coal subsidies. Germany cut its coal subsidies in half between 1989 and 2002, and plans to phase them out by 2018. China cut its coal subsidies by about 73% and has imposed a tax on high-sulfur coal. New Zealand has eliminated virtually all of its agricultural subsidies. Governments could phase in subsidies and tax breaks for pollution prevention, sustainable agriculture, water use, energy conservation, and renewable energy (Miller and Spoolman, 2009: 621). In 2010, some (both broadly and within the Obama administration) were talking about using market incentives and the power of governments to increase the potential for jobs and income from environmentally oriented industries (like producing and installing wind turbines, retrofitting doors, windows, and insulating homes and offices). These incentives will involve difficult new tradeoffs, not unlike those of the past that often had had perverse environmental consequences. The argument is not that subsidies and market incentives are always wrong, but that they could be gradually transformed to serve a positive role for living sustainably.

## Transforming Markets and Consumer Behavior: Green Taxes and Buying Green

How could markets and buying things be reformed to produce a more sustainable economy and society? One idea would be to invert the old system of taxes and subsidies to internalize the full costs of doing business and reassign them to the marketplace where they belong. Doing this would create an economy where business firms prosper by being responsible, both socially and environmentally. In other words, they prosper by competing to be more ecological not because it is the right thing to do, but because it squares with the bottom line of profitability. A common proposal to do this is to shift present taxes on income and payroll to *green taxes*. Governments could gradually and incrementally (not suddenly) decrease taxes on income, savings, and investments ("goods") and increase them on energy and resource use, on polluting emissions to land, air, and water, and on products with a high environmental impact ("bads"). It is important that the purpose of green taxes should *not* be to increase total government revenues (they should be revenue-neutral). Their purpose should be to provide all participants in markets with accurate information about full costs and to undo the perverse distortions produced by the relentless pursuit of low prices. Taxes could then have an environmentally positive impact on consumption patterns and on the cost structure of industry without adding to the overall tax burden on industry and society. Green tax shifts could be graduated so as not to impose an overproportionate burden on low-income people, who gain less by lowering income and investment taxes but still consume at market prices. The purpose of imposing green taxes is to give people and companies positive incentives to avoid them, as they now seek to avoid earning and income taxes. Markets would send different kinds of signals (Hawken, 1993: 167–171; Miller and Spoolman, 2009: 622–623; Speth, 2008: 100–125).

A tax on the carbon content of fuels would give consumers incentives to switch to fuels that produce less pollution or greenhouse gases and would give producers reason to invest in energy efficiency. Besides addressing concerns about global warming, there would be other benefits. I hasten to reemphasize that energy green taxes need to be incremental. If they should go up overnight (as in effect they did during the oil boycotts of the 1970s), they would cause inflation and economic and social chaos. But, phased in over a longer time (20 years), producers and consumers would have time to adapt, plan, and reinvent.

A second idea about transforming markets and consumer behavior is *buying green*. Green consumerism has considerable potential, but only if consumers have adequate information, are insistent and willing to pay a bit more, and have strong government backing. Consumers could insist that the production of goods and services be done in a more environmentally friendly way, and there are provisions for the recycling and reuse of consumer products. When the consumer is finished with a T.V., fridge, or computer, the manufacturer should take it back and see that it is reused, recycled, or disposed of with less damage to the environment. In Europe and Japan, for instance, some "extended producers responsibility laws" require that products be returned to producers "cradle to cradle," which has the effect of encouraging producers to think about reuse of materials from the onset of production.

There is some evidence that American consumers are changing. By 2006, the proportion who were willing to pay more for environmentally benign goods had grown, as did the market for hybrid cars, compact fluorescent light bulbs, and organic foods. Yet, despite these gains, "green" remained a small share of all markets and consumer interests (Speth, 2008: 150–162). There are a number of limitations on the greening of consumption. *First,* greener consumption may be overwhelmed by the growth of consumerism. *Second,* a "rebound effect" may occur when savings— for instance in efficiency and utility bills—get spent in ways that undermine them—like keeping one's house warmer or buying more appliances. *Third,* it suggests that individual consumer choices are the problem, when control of these choices is constrained and shaped by institutions and political forces, which can be changed only by collective citizen action rather than by individual consumer behavior. *Finally,* there is an enormous potential for "greenwashing" that manipulates consumers and perverts the process. It is common that advertising, public relations campaigns, and professional marketers are working hard figuring out how to sell more and more green products.

With all of these problems, just what *are* the long-term potentials for green products and consumerism? Possibly quite large—if government supports it powerfully with clear mandatory requirements uniformly and fairly applied to all. It could, however, be quite small if government stays on the sidelines and counts on major change from the voluntary consumer choices of individuals. With all of the problems of green consumerism, there is another, more fundamental area for action—*reducing consumption.* That is difficult, because consumption can be stimulating, empowering, relaxing, and rewarding. However, as the discussion in Chapter Six about affluence and happiness illustrated, and other research amply documents, market-based consumption is *not* tightly coupled with human welfare or life satisfaction. The bad news is that hyperconsumption is an aspiration, even an addiction, of people around the world, and reducing it would be difficult, but we are not trapped by any means (Speth, 2008: Chap. 6, 153–160).

Eating locally grown food is an important way to reduce people's carbon footprint.

## New Measures of Economic and Social Progress

The economic health of nations is usually measured in terms of changes in the total value of all goods and services bought, a measure called the gross national product (GNP). Economists also use the GNP per capita, which is the GNP divided by the number of people in the population. Such statistical means can be misleading because of the vast inequality that exists among people. Sometimes they use a measure called the gross domestic product (GDP), which factors out the value of imported goods and services. These measures are relatively easy to record and measure, and their *growth* is often taken as a measure of the social as well as economic well-being of a nation. But they are not adequate measures of human well-being. They treat all goods and services as being alike, regardless of externalities, or whether made producing healthful food, treating sick people made ill by pollution, or cleaning up the damage from massive oil spills or nuclear power disasters. They are not, in fact, good measures of social well-being and do not differentiate between goods produced under safe and remunerative labor conditions from those produced under exploitive and hazardous ones. They tell you nothing about the actual distribution of the value of goods and services among individuals or groups within a nation.

To change this, a U.S. NGO, Redefining Progress, created a *genuine progress indicator* (GPI) that adds ignored sectors like unpaid childcare and volunteer work and subtracts uncounted economic costs like traffic, pollution, and crime. In 2004, their calculations showed that the GPI at $4.4 trillion, compared with a GDP of $10.8 trillion, implying that well over half of the economic activity in the United States was unsustainable and did not contribute to genuine progress (Talberth, 2008). Most widely used, the United Nations created a *human development index* (HDI), which combines economic and social indicators to estimate the average quality of life in a country. Measured on a scale from 0 to 1, the HDI aggregates (1) life expectancy at birth, (2) literacy rates, and (3) real GDP per person, based on data that is easily obtainable for most of the world's nations. U.N. analysts rank nations and give them standardized scores.

None of these alternative indicators of economic, social, and environmental well-being is beyond question. What they include for environmental and social costs is notoriously difficult to price. Another barrier to their adoption, I think, is that some interest groups would not *want* presently externalized costs incorporated into routine measures of socioeconomic reporting precisely because they would highlight the human and environmental costs of "business as usual." For instance, poor but overmilitarized nations often object to the HDI.

## Rational-Choice and Human–Environment Problems

These economic arguments have a common theoretical thread that is broader than neoclassical economic theory. A wide variety of scholars from diverse disciplines such as behavioral psychology, economics, political science, sociology, and policy studies created a genuinely transdisciplinary perspective on human behavior, now called *rational-choice theory* (Coleman, 1990; Ritzer, 2010). In this view, humans are rational choice makers. Economic theory argues that they choose economic goods and services in terms of how much they cost and how badly they need them. But rational choice theory argues that—far beyond economic purchases—people make reasoned *social choices*, based on experienced costs and benefits, about all manner of things. These include, for instance, which member of the opposite—or the same—sex is most attractive, whether to maintain a social relationship or let it erode, and whether to see a therapist about your problems or deal with them yourself. Rational-choice theory argues that we choose things that have high benefits relative to their costs. When you say, "I don't really have a choice," what that means is that you think the costs are too high to make a choice. It is not that anyone believes that individuals go around like cost accountants, meticulously calculating the exact numerical costs and benefits of all manner of choices. The assertion is rather that in some more vague but real sense, humans adapt to life by trying to minimize costs and maximize benefits. Some costs and benefits may be given in nature, but others are shaped by culture and perceptions. They may be symbolic as well as material. (People value social honor and spiritual rewards.) Rational choices need not operate in the short term. Over time, we develop a sense of what are roughly fair exchanges of goods, favors, or obligations to each.

Thus, the human cause of environmental degradation is that we get the benefits of unsustainable consumption, but the costs are often invisible or work in such a delayed time frame that we don't take them into account. Furthermore, rational-choice theory argues that many of the change strategies of environmental movements are precisely the wrong ones to produce significant behavior change. The way to avert ecological disaster is not to persuade people to give up their selfish habits for the common good (often for the benefit of generations yet unborn). Typically, appeals are made in terms of sacrifice, selflessness, and moral shame. A more effective strategy is to tap a durable human propensity for thinking mainly of short-term self-interest. Moral appeals to "be good" do not work very well in the absence of real incentives. We should think about "saving the commons" by privatizing it (so the argument goes). Real cooperation, this perspective argues, builds up trust from experience with small-scale tit-for-tat exchanges, not from moral exhortation. The most illustrative case in point of ignoring these powerful mainsprings of human motivation is the fate of the Soviet Union, which tried to make a commons of all economic goods (and administer them "morally"). That turned out to be an environmental, social, and political disaster. External costs are somebody else's business, and we can go for "free rides" on commons resources. Or, so we think.

Most people are aware of environmental problems and agree abstractly with the idea of developing a sustainable society, but the thorny problem is transforming our behavior and the way social systems operate. Rational-choice perspectives suggest that instead of urging us to be "good," we transform incentive systems in economic markets and social life to send concrete signals that make self-interest consistent with what is desirable so that people get real rewards for being good. That is the real logic underlying all of those proposals I discussed. It is a powerful and compelling argument based on an undoubtedly protean dynamic of human behavior. I think it is also slippery and can be misleading. Let me tell you why I think so.

## Markets Alone Are Not *"the"* Answer

All of the preceding ideas about internalizing environmental costs, privatizing the commons, and creating quasimarkets from common property resources imply that our problems are a variety of market failures and the prescription is to get markets functioning like they should. Neoclassical economists and more conservative political thinkers are so enamored with market solutions that they believe that the answer to most human and environmental problems is simply to unhook markets from any undue intervention and just let the market work (DiLorenzo, 1993). That is an attractive but a deeply flawed idea. Problems are deeper than market failures, and even fully functioning markets will not, by themselves, solve our problems.

There are at least four recognized limitations of markets. *First*, markets treat as equal worth (without value judgments) all dollar values, regardless of whether generated by cleaning up toxic wastes; producing nuclear missiles; or producing housing, food, or humanly enriching art. Whether a product was made by well-trained workers in a safe environment or by underpaid labor of unhealthy workers or unhealthy children carries no weight and often misrepresents societal preferences by making the less appropriately produced item less expensive. Markets don't care about these things. But people do.

*Second*, goods that are valued by nonparticipants in formal markets are systematically underpriced. What is the dollar value of a living tree? Usually it is the price at which dead timber can be sold in a market. But what of its value to the person who values it for protecting his or her nearby land from being flooded? Or the person who values it because he or she just likes to look at it, or enjoys its shade? The combined net worth of the tree for all these people may be well above its market price as lumber. But, barring some cooperative arrangement that incorporates the needs of all those who value the tree, cutting the tree and selling it on the market means that the market will have operated in a way that did not optimally represent its value to all those who valued it.

*Third*, markets gauge the real value of resources or products only in present actual exchanges. All other attempts to internalize prices or create quasimarkets from common property resources are *shadow prices*, determined in some speculative way by some expert, planner, administrator, or bureaucrat. They are speculative administered prices. Take, for instance, the common practice of discounting future values. Because of inflation and technological innovation, future values are discounted by some percentage for every year that a resource is conserved. This process conflicts with long-term sustainability and reduces the rights of future generations to near zero (Stern et al., 1992: 86).

A *fourth* limitation of markets has often been noted by those on the political left. Markets may create economic efficiency, narrowly defined, but as they operate over time without some sort of nonmarket restraints, they generate *vast* systems of social inequality that themselves represent significant (but normally externalized) *social costs that affect human welfare and even markets themselves.* The evidence for this effect is overwhelming both within and between nations, as documented in Chapter Six. Some opposition to the creation of quasimarkets of tradeable emission permits from common-pool resources is on exactly these grounds. Rich firms or nations would have the resources to pay surcharges or buy emission permits from poorer firms or nations (who would be under routine pressure to sell them cheaply). Either way, the rich could still afford to pollute, and real reduction would be accomplished on the backs of the poor. In sum, these problems with markets mean that for all their virtues, they do not price all things effectively and do not price many things that people care about.

Pure market strategies have a broader limitation. Some in free-market nations, especially Americans and neoclassical economists in particular, tend to view markets as somehow natural and real systems that arise spontaneously among all people regardless of their differences. Markets seem almost like a part of nature. In contrast, politics and culture are viewed as more obviously socially constructed, arbitrary, whimsical—and often irrational. The GNP is taken as real. The other measures of social and economic progress are seen as arbitrary. Furthermore, when the word *market* is appended to the technical term *economy*, we have the satisfying feeling that we are dealing with forces in the world that function properly without government interference. We think of vast global markets organized by banks and multinational corporations as simply projections of the elemental reality of village markets—even though the scale and connections among market participants is something vastly different and the feedback signals about economic and social value are much more nebulous, abstract, and manipulable.

In fact, markets are no more natural than politics and culture, whether traditional face-to-face or the world market economy. There never has been, nor could ever be, a market that operates beyond the contexts and constraints of politics and culture. The traditional village market was consigned to a specific place in the town, and it was conducted on certain days—assigned by cultural tradition. And even traditional markets were protected from marauders, and local constables or soldiers of the local mandarin, caliph, or duke guaranteed orderly commerce. Certainly in contemporary national and international markets, there is really no such thing as a completely free-functioning market, unconstrained by political regulation or culture. In the global marketplace, every nation expects its government to try to create favorable terms of trade for national firms and products. Even so, as Chapter Six noted, the World Trade Organization is working toward a relatively free global trade system. It is emerging, not because of the "natural operation of markets" themselves, but because of painful and laborious negotiations, between politicians, bureaucrats, and corporate representatives. These efforts are fraught with compromises and opposition. Like politics and culture, markets are social constructions of reality.

*Why do I so belabor this point?* Because, if you look again at the market strategies for dealing with environmental problems discussed earlier (green taxes, privatizing the commons, and creating quasimarkets with tradable emission permits), they all require *political action* to reengineer markets that deliver different signals to producers and consumers. It is *not* a case of going from a regulated market to a free one, but of moving from today's environmentally perverse interventions to a new set of less damaging ones. That is *politically* a tough nut to crack!

It is all well and good to talk about energy taxes, but what politician in an energy-producing state is going to vote for higher taxes on energy? What senator from Wyoming is going to vote to end subsidies like cheap permits for ranchers to graze their animals on public lands (often destroying them)? The principle of rational-choice theory still holds: Politicians operate in different political resource markets (electoral votes and campaign contributions). As discussed in Chapter One, the complex division of labor and occupational specialization in industrial societies produce a *quasispeciation*, which means that different economic groups benefit and bear costs very differently, even in the same physical environment. But rational choice can be broadly as well as narrowly defined. The fact that for many goods, like TVs or electronic appliances,

German consumers are obliged by law to pay a small tax to recycle them, and retailers and manufactures are legally obliged to take them back for proper disposal, recycling, or remanufacture, says more about the influence of the Green political party and German culture than markets per se. Such costs save more in the costs of externalities than in the small costs they add to economic transactions. In 2005 and 2006, the U.S. media were full of reports that in places environmental activists and ranchers were finding common ground in promoting the sustainable use of rangelands in the Western United States rather than defining each other as archenemies. So it is one thing to talk about creating a green economy that makes doing good consistent with doing well: The premise, I think, is sound. Changing market incentives can change behavior. But changing market incentives means looking squarely in the face of politics.

## POLITICS AND POLICY

Like markets, political institutions are also concerned with resource allocation. The classic definition of politics is the process of deciding who gets what, when, and how. But although rational choice theory might understand politics as involving merely a different sort of market (with influence for sale), that is at least partly misleading. Politics involves the mobilization of power to allocate resources for an ostensible collective good and is justified by whether or not it produces public and collective benefits. Markets, on the other hand, are justified in terms of whether or not they produce private gain.

As recently as the late nineteenth century, the American state was a government of "courts and parties" in which conservative congresses blocked attempts to fashion a stronger role for federal intervention in private property prerogatives. But as unregulated modernization proceeded, many of its consequences produced aggrieved constituencies. These include farmers, workers, the elderly, and victims of bank and consumer fraud. The degradation of natural resources also became widely viewed as caused by unregulated private use and profit making. Reformers agitated for protection from monopolistic railroads, banks, and farm machinery firms; middle-class reformers called "progressives" agitated for regulation of banking, finance, food and drugs, and the protection of workers, children, and the elderly, and also for protection of natural resources (as in the conservation movement, discussed earlier). There can be little doubt that the mobilization of public and environmental movements and pressure groups (discussed in Chapter Eight) helped to create the "environmental regulatory state." That, found in the United States and many other nations, illustrates what Max Weber meant by extending rationality and the importance of "managers" in Western democracies (Humphrey et al., 2002: 275; see also Chapter One). But the regulatory state attempts to achieve environmental regulation and management in a variety of ways.

### Strategies for Public Policy

Governments attempt to manage or change behavior by *public policy.* But that is a broad umbrella that encompasses an enormous diversity of agents and modalities that governments use. Let me note some different policy options that governments use and their relevance to environmental problems. Four broad strategies exist by which public policy attempts to produce change. Dunlap described these as different kinds of fixes for environmental problems that involve using public policy to change technology, behavior, ideas, and laws (1992).

*First,* and most often identified as a solution for problems, are *technological fixes.* They include, for instance, more efficient auto engines with emission control devices that use less fuel and pollute less, engineering highways and synchronizing traffic lights to reduce auto accidents, better street lights or burglar alarms to discourage crime, insulating your house to cut your fuel bill, genetic breeding of more productive seed hybrids, biotechnology, and so forth. The list of technological proposals to address problems seems endless. Public policy can stimulate the adoption of new technology in a variety of ways, such as public investment, subsidies, tax policies, or regulatory mandates.

*Second,* in *behavioral fixes,* public policy provides incentives to get us to behave differently. These are (supposedly) more difficult than technological fixes, which require no behavioral modifications. Examples of behavior fixes include getting people to eat lower on the food chain (for ecological and health reasons); use condoms; stop smoking; wear sweaters; turn down thermostats in the winter; install attic fans and use air conditioners less in the summer; and walk, bike, carpool, or use public transportation as alternatives to driving. Whereas technology requires investment, behavioral changes typically require incentives (or penalties). We are not on new ground: This was the whole point of the rational choice perspective developed earlier as well as of the findings about research on energy conservation in Chapter Four.

*Third* are *cognitive fixes* that attempt to create awareness of problems in people's minds. The assumption is that if you change people's minds, they will change their behavior. Cognitive fixes often rely on public education and media campaigns. Cases in point are energy conservation ads telling people "Don't be fuelish," or recycling ads reminding us that "If you're not recycling, you are throwing it all away." The appeal of cognitive fixes is that they rely on voluntary change and are compatible with norms of personal freedom. Unfortunately, there is very little evidence that such strategies work in isolation from others. Even so, the importance of cognitive change as part of more comprehensive policy change strategies is often underrated.

*Fourth* are *legal fixes* that mandate change through laws and regulations rather than incentives, subsidies, or persuasion. Examples include federal speed limits on interstate highways and

A sign on a polluted (oil stained) beach in the United Kingdom warns recreationers.

requirements to remove lead from gasoline, install antipollution devices, or recycle beverage containers or household or industrial wastes. Actually, the first two strategies (technological, behavioral) can be pursued by regulatory or nonregulatory means. Regulatory strategies can be very effective, but they are unpopular in a society that views government regulation negatively. They require great political will, or at least effective mobilization and interest group coalitions, to enact and enforce (Dunlap, 1992). It is a truism among policy scholars that the most effective strategies for change produced by public policy combine all four approaches. In other words, change could be promoted by simultaneously providing better technical means, changing people's minds, providing material incentives, and using regulatory restrictions or targets.

## Policy and the Economic Production Cycle

Policy strategies can apply to different domains of social behavior (as the fixes just described), but policy can also be applied at three different stages of the economic production cycle. *First,* the familiar downstream or "end-of-the-pipe" interventions work after consumption has taken place. Clean air standards, antipollution measures, and recycling are examples. Such end-of-the-economic-cycle strategies obviously work and are, so far, the way most environmental legislation works, by penalties, pollution standards, or providing incentives. Between 1975 and 1995, the world doubled the volume of paper recycled, while the market for air pollution equipment grew to 2% of the *world* GDP, easily outclassing the aerospace industry and approaching the significance of the chemical industry (Matoon, 1998; Renner, 1998). Such strategies are useful, but they do nothing to reduce unsustainable consumption. In people's minds, they may even constitute a rationale for consuming more! *Second,* midstream strategies reduce consumption and not only encourage frugality with trash and effluents, but also include the behavioral changes already noted and industries that use cogeneration processes. *Third,* policy interventions work upstream early in the production process itself, either to make production more environmentally benign or to reduce waste and materials in the production process. The standout example of this in the United States is the engineering of more energy-efficient products, ranging from dishwashers to automobiles. Products that require less packaging are other examples.

History is part of the reason most policy attention has been given to downstream interventions that deal with pollution and toxic emissions. Environmental consciousness in the 1960s focused mainly on pollutants. Awareness of consumption and resource use issues came later, but there are reasons beyond history. Midstream and upstream policies mean intervening in the economy in more fundamental ways than just cleaning up pollution. They mean altering production technologies, consumption patterns, or both. And real upstream policies shift the burden of change from consumers to producers. This is particularly difficult in a political system where producers have more clout than consumers. Even though reducing pollution and waste by end-of-the-pipe controls or recycling is often costly, reducing it through resource efficiency is usually profitable. Again, doing well can be combined with doing good. As you might guess, it was probably politically easier to focus on end-of-the-pipe policies. They provided the comforting illusion that we can go on consuming as we like, as long as we clean up the messes.

## Policy and Social Structure

Political scientist Theodore Lowi worked over decades to develop a framework depicting how public policy articulates with social structure in different ways, and he distinguished between *constituent* and *regulatory policies* (1964, 1972, 1979). Constituent policies provide benefits to particular constituents, clients, or publics, as illustrated by providing tax incentives for the lumber or oil industry. Environmental constituent policies would be those that provide subsidies for solar power for residents of the sunny Southwest or "gasohol" fuel that benefits primarily those who live in corn-growing regions. Even when they regulate, constituent policies are often—grudgingly—welcomed by particular constituent groups and industries as necessary to police their deviants. Examples include the Securities Exchange Commission, which polices the stock market against securities fraud. In the Great Plains states, state legislatures considered enabling legislation to regulate ("meter") water use from the Ogallala aquifer in order to conserve water supplies. While such policies are still embryonic and not very effective, they have met with scattered and surprisingly little opposition from dryland farmers. Constituent policies are politically easy. If they involve subsidies or tax concessions, they are enthusiastically welcomed. If they involve regulation, they may be grudgingly welcomed as a necessary collective security measure for an interest group or industry.

In contrast to constituent policies, true regulatory policies are another matter. *Regulatory policies* attempt to control behavior across a broad spectrum of constituent groups, industries, and economic processes. Related to environmental matters, early legislation from the 1960s that established broad air and water pollution standards are examples of such regulatory policies. Since the 1872 national policies, including some broad regulatory ones, were enacted to protect many environments and ecosystems as noted by Table 7.1.

Virtually all of the legislation shown in Table 7.1 yielded important results, protecting wilderness, forests, and sensitive habitats, and making progress in air and water pollution control and workplace health and safety. When enacted, most of these laws were very controversial among different interest groups. Notice how many environmental regulations were passed in the 1960s and 1970s, and that no major environmental law has been passed since the 1990s. Why do you think that is so?

## Politics and the Limits of Policy

The fragility of regulatory policy is that it tends to devolve into constituent policy through the capture of legislation and enforcement. *Constituent policy* often triggers conflict between *different* constituent groups, meaning that environmental policy often becomes mired in *politics*—the contentious processes of deciding who gets what, when, and how. Emphasizing that policy is embedded in politics underscores faulty technocratic assumptions that often dominate discussions of public policy: that we can simply devise rational, feasible, and cost-effective market interventions and incentive systems that get us to behave properly—and simply enact them. In a pig's eye we can! Not without getting the politics right first.

Political institutions and cultures in different nations are not alike, and the policy process works differently in various nations. In the United States, the constitutional separation of powers provides corporations and nongovernmental organizations (NGOs) with greater opportunities to shape policy through lobbying, litigation, and the judicial system. The more centralized political systems of Japan and France limit participation of citizens' action groups in the political process. While citizens of other more developed countries (MDCs) are likely to have stronger political party affiliations than Americans, they are less likely to join environmental organizations and other NGOs, and are less likely to be connected to policy debates. Environmental policy is relatively centralized at the national level in Great Britain, Japan, and France, but is administered primarily by regional and local governments in Germany (Brickman et al., 1985).

Noted earlier, some European nations have taken a substantial lead in improving human–environment connections. That is where notions of ecological modernization (EM)

| **TABLE 7.1** | Major Environmental Laws of the United States, 1872–1992 |
|---|---|

| | |
|---|---|
| 1872 | Mining Act |
| 1935 | Soil Conservation Act |
| 1963 | Clean Air Act (1965, 1970, 1977, 1990 Amendments) |
| 1964 | Wilderness Act |
| 1965 | Federal Water Pollution Control Act (Clean Water Act) (1972 Amendment) |
| 1968 | Wild and Scenic Rivers Act |
| 1969 | National Environmental Policy Act |
| 1972 | Federal Pesticides Control Act |
| | Marine Protection, Research, and Sanctuaries Act |
| | Marine Mammal Protection Act |
| | Coastal Zone Management Act |
| 1973 | Endangered Species Act (1982, 1985, 1988 Amendments) |
| 1974 | Safe Drinking Water Act (1984 and 1996 Amendments) |
| 1975 | Resource Conservation and Recovery Act (RCRA) |
| | Federal Land Policy Management Act |
| | National Forest Management Act |
| 1976 | Clean Water Act (CWA) |
| | Surface Mining Reclamation Act |
| | Toxic Substances Control Act (TOSCA) |
| | National Forest Management Act |
| 1977 | Soil and Water Conservation Act |
| 1980 | Comprehensive Environment Response, Compensation, and Liability Act (Superfund) |
| | Fish and Wildlife Conservation Act (Nongame Act) |
| 1984 | Hazardous and Solid Waste Amendments (RCRA Amendments) |
| 1987 | Water Quality Act (CWA Amendments) |
| 1988 | Ocean Dumping Acts of 1988 |
| 1990 | Clean Air Act Amendments of 1990 |
| 1992 | Environmental Justice Act |
| 1992 | Energy Policy Act |

*Sources:* Adapted from W. Cunningham and M. Cunningham, 2010: 32; Miller, 2002: A7; Miller and Spoolman, 2009: 641; Kraft, 2001.

thrive and shape national policies (See Chapter Six). Europeans are the leaders in recycling; in tax and subsidy shifting to promote a greener economy; in promoting alternative energy sources, such as wind and solar power; and in supporting international treaties, such as the Kyoto climate treaty. The reasons for the European lead have to do not only with culture, but also with political structure. For one thing, the American electoral system, with its two-party "winner take all" elections, makes it difficult for reform-oriented groups, factions, and movements to be represented in the executive policy-making process. In Germany, by contrast, parliamentary proportional representation of various electoral parties in the formation of governments provides greater access to the political system for parties and groups committed to social reform (Parkin, 1989). The German and Dutch Green parties, for example, had, in their heyday, political influence out of all proportion to their numbers and resources, which made U.S. environmentalists turn green with envy, so to speak. The Dutch and German "Greens" were never a dominant party, but were important parliamentary coalition members of the ruling coalition from the 1990s to 2004 with the leftist Social Democrats. But there are other differences in addition to formal differences between a two-party presidential system and a multiparty proportional representational system.

It is not news that for congressional and presidential candidates, winning elections in the United States is a very expensive process, and the parties and candidates who raise the most money are likely to win. The average U.S. senator will spend millions campaigning; this requires him or her to raise at least $50,000 per week for 312 weeks (six years). Unless they are personally wealthy and willing to spend their own money (some are), candidates can get this money only from very wealthy individuals or corporations. Thus, the American electoral system has become increasingly driven by the money from corporate political action committees and so-called "soft money" from economic elites. Longworth argues that such a system has strong bias toward *shareholder control,* that is, control by corporations and economic elites. By contrast, other democracies have strong bias for *stakeholder influence,* which give more consideration to the interests of a large array of groups with a stake in the system, such municipalities, labor unions, civic, professional, and regional groups (1998). Western European nations give more consideration to diverse stakeholder interests. The German tradition of "codetermination" specifies that labor, local communities, and corporate interests all be represented in the policy process, in about equal proportions (Weinberg et al., 1998).

In spite of their differences, democracies are capable of delivering systemwide reforms. One can think of such system-wide reforms of American past: the Progressive Reforms of the 1900s that regulated banking, interstate commerce, food safety, and labor relations; the New Deal of the 1930s that established Social Security and a government more active in managing the economy (though it did not end the great depression); or the extension of Civil Rights and the War on Poverty of the 1960s. Probably the last great American reform was the passage of the National Environmental Protection Act of 1969, which established the Environmental Protection Agency (EPA) and gave administrative coherence to the plethora of environmental legislation of the 1960s and 1970s noted in Table 7.1.

The establishment of the EPA signaled the American version of a similar change in many nations, which some have called the creation of an *environmental regulatory state* (Fisher and Freudenburg, 2004). Most nations, now, have environmental regulatory departments at the ministerial level. In America the EPA (and agencies in other nations) did produce substantive improvements, or at least slowed environmental degradation for 40 years, but it did a distinct about-face in the recent decade. The American environmental regulatory state was created in an atmosphere of bipartisan cooperation (under the aegis of Richard Nixon, a moderate Republican president) from the 1970s to the 1980s that does not exist today. In fact, the emergence of shareholder politics (in which the major shareholders are the corporate sponsors of conservative—and anti-environmental—politicians) has meant that the national administration in the first decade of the twenty-first century has attempted to roll back many of the environmental protections enacted in the 1960s and 1970s. Such tendencies were visible during the Clinton years, in which conservative congresses dominated, but really became noticeable during the administrations of George W. Bush, who made only the barest pretense of protecting the environment.

---

### BOX 7.1

### Weakening the Environmental Regulatory State, 2000–2009?

After two terms of office, the George W. Bush administration has compiled a record of a destructive campaign against America's environmental established safeguards. For example, the administration attempted to undermine the Clean Air Act by weakening the new source review program that pushed old polluting industries and power plants to clean up. It tried to narrow the scope of the Clean Water Act by stripping environmental protections from thousands of wetlands and streams. It moved to hobble the Endangered Species Act by eliminating habitat protective programs. While nearly every state warns about the threat of mercury poisoning from the consumption of locally caught fish, the administration promoted a scheme that would dramatically weaken mercury pollution control requirements in the existing clean air law. The administration has turned a blind eye to calls from governments and scientists from around the world to limit global warming emissions, and now stands virtually alone in opposing even the most basic effort to move forward cooperatively. Since the Bush administration began, health warnings to avoid eating locally caught fish have doubled, and completed cleanup of toxic wastes at Superfund sites has fallen by 52%. Civil citations to polluters have dropped by 57%. A Knight-Ridder media analysis of the government's own data shows that Americans face a dirtier environment, while polluters largely get a free pass (Kennedy, 2005; National Resources Defense Council, 2006; Pope and Rauber, 2004). One environmental sociologist quipped that in the past half decade, "Bush policies have done more to damage the environment than all other causes combined—including population growth and rampant consumerism." (Dunlap, 2006a)

---

The administration could not actually dismantle the American "environmental regulatory state," because protecting the environment continued to have a broad popular appeal. But they could subtly change the application of such regulations to be less stringent, which they did systematically.

There is ample data to suggest that these policies have had a significant negative effect on the American environment. Here is a sampler of such evidence:

- After years of consistent decline, the most recent annual inventory of industrial toxic releases shows an increase of 5% in the release of toxic substances to the air, water, and land.
- The EPA reports a 36% increase in annual beach closings due to unsafe water quality since 2001.
- More than half of the total area of the national forests has been degraded by logging, mining, and the 440,000 miles of publicly funded roads that make industrial resource extraction possible (Pope and Rauber, 2004: 121).
- While President Carter appointed a presidential commission to study the Three Mile Island nuclear mishap, the Bush administration never asked or commented about a similar nuclear "near miss" at the Besse-Davis reactor near Toledo, Ohio, in 2001 (Pope and Rauber, 2004: 104–105).
- In 2003, 76% of fish samples from U.S. lakes were found to contain mercury levels unsafe for children three years old, and more than 600,000 newborns may have been exposed to levels of mercury exceeding EPA health standards while still in the womb (National Resources Defense Council, 2006).

These consequences are not only failures of the Bush administration, but in a larger context, the "dirty little secret" about public policy in the United States, known among policy scholars but not often publicly discussed. No national administration or political party in recent decades (probably since the 1970s) has been able to mobilize coalitions to support systemwide reforms like those of the past. Increasingly, American public policy is *retail policy,* that is, constituent policy that addresses the need of particular organized client groups, rather than "wholesale" policy in the public interest (Mans, 1994).

## The Recreancy Theorem—Mistrust of Regulatory Agencies in Complex Societies

A sociological tradition argues that citizens in technically advanced societies become more dependent on their technologies rather than in control of their technologies (Alario and Freudenberg, 2003; Barber, 1983). As Chapter Three (about climate change) argued, risk is socially constructed, and depends not only on technologies but also on social relations that bring them into being. There are whole armies of specialists having the competence to judge (where we may not) and control such risks. In public arenas, there are institutional actors (regulatory bodies) that must be perceived as both *competent* and reasonably *responsible to the interests of citizens* (termed "fiduciary responsibility"). Such regulatory agencies are charged with regulating and controlling (in the public interest), for instance, the safety of the U.S. food system, risks in offshore oil drilling, the risks or pollution and environmental toxins, risks of economic collapse in the investment, and lending practices of large banks and financial institutions. Now think about institutional actors like the Food and Drug Administration, the Department of the Interior, the Environmental Protection Agency, and the Federal Exchange Commission charged with assessing and regulating these risks. Freudenburg found that recreancy (mistrust of competency and fiduciary responsibility of regulators) explained about three times as much public mistrust about the handling of nuclear wastes as did any sociodemographic variable (like age, gender, income or education) or political attribute (like party affiliation or political ideology) (1993). Similarly, researchers found among a large sample of more than 2,000 citizens that mistrust of a wide range of issues about agriculture and the safety of the U.S. food system was shaped more by recreancy than any social or demographic characteristic, and that mistrust of the fiduciary responsibility of the regulators was outweighed by mistrust of the competency of regulatory institutions (Sapp et al., 2009).

If limitations of purely market strategies for environmental policy brought us face to face with politics and flawed regulation in contemporary politics, what could work? Is all lost? *I think not.*

## POSSIBLE LEVERS FOR PROGRESS

In spite of these problems, there are possibilities for positive structural transformation.

## The Environmental State and Regulatory Policy

How could these be reasonable levers for progress, given the federal assault on the environmental state sector and regulatory effectiveness since 2000? Furthermore, some research and many scholars have suggested that the consequences of the environmental state are more symbolic and ideological than real, not only recently, and not only in the United States (Bunker, 1996; Freudenburg and Gramling, 1994; Krogman, 1999; Schnaiberg and Gould, 1994: 53). It is a source of hope, however, that worldwide commitment to environmental protection has generated an environmental regulatory state sector in all MDCs and many LDCs. Even in the United States, the assault on environmental protection must often be hidden and covert, because environmental protection remains a vastly popular theme in American culture. There is also real evidence, often over-looked, that state policy and environmental regulations can also have substantive and real consequences for environmental improvement, or at least slowing negative impacts (See Fisher and Freudenburg, 2004; Gardner and Sampat, 1999; Harper, 2005; Perry, 2004; Scheinberg, 2003).

There is a pervasive assumption both popularly and among many scientists that high levels of environmental degradation, toxic emissions, and polluting industries are necessary for economic growth, jobs, and prosperity. This is particularly assumed true for the chemical and primary metals industries that, in combination, produce 60% of the nation's toxic emissions as measured by their Toxic Release Inventory (TRI) required by the EPA. But those industries produce just 4.2% of the nation's economic output, and just 1.4% of the nation's jobs. Furthermore, a single enterprise (the Magnesium Corporation of America, in Rowley, Utah) has been responsible for over 95% of the measured toxic emissions from that industrial sector (Freudenburg, 2006).

The tendency to see polluting resource industries as providing benefits to "capitalism"—rather than to a relatively small number of capitalists—reflects sloppiness in interpreting relevant data. Instead, available data point to "privileged access" by a small number of producers, which produce a vastly disproportionate share of the nation's toxic emissions. "Contrary to the widespread assumptions that environmental improvement could only be possible if societies are willing to accept significant losses of jobs and economic growth, actual research indicates that significant improvements could be made if a small fraction of all economic actors were to reduce their emissions-per-job ratios simply to 'average levels for their economic sector or for the economy as a whole'" (Freudenburg, 2006: 12, 19).

This is contrary to the widespread assumption that environmentally destructive wastes and pollution are regrettable but necessary in many industries for a growing and prosperous economy, and that regulating them to become more environmentally benign would damage the economy. The reality is that environmentally regulated sectors of the economy have done somewhat *better* in terms of international competitiveness than manufacturing firms in general, and the few modest correlations that exist between pollution and profitability have tended to go in the unexpected direction. In other words, establishments that produced more pollution tended to have lower levels of profit than less heavily polluting establishments, even in industry-specific analyses (Freudenburg, 2006; Repetto, 1995). In fact, when comparing areas of the United States (not just particular sectors) with weak environmental regulations with those with more stringent environmental regulations, the more regulated states and regions have more prosperous economies (Freudenburg, 1991a). Economic prosperity is certainly more complex than a single body of regulations, but such stringent environmental regulations are not spoilers of "good business climates" and, if anything, work to improve it. All of these circumstances suggest a significant potential for using broad regulatory policies connected with the environmental state to control the most egregiously damaging enterprises and regions without damaging the entire economy.

## Ecological Modernization

As a process that reforms existing capitalist economies by radically increasing resource productivity, promoting biomimicry, the emergence of a service and flow economy, and dematerialization, EM has the potential to promote positive environmental change. I will not repeat the discussion of EM in Chapter Six, except to note that it has had a greater impact in Europe than in the United States, and is only a structural piece of the puzzle of positive environmental transformation that would not be effective absent behavioral change. It is, however, a program of economic reform that is becoming clearly understood, and has great potential even though it is nowhere the dominant economic practice. That potential is in some ways evident in segments of the corporate economy; there were corporate policy shifts among some of the largest energy firms like British Petroleum (BP) and Royal Dutch Shell, which broke ranks with other fossil fuel firms to take climate change more seriously. They have invested in growing markets in renewable energy, undoubtedly motivated by future profits. These changes remain, in spite of the scandalous BP Alaskan oil spills of 2006, and the unthinkably huge disaster in offshore oil drilling in the Gulf of Mexico in 2010. In western Canada, the giant logging firm MacMillan Bloedel had been the subject of popular protest and litigation for its clear-cutting logging practices throughout the 1990s. In 2000, "McBlow," as it was commonly called, startled the world and other logging firms when it announced that it was giving up the standard forest industry practice of clear-cutting. That practice would be replaced with selective cutting, leaving trees to check runoff and soil erosion and to provide wildlife habitats to regenerate the forest. In the United States, 56% of the steel produced now comes from scrap. As a result, steel mills built in recent years are no longer located in western Pennsylvania, where coal and iron ore are close, but are scattered around the country—in North Carolina, Nebraska, and California—feeding on local supplies of scrap. The new mills produce steel with less energy and far less pollution than did the old mills producing from virgin iron ore. A similar shift occurred in paper mills, once almost exclusively near forested areas, now often built near cities feeding on local supplies of scrap paper. These illustrations illustrate only the potential of EM, not that it has become the dominant economic practice.

## Community Management of Commons Resources

Sustainable community management of commons resources has been practiced in places for many centuries. Yet, it has only recently been "rediscovered" by social scientists, and this suggests that Hardin's "tragedy of the commons" notion—the assumption that people and groups will *always* overuse common pool resources—is not a "law of nature." Consider some illustrations of sustainable community management of commons resources (CRM). Since the fourteenth century, villagers in Torbel, Switzerland, have practiced rules to manage successfully fragile alpine meadowlands and forests, where cattle were grazed in the summer but not in winter. They decided that alpine lands should belong to the community rather than to private owners. No one was permitted to graze more animals in the summer than they could feed in the winter. Cows were sent to alpine meadows all at once and counted, and trees for harvest were marked once a year by a community forester. To manage viable alpine meadowlands, these rules stood the test of time, population growth, and employment outside the village area (Netting, 1981).

Consider an illustration from the United States. Unlike many fishing grounds in the North Atlantic, lobster fisheries along the central coast of the state of Maine have been sustainably maintained for decades. Fishers in small boats drop small lobster traps (or "pots") into identifiable shoreline harbors, moving to deeper water in the winter to do lobstering. CRM is possible because the state limits the number, size, and sex of lobsters that can be harvested and requires lobstermen to get a license and display a license number prominently on the line connected to each particular pot. But most of the credit goes to the lobstermen themselves. In order to maintain their livelihood, communities of lobstermen developed strong unwritten rules governing assigned territories that were defended against outsiders (Acheson, 1981; Gardner and Stern, 2002: 127–128). Are these cases only unusual exceptions to the tragedy of the commons? *No indeed.*

Political scientist Elinor Ostrom and her colleagues studied CRM and found many successful cases (Ostrom, 1990; see also Baland and Platteau, 1996). She focused on the sustainability of common pool resources that were important for livelihoods and geographically large enough to

| **TABLE 7.2** | Conditions Conducive to Successful Community Resource Management |
|---|---|

I. Resource is controllable locally

    A. Definable boundaries (land more than water, water more than air)

    B. Resources stay within boundaries (plants more than animals, lake fish more than ocean fish)

    C. Local CRM rules can be enforced (higher-level governments recognize local control and help enforce rules)

    D. Changes in resource can be adequately monitored

II. Local resource dependence

    A. Perceptible threat of resource depletion

    B. Difficulty in finding substitutes for local resources

    C. Difficulty or expense attached to leaving area

III. Presence of community

    A. Stable, usually small population

    B. Thick network of social interaction and relationships

    C. Shared norms ("social capital"), especially norms for upholding agreements

    D. Resource users have enough local knowledge of the resource to devise fair and effective rules

(*A* facilitates *B*, and both facilitate *C*. All make it easy to share information and resolve conflicts informally.)

IV. Appropriate rules and procedures

    A. Participatory selection and modification of rules

    B. The group controls monitoring, enforcement, and personnel

    C. Rules emphasize exclusion of *outsiders* and the restraint of *insiders*

    D. Congruence of rules and resources

    E. Rules have built-in incentives for compliance

    F. Graduated, easy-to-administer penalties

*Sources:* Adapted from Ostrom, 1990; Gardner and Stern, 1996: 130.

make it difficult, but not impossible, to exclude individuals from benefitting from their use. Ostrom concluded that successful and sustainable CRM systems depend on the characteristics of (1) the resource, (2) the group using the resource, (3) the rules they develop, and (4) the actions of governments at regional and national levels. See a summary of her findings in Table 7.2.

Ostrom found that the success of CRM also depended on factors beyond local communities, particularly the support of local, regional, and national governments. But government may impede as well as facilitate CRM, particularly if officials accept bribes or political favors to allow some to use more than their share. The United States and the state of California helped regional water users in both of these ways. Water management institutions were "nested institutions," in which smaller private and municipal pumping and distribution agencies were nested in larger county and regional associations. They negotiated agreements to restrict pumping as an alternative to expensive lawsuits over water rights. The state helped with the costs of monitoring the agreements, and treated them as legally binding in state courts. Such *comanagement* is a promising idea in CRM (McCay, 1993).

But in MDCs, few people are dependent on local resources like the fishers, woodcutters, and cattle grazers as in the cases just noted. Global markets ensure that people with cash incomes can almost always escape the pain of local shortages and simply buy from elsewhere.

CRM may thus be contrary to powerful social trends in the twentieth century. The emergence of world markets and the world-system often disrupts local CRM. Globalization has been weakening two of the major conditions in Table 7.2 for effective CRM: (1) local resource dependence and (2) the presence of dense, stable community networks. Family farms and ranches in the United States have been owned by individual proprietors practicing relatively sustainable farm management (and leaving productive land to their children, who would support vibrant rural communities). They have sometimes been displaced by farms owned and managed by remote "outsiders." Such investors often have little interest in sustaining resource productivity beyond the "natural life" of the capital invested (about 10 years). There are two lessons to be drawn from this: (1) Commercial development does not "privatize" the commons so much as it shifts community resource control to outside agents, and (2) CRM can sometimes yield social, environmental, and even economic benefits far exceeding commercial commodification that experts and central government officials recognize (Gardner and Stern, 2002: 145). Indeed, the great service of Ostrom and her colleagues was not to disprove Hardin's "tragedy of the commons" but to contest its universality and to offer a powerful set of counterexamples of conservationist social institutions. The problem of the commons is really a problem of *open access*, but where a common resource is limited to a particular group of users, it may suffer no such degradation (Rose, 2001: 234).

There are advantages and limitations of the practice of CRM. The *advantages* are that CRM

1. Builds on long-standing social traditions.
2. Can internalize externalities.
3. Can be effective over very long periods.
4. Can encourage people to move beyond egoism or selfishness.
5. Has low enforcement costs.
6. Is often the "forgotten" strategy.

But CRM *is limited* because

1. It works best with a limited range of resource types.
2. Social trends often destroy the basis for its successful practice. (Gardner and Stern, 2002: 149–150)

The limitations are serious, indeed. They mean that many world environmental problems are not amenable to CRM and that fewer communities have the necessary skills for practicing CRM. Even with these limitations, CRM has great promise for dealing with certain environmental problems as part of a mix of strategies.

## Tradable Environmental Allowances

"Tradable environmental allowances" (TEAs) are another possible way of holding the exploitation of environmental resources or the production of pollutants to a certain level. As a major alternative to the imposition of green taxes, TEAs require that the government establish a maximum allowable level of exploitation (for forestry, or fishing) or for the production of wastes and pollutants, and auction off permits to producers. The government does not establish prices for such permits; rather, in the auction process, some permits would accrue value while others, of less importance to producers, would decline in value. Enterprises that have permits can use them in current production, bank them for future expansion, or sell them to other firms, as their value accrues. TEAs effectively "ration" access to common pool resources. Applied to emissions control, a permit to produce a certain level of emissions carries an economic incentive to figure out ways to maximize units of production per unit of emission resulting. Applied to exploitation of fisheries, as the estimated "maximum sustainable yield" for orange roughy declines and fewer permits are available, they are "bid up." Fishing of that particular species would halt or slow, as fishers are likely to turn to other, more plentiful, commercially viable catches. Once a quantity limit is specified, the government has no responsibility for finding the right price in a tradable permit system; the market defines the price. With a tax system, the government must find the appropriate tax rate—no small task. Hence, when it is desirable to keep environmental destruction at or below a certain level, TEAs are often more effective than green taxes, which have less certain effects.

The strategy has spread to many different kinds of resources in many nations. In 1999, one survey found 9 applications in air pollution control, 75 applications in fisheries, 3 in managing water resources, 5 in controlling water pollution, and 5 in land use control, and that survey failed to consider many applications (OECD, 1999). In one successful application the Australian government, concerned about overharvesting of lobsters, estimated the sustainable yield of the fishery and then issued permits totaling that amount. Lobstermen could then bid for these permits. The government decided how many lobsters could be taken each year and let the market decide how much the permits were worth. Since this TEA was adopted in 1986, lobster fisheries have stabilized and appear to be operating on a sustainable basis. This strategy has been widely applied to fisheries. It is more successful with species like lobster, which have "local" coastal habitats, than with deep-sea fish, particularly fish that span the fisheries of different nations (such as cod in the North Atlantic).

Perhaps the most ambitious and successful application of a TEA system was the U.S. scheme for reducing sulfur emissions by half from 1990 to 2000. Permits were assigned to some 263 of the more sulfur dioxide–intensive electrical plants operated by 61 electric utilities. These were mostly coal-fired power plants east of the Mississippi River. The result was that sulfur emissions were cut in half between 1990 and 1995, well ahead of schedule (Schmalensee et al., 1998). Interestingly, the cost of doing this was one-tenth of the costs projected by industry, because the market-based strategy motivated companies to reduce emissions in more efficient ways (Miller, 2002: 411). As I noted in Chapter Three, a global TEA system was proposed by the United States as a way to reach the carbon reduction goals of the Kyoto Protocol about greenhouse emissions. But there is no precedent for a TEA system *among* nations.

TEAs are less effective when (1) the transaction costs are high, as in the case of the costs of holding and administering an "auction," and (2) enforcement is ineffective, whereby permit holders who don't get caught may gain more by cheating than staying within the constraints imposed on their permit allocation. These would probably be problems with an international TEA. Moreover, if the purpose is to stimulate a long-term trend, then graduated taxes over time may be more effective. If, for instance, the goal is to reduce carbon emissions worldwide, with higher goals for industrial countries that burn disproportionately large amounts of fossil fuels, then governments could set upper limits at a level appropriate to each country's situation (Brown, 2001: 249).

## Comparing Tradable Environmental Allowances and Community Resource Management

Legal scholar Carol Rose has compared the two strategies for environmental protection (2002). To begin, she notes that CRM systems (or "regimes," to use the legal term) are often of long duration, and likely to be quite old and traditional, while TEA regimes are relatively new. CRM

| **TABLE 7.3** | Comparison of Community Resource Management (CRM) and Tradable Environmental Allowance (TEA) Regimes | |
|---|---|---|

| | **CRMs** | **TEAs** |
|---|---|---|
| Scale | Smaller (unless "nested" or coordinated) | Larger |
| Resource complexity | Complex, interactive | Simple, single focus |
| Practices encouraged | Adaptation, long-term stability, risk sharing | Security of investment, innovation |
| Social structure | Close-knit | Loose, stranger relations |
| Adaptation to shifts in the natural environment | More adaptive | Less adaptive |
| Adaptation to shifts in human demand | Less adaptive | More adaptive |
| Typical resource application | Pollution (putting in . . .) | Extraction (taking out . . .) |
| Relation to commerce | Vulnerable to commerce | Accommodates commerce |

*Source:* Adapted from Rose, 2001: 250.

regimes have their history in European and other property right systems in which an environmental resource is held in common among a community that can easily exclude outsiders, and insiders cannot easily sell their rights to outsiders. Because they apply only to a stable set of "insiders," property rights and duties can be quite complex. By contrast, TEA regimes have their origin in Anglo-American property right systems in which the resource is owned by individuals, likely to be commercially traded from one person to the next or outsiders, and hence are typically simple "off-the-shelf" forms of property, so that buyer and strangers will know what they are getting (2001: 247). Rose summarizes the differences between CRM and TEA regimes as if they were pure (or "ideal") types, though she cautions that reality is more complex. See Table 7.3.

CRM and TEA systems are like mirror images, and you can see why TEA systems have been the dominant idea for modern property rights systems, particularly in a global arena. Yet CRM regimes have some positive features, especially at those points where TEA systems tend to be least effective, particularly in coping with locally dense, complex natural systems like forests or wetlands (Salzman and Ruhl, 2000). Environmental managers are now experimenting with ways to provide state assistance and control for CRM systems. I noted earlier the state of California's efforts to assist local water companies in a "nested" system. Another well-known example is the African nation of Zimbabwe's effort to treat local communities as wildlife "owners." Because local communities will receive revenues from tourism and sport hunting, local community members have the incentives, skills, and knowledge to save animals (or harvest them sustainably) rather than deliver them to poachers (Anderson and Grewell, 1999).

## THE GLOBAL POLITICAL ECONOMY AND THE ENVIRONMENT

This chapter focuses mainly (but not entirely) on the economics and politics of the United States, but world market system and the world-system were discussed in several places (particularly in Chapter Six's discussion of globalization). Let me return briefly to that with reference to economic and political structures. International trade is, of course, much older than self-conscious environmentalism. International trade, for instance, brought pasta to Italy; silk to France; Columbus (and all that came with him) to the Americas; polio vaccine to the world; and Coca-Cola, Marlboros, and Ben and Jerry's ice cream to Moscow and Beijing (Zalke et al., 1993: xiv). Though environmental protection, the way we think of it, is a fairly recent concern, international trade is *much* older.

## Organizations, Treaties, and the Environment

Something as important as the emergence of the world market and world-system of nations was connected with multilateral political and economic organizations, many conferences, and treaties. Chapter Six discussed the formation of the World Bank, the International Monetary Fund, and the World Trade Organization. Large international gatherings of governments, corporations, and a multitude of NGOs were convened by the United Nations in Stockholm, Sweden, in 1972; in Rio de Janiero, Brazil, in 1990; and Johannesburg, South Africa, in 2002. The more recent such global gatherings were attended not only by U.N. member states, but also by representatives from interested human rights, labor, and environmental NGOs. See Box 7.2 for some of the more important U.N. agencies and few private ones dealing with global development and environmental issues (not an exhaustive list!).

The 2002 global gathering was known as the Millennium Development Conference, which established goals (and timetables) to improve global human and environmental problems. About human developmental issues, assessments since the meeting found the world's countries on target to meet goals about the reduction of poverty and child mortality, but not about hunger. They found substantial progress about universal child education and mixed progress about gender equality, maternal healthcare, and HIV/AIDS. Progress toward ensuring environmental sustainability was mixed at best. Assessments demonstrated substantial progress in improving access to clean drinking water, but not about improved sanitation facilities (French, 2007–2009: 108–109).

---

### BOX 7.2

### United Nations and Private Multinational Organizations

The United National Environment Programme (UNEP), the Food and Agricultural Organization (FAO), the World Health Organization (WHO), the United Nations Development Programme (UNDP), and the United Nations Conference on Trade and Development (UNCTAD) are agencies of the United Nations. UNCTAD represents the economic and trade interests of LDCs. The UNEP is a small and underfunded agency compared to older, more well-established ones like the WHO, and while U.N. agencies have international legitimacy compared to many private organizations, they often have overlapping concerns and jurisdictions, or ones only partly concerned with environmental issues. A Commission on Sustainable Development (CSD) was founded to monitor progress (or lack thereof) of the programs initiated at the Stockholm, Rio, and Johannesburg meetings.

The Global Environmental Facility (GEF) is a private organization, funded by donors, which makes grants to LDCs for projects about environmental protection and promoting sustainable livelihoods. The World Conservation Union (ICUN) is a global alliance of biologists, conservationists, and environmentalists primarily concerned with the preservation of biodiversity. It has actively sponsored the development of nature reserves around the world.

## Transnational Corporations (TNCs)

TNCs were mentioned in Chapter Six in connection with globalization and sustainability. They are the structural skein of the world market system and the entities that governments most represent in that system. As you might guess, TNCs have many critics among religious, labor, social justice, and environmental groups. To my knowledge, no TNC has ever initially asked whether the introduction of a product into another nation was a social or ethical good without being pressured to do so. At their outrageous worst, TNCs have promoted pharmaceuticals, pesticides, infant formulas, and contraceptives in LDCs after they had been banned as unsafe in their home country. They have imported vegetables for American tables grown in LDCs and sprayed with banned pesticides—thus completing a circle of toxins. They have brokered the international sale of solid and toxic wastes to cash-strapped nations when rich nations regulated against them. Shipments of toxic industrial and pharmaceutical residues arrived in Africa from Europe, and in Central America, the Caribbean, and Latin America from the United States. Where organized local resistance grew, the governments and corporations involved simply moved such dumping elsewhere.

You could create a large catalogue of TNC human and environmental horror stories, for which case material is abundant. But you should also appreciate the more complex big picture of their impacts. According to Organization for Economic Cooperation and Defense (OECD, including most European Nations and the United States and Canada) in research conducted in 1994, TNCs around the world often paid better than did domestic firms. Nor should you overestimate the extent to which corporations will move *for lower environmental regulations alone.* Labor costs are generally more important as a component of total production costs. In the 1990s, for example, environmental compliance costs of OECD TNCs were about 2% of sales income. A 1991 U.S. government interagency task force study found that in Mexico, "U.S. firms, particularly the larger multinational firms most likely to undertake large investments [in Mexico] often hold subsidiaries to a worldwide standard, usually . . . as high as they must comply with in the U.S." An example is the Ford Motor Company, which applied U.S. environmental practices in its Mexican subsidiary (Lasch, 1994: 55). The benefits and costs of foreign direct investment (FDI) around the world, most of it from TNCs, are quite mixed. They can stimulate economic growth, technology transfers, improve efficiency, and reduce environmental impacts. If investments divert production away from traditional sectors toward goods and services that are polluting, unhealthy, or which promote unsustainable lifestyles, then FDI can have overall negative impacts (Gardiner, 2001). Whether a country benefits from FDI depends largely on the regulatory environment in the host country, which is inadequate in many LDCs.

CAUTION: Citing positive and negative illustrations proves no general case. Whether you consider TNCs in general as irredeemably perverse structures or as potentially progressive, humane, and responsible depends on ideology as well as evidence. My own view is that TNCs are neither the chief causes of evil in the world nor the harbingers of a brave new utopia of some sort. The whole truth is more complex.

## Protesting Globalization: Trouble with the World Trade Organization

While promoting free trade among nations and corporations, the WTO must become involved in environmental issues, as well as global labor and human rights issues. It has therefore become a lightning rod attracting strong anti-globalization, environmental, and human rights protests at its meetings, which have been heavily protected by their host governments and sometimes disbanded. As noted in Chapter Six, the global economy and world-system are permeated with powerful contradictions, suspicions, and intense conflicts of interest. It is not surprising that the major promoter of TNCs in world trade, the WTO, is something of a symbol and lightning rod for anger, fears, and criticism of globalization, because it represents the interests of TNCs. Intensifying conflict rather than harmonious integration emerges when the promises of abundance and better living standards meet the realities of environmental constraints and deterioration, deepening income inequality, and threats to human well-being.

It all came to a head in December 1999 in Seattle, Washington, where the WTO, trade ministers, and corporate representatives were to meet (behind closed doors) and negotiate another round of trade agreements. From America and around the world, a motley collection of people representing diverse interests arrived there—labor groups, environmentalists, human rights advocates, advocates of openness and democracy, and people from LDC nations. They had been mobilizing for more than a year and came to Seattle to demonstrate in the streets. Korean farmers protested trade rules that would flood their nation with cheap American and Canadian wheat and beef. Environmentalists from around the world protested the destruction of nature in the name of trade and profits. American labor unions protested the flight of their jobs in the global search for cheap labor. Advocates of democracy protested the closed nature of discussions about many important issues in which most of the world's communities and people were not represented. Activists opposing exploitive conditions and child labor were there, as were a diverse collection of LDC groups protesting the idea that there should *be* some kinds of minimal labor and occupational safety standards (which would disadvantage whatever economic leverage they had). There were also those who came simply to redeem the antiwar activism of the 1960s. Most of the demonstrators were orderly and disciplined, but some were not, smashing windows and looting stores held to be symbols of the global hegemony of TNCs (especially McDonald's and Starbucks). Confrontation on the streets reflected disagreements among the trade ministers inside the hall (over the same issues and cleavages), and the meeting was terminated early without reaching *any* new agreements. The diversity and effectiveness of the opposition, which derailed and shut down the WTO meeting in Seattle, stunned the world. Similar protests, which became predictable, greeted subsequent WTO meetings, in Genoa, Italy; Qatar; Cancun; and Hong Kong.

## International Treaties and Regimes for Environmental Protection

In spite of many problems and strong antiglobalization protests, environmental protection is becoming institutionalized at a global level, transcending national boundaries. There are now 500 or so international environmental agreements (or "conventions") in effect. About 150 are global treaties, while others are agreements among a more limited set of parties (nations) (Cunningham et al., 2005: 24). Some important ones are shown in Table 7.4.

Such treaties and the organizations that create and enforce them are a part of global culture and institutions that Frank and his colleagues think is an emerging "world society" (2000). That concept is based on two intriguing observations: (1) that in spite of the strikingly diverse cultural origins, the global cultural similarities are increasingly impressive (about, for example, the importance of human rights and environmental protection) and (2) that there exists a level of similarity of structural and organizational forms among governments and NGOs around the world that is far too great to be accidental or explainable in terms of some kind of "functional necessity" (Buttel, 2000c: 117). Frank et al. see global forces at work when, for instance, national parks appear in Nepal, when a chapter of the International Council for Bird Preservation opens in The Gambia (a poor African nation), when Mexico joins the International Whaling Commission, when environmental impact assessments begin in Kuwait, and when Romania

**TABLE 7.4**  Some Important International Treaties

Convention on Biological Diversity 1992 (1993)

Convention on International Trade in Endangered Species of Wild Flora and Fauna 1973 (1987)

Convention on the Conservation of Migratory Species of Wild Animals 1979 (1983)

Basel Convention on the Transboundary Movements of Hazardous Wastes and Their Disposal 1989 (1992)

Vienna Convention for the Protection of the Ozone Layer and Montreal Protocol on Substances that Deplete the Ozone Layer 1985 (1992)

U.N. Framework Convention on Climate Change 1992 (1994)

U.N. Convention to Combat Desertification in Those Countries Experiencing Serious Drought and/or Desertification, Particularly in Africa 1994 (1996)

Convention on Wetlands of International Importance, Especially as Waterfowl Habitat 1971 (1975)

Convention Concerning the Protection of the World Cultural and Natural Heritage 1971 (1975)

U.N. Convention on the Law of the Sea 1982 (1994)

*Source:* W. Cunningham and M. Cunningham, 2010: 533.

founds an Environmental Ministry (Frank et al., 2000: 111). Their studies found that that global institutionalization of environmental protection spreads when

- There are greater and "denser" ties between a nation-state and the world society, in terms of national chapters of all kinds of governmental and NGOs.
- The nation-states have many "receptor sites," meaning domestic scientific and ecology organizations, capable of receiving and interpreting global blueprints for environmental protection.

They concluded that large-scale (regional and global) structural processes and forces promote the spread of institutions and treaties for environmental protection, and that "domestic factors" like national opinion and social movements that promote mobilization are mechanisms of change rather than causes of change (Frank et al., 2000: 111).

In a pointed response, Buttel notes that Frank et al. prematurely dismiss the importance of state-level organizations and social movements for environmental protection. He thinks they ignore a vast literature about the importance of state-level organizations and movements (e.g., Yearly, 1996), and suggests that Frank et al. overemphasize the extent of cultural agreement and consistency in the "world society" and underemphasize the extent of tensions and conflict of environmental protection in a vastly unequal and conflict-prone world. Finally, Buttel notes that in many cases there is little evidence that the global spread of organizational forms and treaties has had positive impacts on environmental quality (2000c). Among many critics, James Gustave Speth, a respected environmental expert from Yale University agrees.

> The current international effort to help the environment simply isn't working. . . . The climate convention is not protecting the climate, the biodiversity convention is not protecting biodiversity, the desertification convention is not preventing desertification, and . . . the law of the sea is not protecting fisheries. [Protection of the world's forests has not even] reached the point of a convention. . . . Global environment problems have gone from bad to worse. The problem is not weak enforcement or weak compliance; it is weak treaties. (2004, cited in Miller, 2005: 623–624)

In response to such critics, Frank et al. respond that some studies note evidence that changes in national and global policies *do* in fact improve environmental quality (Dietz and Kalof, 1992; Roberts, 1996). Furthermore, "populations of various endangered species (elephants, wolves, and tigers) are strong and resurgent. CFC emissions, the culprits behind ozone depletion, have declined precipitously. Polluted rivers and bays throughout the industrial world have improved dramatically. Clearly some regulations, national and international, are working. But the 'holes in the system' are legend. Are policies *effective enough* in restoring or maintaining environmental quality? Certainly not. Are policies *effective at all?* The answer is most likely yes. Even a pockmarked system is better than no system at all" (Frank et al., 2000: 123).

## Conclusion

Moving toward sustainability is unthinkable without utilizing the power of market incentives and public policy, though doing so will challenge our collective wisdom and will. *Resilience* was discussed as an important part of sustainability in Chapter Six. Paradoxically, markets and political policies that use rigid control mechanisms to preserve social-environmental systems can only erode resilience and promote collapse. In contrast, resilience-building management can sustain such systems in the face of surprise, unpredictability, and complexity. It is open and flexible to learning, focusing on slowly changing things that enhance memory, diversity, and the capacity to innovate. It conserves and nurtures diverse elements necessary to adapt to novel, unexpected, and changing circumstances, and increases the range of surprises with which systems can cope (Flint, 2010: 48: Pearson, 2008).

In surveying the structural dimensions of change in this chapter, I have taken you into the heart of several academic controversies. But something was missing from this discussion, namely, the impact of ideas and the power of individuals joining forces to advocate change, apply pressure on government, or change markets by selective buying, or economic boycotts. A close reading would find them, in the protests against the WTO and about "McBlow's" clear cutting of timber in British Columbia. It would also find them in the popular protest about the Exxon Valdez Alaskan oil spill and the widespread agitation over the BP oil drilling disaster in the Gulf of Mexico. This chapter focused on the structural side of the agency–structure dialectic of change outlined at the end of Chapter Six. The next chapter turns to the agency side, in the various forms of "environmentalism."

## Personal Connections

*Questions for Review*

1. Economists believe that markets that deliver realistic signals about values, costs, and scarcities, and that many problems (including environmental ones) are market failures. How so? What are some different ways that market failures can generate environmental problems?
2. What are "externalities," and what is an example of one that affects a human or environmental problem?

3. How could a "carbon tax" address environmental problems like pollution and global warming? Why are they so difficult for politicians to enact?

4. What is "green consumption," and how, if widely accepted, could it produce jobs and address environmental issues? What are some things that could limit or enhance the ability of green consumption to make much difference?

5. What are "upstream," "midstream," and "downstream" (or "end of the pipe") interventions to improve the environment? Provide a real-world illustration of each type.

6. Why did America produce so many *major* environmental reforms in the 1960s and '70s, but none since the 1990s? (Hint: Think about the re-alignments in American politics since the 1960s and '70s.)

7. Most contemporary nations, even poor ones, are also "environmental regulatory states," to one degree or another. What does this mean? What are some illustrations of the successes and failures of environmental regulatory states? What is the "recreancy theorem"?

8. Zoologist Garret Hardin thought that an environmental "tragedy of the commons" was a universal condition, but Elinor Ostrom's research about community resource management found conditions under which it was *not* universal. What were some of these conditions, and how does modernization make management of community resources more difficult?

9. Freudenburg found the relationship between the degree of government regulation of the environment and regional prosperity to be counterintuitive. How so?

10. What factors did Frank and his colleagues think makes it more likely that nations would accept international treaties and institutions that protect the environment?

## *Questions for Reflection*

The rational-choice perspective suggests that you do make choices that maximize benefits and minimize costs. Here are some questions to help explore this in terms of some of the ordinary choices that people make.

1. Earlier I argued that there were some benefits in living close to work. What are some of its costs? What are some costs and benefits of living in the suburbs and driving or commuting miles and miles to work? Include in your considerations not only the dollar costs of transportation or the environmental impacts, but things like the social quality of life in various neighborhoods. Are there places close to where people work that they would not like to live in and would bear large costs to avoid? As you can see, deciding what is a net rational choice is not so simple.

2. Many have noted that convenience meals are very expensive per unit price, wrapped in layers of packaging that took an enormous amount of material and energy to produce, and perhaps laced with fat, sugar, salt, chemicals, preservatives, and dyes that make their nutritional and health value questionable. Even knowing this, are there times when the benefits of eating them outweigh the benefits of healthier food? Consider costs and benefits broadly: money, costs imposed by job routines, family roles, time constraints, and market availability. Alternately, consider the costs and benefits of cooking the way most nutritionists and environmentalists advocate: buying unprocessed food in larger quantities and cooking as much from scratch as possible. To quote Kermit the Frog, "It's not easy being green!"

   Think of your own examples. There are many things you could do to be more environmentally frugal. Why do they seem difficult? It is easy to talk glibly about changing lifestyles, but this is often difficult for us to do, even when we want to. What are some of the reasons why?

3. You can see the complexities of the rational-choice perspective in action. Some argue that regulatory strategies are indeed necessary for environmental protection, occupational and safety standards, health, social justice, and many other concerns. The National Environmental Policy Act, which created the EPA, revolutionized the American way of thinking about regulatory policy. Think about this fact concretely. How has your life been impacted, negatively or positively, by environmental or occupational regulation? Talk to some other people for their perspectives: city officials, university administrators, home-makers, your relatives, or small business owners. You will find that hardly anyone likes such regulations. But how do opinions differ about whether they are necessary or not? What do you think shapes divergent opinions?

## What You Can Do

Environmental careers? As environmental problems proliferate, there will be jobs for people with environmental expertise in government, private nonprofit organizations, and companies. There will be opportunities for people with scientific and engineering backgrounds, but also for people with environmental interests combined with backgrounds in other fields, such as business, policy studies, law, the social sciences, ethics, and journalism. An incredible variety of careers that involve environmental and ecological issues exist. Here are just a few:

- *Scientific fields:*   Environmental health and toxicology, environmental geology, ecol-ogy, chemistry, climatology, biology, air and water quality control, solid waste manage-ment, energy analysis, energy conservation, renewable energy technologies, agronomy, urban and rural land-use planning, atmospheric science
- *Resource and land management careers:*   Sustainable forestry and range management, parks and recreation, fishery and wildlife conservation management, conservation biology
- *Engineering and architecture:*   Environmental eningeering, solid and hazardous waste management, environmental design and architecture, product and appliance engineering
- *Humanities, social sciences, and other fields:*   Environmental law, law enforcement, policy, consulting, social science and communications, risk analysis, risk management, demography (population dynamics), environmental economics, psychology or sociology, environmental communications and journalism, environmental marketing, environ-mental policy, international diplomacy, public relations, activism, lobbying, and envi-ronmental writing and journalism

For help, go to

**www.ecojobs.com/index.php**
A newsletter listing 500 jobs every two weeks in various environmental fields

**www.EcoEmploy.com**
Direct links to jobs in the United States and Canada; job listings, help with résumés

## More Resources

Andrews, R. (1999). *Managing the environment, manag-ing ourselves: A history of American environmental policy.* New Haven, CT: Yale University Press.

Brown, L. (2009). *PLAN B 4.0: Mobilizing to save civi-lization.* New York: W. W. Norton.

Hawken, P., Lovins, A., and Lovins, H. (1999). *Natural capitalism: Creating the next industrial revolution.* New York: Little Brown.

Kraft, M. E. (2001). *Environmental policy and politics* (2nd ed.) New York: Longman.

Maddison, A. (2001). *The world economy: A millenial perspective.* Paris: OECD.

Ostrom, E., Dietz, T., Dolsak, N., Stern, P., Stonich, S., and Weber E. (Eds.) (2002). *The drama of the commons.* Washington, DC: National Academy Press.

Stavins, R. (Ed.) (2000). *Economics of the environment: Selected readings.* (4th ed.). New York: W. W. Norton.

## Electronic Resources

**www.unep.org/unep/products/eeu/eeupub.htm**
European Union, environment and economics, topics, papers

**http://directory.google.com/Top/Society/Issues/Environment/Politics**
Google directory; environment and politics, links, e.g., League of Conservation Voters

# CHAPTER 8

# Environmentalism: Ideology and Collective Action

Children picking up trash on Earth Day, which has become the annual celebration of environmentalism.

Lois Gibbs was a housewife and president of the local neighborhood association of Love Canal, a working-class suburb of Niagara Falls, New York, and she was mad as hell. In the 1970s, she and her neighbors complained to local officials about strange smelly chemicals leaking into their basements, gardens, and storm sewers. Local officials listened but ignored their complaints. Children playing on school grounds and around the old canal got strange chemical burns. The Hooker Plastic and Chemicals Company used the old canal for which the subdivision was named, long deserted by barge traffic, as a dumping ground for toxic chemical wastes. Between 1942 and 1953, the company dumped more than 20,000 metric tons of wastes into the canal, mostly in steel drums. In 1953, the company covered the dump site with clay and topsoil and sold it to the Niagara Falls school board for $1 in a sales agreement that specified that the company would have no future liability for injury or property damage caused by the dump's contents. Eventually an elementary school and housing project with 949 homes were built in the 10-square-block Love Canal area.

Informal health surveys conducted by alarmed residents, led by Lois Gibbs, revealed an unusually high incidence of birth defects; miscarriages; assorted cancers; and nerve, respiratory, and kidney disorders among residents. Again, complaints to local officials had little effect. But continued pressure from local residents led New York State officials to conduct more systematic health and environmental surveys, which confirmed the suspicions of the residents (miscarriages were four times higher than normal). They found that the air, water, and soil of the area, as well as the basements of houses, were badly contaminated with toxic and carcinogenic chemicals. In 1978, the state closed the school and relocated more than 200 families living closest to the dump. After outraged protests from the remaining residents and investigations by the Environmental Protection Agency (EPA), President Jimmy Carter declared Love Canal a federal disaster area and relocated all families who wanted to move. About 45 families remained, unwilling or unable to sell their houses to New York State and move. In 1985, former residents received payments from an out-of-court settlement from Occidental Chemical Corporation (which had bought Hooker in 1968), from the city of Niagara Falls, and from the school board. Payments ranged from $2,000 to $400,000 for claims of injuries ranging from persistent rashes and migraine headaches to severe mental retardation. By 1988, a U.S. District Court ruled that Occidental Chemical must pay cleanup costs and relocation costs, which had reached $250 million, but the company appealed that ruling.

Ironically, the dumpsite was covered with a clay cap and surrounded by a drain system that pumped leaking wastes into a treatment plant. By 1990, the EPA renamed the area Black Creek Village and proposed a sale of the 236 remaining dilapidated houses at 20% below market value. However, several environmental organizations filed a federal complaint against the EPA for failing to conduct a health risk survey before moving people back into the Love Canal area. By that time, Lois Gibbs had founded the Citizens' Clearinghouse for Hazardous Wastes, an organization that has helped more than 7,000 citizens environmental organizations. About the effort to relocate people in the old Love Canal subdivision, she said, "It would be criminal. . . . It isn't a matter of if the dump will leak again, but when" (cited in Miller, 2005: 532).

What does this story illustrate about protecting the environment? Two things. Not changing structures, but the other dimension of social change discussed in Chapter Six: change as the practical outcomes (praxis) of the interaction between the purposive actions of individuals and the structures they encounter. Second, it illustrates grassroots mobilization of people for action at its best: In a setting with longstanding problems, a committed organizer and activist arrives on the scene unburdened with blueprints for change and mobilizes the latent talents of community members. From the beginning the community members controlled the process, but they eventually encountered an expanding web of bureaucrats, experts, and politicians in existing organizations (structures).

This chapter is about collective action and human agency related to transforming human–environment relationships. It is, in other words, about *environmentalism*. Environmentalism is an ideology and collective action (as a collection movements for change). After discussing this briefly, the chapter will focus on three broad topics: (1) the varieties of American environmentalism, both historical and contemporary, (2) global environmentalism, and (3) environmentalism and change, raising the question of how successful it has been.

Environmentalism is both ideology and action. (I am not using the term *ideology* in a negative or pejorative sense, but merely to denote a set of beliefs about desirable action about important human activities and perceived sets of problems. You could similarly talk about the ideologies that surround and justify free markets, political conservatism, democracy, or human rights.) Environmentalism is rooted in the worldviews and cognizes the environments of people, as Chapter One noted. But ideologies are not only abstract beliefs and "models about how the world works." They are beliefs that are used, often quite deliberately, to justify change. Environmentalists have produced a social, economic, and philosophical literature of remarkable breadth, depth, and variety that significantly shapes the political values and agendas—if not the actual operation—of most nations today.

Environmentalism is also purposive action intended to change the way people relate to the environment. It includes individual purposive action, but more significantly, it means the *collective action* of many individuals as they form groups and organizations intended to transform the way communities, companies, and societies impact their environments. In other words, collective action results in environmental social movements. They emerge when problems are defined and framed ideologically to mobilize people in collective action (Snow and Benford, 1988). Successful movements require a number of factors: (1) some scientific support for the validation of claims; (2) the existence of activists (or popularizers) who can "frame" the package for journalists and opinion leaders, (3) media attention that defines the problem as important, and dramatizes its symbolic and visual terms, and (4) the emergence of institutional sponsors who can ensure the legitimacy and continuity of the problem (Hannigan, 1995:55). There is a vast sociological literature about social movements (for useful summaries, see Harper and Leicht, 2007; McAdam and Snow, 2010).

## AMERICAN ENVIRONMENTALISM

You might think that American environmentalism is relatively new, but it was the product of over 100 years of collective action and movement organizations. They involved not only historically specific organizations, but different ways of framing environmental problems and different discourses about them, both among environmental movement activists and in the broader arenas of public discourse (the media and political process). Sociologist Robert Brulle identified eight different environmental discourses that shaped different waves and competing manifestations of environmentalism throughout U.S. history, and following Brulle I describe them summarily, in the approximate chronological order of their emergence—along with illustrative environmental movement organizations (2000).

1. *Preservation (1830s):*   Nature is important to support both the physical and spiritual life of humans, hence the continued existence of wilderness and wildlife undisturbed by human action is necessary (Wilderness Society, Sierra Club).
2. *Conservation (1860s):*   Natural resources should be scientifically managed from a utilitarian perspective to provide for the greatest good for people over the longest period of time (Society of American Foresters).
3. *Wildlife management (1890s):*   The scientific management of ecosystems can ensure stable populations of wildlife, viewed as a crop from which excess populations can be harvested, particularly in recreation and sport (Ducks Unlimited).

4. *Reform environmentalism (1870s, but really flourished in the 1960s):*   Human health is linked to ecosystem conditions like water quality and air pollution. To maintain a healthy human society, ecologically responsible actions are required, which can be developed and implemented through the natural sciences (Environmental Defense Fund).

5. *Environmental justice (1970s):*   Ecological problems exist because of the structure of society and its imperatives, and the benefits of environmental exploitation accrue to the wealthy while the poor and marginal bear most of the costs. Hence, the resolution of environmental problems requires fundamental social change (Citizen's Clearinghouse for Hazardous Waste).

6. *Deep ecology (1980s):*   The richness and diversity of life has intrinsic values, so human life is privileged only to the extent of satisfying basic needs. Maintenance of biodiversity requires decreasing the human impact (Earth First!).

7. *Ecofeminism (1980s):*   Ecosystem abuse is rooted in androcentric ideas and institutions. Relations of complementarity rather than domination are required to resolve conflicts between culture/nature, human/nonhuman, and male/female relationships (World Women in Development and Environment).

8. *Ecospiritualism (1990s):*   Nature is God's creation, and humans have a moral obligation to keep and tend the creation, including biodiversity and unpolluted ecosystems (National Council of Churches, as well as most denominational bodies).

It is important to note another human–environment ideological frame, virtually unchallenged in its domination of American environmental discourse from 1620 until the middle of the nineteenth century, which Brulle terms *manifest destiny.* It is a moral and economic rationale for exploiting natural resources, assuming that nature has no intrinsic value, that human welfare depends on the exploitation and development of nature, and that human inventiveness and technology can transcend any resource problem. In effect, the resources of nature are infinitely abundant for human use (Brulle, 2000: 115). We are not on new ground here. He is talking about what Chapter One described as the dominant Western worldview for human–environment relations in industrial societies. It provided a rationale for the European conquest and development of the North American continent, and it continues to serve as the argument and discourse for several waves of countermovements opposed to the goals of environmentalism (McCright and Dunlap, 2000; Meyer and Staggenborg, 1996: 1632). I will return to antienvironmentalism later in the chapter.

The earliest stage of American environmentalism emphasized the conservation and preservation of natural resources and areas, while the 1950s and '60s focused on air and water quality, pollution, and human health issues. While these concerns continue, more recently it developed a more ecological focus on global issues, such as biodiversity problems and climate change (Mertig et al., 2002).

## Early American Environmental Movements, 1870–1950

Preservation and conservation were the first manifestations of American environmentalism, foreshadowing many contemporary environmental concerns. The swift destruction of America's forests and wilderness in the late nineteenth century by the lumber industry was the greatest public concern. Devastating environmental catastrophes turned public opinion against the cutting of large stands of trees. Cutting left pollution from residual bark, branches, and other waste. Worse, it surrounded small hamlets throughout the country with a virtual tinderbox. Approximately 1,500 persons died and 1,300,000 acres of land were burned in a Wisconsin fire in 1871. Related community disasters, such as the famous Johnstown, Pennsylvania, flood, were attributed to clear-cutting, because clear-cut soil does not hold water (Humphrey and Buttel, 1982: 114). Such wanton environmental destruction of America's forests and rangeland produced a broad-based effort to curb the abuses of private ownership and to institute "scientific management" of the nation's environmental resources. There were many individual leaders in this movement (called Progressives or Reformers, as were many leaders for political change in that era). Three were particularly remembered for their influence: President Theodore Roosevelt, John Muir, and Gifford Pinchot. They mobilized public support for conservation and created organizations such as the Sierra Club (founded in 1892 by Muir), the Audubon Society (1905), and many outdoor recreation clubs, such as the Boone and Crockett Club (founded by Theodore Roosevelt).

Conservationism was given intellectual and ideological shape by the writings of three persons. The first was *George Perkins Marsh* (1801–1882), whose work *Man and Nature: Physical Geography as Modified by Human Action* identified the negative impact of human economic activity on forests and rangeland. It documented the connections between cutting of forests and the erosion of soil, between the draining of marshes and lakes and the decline of animal life, between the forced decline of one species and alterations in the population of others, and even between human activity and climate. Marsh's eerily prescient ecological view is all the more remarkable because it was published in 1874, *before* the automobile, the significant use of oil, and the mechanized clearing of forests or modern mining that were to come (Paehlke, 1989: 15). *John Muir* (1838–1914) reacted angrily to the anthropocentrism of those who saw humans as above nature. Nature and wilderness were a spiritual experience, and he saw people, at their best, as part of that spiritual whole. Both politically and intellectually, Muir campaigned tirelessly for the preservation of wilderness areas from human intrusion. For him, the notion that the world was made especially for the uses of man was an enormous conceit (Nash, 1967: 131). *Aldo Leopold* (1886–1948) agreed, but his intellectual achievement was a blending of ecology and ethics. He saw the land itself as a living organism. People, he noted, are the only species that can threaten nature as a whole. If we do so, we will, of course, destroy ourselves. Leopold also pointed out that while most humans imagine that they are sustained by economy and industry, these are in turn sustained, as are all living things, by the land. We are therefore but one part of an interactive global ecosystem, and we injure the land at our own peril (Nash, 1967: 182). In short, the intellectual and ideological basis of contemporary environmentalism was well underway in the latter half of the nineteenth century.

The appeal of *conservationism,* as it was termed, was strongest among the upper and upper-middle classes, who were most concerned about outdoor recreation, the shrinkage of the public domain, and the destruction of forests. Conservationists sought to use the legal and political power of the state to protect forest lands from exploitation, resulting in, for example, the Yellowstone Act (1982), the Adirondack Forest Preserve (1885), and legislation to preserve Yosemite (1890) and Mount Rainier Parks (1890, 1899). Such efforts came to be effectively organized by national movement organizations such as the Audubon Society and particularly by Muir and the Sierra Club (Humphrey and Buttel, 1982: 113–114).

But government officials constantly struggled to balance two different public interests. Organizations such as the Sierra Club and the Audubon Society urged the *preservation of wilderness,* with a minimum of human use for scientific, aesthetic, and "nonconsumptive" recreational use. Others, such as hunters and fishers as well as large ranching, mining, and timber commercial interests, argued for the *utilitarian use of natural resources* subject to "scientific management." The second interest came to be spearheaded by Gifford Pinchot, a private forestry manager on the Vanderbilt Estate in North Carolina. The U.S. Department of Agriculture formed a Forestry

Division, helped Congress to pass the Forest Reserve Act in 1891, and hired Pinchot to study the possibilities of the scientific management of forests. He was appointed chief of the Division of Forestry, and his combination of technical and political skills enabled him to form a close relationship with President Theodore Roosevelt, whose domestic policy advocated the "wise use" of natural resources. Pinchot proved politically far more astute than Muir. In short, *the utilitarians won a decisive political victory over the preservationists*. Such policies enabled commercial interests to use public lands, subject to government regulation. They did protect natural resources, but they also reinforced and rationalized the exploitation of public lands by lumber companies and ranchers (Hays, 1959).

After World War I, the United States was confronted with massive environmental calamities such as flooding and soil erosion in the Great Plains "Dust Bowl" as well as by the Great Depression. A second wave of conservationism that developed during the Franklin Roosevelt administration emphasized both protecting and developing natural resources. New Deal programs such as the Civilian Conservation Corps and the Tennessee Valley Authority worked to protect natural resources as well as to stimulate economic recovery. In the 1950s, more emphasis was placed on preservation of natural beauty and wilderness for public enjoyment. This "wilderness movement," spearheaded by older organizations such as the Sierra Club, developed highly publicized campaigns to save the Grand Canyon and Dinosaur National Monument (Dunlap and Mertig, 1992: 2; McCloskey, 1972).

## American Environmentalism Since the 1950s

By the 1950s, conservationism was an established social force in American life. The 1970s transformed it into a different and greatly expanded environmental movement. This movement, often called *reform environmentalism,* was a complex system of ideas (Brulle, 2000). It was not simply an amplification of conservationism; the newer environmental discourse viewed problems as (1) being more complex in origin, often stemming from new technologies; (2) having delayed, complex, and difficult-to-detect effects; and (3) having consequences for human health and well-being as well as for natural systems. Because they encompassed both pollution and loss of recreational and aesthetic resources, environmental problems were increasingly viewed as threats to the total quality of life (Dunlap and Mertig, 1992: 2–3; Hays, 1987; Mitchell, 1980).

Like earlier movements, the new American environmentalism had important intellectual and ideological foundations. The first was *Silent Spring* (1962) by marine biologist Rachel Carson—an angry and uncompromising analysis of the toxic effects of modern pesticides on every form of wildlife. Carson focused on the politics of science and the exclusion of the public from knowing what risks they were being exposed to by the development and use of synthetic chemicals. *Silent Spring* made bestseller lists and sold more than a million copies—rare for a serious nonfiction book. Indicative of its impact, the American pesticide industry mounted a $250,000 campaign to prove Carson a "hysterical fool." Carson's work enhanced public awareness of the ecological impact of pesticides, and that awareness helped pass the Pesticide Control Act of 1972 (Sale, 1993: 4). Carson's work put the issue of pollution on the environmental agenda.

In 1968, zoologist Garret Hardin rediscovered Malthusian ideas in his famous essay *The Tragedy of the Commons* (The concept of a resource "commons" was discussed in Chapter Seven). Zoologist Paul Ehrlich's book, *The Population Bomb: Population Control or Race to Oblivion?* (1968), was a more popular book that forced the issue of overpopulation into public consciousness in an apocalyptic way, claiming that "the battle to feed all humanity is over." Ehrlich's neo-Malthusian work proved to be the most popular environmental book ever, selling more than 3 million copies in the first decade. Biologist Barry Commoner (1971), the most durable and most political and intellectually sophisticated "framer" of environmental concerns, disagreed with Ehrlich by arguing that the greatest threat to the environment was not population growth per se, but modern technology and the power of corporations that promote consumption.

Environmental events themselves, when publicized by the media, broadened public awareness of problems. In New York City, 80 people died from smog during an air inversion in the summer of 1966. An offshore oil rig near Santa Barbara poured undetermined millions of gallons of oil along the California coastline in January and February of 1969, killing wildlife and soaking beaches with black, oily goo. The industrially polluted Cuyahoga River near Cleveland burst into flames, and in the summer of 1969 nearby Lake Erie was declared a dying sinkhole as a result of sewage and chemical pollutants. As the decade of the 1960s wore on, the mainstream media made environmental events high-visibility ones.

This attention reached a crescendo by 1970 with a spate of front-page articles and cover stories in *Time, Fortune, Newsweek, Life, The New York Times,* and the *Washington Post.* "Ecology" became a word known—if incompletely understood—by the average citizen. Public outcry about such environmental abuses was widespread. Many were no longer willing to accept pollution and environmental disruption as business as usual and complained about the businesses that produced them and the governments that failed to protect against them (Sale, 1993: 19–25).

The event that symbolized this effervescence of environmental consciousness and activism was *Earth Day 1970.* The idea for this observance began with Senator Gaylord Nelson, who proposed a kind of nationwide environmental teach-in on college campuses, following the model of the 1960s antiwar teach-ins about the Vietnam War. He received a federal grant and support from government agencies (e.g., the Interior Department) to organize the event, in spite of critics who saw it as a communist plot and opposition from the Nixon administration. The popular response was overwhelming. *The New York Times* estimated that 20 million people participated, and it represented a surprising demonstration of the depth of feeling about environmentalism at that time (Sale, 1993: 34–35). Earth Day continues today as an annual ritual of environmentalism.

The immense political momentum of the environmental movement continued to build. In 1972, the Apollo 17 crew took a series of photographs of the earth from 22,000 miles away. One of these is on page 160, and it has become an icon of the environmental movement. Using the metaphor "spaceship earth," it came to represent a fragile earth with finite limits and a delicate natural balance—to which the fate of humanity is collectively linked (Brulle, 2000: 187).

Older national conservation organizations were invigorated by this upsurge of consciousness as they attempted to incorporate it. The National Audubon Society, for instance, enthusiastically supported antipesticide campaigns, while the National Wildlife Federation began a legal challenge to polluters (Sale, 1993: 19–20). By 1967, new organizations emerged representing a new wave of environmental movement organizations, such as the Environmental Defense Fund, later renamed Environmental Defense (ED). They marked the beginning of an environmental discourse and movement "frame" based on Rachel Carson's book. Using scientific research and legal action to protect the environment and human health, ED action methods served as an exemplar for many newer organizations. Over time, the environmental movement grew to thousands of movement organizations, over 1,000 of which are relatively large organizations with budgets in excess of $100,000 (Brulle, 2000). Many are led by well-compensated executives; employ scores of professional legal, scientific, and administrative staff; and have the capacity to simultaneously promote multiple goals using diverse techniques at different levels of political action (local, national, and international). In this sense, we do indeed have an "environmental establishment" (Bosso, 2005: 7).

## Reform Environmentalism and the Environmental Lobby

A national network of transformed environmental movement organizations came to dominate the movement's presence in Washington. Known as the "Group of 10," their interests and strategies differed: Some engaged in proenvironment lobbying; some developed the expertise and scientific capability for educational programs and advocacy research; some specialized in litigation to shape the development and enforcement of environmental policy; some purchased land to set aside for wilderness preserves. This core coalition met periodically to discuss common strategies and problems, and worked with other organizations. See Table 8.1.

Collectively, national environmental organizations grew significantly after the 1960s, but it came in spurts interspersed by periods of slow growth or retrenchment. The first growth was in

**TABLE 8.1** Selected National Environmental Organizations, 2003

| Organization | Year Founded | Members** | Revenue (millions) |
|---|---|---|---|
| Sierra Club* | 1892 | 736,000 | 83.7 |
| National Audubon Society* | 1905 | 550,000 | 78.6 |
| National Parks and Conservation Association* | 1919 | 375,000 | 20.9 |
| Izaak Walton League* | 1922 | 45,000 | 4.3 |
| The Wilderness Society* | 1935 | 225,000 | 18.8 |
| National Wildlife Federation* | 1936 | 650,000 | 102.1 |
| Ducks Unlimited | | 656,000 | 125.1 |
| Defenders of Wildlife | | 463,000 | 21.8 |
| Nature Conservancy | | 972,000 | 972.4 |
| World Wildlife Fund—U.S. | | 1,200,000 | 93.3 |
| Environmental Defense* | 1967 | 350,000 | 43.8 |
| Friends of the Earth* | 1969 | 35,000 | 3.8 |
| Natural Resources Defense Council* | 1970 | 450,000 | 46.4 |
| League of Conservation Voters | | 60,000 | 7.0 |
| Greenpeace USA | | 250,000 | 25.9 |
| American Rivers | | 30,000 | 5.5 |
| Sea Shepherd Conservation Society | | 35,000 | 1.0 |
| Earth Island Institute | | 20,000 | 4.9 |
| Environmental Working Group | | — | 1.8 |
| Environmental Policy Institute* | 1972 | Not a membership organization | |
| Total | | 7,799,400 | $2,135 |

*Group of 10
**Includes members or supporters, where possible to estimate.
*Sources:* Adapted from Bosso, 2005: 7; Mertig et al., 2002: 463.

the years just prior to Earth Day in 1970. It slowed during the 1970s but, ironically, as the conservative Reagan administration attacked environmentalism it stimulated a second wave of growth in the 1980s. Visible ecological problems such as toxic wastes, beach contamination, the Exxon *Valdez* oil spill, and global warming stimulated a third surge in membership in the early 1990s. Environmental movement growth plateaued again (and perhaps declined) during the Clinton/Gore administrations that were "green," rhetorically at least. In 2000, national environmental organizations began another period of intense membership mobilization and lobbying with the election of a generally unsympathetic president and a conservative congress. (See Chapter Seven, and BOX 7.1.) This is an interesting and curious dynamic: in democratic polities official hostility can sometimes stimulate the mobilization of oppositional movements. What is beyond question is that by the 1990s, national environmental movement organizations claimed millions of members, or at least "checkbook supporters" (Brulle, 2000: 105; Mitchell et al., 1992: 2–3).

**REFORM ENVIRONMENTALISM, PUBLIC OPINION, AND LEGISLATION**    These national environmental movement organizations—termed *reform environmentalism* by Robert Brulle—channeled and amplified environmental awareness and concerns among broad segments of the population, particularly about the hazards connected with life in industrial society. For instance, national public opinion poll data between 1965 and 1970 demonstrated a growing willingness to define air and water quality as significant problems. Increasingly, these were seen as deserving government attention, serious in respondents' communities, and as government spending areas they would *least* like to see cut. People were increasingly willing to pay modest taxes to address pollution problems. The growth of such proenvironment attitudes can be illustrated even by the most abstract and contentious environmental issue, global warming. In a 1982 survey, only 12% of a national sample saw the greenhouse effect as "very serious," but by 1989, 41% said so, while another 34% said it was "somewhat serious" (Dunlap and Scarce, 1991: 661). By the 1970s, large majorities expressed proenvironmental opinions, which had become a *consensual issue* in the language of public opinion experts. Even so, public opinion polls did not report how important or *salient* environmental concerns were. Reasonable interpretations suggested that a majority of the public had accepted environmentalists' definition of environmental issues as problems and had become sympathetic to environmental protection, but only a minority saw them as among the nation's *most* important problems, compared to issues like crime or unemployment (Dunlap, 1992: 92–96; Smith, 1985).

In the 1970s, when Republicans as well as Democrats attempted to govern from the political center, newly elected Republican President Nixon announced that he was an environmentalist and supported legislation to protect the environment. The EPA required an *Environmental Impact Statement* (EIS) of every federal agency project and had the power to approve or veto projects. Environmental legislation usually included so-called hammer clauses intended to produce strict compliance through mandatory deadlines, explicit and detailed procedural prescriptions, provisions for citizen participation, and citizen legal standing to sue agencies. In fact, almost every major piece of environmental legislation has been challenged in court by industry, environmentalists, or community groups—sometimes simultaneously. But NEPA and the EPA helped to create a transformed new era of administrative law, characterized by the expanding participation of environmental and nontraditional groups in administrative decision making (Miller, 1992: 680–681; Rosenbaum, 1989: 214–219). This influence spread to other agencies concerned with environmental issues, such as the Department of Energy, the Bureau of Land Management, and the Nuclear Regulatory Commission. But importantly this period of the expanding environmental protection did not last. Although the "environmental regulatory state" was not dismantled as some would have liked, no significant environmental legislation was passed since 1990. Environmentalism itself became suspect among large segments of the American public and with outright hostility among the more conservative politicians who came to power in the first decade of the new millennium. Ruling majorities in American politics often viewed environmentalism as "threats to jobs and profits." I will return to this issue.

**THE LIMITS OF REFORM**    Reform environmentalism became the dominant ideological frame for American environmentalism, with the possibility of examining every conceivable environmental or ecological issue. Early reform environmentalism focused mainly on pollution and health-related concerns, while later expanding concerns to global ecological problems, such as the proliferation of endocrine disrupters, biodiversity loss, and global warming. Reform environmentalism's most dramatic successes were in the 1970s. But, for various reasons, limitations in dealing with the "new" issues were apparent by the 1990s.

Reform environmentalism was based primarily on the writings of natural and physical scientists. With the exception of Barry Commoner, most ecological scientists did not examine the social and political causes of ecological degradation. While they had great competence in specific areas of expertise, the discourse obscured the social driving forces of environmental degradation (see Chapters One and Six). The problem is not that their analysis was wrong, but that it was partial. Reform environmentalism was unable to develop a meaningful political vision of how to create a more sustainable society, and without such a vision, it was politically naive and perhaps irrelevant (Taylor, 1992: 136). Environmental reform came in the form of piecemeal efforts, continually mired in technical and legal debates and carried out within a limited community of lawyers and scientists (Brulle, 2000: 192).

In addition, reform environmentalism fostered practices that, however effectively shaping public attitudes, limited its capacity for political mobilization. By practicing piecemeal science-based reforms, movement organizations came to have an oligarchic style because scientists play such a prominent role. Politicians and the public became only bit players—to heed the advice of scientists. There was no real need to involve the public, except for financial support, creating what Brulle called "astroturf" rather than "grassroots" organizations. The Sierra Club and the Audobon Soceity were notable exceptions to this oligarchic top-down management style, because they are national movement organizations that maintain effective grassroots local and regional chapters. Without effective grassroots support, such movement organizations became distant from the very constituencies they claim to represent, and often found their capacity for independent action compromised (Brulle, 2000: 192–193). As reform environmentalism grew from amateur enterprises to ones run by scientists and lawyers, its political clout was accompanied by conservatizing pressures to play by the "rules of the game" in the world of Washington, DC politics. As early as the 1980s, tensions simmered between the nationals and other environmental movement organizations (Mitchell et al., 1992: 24).

## Environmental Justice and Grassroots Movements

Reform environmental organizations in their Washington offices took the soft political road of negotiation, compromising with others about the amount of pollution or environmental disruption that was acceptable. But people living in polluted communities took the hard political road of confrontation, demanding not that the dumping of hazardous waste be slowed, but that it be stopped (Sale, 1993: 58). Grassroots mobilization expanded dramatically in the 1970s and 1980s. As you might suspect, precise numbers of people involved in grassroots environmental movement organizations are informed guesses, but by 1989 national networks that work with local groups reported 8,300 existing groups. Local environmental activism was stimulated by clear and present community health hazards rather than by abstract concerns such as protecting wilderness areas or declining biodiversity. Grassroots organizing has been triggered by toxic waste dumps, radioactive wastes, nuclear plants, and proposals to build garbage incinerators and hazardous waste disposal facilities and a variety of other hazards. Local groups typically document a hazard and link it to a current or potential health problem, such as a cluster of cancer cases or a series of adverse reproductive outcomes. Since corporations usually cause these problems, such environmentalism means redefining environmental hazards as corporate crime. In demanding changes in corporate practices, local activists are inevitably drawn into interaction with public health officials, lawyers, and scientists (Cable and Benson, 1993; Freudenberg and Steinsapir, 1992: 29).

The key organizing frame or discourse for such movements is *environmental justice,* which integrated social with ecological concerns more than reform environmentalism did. Their concerns do overlap with reform environmentalism, but the marginalized people and their spokespersons at the core of environmental justice movements are less likely to see environmental problems as separate from problems of classism, racism, and sexism. They see environmental issues differently, as inherently linked to social justice concerns like self-determination, human rights, and the disproportionate impacts of environmental hazards on worker and family well-being (Taylor, 2000).

That frame pays particular attention to questions of distributive justice, community empowerment, and democratic accountability. It argues that human societies and the natural environment are inextricably linked, and that the health of one depends on the health of the other (Taylor, 1993: 57). Hence, addressing environmental problems effectively means fundamental social change based on the empowerment of local communities.

Reform movement organizations often found their supporters primarily among white middle-class persons. Environmental justice movement organizations have a much broader and well-developed social base. Since they are particularly impacted by environmental hazards, minorities of all kinds—African Americans, Native Americans, and Latinos—as well as working-class homeowners are drawn into grassroots environmental movement organizations. In Warren County, North Carolina, a primarily African-American group struggled to block dumping of PCB-contaminated soil in a landfill. On the Pine Ridge Native American reservation in South Dakota, the Women of All Red Nations sought to force cleanup of contaminated water and land. In California, Mothers of East Los Angeles organized a Mexican-American community to block construction of an oil pipeline through its neighborhood (Freudenberg, 1984).

As discussed in Chapter Six, the unequal impact of environmental hazards is pervasive. A large and growing body of empirical studies documents this fact (see, for instance, Bryant, 1995; Bullard, 1990; Daniels and Friedman, 1999; Mitchell et al., 1999; and, especially, Szasz and Meuser, 1997 for a review of studies). But not all studies find high correlations between environmental hazards and the geographic concentrations of minorities. David Pellow argues that researchers need to look at the process of "environmental inequality formation" over time, as minorities may be drawn to previously unoccupied hazardous areas because of low property values (2000).

Environmental justice movements illustrate a basic human-environmental paradigm (centering on stratification and inequality) as discussed earlier. German social theorist Ulrich Beck, for instance, observed that

> The history of risk distribution shows that, like wealth, risks adhere to the class pattern, only inversely. Wealth accumulates at the top, risks at the bottom. . . . It is especially the cheaper residential areas for low-income groups near centers of industrial

> production that are permanently exposed to various pollutants in the air, the water, and the soil. . . . It is not just this social filtering or amplification which produces class specific afflictions. The possibilities and abilities to deal with risks, avoid them or compensate for them are probably unequally divided among the various occupational and educational strata. (1996: 35)

Lois Gibbs, the organizer of the Love Canal Protest, put it in less academic language:

> [They] all knew that those poisons were in my backyard. . . . And they made a decision . . . that because my husband made $10,000 a year, and because we were working class people, that it was OK to kill us. (cited in Brulle, 2000: 207)

Minority and working-class persons are drawn into grassroots environmentalism because environmental hazards are more likely to be located in their communities. African Americans, for instance, have higher blood levels of carbon monoxide and pesticides, and African-American children have a rate of lead poisoning six times that of white children (National Center for Statistics, 1984; Radford and Drizd, 1982). Not only are they more exposed to environmental hazards, but there also is a growing recognition that they were the targets of hazardous and dangerous projects that more affluent communities were able to resist. Their circumstances are, in other words, related to the pattern of economic and political power in society, and for grassroots groups environmental issues become issues about social and racial justice. *Environmental justice* thus involves questions about political power as well as about public health hazards (Capek, 1993; Freudenberg, 1984).

Unlike the national organizations, environmental justice movements depend almost entirely on volunteers. Women tend to be overrepresented in both the membership and the leadership of such grassroots organizations. Experienced community activists may become involved, but it is a distinguishing characteristic of grassroots environmental movements that new leaders arise, often housewives with no previous organizing experience. Over time, the effect of this experience is the development of considerable scientific and organizational skills and a transformed political consciousness. The reason for this is the typical process through which grassroots efforts develop. After defining environmental hazards as corporate law violation, local activists usually turn to agencies of the state to enforce or create environmental regulation. In doing so, they find that the state is not a neutral player in the process, often being more responsive to corporate than community interests. Therefore, they challenge the democratic responsiveness, credibility, and effectiveness of officials—from city hall to the EPA (Cable and Benson, 1993). As they enter arenas where more is required than personal experience and anecdotal reports, they seek scientists as allies, but their connections with experts and scientists are often ambivalent. Activists in environmental justice movement organizations learn that both government and science can be used against them, often deflecting and trivializing their claims. The outcome is typically significant skepticism and mistrust of both science and officialdom. They tend to reject the image of science as the "objective pursuit of truth" (Freudenberg and Steinsapir, 1992: 29; Pellow, 1994). Grassroots activists learn quickly, perhaps more quickly than most, that environmental problems are not purely, or even primarily, technical problems.

Environmental justice movement organizations are mobilized by people who are frustrated, morally outraged, and passionate about protecting their homes and families, particularly when they feel that the officials have been unresponsive or that they have been manipulated and outmaneuvered by established powers (as illustrated earlier by the quotation from Lois Gibbs). Given their experience and the scarcity of resources to organize, grassroots movement organizations often move beyond the respectable rules of the game available to reform environmentalism (research, lobbying, electoral efforts). They often use the only methods available to them, including *direct action tactics,* such as picketing the homes of key opposition figures or holding sit-ins that block the construction of new facilities. At Love Canal, Lois Gibbs and other residents held two EPA officials hostage for several hours; two days later, President Jimmy Carter declared Love Canal a disaster area (Gibbs, 1982).

Local environmental justice movements did not stay local. Such grassroots movement organizations need allies, both for scientific and technical expertise and political support. Larger movement structures emerged from networks and coalitions between local movement organizations. Most of these are regional, such as the Grassroots Environmental Organization in New Jersey, Citizens' Environmental Coalition in California, Texans United, and the New York Coalition for Alternatives to Pesticides. These groups educate members about scientific and political issues, provide forums for exchanging experiences, and develop broader policy and advocacy strategies. A number of national organizations have emerged from grassroots struggles. These include the Citizen's Clearinghouse for Hazardous Wastes, founded in 1981 by Lois Gibbs (recently renamed the Center for Health, Environment, and Justice), and the Environmental Research Foundation, which provides information about toxic chemicals to local activists. These groups organize national conferences, offer leadership training, publish newsletters and manuals, and provide technical assistance to local groups (Freudenberg and Steinsapir, 1992: 30–31).

Grassroots movement mobilization is inherently difficult and fragile to maintain, partly because groups always wind up fighting city hall in one way or another. Some scholars argue that the most likely outcome of grassroots environmentalism is to be defeated, co-opted, or at best achieve victories that are more symbolic than real (Pellow, 1994). Yet without making any judgment about their net effects, Nicholas Freudenberg, who specializes in the study of such grassroots groups, finds many examples of positive achievements.[1] Critics of grassroots movements often charge that their concerns are narrow and self-interested, ignoring broader obligations to society (hence the derogatory acronym NIMBY, "Not in my back yard!"). What the critics of NIMBYism fail to recognize is the substantial contribution to improved public health by such groups. In addition, they fail to recognize that participation in NIMBY groups is often a consciousness-raising experience. Local activists often graduate to broader concerns. What started out as an attempt to clean up Love Canal wound up being a national toxic waste campaign, and many groups that started by blocking the construction of garbage incinerators became advocates for recycling and waste reduction measures. NIMBY often undergoes a transformation to NIABY ("Not in *anybody's* back yard!"). In a related illustration of moving from particular to broader concerns, 650 grassroots and national leaders concerned about environmental justice met for four days in Washington, DC as the first National People of Color Environmental Leadership Summit. Delegates attended from all 50 states and from Puerto Rico, Chile, Mexico, and the Marshall Islands, along with invited researchers. The summit broadened its scope "beyond its anti-toxics focus to include issues of public health, worker safety, land use, transportation, housing, resource allocation, and community empowerment" (Bullard and Johnson, 2000: 557).

Like reform environmentalism, grassroots environmental justice movements have limitations. In spite of what I just said, environmental justice movements may be successful only in particular instances, and governments may be able to resist pressures for more general environmental reforms. Significant societal change in environmental standards requires a coordinated, nationwide coalition of local environmental organizations. Another limitation is that environmental justice is an exclusively anthropocentric discourse. Its concern with nature is limited to examining how ecological degradation affects the human community. Hence, environmental justice movements cannot inform a cultural practice that could protect nature or biodiversity outside of human-focused utilitarian considerations (Brulle, 2000: 221).

## Other Voices: Deep Ecology and Ecofeminism

As environmentalism developed, it became substantially more diverse, with a broader array of issues, organizations, and strategies. Just as the blending of the earlier frames of conservationism and environmentalism led to greater breadth, by the 1980s other frames and discourses were taking shape. Even though most have no significant mass base (even an astroturf one), they have shaped the intellectual and ideological texture of contemporary environmentalism. This is true because they were often formulated by intellectuals and scholars or by influential refugees from reform environmentalism. Some have a very limited potential for a significant mass base, while others have considerable potential.

**DEEP ECOLOGY**    Originally formulated by Norwegian philosopher Arne Naess in the 1970s, *deep ecology* was brought to the United States primarily by philosopher George Sessions and sociologist Bill Devall, who coauthored its first popular versions (1985). In contrast to what they view as the "shallow environmentalism" of most of the environmental movement, deep ecology thinkers are *biocentric* or *ecocentric* rather than anthropocentric. Deep ecology emphasizes that (1) the richness and diversity of all life on the earth has an intrinsic value, which is threatened by human activities; (2) human life is privileged only to the extent of satisfying vital needs; (3) maintaining biodiversity requires a decrease in human impacts on the natural environment and substantial increases in the wilderness areas of the globe; and therefore (4) economic, technological, and cultural changes are necessary (and perhaps an eventual reduction in the human population size) (Devall and Sessions, 1985). Deep ecology also emphasizes the *self-realization* of humans as belonging to nature, referring to the process whereby one strives for organic wholeness in nature. Those influenced by deep ecology were also determined to reclaim their spiritual identity with nature, some in terms of Buddhist traditions, and some in terms of reviving indigenous "tribal rituals" (Devall, 1992: 56; Sale, 1993: 63).

Although diverse lifestyles and social policies are potentially compatible with deep ecology thinking, its literature emphasizes decentralized and small-scale human communities, self-sufficiency, participatory democracy, and lifestyles that minimize material consumption and maximize the richness of nature. Again, we are not on new ground. Deep ecological thinking was very much influenced by the limits scenario of the future, discussed in Chapter Six, and particularly by the positive possibilities of voluntary simplicity lifestyles. Deep ecologists support the protection of ancient forests and other wild ecosystems, the restoration of biodiversity, and many advocate vegetarianism. Most advocate nonviolent direct action strategies for change of the sort emphasized by Gandhi. They support green consumerism that would minimize the environmental impacts of consumer goods and green politics, meaning the formation of political movements and parties to advocate ecological principles. But most fundamentally for deep ecologists, the path to ecological freedom requires cultivation of an ecological consciousness that permits humans to see through the erroneous and dangerous illusions of Western cultures that justify human dominance over the nonhuman environment (Devall and Sessions, 1985). As complicated and abstract as these ideas are, they gained a diverse following, primarily among intellectuals and activists in the United States as well as in Canada, Australia, and northern Europe. Indeed, many people know about or accept some of these ideas without recognizing the discourse that connects them.

A woman shopping for environmentally friendly "green" cleaning products.

**Deep Ecology Organizations and Action.**    Earth First! (EF!), the most widely known deep ecology organization, was founded by Dave Foreman and a handful of other people disillusioned by their experience in national environmental organizations. EF! advocated civil disobedience combined with absolute nonviolence against humans and other living things, and strategic violence against "things" such as bulldozers, powerlines, and whaling ships (Miller, 1992: 689). Although not committed to any specific political tactics, speaking in many voices, and disavowing bureaucracy, centralized decision making, sexism, and hierarchy, EF! was a vortex of radical environmental action during the 1980s (Devall, 1992: 57). The founders of EF! were inspired by Edward Abbey's novel *The Monkey Wrench Gang* (1975) and advocated militant tactics in defense of nature, eventually including guerrilla theater, media stunts, and civil disobedience. Unofficially, they included ecotage (also called monkey wrenching): sabotaging bulldozers and road-building equipment on public lands, pulling up survey stakes, cutting down billboards, and, famously, "spiking" trees at random to prevent their being cut and milled. The advocacy of such tactics alarmed many, but investigations of actual actions largely found EF! not guilty of the most damaging accusations (Sale, 1993: 66).[2]

Never large in comparison with national reform organizations, EF! and other radical groups try to avoid their professionalization and bureaucratization. Overcoming major fractures, EF! grew from a small group in 1980 to having an estimated following of more than 10,000 from all over the nation and the world, and an annual budget of over $200,000 by the end of its first decade (Lee, 1995). Despite being a national movement with a national journal, local activists and groups affiliated with EF! act largely on their own (Scarce, 1990). As you can imagine, advocating such militant tactics made EF! very controversial and elicited considerable opposition. They were described variously as anarchists, ecowarriors, a tribe, a collection of social deviants, ecoterrorists, and visionaries. The group's founder, Dave Foreman, said that "from one side have come efforts to mellow us out and sanitize our vices; from another efforts to make us radical in a traditional leftist sense, and there are on-going efforts by the powers that be to wipe us out entirely." Indeed there were. The FBI spent three years and $2 million infiltrating EF!, and in 1989 a trumped-up federal suit charged Foreman with conspiracy for helping to finance the destruction of an electric power tower near Phoenix, Arizona. In 1990, two EF! activists were car bombed in California (Devall, 1992: 57; Miller, 1992: 689–690; Sale, 1993: 57).

EF! was not the only manifestation of the deep ecology frame. *First,* it inspired *bioregionalism,* a movement that advocates changing political boundaries of human communities to boundaries defined by ecosystems. Existing political boundaries are defined by many historical accidents of human settlement and control. A *bioregion* is a geographical area defined by ecological commonalities, including soil characteristics, watersheds, climate, and native plants and animals. This perspective would reframe human existence as a part of a natural ecosystem, not apart from it. Many problems could be understood in an ecological focus, such as dealing with water shortages among communities that are located within the same watershed. *Second,* deep ecology inspired the formation of the academic discipline of *conservation biology,* understood as the unification of evolutionary biology and ecology with a normative commitment to preserve biodiversity. That field emerged in 1986 at a national conference in Washington, DC sponsored by the National Academy of Science and the Smithsonian Institute, attended by 14,000 people. At this conference, a group of eminent biologists redefined and publicized the problem of endangered species, coining the term *biodiversity* that I have been using all along (see Chapter Two). They did this to spur political action, based on the belief that "humans and other species with which we share the earth are imperiled by an unparalleled ecological crisis" (Takacs, 1996: 9). The leading organization of this movement among scholars is the Society for Conservation Biology. Conservation biologists formed alliances with financiers to create in 1989 the Foundation for Deep Ecology, which funds activities in support of rainforest preservation, grassroots activism, and indigenous third world people's efforts to protect their natural environment from destruction. In 1997, it had assets of over $35 million. By the 1990s, groups of forest activists were trying to "reinvigorate" the Sierra Club by getting it to lobby for a ban on clear-cut logging on public lands (known as the Zero Cut Campaign). The proposal was passed by a vote of Sierra Club members nationwide. Whether such efforts will revitalize reform environmental movements is not clear, but the Sierra Club and a number of forest protection groups introduced the National Forest Protection and Restoration Act in the House of Representatives in 1997 (HR 2789). Its purpose was to reverse the policy and legislation that since 1897 has allowed commercial logging in national forests (Brulle, 2000: 202–203).

**Limits of Deep Ecology.**    Deep ecology's core themes (biocentric equality and "self-realization" that widens the human understanding of the self to include the natural world) promote overcoming a narrow egoistic (and anthropomorphic) understanding of self-interest and simultaneously developing a sympathy with other living things. But the discourse has a limited appeal because movement organizations shaped by deep ecology focus almost exclusively on the defense of wilderness, with virtually no efforts being extended to reform society. Indeed, deep ecology often vacillates between overt hostility toward the human community and vague appeals to extend that community to the broader natural world. These characteristics limit deep ecology's ability to shape alternative political and social practices (Taylor, cited in Brulle, 2000: 206). They also limit its access to a large popular base of supporters.

**ECOFEMINISM**    The ecofeminist discourse is a blend of feminist and ecological thought that emphasizes conceptual connections between the exploitive domination of women by men and the domination of nature. It sets the problems of women and the ecological crisis in a common framework (Merchant, 1981). Both are seen as products of a patriarchal society in which *domination* has emerged as a pervasive cultural theme and social paradigm. The Western worldview, with its abstract science and the impulse to control "nature" that deep ecologists hold responsible for the ecological crisis, is in fact a historical product of the thinking of men in patriarchal societies. But the domination of both nature and women is not caused by generic human nature but by specific institutional arrangements developed and controlled by men.

*Was this not always so?* Not according to ecofeminist scholars. They sought evidence for this view by retrieving the "full" historical record from our commonly understood history (in patriarchal societies, not surprisingly, a history largely written and interpreted by men). Ecofeminist scholars found evidence that European neolithic societies were largely peaceful, minimally stratified, harmonious, and goddess worshipping until the invasion of patriarchal, militaristic, Indo-European pastoralists in the fourth millennium B.C.E. From this turning point in the prehistory of Western civilization, the direction of our cultural evolution was quite literally turned around. The cultural evolution of societies that worshiped the life-generating powers of the universe was interrupted. There appeared invaders on the prehistoric horizon from peripheral areas of the globe who ushered in a very different form of society. Unlike the neolithic communities they conquered, who considered the earth as a mother and left statues representing fertility all over Europe, the invaders worshiped the "lethal power of the blade." In other words, they emphasized the power to take rather than give life as the ultimate power to establish and enforce domination (Eisler, 1988; Gimbutas, 1977). "Domination" is thus a pervasive mindset that applied to other men and women, and to nature. It is not human nature but a worldview with a history.

By providing a plausible—but still arguable—history, ecofeminist prehistorical scholarship provides an evolutionary depth lacking in deep ecology. But even if you don't accept this historical argument, a more indisputable set of facts support ecofeminist views: the connection among women, development, and environmental disruption in the less developed countries (LDCs). There, economic development replaced ecologically sustainable subsistence agriculture with cash crop monocultures that often appropriated and destroyed the natural resource base for subsistence. Although LDC men as well as women suffer from this, women are the greater losers because, as the primary producers of food, water, and fuel, women were more likely to lose their livelihoods. Moreover, in powerfully patriarchal LDCs, they have less access than do men to land ownership, technology, employment for wages, and small business loans should they desire them. In short, men have been the prime beneficiaries of development, from the colonial era to the contemporary world market system (Mies, 1986; Shiva, 1988: 1–3). Chapter Five noted the consensus among demographers that a key to slowing world population growth is to improve the status of women. Ecofeminists argue more broadly that the ecological crisis is inextricably bound with patriarchal domination and the subordinate status of women—both in its long history and around the world today. Furthermore, survey research over the last decades consistently demonstrates that U.S. women are more concerned than men about health threats posed by environmental and technological problems. This has been found not only in the United States but also around the world. Indeed, when compared with age, class, education, and other social variables, gender is a powerful predictor of environmental concern (Dunlap, 2000b).

Ecofeminism is one of the newer environmental discourses, and its ability to serve as a model for a significant social movement outside of academia has yet to be demonstrated. There are a few ecofeminist movement organizations, but that is not really the point. Ecofeminism has a considerable following, particularly in university circles and women's studies programs. Philosophers and historians have issued a torrent of books about the subject. Moreover, the voice of women is being heard increasingly at international gatherings with environmental implications (such as the 1994 Cairo Conference about population or the subsequent Beijing Conference about the global status of women). As with deep ecology, ecofeminists are not all of one voice, reflecting schisms in the larger feminist movement. They disagree, for example, about whether to emphasize the female "nature of nature" or whether to attempt to transcend gender roles altogether. Given the dominance of patriarchy around the world, the acceptance of the ecofeminist discourse is problematic. But ecofeminism is important as a pervasive discourse and critique of both deep ecology and reform environmentalism.

## Other Voices: Ecotheology and Voluntary Simplicity

The beginnings of *ecotheology* are found in reactions to Lynn White's landmark essay (1967), in which he argued that the Western biblical tradition—on which both Judaism and Christianity are based—was the root of the modern environmental crisis. Man was viewed as the master of, and apart from, the rest of God's creation. According to White, "more science and more technology are not going to get us out of the present ecologic crisis until we find a new religion, or re-think our old one" (White, 1967: 1206). Although an arguable view (as discussed in Chapter One), it did create a problem for Western theologians and religious thinkers. Rejecting radical anthropomorphism, they sought to develop a spiritual vision of the environment combined with the imperative for humans to preserve God's creation.

Several versions of this perspective developed. One stems from the African-American churches of the United States, which linked a spiritual view of the environment with the environmental justice movements. They have been major forces in these movements. For example, the first protest in 1982 against a toxic landfill in North Carolina was led and organized by a local African-American church, and the early influential empirical study of environmental racism was sponsored by the United Church of Christ (Bullard, 1990). Caring for the environment was linked to the creation of just and caring human communities (Brulle, 2000: 229–230). Another perspective, known as *Christian stewardship,* focuses on an evangelical interpretation based on a biblical mandate to care for God's creation. Founded on conservative Christian theology, it creates a moral imperative to preserve God's creation and makes minor adjustments in Christian theology to accommodate environmental concerns. It sees God as a transcendent being, and human nature as fallen, sinful, and in need of redemption. According to an early statement, "Christians, who should understand the creation principle, have a reason for respecting nature, and when they do, it results in benefits to man. Let us be clear: It is not just a pragmatic attitude; there is a basis for it. We treat it with respect because God made it" (Schaeffer, 1970: 76, cited in Brulle, 2000: 232). A third view, usually called *creation spirituality,* sees the need to go beyond the Christian tradition to develop alternative notions of the creation. Creation spirituality seeks a new synthesis of religion and science. One of its founders, Matthew Fox, advocated "the overcoming of dualisms of the western worldview so that we can see the creation as a whole" (Oelschlaeger, 1994: 169). Because he accepted all religions as revelations of the sacred in different contexts, Fox was excommunicated from the Catholic Church. Popular poet and philosopher Wendell Berry advocated a "new story" for humanity, uniting Genesis with scientific knowledge. That "new story" would remove humanity from a position of privilege in the universe. Resonances with deep ecology are obvious.

In the mid-1980s, ecotheology emerged within religious communities that had traditionally not been involved in environmental issues. In 1989, Pope John Paul II wrote an encyclical entitled *The Ecological Crisis: A Common Responsibility.* He urged Catholics to reduce resource consumption and warned farmers to use ethical caution when embracing biotechnology. Statements about religion and the environment were promulgated by other American denominations, culminating in a unified statement by leaders of 24 major religious bodies entitled

*Statement by Religious Leaders at the Summit on the Environment.* Ecumenical Patriarch Bartholomew—the spiritual leader of some 200 million Orthodox Christians—launched an official crusade against pollution, calling it a "sin against creation." He has established an annual day of prayer and action for the planet and environmental training for priests. By 1993, virtually all major religious bodies had issued a proclamation on environmental degradation, and a *National Religious Partnership* was formed that united the major Protestant, Catholic, Jewish, and evangelical communities into one organization focused on developing and implementing religious approaches to combating environmental degradation (Brulle, 2000: 234; Mastny, 2001).

Ecotheology is a new and emerging discourse. Since most Americans have religious affiliations (at least nominal ones), it would seem to have a huge potential to mobilize a popular base. It is also connected with established institutions that have vast educational and media networks, which strategically position them to facilitate environmental consciousness raising and mobilization. But ecotheology has some limitations. First, it will be limited to the extent that its carriers are agents for preserving the status quo rather than agents of social and political transformation. Second, since one version calls for humans to value nature not for its own sake, but because of its divine origins, it may have limited acceptance outside of communities of believers.

**VOLUNTARY SIMPLICITY AGAIN?**    As noted in Chapter Six, philosopher Duane Elgin coined the term *voluntary simplicity* in the 1970s to describe and promote a movement away from materialism, excessive consumerism, and unsustainable consumption. That early VS movement was linked to New Age spirituality, the themes of the 1960s counterculture, and moving "back to nature." Its rhetoric was primarily moralistic, presenting idyllic images of romantic asceticism and living in nature or rebuking consumers for overindulgence. It had a limited appeal and was overwhelmed by the more powerful forces promoting consumerism, living on credit, shopping at malls, and buying SUVs. But the idea of voluntarily simplifying lifestyles was more than just a passing fad. It returned in the 1990s, along with a movement to promote it. Most Americans think that they consume more than they need, produce too much waste, and focus too much on consuming now at the expense of future generations. A wide variety of groups sprang up dedicated to plain living, frugality, "downshifting," and living lightly on the earth. Amy Dacyczyn's newsletter *Tightwad Gazette,* devoted to spending less and living more, had 100,000 subscribers before she got tired of producing it. Similar publications exist, such as *Frugal Gazette, Miser's Gazette,* and the *Something for Nothing Journal.* People interested in voluntary simplicity make contact through a wide variety of local discussion groups ("simplicity circles"), publications, and Web pages. Simplicity circles, which started in Seattle, now exist in many states. You can easily find them.[3] VS organizations include the Northwest Earth Institute in Portland, Oregon, and the New Roadmap Foundation in Seattle, Washington. The Center for a New American Dream (CNAD), in Tacoma Park, Maryland, seeks to change North American attitudes about overconsumption in a "throwaway" culture (Bell, 2004: 29–30; CNAD, www.newdream.org). There are a number of such organizations in Europe, such as the Northern Alliance for Sustainability, which has organizations in six nations (Humphrey et al., 2002: 235).

So there is a second VS movement, but its power and pervasiveness still pales compared to opposing urgings of marketers, advertisers, and the mass media. If the new VS movement is to have greater appeal and impact, it needs to be promoted differently than was the earlier movement. High mass consumption is more complex than promoters of simple lifestyles often think. Consumption is related to the creation and transmission of meaning in modern societies. Consumption defines identity, status, and privilege more clearly than production in increasingly large and uncontrollable global systems of production. It is not just a psychological blight or "sick culture" (Cohen, 1995). Most important, voluntary simplicity would have broader appeal if seen as a means of improving the quality of life in a society where many experience life as overly complex and hectic and in which "life in the fast lane" provides little satisfaction or leisure. Voluntary simplicity could be seen as a means of reclaiming something important rather than depriving oneself and one's family.

To summarize, I have sketched the varieties of contemporary environmental movements in broad strokes. Having different ideological frames and discourses with different organizational structures, action strategies, and diverse clienteles, they can all claim successes, but all have limitations. Such fractious movements need a *metanarrative,* or master frame, that could enable them to work in complementary fashion, rather than in contradictory ways that blunt the effectiveness of the larger movement. An environmental metanarrative would provide common discourse, enabling people to unite around actions creating just, democratic, and sustainable societies. It would not destroy existing discourses, but rather would incorporate them, creating a larger capacity for collective action. If you think that is impossible, consider a more limited version of a metanarrative that did just that, about biodiversity, discussed earlier as a fairly recent invention of conservation biologists. It incorporated separate preexisting environmental discourses about deforestation, overfishing, habitat destruction, the introduction of exotic species, and endangered species. It did not destroy other discourses; it expanded the concerns of various groups to see their common purpose and created the potential for greater collective action (Brulle, 2000: 200–201).

## Movement Activism: Grassroots and Astroturf

A visible change in the United States after World War II was the growth of "movement activism," meaning the popular mobilization of many ordinary people to work for worthy causes and fight perceived injustices. Think not only of the emergent "environmentalisms," but also the civil rights, antipoverty, antiwar, and feminist movements of the 1960s, called the "decade of movements." What motivates ordinary people to be courageous enough to be active supporters of such causes, often with considerable risks and costs? A study examined that question among 64 environmental activists and whistleblowers (who spoke out against powerful institutions) in the United States, Israel, and the former Czechoslovakia. They faced firing, being blacklisted and character assassination. The research found four powerful factors among such people. First, they had strong social networks (or "social capital"); second, they believed that they could make a difference; third, they were willing to accumulate evidence and experience; and fourth, they were able to overcome fear and intimidation (M. Glazer and P. Glazer, 1999).

Such activism, however, is not only from the "grassroots," meaning, the ways that the weak and outsiders mobilize about their concerns. Elite "insiders," institutions, and corporations (like hospitals, pharmaceutical companies) have few voluntary "members" or connected groups, and often find it difficult to influence public opinion or shape public policy. They have developed an arsenal of tactics for mobilization to give the appearance of widespread popular support. For instance, they can use television advertisements that encourage the spin-off of semi-autonomous support groups. They can organize consumers, work with leaders of existing voluntary groups in what has been called a "grass tops" strategy, activate employees, and build third-party organizations. But protest groups almost always have outside sponsors or patrons to help organizers get things started, so the dividing line between "grassroots" and "Astroturf" may be more of a political Rorschach test than a precisely measurable concept. The expansion of institutional and industry-driven public participation reflects a society in which civic ties are increasingly indirect, and mediated by communication technologies like e-mail, texting, and social network Web sites (Walker, 2010). Having discussed environmental discourses, movements, and movement activism, I return to the durable and important human–environment discourse, noted earlier, which is typically connected with astroturf and grass top mobilization.

## Antienvironmentalism: Manifest Destiny and Countermovements

The oldest and most pervasive human–environment discourse derives from the Western world-view of America and industrial societies. Termed *manifest destiny,* it provides a moral and economic rationale for exploiting the natural environment. Manifest destiny and the human exemptionalism paradigm to which it was connected assumes that nature (1) has no intrinsic value, (2) is unproductive and valueless without human labor that transforms it into commodities upon which human welfare depends, and (3) has abundant natural resources for humans—who have rights to use it to meet their needs. In addition to providing a rationale for the development of the North American continent by European settlers, manifest destiny provided the ideological discourse or frame for several waves of countermovements opposed to the goals of environmentalism (Brulle, 2000: 116). As I noted at the beginning of this chapter, countermovements share many objects of concern with the movements they oppose and make competing claims that vie for attention of the media, politicians, and broader publics.

The most significant early manifestation of manifest destiny countermovements erupted when President Grover Cleveland created 23 new national forests (bringing the total to 39 million acres) in 1897. Protests happened in the West, including a mass rally that attracted 30,000 people in Deadwood, South Dakota. A Montana senator accused the president of "contemptuous disregard" for people's interest, and a Washington state senator asked: "Why should we be everlastingly and eternally harassed and annoyed and bedeviled by these scientific gentlemen from Harvard College?" (Robbins, cited in Brulle, 2000: 120). Another series of Western protests over federal land policy happened between 1925 and 1934. Known as the Stansfield Rebellion, it was led by Oregon Senator Stansfield and focused on opposition to the imposition of grazing fees in the national forests. The Taylor Grazing Act as amended in 1939 resolved the issue in a series of compromises between the interests of ranchers and conservationists. I noted earlier the opposition to Rachel Carson's book *Silent Spring* and industry attempts to defame her character in the media. That publicity campaign backfired. The sales of the book soared, and legislation subsequently banned the most objectionable pesticides.

By the 1970s, laws governing land use had shifted in favor of environmentalism, as movements with wilderness protection and endangered species acts that permanently locked up parts of national forests and placed limits on land use, even by private property owners. Ranchers, miners, lumber corporations, and the business community bore the most obvious and most direct costs of environmental protection. The previous chapter said quite a lot about *internalizing* environmental costs that are presently unaccounted for. Economic interest groups made major efforts to return control of federal lands to local enterprises. The Sagebrush Rebellion, as it was known, was a reincarnation of earlier land use issues. Several movement organizations emerged, such as the Center for the Defense of Free Enterprise, which protested environmental restrictions being imposed on the free enterprise system, and the Mountain States Legal Defense Fund, a business-supported antienvironmental law firm. Its president and chief legal officer was James Watt, later to be appointed director of the EPA under President Reagan (Brulle, 2000: 124–126).

When it was obvious that environmentalism was not a passing fad and they were faced with threats to profits, many corporations took an offensive position. Companies spent massively on public campaigns to depict themselves as good environmental corporate citizens, while environmentalists were depicted as unrepresentative nuts who needlessly threatened economic prosperity, jobs, and human well-being. Corporate-sponsored attacks on environmentalists took a variety of forms: political lobbying, public relations campaigns with hired public relations firms, and advertising. By 1995 American firms were spending $1 billion a year on antienvironmental activities (Beder, 1998: 108). Such campaigns also included "sponsored research" designed to refute the claims of environmentalists and regulatory agencies.[4] Except for the direct action tactics of grassroots movements and the radicals, corporate strategies were often a mirror image of those of the environmentalist groups. Increasingly, corporations are likely to use litigation tactics against anyone who publicly opposes their use of the environment (Clyke, 1993: 87–88; Sale, 1993: 102). Such suits, called *strategic lawsuits against public participation* (SLAPPs), have the intention of silencing activists or diverting their attention away from the issues. SLAPPs charge environmental groups and grassroots activists with defamation of character, interference with contracts or business, or conspiracy. An earlier study of them found that about 25% of SLAPPs were about development and zoning issues, and another 20% surrounded pollution and animal rights issues. In the 1990s, the average SLAPP was for $9 million; some have been for as much as $100 million. Most of these suits are unsuccessful and eventually dropped, but in the meantime they create many problems for activists (for instance, financial troubles and fears of retribution and for exercising constitutionally guaranteed free speech). Corporate America has found SLAPPs an effective strategy for neutralizing opponents (Dold, 1992).

Where legal methods did not suffice, environmentalists were harassed by extralegal methods—offices trashed, cars smashed, homes entered, death threats. The home of a Greenpeace worker in Arkansas was burned, and two EF! workers were firebombed in California. Karen Silkwood, a worker in an ARCO nuclear fuel processing plant in Oklahoma, was harassed and possibly killed by agents of the company when she tried to "blow the whistle" on fraudulent safety reporting procedures. In the most egregious and well-documented case, a congressional committee discovered in 1991 that the corporate managers of the Trans-Alaska Pipeline paid hundreds of thousands of dollars for a nationwide hunt to find and silence critics of the Alaska oil industry—complete with eavesdropping, theft, surveillance, and sting operations—and harassed its own employees to cover up leaks about its environmental and safety errors. The point is, I think, that not all of the illegal "radical" action is in defense of the environment. Corporation actions are sometimes supported by government agencies. Government agents have infiltrated environmental groups (I mentioned the case of EF! earlier) and have used tactics of surveillance, intimidation, anonymous letters, phony leaflets, telephone threats, police overreaction, and dubious arrests (Dowie, 1995; Helvarg, 1994; Sale, 1993: 102–103).

By the 1980s and 1990s, renewed and coordinated countermovements were underway. A new strand of antienvironmentalism was the collection of energy, lumber, and mining industry associations, along with conservative foundations and think tanks that emerged to delegitimize the status of global warming as a real problem, and to oppose the ratification of the Kyoto accords (see Chapter Three) (Lutzenhiser, 2001; McCright and Dunlap, 2000; McCright and Dunlap, 2003). This countermovement of organizations and interest groups, although powerful, can hardly be said to have much of a popular base.

The other stream of reinvigorated antienvironmentalism is commonly termed the *Wise Use Movement* (WUM). The WUM is supported by conservative/right-wing politicians and media spokespersons (e.g., Rush Limbaugh, George Will) and sees itself as waging war on environmentalists, who want, they claim, to destroy free enterprise, private property rights, and jobs by misguided efforts to increase government regulations. Like the Sagebrush Rebellion before it, the primary constituency of the WUM comprises those who blame industry cutbacks on excessive environmental regulations and feel threatened by environmental reforms: loggers, miners, ranchers, farmers, hunters, industrialists, motorized recreationists, property owners, and factory workers (Helvarg, 1994). In 1988, the WUM convened a meeting in Reno, Nevada, to coordinate the growth of "wise use" organizations and draw up an agenda. By 1995, there were about 1,500 different groups coordinated by Ron Arnold and his Center for the Defense of Free Enterprise in Bellevue, Washington. WUM movement leaders claim millions of followers, but dues-paying and active members probably number much fewer than 100,000 (Helvarg, 1994; Mertig et al., 2002: 460). For a national movement, this is rather small, about the size of EF!, but its influence is greater because of its connections to conservative foundations (e.g., the Heritage Foundation and the Cato Institute) and legal and lobbying organizations.

WUM and related countermovement organizations have curious names:

- National Wetlands Coalition (oil drillers and real estate developers)
- The U.S. Council on Energy Awareness (the nuclear power industry)
- Friends of Eagle Mountain (a mining company that wants to create landfills in open pit mines)
- Wilderness Impact Research Foundation (logging and ranching interest groups in Nevada)
- American Environmental Foundation (a Florida property owners' group)
- Global Climate Coalition (corporations opposed to regulations to control global warming)

From their names, you would think that these *were* environmental organizations! A weakness of antienvironmentalism is that its organizations *must* often be given deceptive names if they are to succeed publicly (a phenomenon that environmentalists termed *greenscamming*). Imagine the public relations problems of a group calling itself something like the "Coalition to Trash the Environment for Profit." The WUM adopted a formal agenda that declared, "all public lands including wilderness and national parks shall be open to mineral and energy production" and that the endangered species act be amended to "exclude relic species in decline before the appearance of man" (Gottleib, cited in Brulle, 2000: 127).

*Tough opposition indeed!* Such countermovements are a measure of *both* the power and success of environmental movements *and* their difficulties in that they elicit powerful and sustained opposition. Protecting the environment may well be a consensual value, as public opinion polls indicate, but the costs and benefits of doing so are very unevenly distributed. Antienvironmental movements have not derailed, but have certainly deflected and blunted the impact of environmental movements. But such countermovements also have their weaknesses and vulnerabilities. One is that it has always been difficult for antienvironmental movements to co-opt the moral high ground. Who wants to "dance with the devil" and openly advocate economic practices that destroy the planet's natural resource base or kill humans? This is why antienvironmental movements must often operate under a cover of deception that makes them vulnerable to public disclosure. Greenscamming is a strategy that exposes a vulnerability. Moreover, given the consensual nature of proenvironmental attitudes, such countermovements are likely to backfire. Such was the case in the first part of the conservative Reagan administration. Legislation proposed at the urging of environmental countermovements to weaken environmental laws and reduce budgets of programs protecting the environment has often failed. It is important to note that business reaction has not been uniform. For understandable reasons, opposition was always stronger in capital-intensive and extractive industries and weaker in retail industries that are more directly connected to public opinion.

## GLOBAL ENVIRONMENTALISM

As in the United States, environmentalism grew in virtually every more developed country (MDC) nation during the 1960s and 1970s, but particularly in Western Europe. I mentioned the influence of the German "Greens" on German environmental politics and policy, but in fact, environmentalism in Germany has a long history, reaching back to the turn of the last century in "conservation" movements similar to those in the United States (Dominick, 1992). Environmentalism visibly emerged in Eastern Europe and the Soviet Union as those systems began to unravel in the 1980s. As in the United States, heightened public awareness everywhere led to collective action and pressure on public officials. A multitude of environmental and other private organizations became internationally linked or networked as nongovernmental organizations (INGOs in the parlance of diplomats and international agencies).

Global environmentalism was stimulated by increasing cooperation among the world's scientific communities to study things at biospheric and planetary levels, including the International Geophysical Year (1957–1958), the International Biological Programme (1963–1974), and the Scientific Committee on Problems of the Environment (SCOPE). Agencies noted earlier helped, including the World Meteorological Organization (WMO) and the Food and Agriculture Organization (FAO), and particularly NGOs like the International Union for Conservation of Nature and Natural Resources (IUCN). At both national and international levels, there was scientific progress in atmospherics, soil science, oceanography, environmental toxicology, and ecology. Although organized by MDCs, scientists from LDCs emerged as leaders in the diffusion of environmental awareness in their nations, and in 1971 SCOPE convened a meeting of LDC scientists in Australia to consider environmental issues from their perspective (Caldwell, 1992: 65).

Another stimulus for the globalization of environmental consciousness was the emergence of problems that transcend national boundaries. These included concerns about nuclear radiation; pollution of the air and water; transborder shipment of hazardous materials; the global reduction of biodiversity (especially tropical deforestation); the spread of contagious disease; and dilemmas about use of outer space, the seas, and the Antarctic region. International environmental awareness was also amplified by high drama media-enhanced disasters. These include, for instance, the disastrous escape of toxic gases at a Union Carbide plant in Bhopal, India, in which an MDC corporation killed people in third world communities, the diffusion of radioactivity from the atomic nuclear reactor disaster at Chernobyl in the USSR in 1986, and disastrous ocean oil spills. These disasters were widely reported in the international press, dramatizing that environmental vulnerabilities are ultimately global. Equally important to the emergence of global environmentalism were the more general threats of the 1990s: the international shipment of hazardous material, chiefly wastes; the disintegration of the stratospheric ozone layer; and the threat of global climate change. In each case, scientific findings publicized in the media preceded public awareness, and eventually led to popular calls for governmental and international action (Caldwell, 1992: 67).

Environmentalism was not limited to the affluent MDCs or stimulated only by global problems. As in the United States with grassroots and environmental justice movements, environmental movement organizations proliferated in the LDCs, most remarkably among the world's poorest and most marginal to the modern world economy.

---

## BOX 8.1

### Tree Huggers?

The most acclaimed LDC grassroots movement grew in the hills of Uttar Pradesh, India, in 1993, when a timber company headed for the woods above an impoverished village, and local men, women, and children rushed ahead of them to *chipko* (literally "hug" or "cling to") the trees, daring the loggers to let the axes fall on their backs. Maybe you've heard the word "tree hugger" as American slang for environmentalist. That's where the term came from (Bell, 1998: 190). The Chipko movement has gone beyond resource protection to ecological management. The women who first guarded trees from loggers now plant trees, build soil-retention walls, and prepare village forestry plans. Similarly, communities of traditional fishers in Brazil, the Philippines, and the Indian states of Goa and Kerala organized to battle commercial trollers and industrial polluters who deplete their fisheries.

---

The people of the world's disappearing tropical forests have begun to defend their homes despite a pace of destruction that has made their task a daunting one. In the late 1970s, a union of 30,000 Brazilian rubber tappers in the rainforest decided to draw the line.[5] Their tactics were simple and direct: Where the chainsaws were working, men, women, and children would peacefully occupy the forest, putting their bodies in the path of destruction. This action was met with violent reprisals that continue today. In 1988, opponents gunned down Chico Mendez, the national leader of the rubber tappers—later to become a powerful symbolic martyr of rainforest protection for environmentalists around the world. At a high price, the tappers made modest gains: They helped reshape World Bank development policy, and international environmental organizations have called on the Brazilian government to set off large "extractive reserves" where tappers could continue their traditional livelihood. Across the Pacific, Borneo's Dayak tribe was less fortunate. Living in Malaysia's dense forest, they opposed cutting the tropical hardwood, the heart of Malaysia's export strategy. The Dayaks wanted it cut only sustainably and have battled timber contractors by constructing roadblocks and appealing to European consumers to boycott Malaysian lumber. Government intransigence has stymied their effort.

An African federation known as *Naam* is among the most successful of the world's grassroots movements at mobilizing people to protect and restore overused agricultural resources. Building on precolonial self-help traditions, Naam taps vast stores of peasant knowledge and creativity to halt the deterioration of the drought-prone Sahel (in western sub-Saharan Africa). Naam originated in Burkina Faso and now extends under different names into Mauritania, Senegal, Mali, Niger, and Togo. Each year during the dry season, thousands of Naam villagers undertake projects that they initiate with minimal external assistance. They build large dams and a series of check dams to trap drinking and irrigation water and to slow soil erosion. Hundreds of Naam farmers have adopted a simple technique of soil and water conservation, developed by Oxfam UK (a multinational NGO), in which stones are piled in low rows along the contour to hold back the runoff from torrential rains. While halting soil loss, these structures dramatically increase crop yields (Durning, 1989: 34–39; Harrison, 1987).

In Kenya, East Africa, the idea of a grassroots environmental movement was conceived during political campaigns in the early 1970s. In 1974, an articulate and enthusiastic Kenyan woman, Wangari Maathai, attended an international U.N. meeting where she met and developed connections with women active in environmental and social justice NGOs. Returning to Kenya, she started a reforestation "Green Belt" movement, primarily among Kenyan women, for small farmers to plant trees. The goals of the movement were not only to stanch soil erosion, but also to educate people about the interrelations of the environment to other issues, such as food production and health. The *Green Belt movement* intended to improve the income and sense of efficacy of women in particular. Remarkably, the Green Belt movement slowly thrived in a hostile and authoritarian political climate by using consensus and nonconfrontational strategies (vs. conflict strategies) and by developing support among international organizations. By 1992, 10 million trees had been planted that survived (a 70% to 80% survival rate), and as many as 80,000 women were involved in work at nursery sites. Gradually people learned that trees prevented soil erosion and loss of fertility. They came to see the link between loss of soil fertility, poor crop yields, and famine. At the local level, the Green Belt movement increased farm income and also helped to transform Kenyan communities by empowering them to help themselves. At the societal level, environmental degradation gained widespread recognition as an important issue. In 1989, environmental leaders from other African nations attended workshops conducted by the Kenyan Green Belt movement; and in 1992, after a U.N. environment conference in Rio de Janeiro, a Pan-African Green Belt Movement was launched (Michaelson, 1994). As you can see from these illustrations, protection of the environment in the LDCs is clearly and directly linked to the need for improved economic and material security. For obvious reasons, improved material security is often a more pressing issue among the poor in the LDCs than environmental protection per se. But people everywhere have come to understand a relationship between protecting and improving material security and protecting the environment.

As such concerns became visible on a worldwide basis, the United Nations sponsored a series of conferences about environment and development concerns beginning in 1972 (mentioned in Chapter Seven). Disappointingly, the 1992 Rio conference (United Nations Conference on Environment and Development [UNCED]) did not produce enforceable treaties about environmental problems, but generated a broad consensus about issues like pollution, biodiversity, and global warming. A series of more specific conferences followed UNCED related to environmental particular issues about, for instance, population, the rights of women, global warming, human habitat (housing), and the growth of urban areas. The global warming (Kyoto) and population (Cairo) conferences were discussed in earlier chapters. Real progress remained painstakingly slow, and new international challenges—terrorist attacks, war, and mounting tensions around the world—threatened to sidetrack growing world momentum to address environmental problems (Runyan and Norberhaug, 2002: 30). Steps taken toward a more just and ecologically resilient world were too small, too slow, and too narrowly rooted. In 2002, 20 years after UNCED, the World Summit on Sustainable Development (WSSD) in Johannesburg, South Africa, while noting areas of progress and problems, produced a consensus that sustainable development and environmental protection were more difficult and complex than thought in 1992 (Associated Press, 2002).

An important point is that in recent decades, a truly global concern about environmental hazards emerged, stimulated by a combination of more global scientific knowledge, the impacts of international environmental degradation, the globalization of poverty, the growth of international environmental activism in both MDCs and LDCs, and a series of U.N. conferences. As evidence for such global concern, consider the Gallup Organization's survey about the Health of the Planet (HOP) that compared the public's views of environmental issues and concerns among representative samples in 24 economically and geographically diverse nations. The HOP survey found significant levels of environmental concern among people in all nations, including rich ones (like the United States and Denmark) and poor ones (like Nigeria and India). But concerns were not identical around the world. Surprisingly, people in poor nations were more likely to rate the environment as a serious problem than do their counterparts in rich nations.

Understandably, however, they rated it less serious relative to other national problems, such as poverty and malnutrition (Gallup et al., 1993). Some have argued that poor people are not as concerned about the environment as the affluent because they have yet to experience the material security and the "postmaterialist values" said to spawn environmentalism (Inglehart, 1990). But, as the discussion of grassroots environmentalism demonstrates, that it is not true in the United States, nor is it true around the world. The preponderance of evidence from HOP and other research contradicts the common idea that environmental concerns are a luxury reserved for affluent people and nations (Dunlap and Mertig, 1995; Mertig and Dunlap, 2001).

## ENVIRONMENTALISM: POPULAR SUPPORT AND CHANGE

Given extensive mobilization over 40 years, for what kinds of change has environmentalism been at least partly responsible? What have the actual impacts been for the environment and for those of us who are not activists? Fair questions.

### People and Environment: Attitudes, Commitments, and Behaviors

There is evidence of changing attitudes and behavior about environmental concerns.

In contrast to the dominant Western Worldview and its connected Human Exceptionalism paradigm, Dunlap and colleagues proposed an alternative New Ecological Paradigm (NEP) for "seeing the world ecologically." (See Chapter One.) Dunlap and Van Liere concretized the question for empirical research by developing a 12-item NEP scale containing such items as (1) the importance of maintaining the balance of nature, (2) the reality of limits to growth, (3) the need for population control, (4) the seriousness of anthropogenic environmental degradation, and (5) the need to control industrial growth (1978, 1984). Among random samples in several states, they found the general public accepted the context of the emerging NEP much more than expected (1978), and that this acceptance has grown since then (Dunlap et al., 2000). Subsequently, other researchers found support for the NEP and similar concepts in a variety of public samples in the United States and Canada (e.g., Caron, 1989; Cooper et al., 2004; Edgell and Nowell, 1989; Pierce et al., 1999).

What kinds of people are likely to be more concerned about environmental problems? Research suggests that educated people are more concerned than less educated people, younger adults are more concerned than older adults, and people whose lives are more directly impacted by environmental hazards are more concerned than those whose lives are less directly impacted. *These differences are not statistically very powerful ones* (Gould et al., 1988; Samdahl and Robertson, 1989; Van Liere and Dunlap, 1980). Gender is a powerful predictor of *some* environmental attitudes. Women are more concerned than men about health and safety issues and technological risks, but evidence of similar gender differences is weak about other concerns, such as global warming and biodiversity. Furthermore, women are not more likely than men to participate in environmental movement activities (Caiazza and Barrett, 2003; Freudenburg and Davidson, 1996; Stern et al., 1993). Research generally shows urban people to be more environmentally concerned than rural people, possibly because urbanites live in more visibly degraded and polluted environments. Other studies suggest that farmers are more concerned than nonfarm rural residents are, and owner-operator farmers are more concerned than absentee owners or farmers who lease land. Furthermore, depending on the *kind* of environmental issue, some urban people are less concerned than are rural people. In short, urban–rural differences exist, but in complex rather than simple ways (Constance et al., 1994; Freudenburg, 1991a; Williams and Moore, 1994).

Political and ideological differences exist about environmental protection. Liberals have more proenvironmental attitudes than do conservatives, and Democrats and political liberals

An environmental activist wears a shirt saying "more trees please" at an international demonstration about climate change.

consistently report stronger proenvironmental attitudes than do Republicans (though as with the social variables above, differences are not very great). It is not an exaggeration to say that since the 1980s the Democrats have become the "environmental party" and the Republicans the "antienvironmental party," although the Republicans don't describe themselves this way. Instead, they prefer to talk about the need for "balance" between economic growth and environmental protection, and so on (Dunlap, 2000b).

The Gallup Organization tracks public opinion over time about the environment and many other issues. In 2007, it found among random samples of Americans that more gave a higher priority to protecting the environment (58%) than for energy production (34%). By 2010, those favoring a higher priority to protecting the environment had declined to 43%, while those favoring a higher priority for producing energy had increased to 50%. But between March and May of 2010, the oil spill in the Gulf of Mexico sharply altered American's views. By May a majority again favored environmental protection (55%) over energy production (39%), the second largest percentage favoring the environment in the 10-year history of asking the question. These March to May shifts were much stronger among self-described Democrats and Independents, but negligible for Republicans (Jones, 2010). This dramatically illustrates the impact of environmental events, like the oil spill, to shape human attitudes and culture, and that given events, environmental protection and producing more energy will probably compete as significant public concerns.

Continuing with Gallup poll data, on April 22, 2010, the 40th Earth Day, poll data found that 19% Americans said they were active participants in the environmental movement, while 42% were sympathetic but not active. At the same time, 28% were neutral and 10% were unsympathetic. The combined activists and sympathizers have declined somewhat since 2000, but at 61% remains high. Attitudes about the impact of environmentalism were similar. The percentage of respondents who believed that environmentalism had done more good than harm declined from 75% to 62% from 2000 to 2010, and those who believed that it had done more harm than good increased from 21% to 36%. On both issues (participation and beliefs about its impact), those more supportive of the environmental movement were the young (aged 18–32), those with college degrees, Democrats, and self-described liberals. There were no differences between men and women, but women were more likely to personally identify with the environmental movement (Dunlap, 2010).

Measures of "proenvironmental behaviors" were very stable over the first decade of 2000. In various years, large majorities (80%–90%) engaged in the most popular and easy-to-perform behavior (recycling) or increased negligibly from 70% to 80% of the respondents (e.g., reducing household energy or making "green purchases"). Over the decade, there were small declines in contributing money to an environmental group (from 40% to 36%, a decline not surprising given the economic conditions of the decade). Over the decade, 28% to 30% reported working for a political candidate because of their position on environmental issues. There were also small declines in contacting a public official about an environmental issue (from 18% to 17%), and in contacting a business to complain about a harmful product (from 13% to 8%, the least common of all behaviors) (Dunlap, 2010).

The overall implications of these data suggest that after 40 years environmentalism endures, but with much less consensus than it had at 2000. But I noted earlier that this period of expanding environmental protection did not last. Between 2008 and 2009 belief that the environment (including global warming) was a very significant problem declined sharply, along with a political polarization of attitudes and political support for environmental protection. Favorable attitudes toward protecting the environment became concentrated among Democrats and political liberals, while support for environmental protection was much less evident among Republicans and political independents. Political ideology moderated whatever benefits higher education may have had in producing more proenvironmental attitudes. These shifts are particularly significant because Republicans and independents had become the dominant American attitudinal and governing majorities by the late 1990s. The "environmental regulatory state" was not dismantled, as some would have liked. Outright hostility toward environmental problems grew among parts of the American people, including global warming—in spite of massive scientific consensus to the contrary. Environmentalism itself became suspect as "threats to jobs and profits" among many Americans and particularly among the more conservative politicians who came to power by the first decade of the new millennium (McCright and Dunlap, 2011).

## ENVIRONMENTALISM: HOW SUCCESSFUL?

It could be argued that environmentalism has not been successful because of ongoing problems in the biophysical environment itself and limited success in policy arenas. In 2004 at a meeting of environmental grantmakers, journalists Michael Schellenberger and Ted Nordhaus delivered a stunning and widely distributed essay entitled the "Death of Environmentalism" (2004). They argued that, after decades of mobilizing and great investment, the environmental movement has little to show for its efforts. Speaking particularly about the United States, environmental movements represent special interest groups, speak in an elitist technocratic language, have failed to develop a public vision or strategy for change, and do not connect in any meaningful way with American social values. They claim that environmental protection has measurably lost support in public opinion, and that the Bush era exposed it as something of a paper tiger. They advocate a "New Apollo Project," using cognitive linguistics to "reveal the underlying frames of American political discourse and would use various rhetorical strategies to generate support for progressive policies." Their critics saw this as a one-size-fits all approach that mimics the political right and simply reframes their arguments (Brulle and Jenkins, 2006: 83). Dunlap asked "Where's the data?" and cited evidence that in spite of decline and limitations there is little evidence of a thorough failure. As much as the environmentalism they criticize, Schellenberger and Nordhaus advocate an elitist and technocratic approach, without addressing questions of hard tradeoffs, or having a real vision of political and economic change (Brulle and Jenkins, 2006).

Schellenberger and Nordhaus's obituary not only produced defensive reactions among leaders of national environmental organizations (though it did do that), but also produced serious soul-searching. Defenders of environmentalism had to admit that some of Schellenberger and Nordhaus's critique rang true. With the exception of the Sierra Club and the League of Conservation Voters, national organizations have eschewed electoral politics and grassroots organizing. "Our movement has been apolitical," said Brent Blackwelder, president of Friends of the Earth (Hertzgaard, 2006). Most environmental organizations treated supporters as donors rather than as citizens, and have little engagement or interest in grassroots organizing. Yet the decade of decline may re-invigorate environmentalism, for it has led even the national movement organizations to recognize that something new is needed. A more successful approach would have several common themes. It would focus on economically attractive solutions rather than downbeat warnings of disaster. It would reach out to new and sometimes ideologically or culturally "distant" constituencies, and do so in plain language that ordinary people can grasp. It would emphasize sustained local organizing that "grows" the movement's base and supports the skills in lobbying, litigation, and other tactics (Hertzgaard, 2006). Instead of endorsing private rhetorical initiatives, Luke (2005) called for a *public ecology* that would engage citizens in a collective effort to rebalance the sociotechnical order with human and natural needs. One of its first jobs would be a democratization of the environmental movement, making it capable of engaging citizens and developing a healthy dialogue about long-term solutions (Brulle and Jenkins, 2006). There is ample evidence that this strategy would have a greater likelihood of success (Shaiko, 1999).

It was a good time to be making this argument. Global warming has finally been widely acknowledged as an urgent problem, and fighting it can be very profitable. The more that fossil fuel energy prices go up, the more profitable it will be to invest in green energy—above all, in energy efficiency (Hertzgaard, 2006).

## Personal Connections

*Questions for Review*

1. How does "environmentalism" combine various discourses about the environment, ideology, and advocacy organizations?
2. What are some important environmental discourses in the history of the United States that define differently issues about human–environment relations and have given rise to different groups and organizations?
3. The earliest environmental discourse has been termed "manifest destiny," and it played an important role in the settling and development of North America by Europeans. How so?
4. How did the rise of an urban industrial society in the United States, particularly from the 1950s onward, transform movements to protect the environment?
5. As the awareness of the importance of the natural environment grew in the United States, what are some large environmental advocacy organizations that emerged that are important sources of education, recreation, reform, and political lobbying on behalf of environmental causes?
6. What has emerged as the ritual celebration of the environment in American culture?

7. Why are the goals of environmental movements (even moderate ones) always controversial, and why do they engender strong (often organized) opposition? What forms do "manifest destiny" and anti-environmentalism take today?

8. What are some of the natural and social causes of the emergence of *global* environmental consciousness and movements?

9. What impact has environmentalism had on the behavior and attitudes of people in the United States and around the world?

10. In the last 100 years, how has environmentalism succeeded and failed?

*Questions for Reflection*

1. How do your acquaintances view environmental activists or organizations? Ask a variety of people in different walks of life (your friends, several professors, clergy, businesspeople, your relatives). What kinds of different responses and perceptions do people have? Do people differentiate between "responsible" and "radical" environmentalism? Do people see environmentalism as a threat? To what?

2. This chapter has argued that environmentalism would be better served by emphasizing attractive alternatives rather than warnings of disaster. Can you envision any? Think about energy, transportation, consumption, food issues, water, maintaining biodiversity, global warming, etc. I have suggested several in places.

3. In what senses do you think environmentalism has succeeded or failed?

## What You Can Do

While this book has treated the abstract big issues, I hope you recognize that there has been another theme: that individuals matter. Often significant social change comes from the bottom up, not from the top down. I began this section in the introductory chapter by noting (with some misgivings) the established slogan of environmentalism: "Think globally, act locally." Individuals can matter in several ways. You can change your own lifestyle to be more environmentally benign (which is good in itself but may also demonstrate to others the possibility of positive change). Many of the "what you can do" suggestions that I have offered so far are about these kinds of possibilities. If the idea of voluntary simplicity intrigues you and you want to find out more about how people are doing it or make contact with others, try these Web sites: www.simplicitycircles.com; www.newdream.org; www.adbusters.org. Changing yourself is important, but I also think it's important that you join with others to act or raise consciousness about human and environmental issues. There are many ways of doing so.

## More Resources

Brulle, R. J. (2000). *Agency, democracy, and nature: The U.S. environmental movement from a critical theory perspective.* Cambridge, MA: MIT Press.

De Steiguer, J. E. (1997). *The age of environmentalism.* New York: McGraw-Hill.

Dobson, A. (2000). *Green political thought.* London, UK: Routledge.

Dalton, R. J. (1994). *The green rainbow: Environmental groups in Western Europe.* New Haven, CT: Yale University Press.

Dryzek, J., Downes, D., Hunold, C, and Schlosberg, D. (2003). *Green states and social movements: Environmentalism in the United States, United*

*Kingdom, Germany, and Norway.* New York: Oxford University Press.

Florina, A. M. (Ed.) (2000). *The third force: The rise of transnational civil society.* Tokyo and Washington, DC: Japan Center for International Exchange and the Carnegie Endowment.

Helvarg, D. (1994). *War against the greens: The "Wise Use" movement, the New Right, and antienvironmental violence.* San Francisco, CA: Sierra Books.

Kline, B. (2000). *First along the river: A brief history of the U.S. environmental movement* (2nd ed.). San Francisco, CA: Arcada Books.

Littig, B. (2001). *Feminist perspectives on environment and society.* New York, London, UK: Prentice Hall.

Switzer, J. V. (1997). *Green backlash: The history and politics of environmental opposition in the U.S.* Boulder, CO: Lynne Rienner.

## Endnotes

1. Freudenberg and Steinsapir list seven kinds of outcomes: (1) blocking the construction of waste disposal facilities, forcing the cleanup of toxic dumps, banning aerial spraying of pesticides, and so forth; (2) altering corporate practices, particularly through product liability suits; (3) applying increased popular economic and political pressure for the prevention of environmental hazards; (4) winning legislative victories about rights for citizen participation in environmental decision making; (5) increasing community mobilization; (6) linking environmental problems with problems of social justice; and (7) promoting broader public environmental consciousness (1992: 33–35).

2. The only known injury from tree spiking was to a millworker at a Louisiana Pacific mill in California in 1987, when a bandsaw struck an embedded spike. The company blamed it on EF! and the media broadcasted the allegation with great fanfare. EF! was never charged or even investigated, however, and no evidence ever connected it to the spiking. Furthermore, the tree was not in an old-growth area that activists had been defending, nor was it even standing when it was spiked, not a monkey wrench tactic (Sales, 1993: 66).

3. In a few minutes on my computer, I located 22 in California, 7 in Minnesota, 4 in New York, and 4 in Missouri. The Web site address for the voluntary simplicity network is www.simplicitycircles.com.

4. Consider a March 1998 article entitled "Environmental Effects of Increased Atmospheric Carbon Dioxide," in a format closely resembling a reprint of the *Proceedings of the National Academy of Sciences* (which it was not). The article concluded that predictions of global warming are in error and that increased $CO_2$ levels greatly benefit plants and animals. In fact, this article was in a nonreferred publication funded by the George C. Marshall Institute, an antienvironmental think tank (Brulle, 2000: 128).

5. Rubber tappers make their living in the Amazon basin by harvesting latex from rubber trees spread throughout the region. They also gather Brazil nuts, fruits, and fibers in the forest and cultivate small plots near their homes. A 1988 study showed that sustainable harvesting of such nonwood products *over 50 years* would generate twice as much revenue per hectare as timber production and three times as much as cattle ranching (Miller, 1992: 261).

# In Conclusion: A Short Epilogue

Britain's First Carbon Neutral Village

The dismal litany of human–environment problems seems overwhelming, doesn't it? But I have also tried to note progress. Let me do so again in closing. Many cities, particularly in Europe and North America, are cleaner and more livable than they were a century ago. In the last 20 years, the average number of children per woman worldwide has decreased from 6.1 to 3.4. By 2050, the United Nations predicts that all developed countries and 75% of the developing world will experience a below-replacement fertility rate (2.1), meaning that the world population would stabilize at about 8.9 billion rather than 9.3 billion, as previously predicted. During the past century, the incidence of life-threatening diseases has been reduced in most countries. In spite of population growth that added a billion people in the 1990s, the number of people facing food insecurity and chronic hunger declined by about 40 million. Deforestation has slowed in Asia, from 8% per year in the 1980s to less than 1% in the 1990s. Nature preserves and protected areas grew fivefold in the last 20 years, to about 8.2% of all land area—less than the 12% thought necessary to protect the world's biodiversity, but a dramatic increase nonetheless. The European Union announced a goal of getting 22% of its electricity and 12% of all energy from renewable sources by 2010. The world's *carbon intensity*—how much carbon emissions it takes to produce a unit of economic output—has declined by 40% since 1950, and most of this since 1985 (Dunn, 2002: 52). Because democracy and the environment were a major focus of the 2002 Johannesburg World Symposium on Sustainable Development, it is worth noting that some 81 countries took significant steps toward democracy in the last two decades, and that nearly three-quarters of the world's 200 countries now hold multiparty elections (Cunningham et al., 2005: 23–24).

While these may be signs of progress, there is still plenty of bad news to go around. Environmental activist Mark Dowie captured the mixed picture this way:

> There's clearly measurable progress. People on a broad level are more aware of environmental issues. But awareness may not be enough. It's hard escaping the conclusion that it's all too little, too late. We protect one forest, and lose five, one species is brought back from the brink, but 100 quietly disappear. We controlled damage to the ozone layer, but lost ground on global warming. (cited in Motavalli, 2000: 29)

We should not fool ourselves—the costs of addressing such problems are very great, yet many are not simply costs, but rational choices that invest our energies and resources in a more sustainable world.

We know *what* needs to be done. It's a remarkably simple list of things. We need to promote three sets of ideas:

1. That cohabitation with nature is necessary
2. That there are limits to the scope of human activity
3. That the benefits of human activity need to be more widely shared (Kates, 1994: 118)

More specifically, we need to

1. Stabilize human populations
2. Reduce excess material consumption
3. Change damaging technologies into environmentally more benign ones

It is easy to say these things, but very hard to figure out how to do them, and particularly hard to muster the political will to achieve them. The depth of our environmental problems, our awareness, our rational-choice-making capacity, and our technological inventiveness makes it more likely that we will cross a threshold to global sustainability. If I am pessimistic, I remain a hopeful pessimist. Let me close by sharing something from Jared Diamond, who has written eloquently about the "collapse" of societies:

> People often ask if I am an optimist or a pessimist about our future. I answer that I'm cautiously optimistic. We face big problems that will do us in if we don't solve them. But we are capable of solving them. The risk we face isn't that of an asteroid collision

beyond our ability to avoid. Instead our problems are of our own making, and so we can stop making them. The only thing lacking is the necessary will power. We can learn from understanding [environmental problems] of remote places and times. [Past societies] didn't have that option. Knowing history, we are not doomed to repeat it. (2002: A35)

## A Final Reflection Question

Do a summary reflection: Thinking back over your reading and discussions, what stand out as some of the most important things that you learned? How have your perspectives and opinions about environmental issues changed since the beginning (if they have)?

# GLOSSARY

**Adaptation** [Ch 3, p. 75] Modifying human activities, communities, and subsistence practices to adapt to the climate change that has or will take place.

**Agroecology** [Ch 5, p. 152] Growing a variety of crops and livestock in a manner that mimics a natural ecosystem

**Anthropogenic** [Ch 1, p. 27] Environmental changes caused by humans

**Anti-environmentalism** [Ch 8, p. 243] Ideologies and movements that oppose environmental movements.

**Anti-global warming movement** [Ch 3, p. 78] The organizations and foundations that lobby against measures to address climate change. Some, like the Heartland Institute, have extensive publishing operations, and are funded by some industries (particularly energy and refining industries).

**Astroturf** [Ch 8, p. 232] A flippant term to describe environmental organizations that collect money and lobby on for environmental causes, but have a nonexistent or weakly developed base of popular support.

**Attitude-behavior consistency model** [Ch 4, p. 108] A social psychological framework for studying energy conservation that focuses on the efficacy of proconservation attitudes and behaviors.

**Biodiversity** [Ch 2, p. 40] The degree of genetic and species diversity in an ecosystem. For example, a rainforest is more diverse than a corn field.

**Biofuels** [Ch 4, p. 114] Fuels such as ethanol produced from the fermentation of plant materials like corn, grasses, algae, or sugarcane.

**Biome** [Ch 1, p. 3] A broad, regional ecosystem, with distinctive climate, soil conditions, and living things, for examples, desert, temperate forest, or Arctic biomes.

**Biomimicry** [Ch 6, p. 177] The idea of constructing an economy with many feedback loops like natural systems, rather than just extracting resources and generating wastes.

**Bioprospecting** [Ch 2, p. 48] The practice, often practiced by pharmaceutical firms, of looking pharmacologically active compounds produced by rainforest species.

**Biosphere** [Ch 1, p. 3] The entire "layers of life" on the planet, from deep in the oceans to high in the stratosphere.

**Carrying capacity** [Ch 1, p. 5] The capacity of an environment to support life.

**Chlorofluorocarbons (CFCs)** [Ch 3, p. 64] Chlorinated carbon compounds, used in refrigeration and air-conditioning units. When they "leaked" (as they all did), they rose to the stratosphere where they destroyed ozone molecules that absorbed ultraviolet solar radiation.

**Circle of toxins** [Ch 2, p. 50] Toxic agrochemicals banned in industrial nations are "re-imported" with food from the less developed nations, where their use is still widespread.

**Classical economic theory** [Ch 1, p. 17] Founded by Adam Smith in the 1700s, and based on the idea that the interplay of supply and demand in economic markets meant that they are naturally and benignly self-regulating without human intervention.

**Climate** [Ch 3, p. 62] The average weather conditions experienced on the earth over a long time. Unlike the weather, climate changes are usually not accessible unaided human senses.

**Club of Rome** [Ch 6, p. 172] The name of an organization of computer modelers whose simulations about the earth's future were published in the 1970s as "the Limits of Growth." Updates of this report are used today.

**Coevolution** [Ch 1, p. 6] The complementary evolution of closely associated species, such as the interlocking adaptation of flowering plants and their pollinating insects. Humans are thought to have similarly co-evolved with the earth's climate.

**Cogeneration (See combined heat and power)** [Ch 6, p. 177]

**Combined heat and power systems (cogeneration)** [Ch 4, p. 120] Using the heat produced by an economic process to power another, widely used for its efficiencies in some parts of the world (e.g., Scandinavia and Eastern Europe).

**Common-property resource** [Ch 7, p. 193] Resources like air and oceans that cannot be individually owned or preserved. Common resources are commonly abused and degraded (but see Community Management of Environmental Resources).

**Community** [Ch 1, p. 3] A system of organisms or people that interact in a particular region or place.

**Community management of common resources (CRM)**  [Ch 7, p. 210] The conditions, studied by Elinor Ostrum, under which community resources are sustainably managed, including (1) local resource dependency, (2) stable community ties, and (3) effective rules governing resource use.

**Conflict theory**  [Ch 1, p. 23] A major sociological perspective with its history the ideas of Karl Marx (though greatly modified) emphasizing the role of conflict in the structure of society and social change.

**Conservation biology**  [Ch 8, p. 238] A subdiscipline of biology focusing on the study of the maintenance of biodiversity (see deep ecology).

**Conservation environmental movement**  [Ch 8, p. 226] A historic American environmental movement, organized around the conservation and "scientific management" of nature, associated with Gifford Pinchot and the foundation of the national forests, grassland, and parks of the federal Interior Department.

**Conservatories**  [Ch 2, p. 48] Institutions like zoos, botanical gardens, nurseries, and gene banks established to protect and preserve "wild" species of plants and animals (see gene bank).

**Constituent policy**  [Ch 7, p. 204] A policy that gives benefits or tax incentives to particular constituent groups, regions, or communities.

**Cost-benefit analysis**  [Ch 3, p. 87] A risk assessment method that compares economic costs and benefits.

**Countermovement**  [Ch 3, p. 74; Ch 8, p. 243] A social movement that develops in opposition to another movement and/or the changes it produced.

**Culture**  [Ch 1, p. 9] The total way of life of a group of people, including their customs, habits, symbols, and material things.

**Debt for nature swap**  [Ch 2, p. 48] Programs where nations act as custodians of their natural resources in exchange for debt relief from lenders.

**Deep ecology**  [Ch 8, p. 236] An ecocentric (vs. anthropocentric) environmental movement emphasizing the maintenance of biodiversity and wilderness, and that the rights of humans include only meeting basic needs. Scientists influenced by deep ecology founded conservation biology (see conservation biology).

**Dematerialization**  [Ch 2, p. 53] The extent to which an economy can maximize its results while minimizing material resources.

**Demographic transition**  [Ch 5, p. 130] Related to social development, a complex and lengthy process whereby human populations change from ones with high birth and death rates to ones with low birth and death rates. Between these points, there is a period of rapid population growth.

**Demography**  [Ch 5, p. 138] The study of the size, change, and characteristics of human populations.

**Devolution**  [Ch 1, p. 14] The process of reversal of the evolution of human societies, usually meaning the collapse of large complex structures into simpler ones (see evolution).

**Dialectec**  See societal-environmental dialectic.

**Discourse**  [Ch 8, p. 238] A narrative that tells the story of something.

**Discounting the future**  [Ch 7, p. 199] Reducing future profits by anticipating inflation and technological improvements.

**Disproportionality**  [Ch 6, p. 178] When, after controlling for differences between firms, a small number produces much more than their "share" of pollutants or toxic wastes.

**Distribution problem**  [Ch 4, p. 97] Related to energy, the problem of getting energy from where it is produced to the people and communities that need to use it. Related to food, a similar problem (maldistribution) is a cause of hunger, malnourishment, and famine.

**Division of labor**  [Ch 1, p. 12] An older term meaning *specialization*.

**Ecofeminism**  [Ch 8, p. 238] An environmental movement based on assumptions and archeological evidence that human domination of the environment is related to male domination of females

**Ecological economics**  [Ch 1, p. 19] The subdiscipline of economics that focuses on how the environment and ecosystems relate to economic processes.

**Ecological footprint**  [Ch 6, p. 175] A method of calculating the human impact on the earth, which can be done for individuals, households, communities, regions, and nations.

**Ecological modernization**  [Ch 6, p. 177; Ch 7, p. 209] A perspective maintaining that economic and social progress without disastrous growth can occur within capitalistic markets by incorporating enough "green" consumption and environmentally benign technology.

**Ecological niche**  [Ch 1, p. 5] The role in the community for animals that live in an ecosystem

**Economic nationalism**    [Ch 6, p. 162] Using means like armies, trade rules, taxes, and subsidies to benefit a nation's economic products over those of other nations (see mercantilism).

**Economic-rationality model**    [Ch 4, p. 108] A strategy of reducing energy consumption by making it more expensive

**Ecosocial system**    [Ch 2, p. 57] An environment that has been shaped so much by human–environment relations

**Ecospiritualism**    [Ch 8, p. 226] Environmental movements that view the environment as permeated by spiritual realities (similar but not identical to ecotheology)

**Ecotheology**    [Ch 8, p. 240] Environmental movements that use religious literature and mobilize religious people and organizations on behalf of the environment (related to ecospiritualism).

**Efficiency**    [Ch 4, p. 119] The ratio between energy input and productive output for consumption, with such possibilities for improvement that it is now viewed as an overlooked source of more energy.

**Energetics**    [Ch 4, p. 96] Related to energy.

**Energy regime**    [Ch 4, p. 122] A system of producing energy from particular fuels and their infrastructure (e.g., the coal or gasoline energy regimes).

**Entropy**    [Ch 1, p. 5; Ch 4, p. 101] Combustion or metabolism degrades high-quality organized forms of energy to low-quality less organized forms, such as heat (a law of thermodynamics).

**Environment**    [Ch 1, p. 1] The total surroundings of living things, with many dimensions (e.g., physical, geo-chemical, biological, sociocultural).

**Environmental justice movement**    [Ch 8, p. 233] A movement that grows from the experience of the unequal distribution environmental costs and benefits by different groups and social classes.

**Environmental Kuznets curve**    [Ch 6, p. 175] The hypothesis that at the highest levels of technological development, human impact on the environment declines somewhat, which is an environmental adaptation of the ideas of economist Simon Kuznets.

**Environmental movement**    [Ch 1, p. 17] A social movement aimed at addressing environmental problems (see environmentalism, social movement).

**Environmental possibilism**    [Ch 1, p. 13] The idea that certain kinds of material, social, and cultural factors are *likely* to produce other things, which is an alternative to a deterministic view.

**Environmental Regulatory State**    [Ch 7, p. 206] States that attempt to regulate the variety of ways humans use the environment, which includes most contemporary states.

**Environmentalism**    [Ch 8, p. 224] Ideology and collective action concerning various aspects of the environment.

**Evolution**    [Ch 1, p. 6] Change by the survival of organisms or groups that are best adapted for particular environments, sometimes associated with the emergence of greater complexity (see devolution).

**Exchange**    [Ch 1, p. 3] A way of speaking of cycles of nutrients or minerals, such as the carbon cycle. May mean economic exchange (see reciprocal exchange, exchanges of redistribution, and market exchanges).

**Exchanges of redistribution**    [Ch 1, p. 12] Economic exchanges that shift goods and services to different social levels (see exchange).

**Fault tree analysis**    [Ch 3, p. 86] A method of risk analysis for a complex system that calculates the number of separate components that need to break down before the total system collapses.

**Food pyramid (or food chain)**    [Ch 1, p. 5] The way that organisms feed on others in an ecosystem depicting the flow of energy and minerals within an ecosystem.

**Fossil fuels**    [Ch 4, p. 110] Fuel formed by the sedimentation and decay of organic material over long periods of time (e.g., coal, natural gas, and oil).

**Framing**    [Ch 4, p. 109] The symbols and discourses that surround and give meaning to a social issue.

**Functionalism**    [Ch 6, p. 185] A sociological perspective that emphasizes the way that subsystems such as operate to integrate and support the persistence (see social institutions and functions of the environment).

**Functions of the environment**    [Ch 1, p. 25] The environment "functions" for society by providing a supply depot, a waste repository, and living space.

**Gene bank**    [Ch 2, p. 48] A conservatory that preserves the genes and DNA of wild and historic species (see conservatories).

**General Circulation Models (GCMs)**    [Ch 3, p. 68] Simplified computer simulations that can be "run" over time simulate the dynamic changes in the earth's climate.

**Genuine Progress Indicator (GPI)**    [Ch 7, p. 197] A measure of social progress that, in addition to the gross domestic product, adds the value of unpriced social benefits (like volunteerism and housekeeping) and subtracts unpriced costs (like pollution and crime).

**Geoengineering** [Ch 3, p. 77] Ideas thought to be effective but unproven about addressing climate change by changing the nature of the planet, like putting minerals in the oceans to maintain the circulation of ocean thermal currents, and seeding the stratosphere with reflective objects.

**Geopolitical problem** [Ch 4, p. 98] A problem having to do with world politics and conflict, and trade among nations.

**Global environmentalism** [Ch 8, p. 246] World consciousness and action about environmental issues; an element of contemporary global culture stimulated, for instance, by trans-boundary problems (like drought, pollution, and global warming), the internationalization of the mass media, science, and activism.

**Globalization** [Ch 6, p. 160] The pervasive trends toward the integration of distinct national cultures, economies, politics, and problems into a worldwide—but highly volatile—world order. This has both positive and negative causes and consequences.

**Grassroots** [Ch 8, p. 232] The extent to which an organization, community initiative, or movement has broad-based support from non-elites.

**Green Belt Movement** [Ch 8, p. 248] A successful reforestation movement started by Kenyan women in the 1990s.

**Green consumption** [Ch 7, p. 196] Deliberately purchasing goods and consuming energy in ways that minimize their environmental impact.

**Green Imperialism** [Ch 6, p. 170] When the advice of wealthy nations to less developed nations ("preserve the rainforest; avoid unsustainable growth") is perceived as a form of imperialism justified by environmental issues.

**Greenwashing** [Ch 7, p. 196] Marketing and advertising products as "green" on questionable grounds to promote sales.

**Heuristic** [Ch 6, p. 174] Using an easily understood metaphor to explain an abstract and complex reality (e.g., "greenhouse gases" understand climate change, or a "dustbowl" to describe prolonged drought).

**Human development Index (HDI)** [Ch 7, p. 197] A measure of development, created by the United Nations, that combines data for nations about life expectancy, literacy, and real GDP per person.

**Human Exemptionalism Paradigm (HEP)** [Ch 1 p. 21] A paradigm for human–environment relations suggesting that human technological inventiveness makes them exempt from most environmental restrictions and limits (see New Ecological Paradigm).

**Human–environment relations** [Ch 2, p. 15] The relationships between people and their biophysical environments.

**I = PAT** [Ch 6, p. 174] A way of calculating human environmental impact, in which impact equals population size multiplied by the level of consumptive affluence, times the level of technology

**Ideology** [Ch 1, p. 11] A system of ideas that explains a situation and justifies action (e.g., free markets, individualism, nationalism, environmentalism).

**Incentive shifting** [Ch 6, p. 177] Changing economic incentives so that production an consumption have minimal environmental impacts. This can be accomplished, for instance, through taxing things like wasteful use of resources and pollution.

**Inelastic economic demand** [Ch 4, p. 108] When the price of goods or services goes up, demand is not much effected (the opposite of elastic demand, which is sensitive to changes in price).

**Infrastructure** [Ch 4, p. 112] The system of mechanisms for delivering a product. For fossil fuels, all the wells, mines, refineries, trucks, tankers, and pumping facilities, pipelines, transmission lines, etc.

**Intergenerational equity** [Ch 6, p. 170] Equity between generations, as in consumption at the expense of future generations (compare with intragenerational equity)

**International Monetary Fund (IMF)** [Ch 6, p. 163] A fund created by donor nations to stabilize international currencies through rapid inflation and recessions.

**Issue attention cycle** [Ch 4, p. 121] Cycles in media attention (or inattention) to issues. In 2010, for instance, the media was flooded with stories about the Gulf oil spill, but there were few stories about species extinction.

**Kyoto protocol** [Ch 3, p. 79] An international accord, signed at the ancient Japanese city of Kyoto, for nations to address climate change by reducing greenhouse gas emissions. The accord was revisited (inconclusively, without reaching quantitative national targets) at Copenhagen in 2009. The United States is not a signatory to the accord.

**Landscapes and flows** [Ch 6, p. 165] An anthropological perspective about globalization that understands it as global "flows" of people, ethnic cultures, technologies, money, and ideas.

**Less developed country (LDC)** [Ch 3, p. 72; Ch 4, p. 94] A country that is poor, typically agrarian, and relatively less developed in economic and technological terms. Collectively, LDCs were referred to as the "third world," but now sometimes as the "global South," since most are in the Southern Hemisphere. Contrast with wealthier industrial nations, the MDCs.

**Limits to growth (LG)** [Ch 6, p. 172] The notion that there are limits to continual population, consumption, and economic growth in a finite world of resources.

**Love Canal** [Ch 8, p. 223] A famous community in upstate New York, where a housing development was built on top of a toxic waste dump, which resulted in an epidemic of disease, cancers, and deaths. Activists (especially Lois Gibbs) went on to create a national toxic wastes campaign.

**Malnourishment (See distribution problem)** [Ch 5, p. 139]

**Manifest destiny** [Ch 8, p. 226] An ideological frame that provided justification for widespread and destructive environmental exploitation as Europeans settled North America.

**Market exchange** [Ch 1, p. 12] Exchanges for money that accumulate wealth, rather than for use, in which social relationships may become embedded in economic ones (See exchange).

**Material Flow analysis (MFA)** [Ch 6, p. 175] A methodology developed by Ayers and Kneese that estimates the environmental impact of economic growth by separating the "material throughput" from non-material aspects of economic production.

**Megaproblem** [Ch 3, p. 63] A problem that is on such a vast scale that it is difficult to observe by ordinary human senses, as in the cases of climate change or the "population explosion."

**Mercantilism** [Ch 6, p. 162] In European history, when kings tried to protect their nations' products by royal decrees and military force (see economic nationalism).

**Metanarrative** [Ch 8, p. 242] A "grand narrative" that can integrate more particular narratives and frames. An environmental metanarrative would, for instance, address issues about biodiversity, climate change, resource exhaustion, and justice

**Mitigation** [Ch 3, p. 75] Curtailing greenhouse gas emission to curb further global warming.

**Monoculture** [Ch 1, p. 7] An area where primarily one kind of organism grows, for instance, a corn field, or an urban lawn of bluegrass.

**More developed country (MDC)** [Ch 1, p. 17] A wealthy industrial nation, more developed in economic

and technological terms. Historically known as "first world nations." MDCs are mainly in the Northern Hemisphere.

**Multinational Corporation** (Ch 7, p. 200) A corporation that has investors, production facilities, and offices in several nations (see transnational corporation).

**Naam** [Ch 8, p. 247] A widespread indigenous agricultural movement in sub-Saharan Africa aimed at stopping soil erosion.

**Natural capital** [Ch 2, p. 40] Viewing "nature" as capital, compared with economic or social capital.

**Natural selection** [Ch 1, p. 6] The mechanisms by which "nature" selects the most well-adapted species for survival, assumed to be a major process in organic evolution.

**Neoclassical economic theory** [Ch 1, p. 18] Contemporary economic theory, which, in contrast to classical theory, assumes the need for some regulation of "free" markets for the public good.

**Neoliberalism** [Ch 6, p. 161] The perspective, primarily shared by Western economists, bankers, and finance ministers, that world economic growth will come about if world trade is unfettered by government labor policies, tariffs, or environmental restrictions,

**Net primary production (NPP)** [Ch 2, p. 56] The total photosynthetic product of green plants as they capture sunlight and manufacture living tissue, the base of all food chains. Human use accounts for about 40% of the land-based NPP, and about 25% of the earth's total NPP.

**Netherlands fallacy** [Ch 2, p. 57] When a nation is environmentally protective and frugal, but imports many resources so that its environmental impacts spread far beyond its borders.

**New Ecological Paradigm (NEP)** [Ch 1, p. 22; Ch 8, p. 249] The view that humans, like all other species, are subject to environmental limits in a finite world. Contrast this view with the "human exemptionalism paradigm," which views humans as so culturally and technologically creative that most limits can be transcended.

**NIMBY** [Ch 8, p. 235] A slogan of grassroots movements, referring to toxic and nuclear waste dumps: "Not in my back yard."

**Oil peak** [Ch 4, p. 97 ] The observation of geologist M. King Hubbard that oil production follows a "bell shaped curve" increasing rapidly, peaking, and then declining to exhaustion. Production peaked in the

United States in the 1970s, and the world peak will occur in this century.

**Outbreak crash**   [Ch 6, p. 172] A process familiar to population biologists; when a population grows beyond its environmental "carrying capacity," it experiences a rapid decline. Human communities have experience sudden collapses for similar reasons, as was the fate of the Easter Islanders, the Western Roman Empire, and Mesopotamian civilizations.

**Paradigm**   [Ch 1, p. 21] A mental image of "the way the world works," a term coined by philosopher Thomas Kuhn to describe the Newtonian ("quantum mechanics") view of the universe. Paradigms may be held unwittingly, and they may be elements of popular culture or scholarly/scientific ones.

**Perverse subsidy**   [Ch 7, p. 195] A subsidy that makes an economic commodity artificially cheap, and leads to its overuse. For examples, water in the Western United States is highly subsidized and if overused in a dry region, and subsides to farmers (in many countries) encourage them to "overfarm" and farm on marginal lands,

**Photovoltaic electricity (PVE)**   [Ch 4, p. 117] When semiconductor cells absorb sunlight and produce an electric current.

**Policy**   [Ch 7, p. 201 ] A set of rules or procedures to address an important problem or concern. Policy may be public (governmental) or private.

**Precautionary principle**   [Ch 3, p. 74] Addressing a potential high cost problem, even though its occurrence may be unlikely, as, for instance, in mortgage insurance.

**Preservation environmental movement**   [Ch 8, p. 226] An original form of American environmentalism, dedicated to protecting nature from human intrusion. Associated with John Muir and nature photographer Ansel Adams.

**Private-property resource**   [Ch 7, p. 193] A resource that can be privately owned, and may be more likely to be sustainably used.

**Public-property resource**   [Ch 7, p. 193] A resource that could be privately owned, but is often owned by governments having exclusive rights to control their use (e.g., national parks, public education, prisons, jet fighters).

**Rational-choice theory**   [Ch 7, p. 198] A recent perspective that can integrate substantial bodies of theory in economics, biology, and psychology, that humans (both individually and collectively) are rational choice makers, who seek to minimize costs and maximize rewards or benefits

**Rationality**   [Ch 1, p. 26 ] As used by Max Weber, "rationality" means an efficient linkage between means and ends, that is, minimizing inputs (of cost, resources, or labor) and maximizing output.

**Rebound effect**   [Ch 7, p. 196] When efficiency (for instance, in the operation of home appliances) saves money that gets spent in other ways, perhaps increasing consumption.

**Reciprocal exchange**   [Ch 1, p. 12] Mutual benefit exchanges, as in symbiosis.

**Recreancy**   [Ch 7, p. 208] The idea that as people become more dependent on "experts," they become suspect for their lack of competence, or lack of commitment to the pubic good.

**Regulatory policy**   [Ch 7, p. 208] Policy that attempts to control behavior over a broad spectrum of economic processes, institutions, and communities.

**Renewable energy source**   [Ch 4, p. 114] Energy from sources that are hypothetically renewable, like solar, wind, or energy driven by tidal motion, unlike fossil fuels.

**Resilience**   [Ch 7, p. 219] The ability of a social-ecological system to absorb change and persist. Resiliant systems have a greater capacity to learn, undergo transformation, and stay within a desired state.

**Resource allocation paradigm**   [Ch 7, p. 193] The notion of neoclassical economists that markets allocate resources efficiently, by the interplay of supply and demand.

**Resource partitioning**   [Ch 1, p. 5] Mechanisms that make it possible for different species to share the same resource base without much conflict or competition, for example, in lakes and seas, bottom feeders versus top feeders, or day versus nocturnal feeders. In human communities, the segmentation of labor markets does much the same.

**Salinization**   [Ch 2, p. 51] When soil becomes too salty by over-irrigation, water evaporates, leaving mineral salts behind in the soil. A major cause of the decline of soil fertility.

**Service and flow economy**   [Ch 6, p. 177] Instead of being based on ownership, an economy where many goods and services can be leased or rented. In Paris, there are stations where you can rent a car or bicycle by the hour, and in some places you can rent the services of a nurse or an attorney for a short time. Such a system multiplies re-use and recycling of resources.

**Sink** [Ch 2, p. 34] A waste repository—landfill, dump. Pollution makes environmental sinks out of air or bodies of water.

**Sink problem** [Ch 4, p. 99] Related to energy, the "sink problem" is about the combustion byproducts of fuels, as in smoke, smog, or greenhouse emissions.

**Social construction** [Ch 1, p. 26] The perspective that realities are not only external, but constructed by people who define, discuss, and experience them

**Social impact assessment** [Ch 3, p. 86] A method of assessing the community impacts of major new projects like mines, power plants, and hydroelectric dams.

**Social institution** [Ch 1, p. 10] Long established parts of society that address important concerns (e.g., families, politics, the economy, healthcare).

**Social movement** [Ch 8, p. 225] Ideology and collective action about promoting or preventing change.

**Social stratification** [Ch 1, p. 22] Layers of social inequality arranged in layers. The basic "building blocks" of society, such as status-roles, groups, organizations, and social classes.

**Societal-environmental dialectic** [Ch 1, p. 23] A three-part process of change in human–environmental relations consisting of a direction (or thesis), its opposite (or an antithesis), and a fusion (or synthesis) (see treadmill of growth).

**Passive solar heating system** [Ch 4, p. 117] A solar space heating system that uses walls or windows to collect solar radiation.

**Active solar heating system** [Ch 4, p. 117] A solar space heating system that uses panels mounted on rooftops that pipes warm water to water tanks or living space.

**Retrofit** [Ch 4, p. 117] Making a building more energy efficient, for instance, by installing more insulation or more efficient appliances.

**Source problem** [Ch 4, p. 96] As related to energy, having to do with the adequacy of supplies.

**Status-role** [Ch 1, p. 10] The most elementary units of social structure. Statuses are structures, and roles are expectations and/or behaviors (see social structure).

**STIRPAT** [Ch 6, p. 174] The stochastic regression of impacts on population, affluence, and technology: A method of studying environmental impacts using data from a large sample of nations over time, rather than summary numbers in an "accounting" equation.

**Stochastic** [Ch 6, p. 174] Probabilistic, rather than deterministic.

**Supply side energy policies vs demand side** [Ch 4, p. 98] Policies to address energy problems by increasing the supply of fuels.

**Sustainability** [Ch 6, p. 170] When a process can be carried on indefinitely without collapse.

**Symbiosis** [Ch 1, p. 6] When two or more species live in a closely associated way that may or may not be mutually beneficial.

**Symbolic interactionism** [Ch 1, p. 26] A social psychological perspective emphasizing that behavior and self-concepts are critically influenced by language and symbols.

**System** [Ch 1, p. 3] A network of interconnected parts, so that a change in one element of a system has implications for other parts of the system.

**TRI (Toxic Release Inventory)** [Ch 7, p. 209] Under the provisions of the National Environmental Protection Act (NEPA), in the United States industrial firms are obliged to publish an annual estimate of the volume of toxins that produce and release into the environment.

**The Three E's** [Ch 6, p. 170] Understanding sustainability as involving ecology, economics, and (social) equity. Any of the three can be a starting place for policy to address environmental sustainability, but it makes a big difference that you start with.

**Third World nations** [Ch 6, p. 173] See less developed country (LDC).

**Tradable Environmental Allowances (TEAs)** [Ch 7, p. 212] A system of giving producers permits for limits on their impact on common property resources (e.g., industrial emissions or fish catch from an ocean fishing ground). Producers who exceed their permits buy permits from more efficient producers in a special auction. Known as a "cap and trade" system, it provides incentives for using fewer resources and efficiency (see common property resources).

**Tragedy of the commons** [Ch 7, p. 194] Garrett Hardin's observation that common property (or common pool) resources are often exploited beyond sustainable levels.

**Transnational corporation (TNC)** [Ch 7, p. 216] A corporation that produces goods and services in more than one country, to reduce production costs, or avoid taxes, or both (see multinational corporations).

**Treadmill of production** [Ch 1, p. 23; Ch 7, p. 173] The observation that in market economies continual growth is universally desirable (to avoid unemployment and recessions), but—ironically—continual growth undermines the environmental resources that make growth possible.

**Tree huggers**   [Ch 8, p. 247] A label applied to environmentalists, deriving from rural Indians who surrounded forest trees, attempting to prevent logging companies from cutting them.

**Volatile Organic Compounds (VOCs)**   [Ch 3, p. 54] A harmful collection of more than 100 organic compounds remaining from the incomplete combustion of hydrocarbons from transportation and industry. Urban "smog."

**Voluntary simplicity**   [Ch 6, p. 180; Ch 8, p. 240] A recurring but minor theme (and movement) in contemporary societies advocating the less consumption, simpler lifestyles, and less environmentally damaging technologies.

**Wedge Analysis**   [Ch 3, p. 76] Addressing a large, complex problem like the mitigation of global warming by breaking it down into smaller, manageable ("bite sized") parts or pieces.

**Wind farm**   [Ch 4, p. 116] A large array of wind turbines in a particular place linked to an energy grid.

**Wind turbine** [Ch 4, p. 116]   The contemporary version of windmills that are complex and highly engineered machines with many moving parts, metal alloys and gears.

**World Bank for Development and Reconstruction** [Ch 6, p. 163] The international agency that provides loans and assistance for development to poor nations.

**World market economy**   [Ch 6, p. 161] The emerging system of international trade, labor relations, and currency exchange that is the key to understanding globalization.

**World Trade Organization (WTO)**   [Ch 6, p. 163] The organization created by nations and large banks to promote, establish policy for, and monitor world trade.

**World-system**   [Ch 6, p. 163] Wallerstein's theory about the integration of economies, politics, and culture into a connected hierarchy of nations, which began to replace older colonialism in the twentieth century. When not hyphenated, world system is a synonym for globalization.

**Worldview**   [Ch 1, p. 11] The total understanding of the world and universe that people have, which includes all dimensions of their knowledge, beliefs, and experience.

# REFERENCES

ACHESON, J. (1981). The lobster fiefs, revisited: Economic and ecological effects of territoriality in the Maine lobster industry. In B. McCay and J. Acheson (Eds.), *The question of the commons* (pp. 37–65). Tucson, AZ: University of Arizona Press.

ADEOLA, F. (2004). Boon or bane? The environmental and health impacts of persistent organic pollutants (POPs). *Human Ecology Review, 11* (1), 27–35.

ALARIO, M., and FREUDENBURG, W. (2003). The paradoxes of modernity: Scientific advances, environmental problems, and risks to the social fabric. *Sociological Forum, 18,* 193–214.

ALEKLETT, K. (2006). Oil: A bumpy road ahead. *Worldwatch, 19* (1), 10–11.

ALEXANDER, J. (1985). *Neofunctionalism.* Beverly Hills, CA: Sage.

ALEXANDER, S., SCHNEIDER, S., and LAGERQUIST, K. (1997). The interaction of climate and life. In G. Daily (Ed.), *Nature's services: Societal dependence on natural ecosystems* (pp. 71–92). Washington, DC: Island Press.

ALTIERI, M. (1995). *Agroecology: The science of sustainable agriculture.* Boulder, CO: Westview Press.

ALTIERI, M. (1998). Ecological impacts of industrial agriculture and the possibility for a truly sustainable farming. *Monthly Review, 50* (3), 60–71.

AMANO, A. (1990). Energy prices and $CO_2$ emissions in the 1990s. *Journal of Policy Modeling, 12,* 495–510.

ANDERSON, T., and GREWELL, J. (1999). Property rights solutions for the global commons: Bottom up or top down? *Duke Environmental Law and Policy Forum, 10,* 73–101.

APPADURAI, A. (1996). *Modernity at large: Cultural dimensions of globalization.* Minneapolis, MN: University of Minnesota Press.

ARMILLAS, P. (1971). Gardens on swamps. *Science, 174,* 653–661.

ASSADOURIAN, E. (2005). Toxic chemicals. In Prugh, T. (Ed.), *State of the world, 2005: Redefining global security* (pp. 78–79). New York: W. W. Norton.

ASSOCIATED PRESS. (1994, October 20). EPA reports improvements in air quality. *The Omaha World Herald,* p. 19.

ASSOCIATED PRESS. (2002, August 25). "Show me the money" replaces climate change as summit theme, *The Omaha World Herald,* p. 17a.

ASSOCIATED PRESS. (2006, June 23). Report says world now warmest in 2000 years. *The Omaha World Herald,* p. 3A.

ASSOCIATED PRESS. (2010a). Millennium's first decade sets heat record. In *The Omaha World Herald,* 5A, Jan 20, 2010.

ASSOCIATED PRESS. (2010b). Hurricanes predicted to be fewer, stronger. In *The OmahaWorld Herald,* Feb 22, 3A.

ASSOCIATED PRESS. (2010c). Nuclear plants get $8 billion boost. In *The Omaha World Herald,* Feb 17, 1A–2A.

AYRES, J., and KNEESE, A. (1968). *Environmental pollution.* Washington DC: Federal Programs for the Development of Human Resources.

AYRES, R. (2001). The energy we overlook. *Worldwatch, 14* (6), 30–39.

BALAAM, D., and VESETH, M. (1996). *Introduction to international political economy.* Upper Saddle River, NJ: Prentice Hall.

BALAND, J., and PLATTEAU, J. (1996). *Halting degradation of natural resources: Is there a role for rural communities?* Oxford, UK: Clarendon Press.

BARASH, D. (1979). *Sociobiology: The whisperings within.* New York: HarperCollins.

BARBER, B. (1983). *The logic and limits of trust.* Rutgers, NJ: Rutgers University.

BASKIN, L., HIMES, K., and COLBURN, T. (2001). Hypospadias and endocrine disruption: Is there a connection? *Environmental Health Perspectives, 109* (11), 1175–1183.

BECK, U. (1995). *Ecological politics in an age of risk.* New York: Polity Press.

BECK, U. (1996). World risk society as cosmopolitan society? Ecological questions in a framework of manufactured uncertainties. *Theory, Culture, and Society, 13,* 4.

BEDER, S. (1998). *Global spin: The corporate assault on environmentalism.* White River Junction, VT: Chelsea Green.

BELL, M. (1998). *An invitation to environmental sociology.* Thousand Oaks, CA: Pine Forge Press.

BELL, M. (2004). *An invitation to environmental sociology* (2nd ed.). Thousand Oaks, CA: Pine Forge Press.

BENDER, W., and SMITH, M. (1997). Population, food, and nutrition. *Population Bulletin, 51* (4), 2–43.

BENTON, T. (1989). Marxism and natural limits: An ecological critique and reconstruction. *New Left Review, 178,* 51–86.

BERGER, P., and LUCKMANN, T. (1976). *The social construction of reality.* New York: Doubleday.

BIRDSALL, N. (1980). Population and poverty in the developing nations. *Population Bulletin, 35,* 1–48.

BLACK, J. et al. (1985). Personal and contextual influences on household energy adaptations. *Journal of Applied Psychology, 70,* 3–21.

BLEVISS, D. L., and WALZER, P. (1990). Energy for motor vehicles. *Scientific American, 263* (3), 103–109.

BLOCK, B. (2010). Covering climate change. *Worldwatch, 23* (2), 20–25.

BOOKCHIN, M. (1982). *The ecology of freedom: The emergence and dissolution of hierarchy.* Palo Alto, CA: Cheshire Books.

BOSERUP, E. (1981). *Population and technological change: A study of long-term trends.* Chicago: University of Chicago Press.

BOSSO, C. (2005). *Environment, Inc.* Lawrence, KS: University of Kansas Press.

BRICKMAN, R., JASANOFF, S., and ILGEN, T. (1985). *Controlling chemicals: The politics of regulation in Europe and the United States.* Ithaca, NY: Cornell University Press.

BROWN, L., and FLAVIN, C. (1999). A New economy for a new century. In L. Brown, C. Flavin, and H. French (Eds.), *State of the world 1999.* New York: W. W. Norton.

BROWN, L. (1988). *The changing world food prospect: The nineties and beyond.* Worldwatch Institute Paper No. 85. Worldwatch Institute.

BROWN, L. (1991). The new world order. In L. Starke (Ed.), *State of the world 1991.* New York: W. W. Norton.

BROWN, L. (1994). Who will feed China? *Worldwatch, 7* (5), 10–22.

BROWN, L. (1999). Feeding nine billion. In L. Starke (Ed.), *State of the world, 1999.* New York: W. W. Norton.

BROWN, L. (2001). *Eco-economy: Building and economy for the earth.* New York: W. W. Norton.

BROWN, L. (2004). *Outgrowing the earth: The food scarcity challenge in an age of falling water tables and rising temperatures.* New York: W. W. Norton.

BROWN, L. (2008). *Plan B 3.0: Mobilizing to save civilization.* New York: W. W. Norton.

BROWN, L. (2009). *Plan B 4.0: Mobilizing to save civilization.* New York: Earth Policy Institute.

BROWN, L., FLAVIN, C., and KANE, H. (1992). *Vital signs: Trends that are shaping our future.* New York: W. W. Norton.

BROWN, L., FLAVIN, C., and POSTEL, S. (1990). Picturing a sustainable society. In L. Starke (Ed.), *State of the world, 1990.* New York: W. W. Norton.

BRULLE, R. J. (2000). *Agency, democracy and nature: U.S. environmental movements from the perspective of critical theory.* Cambridge, MA: MIT Press.

BRULLE, R. J., and JENKINS, C. (2006). Spinning our way to sustainability? *Organization and Environment, 19* (1), 82–87.

BRUNO, M. (2010). Disaster contingency plans are "fantasy documents" when it comes to oil spills. http:// grist.org. Accessed 2010/05/11.

BRYANT, B. (1995). *Environmental justice: Issues, policies, and solutions.* Washington, DC: Island Press.

BULLARD, R. D. (1990). *Dumping in Dixie: Race, class, and environmental quality.* Boulder, CO: Westview.

BULLARD, R. D. (Ed.) (1993). *Confronting environmental racism: Voices from the crossroads.* Boston: South End Press.

BULLARD, R., and JOHNSON, G. (2000). Environmental justice: Grassroots activism and its impact on public policy decision making. *Journal of Social Issues, 56,* 555–578.

BUNKER, S. (1996). Raw materials and the global economy: Distortions in industrial ecology. *Society and Natural Resources, 9,* 419–429.

BURINGH, P. (1989). Availability of agricultural land for crop and livestock production. In D. Pimentel and C. W. Hall (Eds.), *Food and natural resources.* San Diego, CA: Academic Press.

BURNS, T. R., and DIETZ, T. (1992). Cultural evolution: Social rule systems, selection and human agency. *International Sociology, 7* (3), 259–283.

BUTTEL, F. (1986). Sociology and the environment: The winding road toward human ecology. *International Social Science Journal, 109,* 337–356.

BUTTEL, F. (2000c). World society, the nation-state, and environmental protection: Comment on Frank, Hironaka, and Schofer. *American Sociological Review, 65* (February), 117–121.

BUTTEL, F. (2000a). Ending hunger in developing countries. *Contemporary Sociology, 29* (1), 13–27.

BUTTEL, F. (2000b). *The adoption and diffusion of GM crop varieties: The "gene revolution" in global perspective.* PATS Paper Series, Program on Agricultural Technology Studies, College of Agricultural Life Sciences, Paper no. 6, March. Madison, WI: University of Wisconsin–Madison.

BUTTEL, F. (2002). Ecological modernization as a social theory. *Geoforum, 31,* 57–76.

BUTTEL, F., HAWKINS, A., and POWER, A. (1990). From limits to growth to global change: Contraints and contradictions in the evolution of environmental science and ideology. *Global Environmental Change, 1190* (December), 57–66, cited on p. 53 in A. Mol (2003). *Globalization and environmental reform: The ecological modernization of the global economy.* Cambridge, MA: MIT Press.

CABLE, S., and BENSON, M. (1993). Acting locally: Environmental injustice and the emergence of grassroots environmental organizations. *Social Problems, 40* (4), 464–477.

CAIAZZA, A., and BARRETT, A. (2003). *Engaging women in environmental activism: Recommendations for Rachel's Network.* Washington, DC: Institute for Women's Policy Research.

CALDWELL, L. (1992). Globalizing environmentalism: Threshold of a new phase in international relations. In R. E. Dunlap and A. G. Mertig (Eds.), *American environmentalism: The U.S. environmental movement, 1970–1990* (pp. 63–76). New York: Taylor & Francis.

CAMP, S. L. (1993, Spring). Population: The critical decade. *Foreign Policy, 90,* 126–144.

CAPEK, S. (1993). The "environmental justice" frame: A conceptual discussion and application. *Social Problems, 40* (1), 5–24.

CARON, J. (1989, Spring). Environmental perspective of blacks: Acceptance of the new environmental paradigm. *Journal of Environmental Education, 20,* 21–26.

CARRUS, K. (2006). Birds remain threatened. In L. Starke (Ed.), *Vital signs 2006–2007: Trends that are shaping our future* (pp. 96–97). New York: W. W. Norton.

CARSON, R. (1962). *Silent spring.* Boston: Houghton Mifflin.

CARVER, T. N. (1924). *The economy of human energy.* New York: Macmillan.

CASTELLS, M. (2000). *The rise of the network society.* Oxford, UK: Blackwell.

CASTEN , S. (2009). The perfect market fallacy. *The recycled energy blog.* Accessed March 30, 2011.

CATTON, W. (1993/1994). Let's not replace one set of unwisdoms with another. *Human Ecology Review, 1* (1), 33–38.

CATTON, W. (1997). Redundancy anxiety. *Human Ecology Review, 3* (2), 175–178.

CATTON, W. R., and DUNLAP, R. E. (1986). Competing functions of the environment: Living space, supply depot, and waste repository. Paper presented at the 1986 meeting of the Rural Sociological Society, Salt Lake City, UT.

CATTON, W., and DUNLAP, R. E. (1978). Environmental sociology: A new paradigm? *The American Sociologist, 13,* 41–49.

CHARLES, D. (1999, October 15). Hunger in America. *Morning Edition.* Washington, DC: National Public Radio.

CHARMAN, K. (2006). Brave nuclear world. *Worldwatch 19* (4), 12–18.

CHASE-DUNN, C. (1989). *Global formation: Structures of the world economy.* Oxford, UK: Blackwell.

CHIU, A. (2009). One twelfth of global electricity comes from combined heat and power systems. In L. Starke (Ed.), *Vital signs 2009: Trends that are shaping our future* (pp. 50–52). New York: W. W. Norton.

CICCANTELL, P. (1999). It's all about power: The political economy and ecology of redefining the Brazilian Amazon basin. *Sociological Quarterly, 40* (2), 293–315.

CLAPP, J. (2002). The Distancing of waste: Overconsumption in a global economy. In Princen, T., Maniates, and Conca, K. (Eds.), *Confronting consumption* (pp. 155–176). Cambridge, MA: MIT Press.

CLARKE, L. (1993). The disqualification heuristic: When do organizations misperceive risk? *Research in Social Problems and Public Policy, 5,* 289–312.

CLARK, L. (1998). Explaining choices among technological risks. *Social Problems, 35* (1), 22–35.

CLARK, M. (1991). Rethinking ecological and economic education: A gestalt shift. In R. Costanza (Ed.), *Ecological economics: The science and management of sustainability* (pp. 400–414). New York: Columbia University Press.

CLARK, W. (1990). Managing planet earth. In *Managing planet earth: Readings from* Scientific American (pp. 1–12). New York: W. H. Freeman.

CLYKE, F. (1993). *The environment.* New York: HarperCollins.

COHEN, J. E. (1995). *How many people can the earth support?* New York: W. W. Norton.

COLEMAN, J. S. (1990). *Foundations of social theory.* Cambridge, MA: Harvard University Press.

COLES, C. (2004). Water without war. *Futurist, 38,* 2.

COLLINS, J., and PORRAS, J. (2002). *Built to last: Successful habits of visionary companies.* New York: Harper Business.

COLLINS, R. (1975). *Conflict sociology: Toward an explanatory science.* New York: Academic Press.

COMMONER, B. (1971). The *closing circle.* New York: Knopf.

COMMONER, B. (1992). *Making peace with the planet.* New York: The New Press.

CONDORCET, M. DE (1979). *Sketch for a historical picture of the progress of the human mind.* (J. Barraclough, Trans.) London: Wiedenfield and Nicholson. (Original work published in 1795.)

CONSTANCE, D., RIKOON, J., and HEFFERNAN, W. (1994). Groundwater issues and pesticide regulation: A comparison of Missouri urbanites' and farm operators' opinions. Presented at the annual meeting of the Midwest Sociological Society, St. Louis, MO.

COOK, E. (1971). The flow of energy in an industrial society. *Scientific American, 224* (3), 134–147.

COOPER, P., POE, G., and BATEMAN, I. (2004). The structure of motivation for contingent values: A case study of lake water quality improvement. *Ecological Economics, 50,* 69–82.

COSTANZA, R., CUMBERLAND, J., DALY, H., GOODLAND, R., and NORGAARD, R. (1995). *An introduction to ecological economics.* Boca Raton, FL: St. Lucie Press.

COTTRELL, F. (1955). *Energy and society.* New York: McGraw-Hill.

CRAIG, J. R., VAUGHAN, D. J., and SKINNER, B. J. (1988). *Resources of the earth.* Englewood Cliffs, NJ: Prentice Hall.

CROSSON, P., and ROSENBERG, N. (1990). Strategies for agriculture. In *Managing planet earth: Readings from* Scientific American. New York: W. H. Freeman.

CUNNINGHAM, W., and CUNNINGHAM, M. (2010). *Environmental science: A global concern* (11th ed.). Boston: McGraw Hill Higher Education.

CUNNINGHAM, W., CUNNINGHAM, M., and SAIGO, B. (2005). *Environmental science: A global concern* (8th ed.). Boston: McGraw Hill Higher Education.

DAHRENDORF, R. (1959). *Class and class conflict in industrial society.* Stanford, CA: Stanford University Press.

DAILY, G. (Ed.). (1997). *Nature's services: Societal dependence on natural ecosystems.* Washington, DC: Island Press.

DAILY, G., and ELLISON, K. (2002). *The new economy of nature.* Washington, DC: Island Press.

DAILY, G., MATSON, P., and VITOUSEK, P. (1997). Ecosystem services supplied by soil. In G. Daily (Ed.), *Nature's services: Societal dependence on natural ecosystems* (pp. 113–150). Washington, DC: Island Press.

DALY, H., and COBB, J. (1989). *For the common good: Redirecting the economy towards community, the environment, and a sustainable future.* Boston: Beacon Press.

DALY, H., and TOWNSEND, K. (Eds.). (1993). *Valuing the earth: Economics, ecology, and ethics.* Cambridge, MA: MIT Press.

DANIELS, G., and FRIEDMAN, S. (1999). Spatial inequality and the distribution of industrial toxic releases: Evidence from the 1990 TRI. *Social Science Quarterly, 80* (2), 244–262.

DAVIS, M. (2007). *Planet of Slums.* New York: Verso Press.

DE BLIJ, H. J. (1993). *Human geography: Culture, society, and space* (4th ed.). New York: John Wiley and Sons.

DEJONG, G. (2000). Expectations, gender, and norms in migration decision-making. *Population Studies, 54,* 307–319.

DECONINCK, S. (2004). Israeli water policy in a regional context of conflict: Prospects for sustainable development for Israelis and Palestinians? Available at http://waternet.ugent.be/waterpolicy.htm.

*Der Spiegel* (1992). May 25, p. 77. Reprinted in *Utne Reader,* May/June 1993, 57.

DEROSE, L., MESSER, E., and MILLMAN, S. (1998). Who's hungry? And how do we know? *Food shortage, poverty, and deprivation.* New York: United Nations University Press.

DEVALL, B. (1992). Deep ecology and radical environmentalism. In R. E. Dunlap and A. G. Mertig (Eds.), *American environmentalism: The U.S. environmental movement, 1970–1990* (pp. 51–62). Philadelphia: Francis Taylor.

DEVALL, B., and SESSIONS, G. (1985). *Deep ecology.* Salt Lake City, UT: Peregrine Smith.

DEVEREAUX, S., and EDWARDS, J. (2004). Climate change and food security. *IDS Bulletin, 35* (3), 22–30.

DIAMOND, J. (2002). Lessons from lost worlds. *Time, 160* (9), August 26, A54–A55.

DIAMOND, J. (2003). The last Americans. *Harper's Magazine.* June, 34–51.

DIAMOND, J. (2004), *Collapse: How societies choose to fail or succeed.* New York: Viking Press.

DIETZ, T. (1996/1997). The human ecology of population and environment: From utopia to topia. *Human Ecology Review, 3* (3), 168–171.

DIETZ, T., and KALOF, L. (1992). Environmentalism among nation-states. *Social Indicators Research, 26,* 353–366.

DIETZ. T., and ROSA, E. (1994). Rethinking the environmental impacts of population, affluence, and technology. *Human Ecology Review, 1,* 277–300.

DIETZ, T., STERN, P., and RYCROFT. R. (1989). Definitions of conflict and the legitimatization of resources: The case of environmental risk. *Sociological Forum, 4,* 47–50.

DIETZ, T., and VINE, E. L. (1982). Energy impacts of a municipal conservation program. *Energy, 7,* 755–758.

DIETZ, T., BURNS, T., and BUTTEL, F. (1990). Evolutionary thinking in sociology: An examination of current thinking. *Sociological Forum, 5,* 155–185.

DIETZ, T., STERN, P., and RYCROFT, R. (1989). Definitions of conflict and the legitimization of resources: The case of environmental risk. *Sociological Forum, 4,* 47–70.

DILLMAN, D., ROSA, E., and DILLMAN, J. (1983). Lifestyle and home energy conservation in the United States: The poor accept lifestyle cutbacks while the wealthy invest in conservation. *Journal of Economic Psychology, 3,* 299–315.

DILORENZO, T. J. (1993, September/October). The mirage of sustainable development. *The Futurist, 27* (5), 14–19.

DOLD, C. (1992, July/August). Slapp back! *Buzzworm, 4* (4), 34–41.

DOMINICK, R. H. (1992). *The environmental movement in Germany.* Bloomington, IN: Indiana University Press.

DOWIE, M. (1995). *Losing ground: American environmentalism at the close of the twentieth century.* Cambridge, MA: MIT Press.

DOWNS, A. (1972). Up and down with ecology—the "issue-attention cycle." *Public Interest, 28,* 38–50.

DUNLAP, R. E. (1992). From environmental to ecological problems. In C. Calhoun and G. Ritzer (Eds.), *PRIMIS: Social Problems.* New York: McGraw Hill.

DUNLAP, R. E. (2000a). Paradigms, theories, and environmental sociology. In R.E. Dunlap, F. Buttell, and A. Gijswijt (Eds.), *Sociological theory and the environment* (pp. 329–350). New York: Roman and Littlefield.

DUNLAP, R. E. (2000b). Americans have positive image of the environmental movement. *Gallup Poll Monthly, 415,* April.

DUNLAP, R. E. (2006a). Personal Comment.

DUNLAP, R. E. (2006b). Where's the data? An examination of the death of environmentalism's ambiguous empirical foundations. *Organization and Environment, 19* (1), 1–15.

DUNLAP, R. E. (2010). At 40, environmental movement endures, with less consensus. http://www.gallop.com/poll/127487/environmental-movement-endures-less-consensus.aspx. Accessed 6/1/2010.

DUNLAP, R. E., and CATTON, R. (2002). Which function(s) of the environment do we study? A comparison of environmental and natural resource sociology. *Society and Natural Resources, 15,* 239–249.

DUNLAP, R. E., and CATTON, W. (1983). What environmental sociologists have in common. *Sociological Inquiry, 33,* 113–135.

DUNLAP, R. E., and MARSHALL, B. (2006). Environmental sociology. Manuscript, forthcoming in D. Bryant and D. Peck (Eds.), *The handbook of 21st century sociology.* Thousand Oaks, CA: Sage.

DUNLAP, R. E., and MERTIG, A. G. (1992). The evolution of the U.S. environmental movement from 1970 to 1990: An overview. In R. Dunlap and A. Mertig (Eds.), *American environmentalism: The U.S. environmental movement, 1970–1990* (pp. 1–10). Philadelphia: Francis Taylor.

DUNLAP, R. E., and MERTIG, A. G. (1995). Global concern for the environment: Is affluence a prerequisite? *Journal of Social Issues, 51,* 121–137.

DUNLAP, R. E., and SCARCE, R. (1991). The polls—poll trends: Environmental problems and protection. *Public Opinion Quarterly, 55,* 651–672.

DUNLAP, R. E., and VAN LIERE, K. (1984). Commitment to the dominant social paradigm and concerns for environmental Q: An empirical examination. *Social Science Quarterly, 65,* 1013–1028.

DUNLAP, R. E., VAN LIERE, K., MERTIG, A., and JONES, R. (2000). Measuring endorsement of the new ecological paradigm: A revised NEP scale. *Journal of Social Issues, 56* (3), 425–442.

DUNLAP, R. E., and VAN LIERE, K. (1978, Summer). The new environmental paradigm: A proposed measuring instrument and preliminary results. *Journal of Environmental Education, 9,* 10–19.

DUNN, S. (1998). After Kyoto: A climate treaty with no teeth. *Worldwatch, 11* (2,4), 33–35.

DUNN, S. (1999). Automobile production drops. In L. Starke (Ed.), *Vital signs 1999: The environmental signs that are shaping our future.* New York: W. W. Norton.

DUNN, S. (2002). Carbon emissions reach new high. In L. Starke (Ed.), *Vital signs 2002: The trends that are shaping our future.* New York: W. W. Norton.

DURKHEIM, E. (1964). *The division of labor in society.* (G. Simpson, Trans.) New York: Macmillan. (Original work published in 1893.)

DURNING, A. (1989). *Poverty and the environment: Reversing the downward spiral.* Worldwatch paper no. 92. Washington, DC: Worldwatch Institute.

DURNING, A. (1992). *How much is enough? The Consumer society and the future of the earth.* New York: W. W. Norton.

DURNING, A. (1993). Can't live without it: Advertising and the creation of needs. *Worldwatch, 6* (3), 10–18.

DURNING, A. (1994, March/April). The seven sustainable wonders of the world. *Utne Reader, 62,* 96–99.

ECKERELE, K. (2006). Plant diversity endangered. In Starke, L. (Ed.), *Vital signs 2006–2007: Trends that are shaping our future* (98–99). New York: W. W. Norton.

ECKHOLM, E. (1976). *Losing ground: Environmental stress and world food prospects.* New York: W. W. Norton.

EDGELL, M., and NOWELL, D. (1989). The new environmental paradigm scale: Wildlife and environmental beliefs in British Columbia. *Society and Natural Resources, 2,* 285–296.

EDITORS. (2006a). We have been warned: Now everyone should understand why we have to combat climate change. *NewScientist,* Nov. 10–14, 5.

EDITORS. (2006b). Low carbon now. *NewScientist,* Nov. 4–10, 7.

EDWARDS, B. (2000, November 19). Genetically engineered rice. *Morning Edition.* Washington, DC: National Public Radio.

EHRLICH, P. (1968). *The population bomb.* New York: Ballantine Books.

EHRLICH, P., and EHRLICH, A. (1992). *The population explosion.* New York: Doubleday.

EHRLICH, P., and HOLDREN, J. (1974). Impact of population growth. *Science, 171,* 1212–1217.

EHRLICH, P., and HOLDREN, J. (1988). *The Cassandra conference: Resources and the human predicament.* College Station, TX: Texas A & M Press.

EISLER, R. (1988). *The chalice and the blade.* New York: Harper and Row.

EITZEN, S., and BACA ZINN, M. (1992). *Social problems* (5th ed.). Boston: Allyn and Bacon.

ELGIN, D. (1982). *Voluntary simplicity: Toward a way of life that is outwardly simple, inwardly rich.* New York: Morrow.

FALKENMARK, M., and WIDSTRAND, C. (1992). Population and water resources: A delicate balance. *Population Bulletin, 47,* 3.

FALLOWS, J. (2010). Dirty coal, clean future. *The Atlantic, 306* (4, December), 64–78.

FARHAR, B. (1994). Trends: Public opinion about energy. *Public Opinion Quarterly, 58,* 603–632.

FICKETT, A., GELLINGS, C., and LOVINS, A. (1990). Efficient use of electricity. *Scientific American, 263* (3), 64–75.

FIELD, J. (1993). *The challenge of famine.* West Hartford, CT: Kumarian Press.

FISCHER, C. (1976). The *urban experience.* New York: Harcourt Brace Jovanovich.

FISCHOFF, B. (1990). Psychology and public policy: Tool or toolmaking? *American Psychologist, 45,* 647–663.

FISCHOFF, B., SLOVIC, P., and LICHTENSTEIN, S. (1980). Lay foibles and expert fables in judgments about risk. *American Statistician, 36,* 240–255.

FISHER, D. (2004). *National governance and the global climate change regime.* New York: Roman and Littlefield.

FISHER, D., and FREUDENBURG, W. (2004). Postindustrialization and environmental quality: An empirical analysis of the environmental state. *Social Forces, 83* (1), 157–188.

FISHER, J. (1993). *The road from Rio: Sustainable development and the nongovernmental movement in the Third World.* Westport, CT: Prager.

FISCHER-KOWALSKI, M. (1998). Society's metabolism: The intellectual history of flow analysis. *Journal of Human Ecology, 2 (1),* 61–78.

FISCHER-KOWALSKI, M., and AMANN, C. (2001). Beyound IPAT and Kuznets curves: Globalization as a vital factor in analysing the environmental impact of socio-economic metabolism. *Population and Environment, 23* (1), 7–47.

FLAVIN, C. (1986). Moving beyond oil. In L. Starke (Ed.), *State of the world, 1986.* New York: W. W. Norton.

FLAVIN, C. (1997). Storm damages set record. In L. Starke (Ed.), *Vital signs 1997: The environmental trends that are shaping our future* (pp. 70–71). New York: W. W. Norton.

FLAVIN, C. (1998). Last tango in Buenos Aires. *Worldwatch, 11* (6), 10–18.

FLAVIN, C. (1999). Wind power blows to new records. In L. Starke (Ed.), *Vital signs 1999: The environmental trends that are shaping our future* (pp. 52–53). New York: W. W. Norton.

FLAVIN, C. (2001a). Wind energy growth continues. In L. Starke (Ed.), *Vital signs 2001: The trends that are shaping our future* (pp. 44–45). New York: W. W. Norton.

FLAVIN, C. (2001b). Rich planet, poor planet, In L. Starke (Ed.), *State of the world, 2001.* New York: W. W. Norton.

FLAVIN, C. (2005). Fossil fuel surges. In Starke L. (Ed.) *Vital signs 2005: The trends that are shaping our future* (pp. 30–31). New York: W. W. Norton.

FLAVIN, C. (2006). Nuclear revival? Don't bet on it. *Worldwatch, 19* (4), 19.

FLAVIN, C., and DUNN, S. (1999). Reinventing the energy system. In L. Stark (Ed.), *State of the world, 1999.* New York: W. W. Norton.

FLAVIN, C., and YOUNG, J. E. (1993). Shaping the next industrial revolution. In L. Starke (Ed.), *State of the world, 1993.* New York: W. W. Norton.

FLINT, R. (2010). Seeking resiliency in the development of sustainable communities. *Human Ecology Review, 17* (1), 44–57.

FORTUNE MAGAZINE. (2008). *The Fortune Global 500.* Cited in Giddens, A., Dunier, M. Applebaum, R. and Carr, D., *Introduction to Sociology* (7th ed., pp. 439–440). New York: W. W. Norton.

FOSTER, J. (1999). Marx's theory of metabolic rift: Classical foundations for environmental sociology. *American Journal of Sociology, 105* (2), 366–405.

FRANK A. (1997). *Capitalism and development in Latin America.* New York: Monthly Review Press.

FRANK, D. (1999). The social bases of environmental treaty ratification, 1900–1990. *Sociological Inquiry, 69,* 523–550.

FRANK, D., HIRONKA, A., and SCHOFER, E. (2000). The nation-state and the natural environment over the twentieth century. *American Sociological Review, 65,* 96–116.

FRENCH, H. (1990). *Green revolutions: Environmental reconstruction in Eastern Europe and the U.S.S.R.* Washington, DC: Worldwatch Institute.

FRENCH, H. (1993). Reconciling trade and the environment. In L. Starke (Ed.), *State of the world, 1993.* New York: W. W. Norton.

FRENCH, H. (1994). The World Bank: Now fifty, but how fit? *Worldwatch, 7* (4), 10–18.

FRENCH, H. (1999, November/December). Challenging the WTO. *Worldwatch, 12,* 22–27.

FRENCH, H. (2007–2008). Progress toward the MGDs is mixed. In L. Starke (Ed.), *Vital signs 2007–2008: The Trends that are shaping our future* (pp. 108–109). New York: W. W. Norton.

FREUDENBERG, N. (1984). *Not in our backyards! Community action for health and the environment.* New York: Monthly Review Press.

FREUDENBERG, N., and STEINSAPIR, C. (1992). Not in our backyards: The grassroots environmental movement. In R. E. Dunlap and A. G. Mertig (Eds.), *American environmentalism: The U.S. environmental movement, 1970–1990* (pp. 27–37). Philadelphia: Francis Taylor.

FREUDENBURG, W. R. (1984). Boomtown's youth: The differential impacts of rapid community growth on adolescents and adults. *American Sociological Review, 40,* 697–705.

FREUDENBURG, W. R. (1991a). Rural–urban differences in environmental concern: A close look. *Sociological Inquiry, 61* (2), 167–198.

FREUDENBURG, W. R. (1991b). A "good business climate" as bad economic news? *Science and Natural Resources, 3,* 313–331.

FREUDENBURG, W. R. (1992). Addictive economies: Extractive industries and vulnerable localities in a changing world economy. *Rural Sociology, 57* (3), 305–332.

FREUDENBURG, W. R. (1993). Risk and recreancy: Weber, the division of labor, and the rationality of risk perceptions. *Social Forces, 71,* 909–932.

FREUDENBURG, W. R. (2005). Privileged access, privileged accounts: Toward a socially structure theory of resources and discourses. *Social Forces, 84* (1), 89–114.

FREUDENBURG, W. R. (2006). Environmental degradation, disproportionality, and the double diversion: Reaching out, reaching ahead, and reaching beyond. *Rural Sociology, 71* (1), 3–32.

FREUDENBURG, W. R., and DAVIDSON, D. (1996). Gender and environmental risk concerns: A review and analysis of available research. *Environment and Behavior, 28* (3), 332–339.

FREUDENBURG, W. R., and FRICKEL, S. (1994). *Digging deeper: Mining-dependent regions in historical perspective.* Paper presented at the 1994 meeting of the Midwest Sociological Society, St. Louis, MO.

FREUDENBURG, W. R., and FRICKEL, S. (1995). Beyond the nature/society divide: Learning to think about a mountain. *Sociological Forum, 10,* 361–392.

FREUDENBURG, W. R., and GRAMLING, R. (1994). Natural resources and rural poverty: A closer look. *Society and natural resources, 7,* 5–22.

FREY, B., and STUTZER, A. (2002). *Happiness and economics.* Princeton, NJ: Princeton University Press.

FROSCH, R., and GALLOPOULOS, N. (1990). Strategies for manufacturing. *Managing planet earth: Readings from* Scientific American (pp. 97–108). New York: W. H. Freeman.

FRY, R. (2010). Methane threat imperils climate. *The Omaha World Herald,* June 6, 7B.

FULKERSON, W., JUDKINS, R., and SANGHVI, M. (1990). Energy from fossil fuels. *Scientific American, 263* (3), 128–135.

GALLUP, G., DUNLAP, R. E., and GALLUP, A. (1993). *Health of the planet.* Princeton, NJ: Gallup International Institute.

GARDINER, R. (2001). Foreign direct investment: A lead driver for sustainable development? *Towards Earth Summit 2002* (p. 3). London: UNED Forum–UK Committee.

GARDNER, G. (1998). Organic waste reuse surging. In L. Starke (Ed.), *Vital signs 1998: Environmental trends that are shaping our future* (pp. 130–131). New York: W. W. Norton.

GARDNER, G. (2000). Fish harvest down. In Starke, L. (Ed.) *Vital signs 2000: Environmental trends that are shaping our future.* New York: W. W. Norton.

GARDNER, G. (2002). The challenge for Johannesburg. In L. Starke (Ed.), *State of the world, 2002* (pp. 3–23). New York: W. W. Norton.

GARDNER, G. T., and STERN, P. (1992). *Environmental problems and human behavior* (2nd ed.). Boston, MA: Pearson Custom Publishing.

GARDNER, G., and SAMPAT, P. (1999). Forging a sustainable materials economy. In L. Starke (Ed.), *State of the world, 1999* (pp. 41–59). New York: W. W. Norton.

GARDNER, G., and STERN, P. (1996). *Environmental problems and human behavior.* Needham Heights, MA: Allyn and Bacon.

GARDNER, G., and STERN, P. (2002). *Environmental problems and human behavior* (2nd ed.). Boston: Pearson Custom Publishing.

GARRIGUES, L. (2010). Why is Costa Rica smiling. *Yes!* Winter: 12–15.

GEDDES, P. (1979). *Civics as applied to sociology.* Leicester, England: Leicester University Press. (Original work published in 1890.)

GELBARD, A., HAUB, C., and KENT, M. (1999). World population beyond six billion. *Population Bulletin, 3* (54), 1.

GELBSPAN, R. (1997). *The heat is on.* Reading, PA: Addison-Wesley.

GIBBONS, J., and GWIN, H. (1989). Lessons learned in twenty years of energy policy. *Energy Systems and Policy, 13,* 9–19.

GIBBONS, J., BLAIR, P., and GWIN, H. (1990). Strategies for energy use. In *Managing planet earth: Readings from* Scientific American (pp. 85–96). New York: W. H. Freeman.

GIBBS, L. (1982). *Love Canal: My story.* Albany, NY: State University of New York Press.

GIDDENS, A. (1991). *Modernity and self-identity: Social and society in the later modern age.* Stanford, CA: Stanford University Press.

GIDDENS, A. (1995) *Beyond left and right: The future of radical politics.* Stanford, CA: Stanford University Press.

GIMBUTAS, M. (1977, Winter). The first wave of Eurasian steppe pastoralists into Copper Age Europe. *Journal of Indo-European Studies, 5,* 281.

GLACKEN, C. (1967). *Traces on the Rhodian shore: Nature and culture in western thought from ancient times to the end of the eighteenth century.* Berkeley, CA: University of California Press.

GLAZER, M., and GLAZER, P. (1999). On the trail of courageous behavior, *Sociological Inquiry, 69* (2, Spring), 276–295.

GLEICK, P. (1991, April). Environment and security: The clear connection. *The Bulletin of Atomic Scientists, 47,* 17–21.

GLEICK, P. (2009). Water use is lower than it was 30 years ago. Interviewed by Renee Montaigne on *The Morning Edition, National Public Radio.* Nov 18, 2009.

GOESLING, B. (2001). Changing income inequalities within and between nations: New evidence. *American Sociological Review, 66* (October), 745–761.

GOLDFRANK, W., GOODMAN, D., and SZASZ, A. (Eds.) (1999). *The global environment and the world system.* Westport, CT: Greenwood Press.

GOLDSTEIN, D. (2004). Cited in Roberts, P., *The end of oil: On the edge of a perilous new world.* (p. 225). Boston, MA: Houghton Mifflin.

GOODLAND, R., and ANHANG, J. (2009). Livestock and climate change. *Worldwatch, 22* (6, November/ December), 10–19.

GOODLAND, R., DALY, H., and KELLENBERG, J. (1993, June 27–July 1). *Burden sharing in transition to environmental sustainability.* Paper presented at the Seventh General Assembly of the World Future Society, Washington, DC.

GOODMAN, H., and ARMELAGOS, G. (1985). Disease and death at Dr. Dickson's mounds. *Natural History, 94,* 9.

GOODSTEIN, D. (2004). *Out of gas: The end of the age of oil.* New York: W. W. Norton.

GOULD, K. (1991). The sweet smell of money: Economic dependency and local environmental political mobilization. *Society and Natural Resources, 4,* 133–150.

GOULD, K. (1998, Spring). Nature tourism, environment, and place in a global economy. *Environment, Technology, and Society, 89,* 3–5.

GOULD, L., GARDNER, G., DELUCA, D., TIEMANN, A., and DOOB, L. (1988). *Perceptions of technological risks and benefits.* New York: Russell Sage Foundation.

HAIMSON, L. (2002a, March 8). This just in . . . *Grist Magazine, www.gristmagazine.com.*

HAIMSON, L. (2002b, January 24). This just in… *Grist Magazine, www.gristmagazine.com.*

HALWEIL, B. (1999). The emperor's new clothes. *Worldwatch, 12* (6), 21–29.

HALWEIL, B. (2000). Where have all the farmers gone? *Worldwatch, 13* (5), 13–28.

HALWEIL, B. (2003). High farm subsidies persist. In Starke L. (ed.), *Vital signs: Trends that are shaping our future* (pp. 96–97). New York: W. W. Norton.

HALWEIL, B. (2006). Can organic farming feed us all? *Worldwatch, 19* (3).

HALWEIL, B. (2006). Grain harvest flat. In L. Starke (Ed.), *Vital signs: The trends that are shaping our future* (pp. 22–23). New York: W. W. Norton.

HAMLIN, J., HUMMEL, H., and CANPA, R. (2007). *Review of renewable energy in global scenarios.* Prepared for the IEA. San Francisco: Center for Resource Solutions, 1.

HANNIGAN, J. (1995). *Environmental sociology: A social constructionist perspective.* New York: Routledge.

HARDIN, G. (1968). The tragedy of the commons. *Science, 162,* 1243–1248.

HARDIN, G. (1993). Second thoughts on the tragedy of the commons. In H. E. Daly and K. N. Townsend (Eds.), *Valuing the earth: Economics, ecology, and ethics.* Cambridge, MA: MIT Press.

HARMAN, W. W. (1979). *An incomplete guide to the future.* New York: W. W. Norton.

HARPER, C. (1998). *Exploring social change* (3rd ed.). Englewood Cliffs, NJ: Prentice Hall.

HARPER, C. (2005). Limits to growth and ecological modernization: The case of food and agriculture. Presented to the Annual Meeting of the Midwest Sociological Society, March, Kansas City, MO.

HARPER, C. (2007). *Food, society, and environment* (2nd ed.). Victoria, BC, Canada: Trafford.

HARPER, C., and LEICHT, K. (2002). *Exploring social change* (4th ed.). Upper Saddle River, NJ: Prentice Hall.

HARPER, C., and LEICHT, K. (2007). *Exploring social change* (5th ed.). Upper Saddle River, NJ: Prentice Hall.

HARRIS, M. (1971). *Culture, man, and nature.* New York: Thomas Crowell.

HARRIS, M. (1979). *Cultural materialism.* New York: Vintage.

HARRISON, P. (1987). *The greening of Africa.* New York: Viking/Penguin.

HARRISON, P. (1993). *The third revolution: Population, environment, and a sustainable world.* London: Penguin.

HAWKEN, P. (1993). *The ecology of commerce: A declaration of sustainability.* New York: HarperCollins.

HAWKEN, P., LOVINS, A., and LOVINS, H. (2000). *Natural capitalism: Creating the next Industrial Revolution.* Boston: Back Bay Books.

HAYES, D. (1990, April). Earth Day 1990: The threshold of the green decade. *World Policy Journal, 7*(2).

HAYS, S. (1959). *Conservation and the gospel of efficiency.* New York: Atheneum.

HAYS, S. (1972). *Conservation and the gospel of efficiency: The progressive conservation movement, 1890–1920.* New York: Atheneum.

HAYS, S. (1987). *Beauty, wealth, and permanence: Environmental problems and human behavior.* Needham Heights, MA: Allyn and Bacon.

HEBERLEIN, T. (1975). Conservation information: The energy crisis and electricity consumption in an apartment complex. *Energy Systems Policy, 1,* 105–118.

HEBERLEIN, T., and WARRINER, G. (1983). The influence of price and attitudes on shifting residential electricity consumption from on to off peak periods. *Journal of Economic Psychology, 4,* 107–131.

HEILBRONER, R. (1974). *An inquiry into the human prospect.* New York: W. W. Norton.

HEILBRONER, R. (1985). *The making of economic society* (7th ed). Englewood Cliffs, NJ: Prentice Hall.

HELVARG, D. (1994). *War against the greens: The "wise use" movement, the new right, and anti-environmental violence.* San Francisco, CA: Sierra Books.

HENDRY, P. (1988). Food and population: Beyond five billion. *Population Bulletin, 43,* 2.

HERTZGAARD, M. (2006). Green grows grassroots, *The Nation,* http://www.thenation.com/doc/2006731/hertzgaard.

HIRSCH, R. (1987). Impending United States energy crisis. *Science, 235,* 1471.

HOLDREN, J. (1990). Energy in transition. *Scientific American, 263* (3), 156–164.

HOLDREN, J., and EHRLICH, P. (1974). Human population and the global environment. *American Scientist, 26* (6), 6–7.

HOLLING, C. (1973). Resilience and stability of ecological systems. *Annual Review of Ecology and Systematics, 4,* 1–23.

HOMER-DIXON, T. (1996). Environmental scarcity, mass violence, and the limits of ingenuity. *Current History, 95* (604), 359–365.

HOMER-DIXON, T. (2006). *The upside of down: Catastrophe, creativity, and the renewal of civilization.* Washington, DC: Island Press.

HUMPHREY, C., and BUTTEL, F. (1982). *Environment, energy, and society.* Belmont, CA: Wadsworth.

HUMPHREY, C., LEWIS, T., and BUTTEL, F. (2002). *Environment, energy, and society: A new synthesis.* Belmont, CA: Wadsworth.

HUNT, S., and STAIR, P. (2006–2007). Biofuels hit gusher. In L. Starke, (Ed.) *Vital signs 2006–2007: Trends that are shaping our future* (pp. 40–41). New York: W. W. Norton.

HUTCHINSON, E. (1967). *The population debate.* Boston: Houghton Mifflin.

HUTCHINSON, G. (1965). *The ecological theater and the evolutionary play.* New Haven, CT: Yale University Press.

INGLEHART, R. (1990). *Culture shift in advanced industrial society.* Princeton, NJ: Princeton University Press.

INTERGOVERNMENTAL PANEL on CLIMATE CHANGE (IPCC) (2001). *Climate change 2001: Impacts, adaptation and vulnerability* (McCarthy, J., Canziani, O., Leary, N., Dokken, D., and White, K., Eds.). Cambridge, UK: Cambridge University Press.

INTERGOVERNMENTAL PANEL on CLIMATE CHANGE (IPCC) (2007). Summary for policy makers. *Climate change 2007: Mitigation of climate change.* Cambridge, UK: Cambridge University Press, p. 13.

INTERNATIONAL ENERGY AGENCY (IEA) (1987). *Energy conservation in the IEA countries.* Paris: OECD.

INTERNATIONAL ENERGY AGENCY (IEA) (2007). *World energy outlook 2007.* Paris: IEA.

INTERNATIONAL ENERGY AGENCY (IEA) (2008). *Energy technology perspectives 2008: Scenarios and strategies 2008.* Paris: IEA.

JACOBSON, M., and DELCUCCHI, M. (2009). A path to sustainable energy by 2030. *Scientific American, 301* (5), 58–65.

JONES, J. (May 27, 2010). Oil spill alters views on environmental protection. http://www.gallup.com/poll/137882/oil-spill-alters-views-environmental-protection.asx

JORGENSON, A. (2003). Consumption and environmental degradation: A cross-national analysis of the ecological footprint. *Social Problems, 50,* 374–394.

JOSKOW, P. (2002, March). United States energy policy during the 1990s. *Current History, 101* (653), 105–124.

JOWIT, J., and WINTOUR, P. (2008). The costs of tabling climate change has doubled, warns Stern. *The Guardian,* June 26, London: United Kingdom.

KATES, R. (1994). Sustaining life on the earth. *Scientific American, 271* (4), 114–122.

KEMP, W. B. (1971). The flow of energy in a hunting society. *Scientific American, 224,* 104–105.

KENNEDY, R. (2005). *Crimes against nature: How George W. Bush & his corporate pals are plundering the country & hijacking our democracy.* New York: Harper Perennial.

KENT, M. (1984). *World population: Fundamentals of growth.* Washington, DC: Population Reference Bureau.

KEYFITZ, N. (1990). The growing human population. *Managing planet earth: Readings from* Scientific American (pp. 61–72). New York: W. W. Freeman.

KING, T., and KELLY, A. (1985). *The new population debate: Two views on population growth and economic development.* Population Trends and Public Policy Paper no. 7. Washington, DC: Population Reference Bureau.

KINGSLEY, G. (1992). U.S. energy conservation policy: Themes and trends. *Policy Studies Journal, 20* (1), 114–123.

KLARE, M. (2002, March). Global petro-politics: The foreign policy implications of the Bush administration's energy plan. *Current History, 101* (653), 99–104.

KLEIN, D. (1968). The introduction, increase, and crash of reindeer on St. Matthew Island. *Journal of Wildlife Management, 32,* 350–367.

KNORR-CETNINA, K. D. (1981). *The manufacture of knowledge: An essay on the constructivist and contextual nature of science.* Oxford, England: Pergamon.

KORMONDY, E., and BROWN, D. (1998). *Fundamentals of human ecology.* Upper Saddle River, NJ: Prentice Hall.

KORTEN, D. (1995). *When corporations rule the world.* West Hartford, CT: Kumarian.

KOTOK, D. (1993, December 6). Arab oil embargo changed habits. *The Omaha World-Herald,* pp. 1–2.

KRAFT, M. (2001). *Environmental policy and politics* (2nd ed.). New York: Longman.

KRAUSE, F., BACH, W., and KOOMEY, J. (1992). *Energy policy in the greenhouse.* New York: John Wiley and Sons.

KROGMAN, N. (1999). Bureaucratic slippage in environmental agencies: The case of wetlands regulation. *Research in Social Problems and Public Policy, 7,* 163–181.

KUHN, T. (1970). *The structure of scientific revolutions.* Chicago: University of Chicago Press.

KUZNETS, S. (1955). Economic growth and inequality. *American Economic Review, 45,* 1–28.

LANE, R. (2000). *The loss of happiness in market democracies.* New Haven, CT: Yale University Press.

LAPPÉ, F., COLLINS, J., and ROSSET, P. (1998). *World hunger: Twelve myths.* New York: Grove Press.

LASCH, W. H. (1994, May/June). Environment and global trade. *Society, 31* (4), 52–58.

LAYZER, J. (2007). Deep freeze: How business has shaped the global warming debate in Congress. In M. Kraft and S. Kamieniecki (Eds.), *Business and Environmental Policy: Corporate Interests in the American Congress.* New Haven CT: Yale University Press.

LEE, M. (1995). *Earth first! Environmental apocalypse.* Syracuse, NY: Syracuse University Press.

LEE, R. (1969). !Kung bushmen subsistence: An input–output analysis. In A. Vayda (Ed.), *Environment and cultural behavior* (pp. 47–78). Garden City, NJ: Natural History Press.

LEON-GUERRERO, A. (2009). *Social problems: Community, policy, and social action* (2nd ed.). Thousand Oaks, CA: Pine Forge Press.

LENSKI, G., and NOLAN, P. (1999). *Human societies: An introduction to macrosociology.* New York: McGraw-Hill.

LEWIS, M. (1994). Environmental history challenges the myth of a primordial Eden. *The Chronicle of Higher Education, 40* (35), A56.

LI, L. (2007–2008). Bottled water consumption jumps. In L. Starke (Ed.), *Vital signs: The trends that are shaping our future* (pp. 102–103). New York, W. W. Norton.

LI, Z. (May, July, August, 2006). Capturing the sun: The future of China's solar power. *Worldwatch, 18* (4), 10–11.

LIU, Y. (2006). Groundwater overdraft problem persists. In L. Starke (Ed.), *Vital signs 2006–2007: Trends that are shaping our future* (pp. 104–105). New York: W. W. Norton.

LONGWORTH, R. (1998). *Global squeeze: The coming crisis for first-world nations.* Skokie, IL: NTC/Contemporary Books.

LOTKA, A. (1922). Contribution to the energetics of evolution. *Proceedings of the National Academy of Sciences, 8,* 147–151.

LOTKA, A. (1924). *Elements of physical biology.* New York: Williams and Wilkins. [Republished in 1956 as *Elements of mathematical biology.* New York: Dover.]

LOTKA, A. (1945). The law of evolution as a maximal principle. *Human Biology, 14,* 167–194.

LOVINS, A. (1977). *Soft energy paths.* Cambridge, MA: Ballinger.

LOVINS, A. (1993). Letter to the editor. *Atlantic Monthly, 272,* 6.

LOVINS, A. (1998). Energy efficiency to the rescue. In T. Miller (Ed.), *Living in the environment* (10th ed., p. 378). Belmont, CA: Wadsworth.

LOWI, T., JR. (1964). American business, public policy, case-studies, and political theory. *World Politics, 16,* 677–715.

LOWI, T., JR. (1972). Four systems of policy, politics, and choice. *Public Administration Review, 32,* 298–310.

LOWI, T., JR. (1979). *The end of liberalism* (2nd ed.). New York: W. W. Norton.

LUKE, T. (2005). The death of environmentalism or the advent of public ecology? *Organization and Environment, 18,* 489–494.

LUTZENHISER, L. (1993). Social and behavioral aspects of energy use. *Annual Review of Energy and the Environment, 18,* 247–289.

LUTZENHISER, L. (2001). The contours of U.S. climate non-policy. *Society and Natural Resources, 14,* 511–523.

LUTZENHISER, L., and HACKETT, B. (1993). Social stratification and environmental degradation: Understanding household $CO_2$ production. *Social Problems, 40* (1), 50–73.

LUTZENHISER, L., HARRIS, C., and OLSEN, M. (2002). Energy, society, and environment. In R.E. Dunlap and W. Michelson (Eds.), *Handbook of environmental sociology* (pp. 222–271). Westport, CT: Greenwood Press.

MACK, R., and BRADFORD, C. P. (1979). *Transforming America* (2nd ed.). New York: Random House.

MACNEILL, J., WINSEMIUS, P., and YAKUSHIJI, T. (1991). *Beyond interdependence: The meshing of the world's economy and the earth's ecology.* New York: Oxford University Press.

MAMDANI, M. (1972). *The myth of population control.* London: Reeves and Turner.

MANS, T. (1994). Personal communication.

MARSH, G. (1874). *The earth as modified by human action.* New York: Scribner and Armstrong.

MARTIN, M. (2009). Income Gap between Whites and Blacks Continues to Grow. *Tell Me More.* National Public Radio, March 23.

MARTIN, P., and MIDGLEY, E. (1999, June). Immigration to the United States. *Population Bulletin, 54,* 2.

MARTIN, P., and MIDGLEY, E. (2006). Immigration: Shlaping and reshaping America, 2nd Ed. *Bulletin: A publication of the population reference bureau, 61,* 4.

MARTIN, R. (2010). The New Nuke. *Wired,* January 4: 114–119.

MARYANSKI, A. (1998). Evolutionary sociology. In L. Freese (Ed.), *Advances in human ecology,* vol. 7 (pp. 1–56). Greenwich, CT: JAI Press.

MASON, J., and ENNIS, D. (2009). G 20 agrees on phase out of fossil fuel subsidies. *Reuters, U.S. Edition.* Sept 25.

MASTNEY, L. (2006). Coral reef losses increasing. In L. Starke (Ed.), *Vital signs 2006–2007: Trends that are shaping our future* (pp. 94–95). New York: W. W. Norton.

MASTNY, L. (2001). Religious environmentalism rises. In L. Starke (Ed.), *Vital signs 2001: The trends that are shaping our future* (pp. 146–147). New York: W. W. Norton.

MASTNY, L., and CINCOTTA, R. (2005). Examining the connections between population and security. In L. Starke (Ed). *State of the world: 2005* (pp. 22–39). New York: W. W. Norton.

MATOON, A. (1998). Paper recycling climbs higher. In L. Starke (Ed.), *Vital signs 1998: The environmental trends that are shaping our future* (pp. 144–145). New York: W. W. Norton.

MAZUR, A. (1981). *The dynamics of technological controversy.* Washington, DC: Communications Press.

MAZUR, A. (1991). *Global social problems.* Englewood Cliffs, NJ: Prentice Hall.

MAZUR, A., and ROSA, E. A. (1974). Energy and lifestyle: Cross-national comparison of energy consumption and quality of life indicators. *Science, 186,* 607–610.

McADAM, D., and SNOW, D. (2010). *Readings on social movments: Origins, dynamics, outcomes.* Los Angeles: Oxford University Press.

McCAY, B. J. (1993). *Management regimes.* Presented at the conference on Property Rights and Performance of Natural Resource Systems. Stockholm, Sweden: The Biejer Institute.

McCLOSKEY, M. (1972). Wilderness movement at the crossroads. *Pacific Historical Review, 41,* 346–364.

McCRIGHT, A., and DUNLAP, R. E. (2000). Challenging global warming as a social problem: An analysis of the conservative movement's counter-claims. *Social Problems, 47,* (4), 499–522.

McCRIGHT, A., and DUNLAP, R. E. (2003). Defeating Kyoto: The conservative movement's impact on U.S. climate change policy. *Social Problems, 50* (3), 348–373.

McCRIGHT, A. and DUNLAP, R. E. (2011). The politicization of Climate change and polarization in the American public's views of Global Warming, 2001-2010. *The Sociological Quarterly,* 52, pp. 155–194.

McDONOUGH, W., and BRAUNGART, M. (2002). *Cradle to cradle: Remaking the way we make things.* New York: North Point Press.

McKEOWN, A. (2009). Genetically modified crops only a fraction of primary global crop production. In L. Starke (Ed.), *Vital signs 2009: Trends that are shaping our future* (pp. 18–19). New York: W. W. Norton.

McNAMARA, R. (1992, November/December). The population explosion. *The Futurist,* 9–13.

MEAD, G. (1934). *Mind, self, and society: From the standpoint of a social behaviorist.* Chicago: University of Chicago Press.

MEADOWS, D. H., MEADOWS, D. L., and RANDERS, J. (1992). *Beyond the limits: Confronting global collapse and envisioning a sustainable future.* Post Mills, VT: Chelsea Green.

MEADOWS, D. H., MEADOWS, D. L., RANDERS, J., and BEHRENS, W. (1972). *The limits of growth: A report for the Club of Rome's project on the predicament of mankind.* New York: New American Library.

MEADOWS, D., RANDERS, J., and MEADOWS, D. (2004). *Limits of growth: The 30-year update.* White River, VT: Chelsea Green.

MERCHANT, C. (1981). *The death of nature: Women, ecology, and the scientific revolution.* San Francisco, CA: Harper and Row.

MERRICK, T. (1986). World population in transition. *Population Bulletin, 41,* 2.

MERTIG, A., and DUNLAP, R. E. (2001). Environmentalism, new social movements, and the new class: A cross national investigation, *Rural Sociology, 66* (1), 115–136.

MERTIG, A., DUNLAP, R. E., and MORRISON, D. (2002). The environmental movement in the United States. In R. E. Dunlap and W. Michelson (Eds.), *Handbook of environmental sociology* (pp. 448–481). Westport, CT: Greenwood Press.

MESSER, E. (1998). Conclusions. In L. DeRose, E. Messer, and S. Millman (Eds.), *Who's hungry? And how do we know?* New York: United Nations University Press.

MEYER, D., and STAGGENBORG, S. (1996). Movements, countermovements, and the structure of political opportunity. *American Journal of Sociology, 101,* 6.

MICHAELSON, M. (1994). Wangari Maathai and Kenya's green belt movement: Exploring the evolution and potentialities of consensus movement mobilization. *Social Problems, 41* (4), 540–561.

MIES, M. (1986). *Patriarchy and accumulation on a world scale.* London: Zed Books.

MILBRATH, L. (1989). *Envisioning a sustainable society: Learning our way out.* Albany, NY: State University of New York Press.

MILLER, G. T., JR. (1992). *Living in the environment* (7th ed.). Belmont, CA: Wadsworth.

MILLER, G. T. (1998). *Living in the environment* (10th ed.). Belmont, CA: Wadsworth.

MILLER, G. T., JR. (2002). *Living in the environment* (12th ed.). Belmont, CA: Wadsworth.

MILLER, G. T., JR. (2005). *Living in the environment* (14th ed.). Belmont, CA: Wadsworth.

MILLER, G. T., and SPOOLMAN, S. (2009). *Living in the environment* (16th ed.). Belmont, CA: Brooks/Cole.

MITCHELL, J., THOMAS, D., and CARTER S. (1999). Dumping in Dixie revisited: The evolution of environmental injustices in South Carolina. *Social Science Quarterly, 80* (2), 229–243.

MITCHELL, R. (1980). Public opinion on environmental issues. In *Environmental quality: The eleventh annual report of the Council on Environmental Quality.* Washington, DC: U.S. Government Printing Office.

MITCHELL, R., MERTIG, A., and DUNLAP, R. E. (1992). Twenty years of environmental mobilization: Trends among national environmental organizations. In R. E. Dunlap and A. G. Mertig (Eds.), *American environmentalism: The U.S. environmental movement, 1970–1990* (pp. 11–26). Philadelphia: Francis Taylor.

MOL, A. (2003). *Globalization and environmental reform: The ecological modernization of the global economy.* Cambridge, MA: MIT Press.

MOL, A., and SONNENFELD, D. (Eds.) (2000). *Ecological modernization around the world: Perspectives and critical debates.* Ilford, UK: Frank Cass.

MONFORT, J. (2009). Despite obstacles, biofuels continue surge. *Vital signs 2009* (pp. 35–37). Washington DC: Worldwatch Institute.

MONTGOMERY, D. (2010). Dirt: The erosion of civilizations. *Worldwatch Magazine.* January–February, p. 32.

MOTAVALLI, J. (2000, January/February). Flying high, swooping low. *E Magazine, 11* (1), 20–30.

MOTAVALLI, J. (January/February, 2006). The outlook on oil. *E Magazine, 17* (1), 27–37.

MURPHY, R. (1994). *Rationality and nature: A sociological inquiry into a changing relationship.* Boulder, CO: Westview Press.

MYERS, D., and DIENER. (1995). Who is happy? *Psychological Science, 6* (1), 10–19.

MYERS, N. (1989). *Deforestation rates in tropical forests and their climatic implications.* London: Friends of the Earth.

MYERS, N. (1996). The biodiversity crisis and the future of evolution. *The Environmentalist, 16,* 37–47.

MYERS, N. (1997). The world's forests and their ecosystem services. In G. Daily (Ed.), *Nature's services: Societal dependence on natural ecosystems* (pp. 215–236). Washington, DC: Island Press.

MYERS, N., and KENT, J. (2001). *Perverse subsidies: How tax dollars can undercut the environment and the economy.* Washington, DC: Island Press.

NASH, R. (1967). *Wilderness and the American mine.* New Haven, CT: Yale University Press.

NATIONAL CENTER FOR STATISTICS. (1984). Blood levels for persons 6 months to 74 years of age: United States, 1976–1980. *Vital Statistics,* no. 79. Hyattsville, MD: National Center for Health Statistics.

NATIONAL PUBLIC RADIO NEWS. (2006). *The Morning Edition,* April 18.

NATIONAL PUBLIC RADIO NEWS. (2010a). The Gulf oil spill, containment and cleanup. *The Morning Edition.* May 17.

NATIONAL PUBLIC RADIO NEWS. (2010b). Renee Montaigne, on the Gulf oil spill. *The Morning Edition.* June 1.

NATIONAL RESEARCH COUNCIL. (1986). *Population growth and economic development: Policy questions.* Committee on Population, Working Group on Population and Development. Washington, DC: National Academy Press.

NATURAL RESOURCES DEFENSE COUNCIL. (2006a). *http://www.nrdc.org/legislation/rollbacks/ execsum.asp.*

NATURAL RESOURCES DEFENSE COUNCIL. (2006b). Cited in *The Page that Counts, YES!* Winter 2010.16.

NELSON, T. (1996). Urban agriculture. *Worldwatch, 9* (22), 110–17.

NETTING, R. (1981). *Balancing on an Alp: Ecological change and continuity in a Swiss mountain community.* Cambridge, UK: Cambridge University Press.

NEW YORK TIMES. (2009). If we grow it, can we feed the hungry? In *The Omaha World Herald,* October 26, p. 4A.

NEW YORK TIMES. (2010). U.N. official says climate accord already in danger. In *The Omaha World Herald,* January 21, 2A.

NEWELL, P. (2000). *Climate for change.* Cambridge, UK: Cambridge University Press.

NORDSTROM, H., and VAUGHN, S. (1999). *Trade and environment.* Geneva, Switzerland: World Trade Organization.

NORSE, D. (1992). A new strategy for feeding a crowded planet. *Environment, 43* (5), 6–39.

O'CONNOR, J. (1994). Is sustainable capitalism possible? In M. O'Connor (Ed.), *Political economy and the politics of ecology* (pp. 152–175). New York: The Guilford Press.

O'MEARA, M. (1999). Urban air taking lives. In L. Starke (Ed.), *The state of the world, 1999* (pp. 128–129). New York: W. W. Norton.

O'MEARA, M. (2002). CFC use declining. In L. Starke (Ed.), *The state of the world, 1999* (pp. 54–55). New York: W. W. Norton.

ODUM, E. P. (1971). *Fundamentals of ecology* (3rd ed.). Philadelphia: W. B. Saunders.

OECD (Organization for Economic Development and Cooperation) (1999). *Implementing domestic tradeable permits for environmental protection.* Paris: OECD.

OELSCHLAEGER, M. (1994). *Caring for creation: An ecumenical approach to the environmental crisis.* New Haven, CT: Yale University Press.

OLSEN, M. (1968). *The process of social organization.* New York: Holt, Rinehart, & Winston.

OLSEN, M., and CLUETT, C. (1979). *Evaluation of Seattle city light neighborhood conservation program.* Seattle, WA: Battelle Human Affairs Research Center.

OLSEN, M., LODWICK, D., and DUNLAP, R. E. (1992). *Viewing the world ecologically.* Boulder, CO: Westview Press.

OSTROM, E. (1990). *Governing the commons: Evolution of institutions for collective action.* Cambridge, England: Cambridge University Press.

OSTWALD, W. (1909). *Energetische grundlagen der kulturwissenshaften.* Leipzig, Germany: Vorvort.

PAEHLKE, R. (1989). *Environmentalism and the future of progressive politics.* New Haven, CT: Yale University Press.

PARKIN, S. (1989). *Green parties: An international guide.* London, UK: Heretic Books.

PARRICK, D. W. (1969). An approach to the bioenergetics of rural West Bengal. In A. Vayda (Ed.), *Environment and cultural behavior* (pp. 29–46). Garden City, NJ: Natural History Press.

PARSONS, T. (1951). *The social system.* Glencoe, IL: Free Press.

PASCALA, S., and SOCOLOW, R. (2004). Stabilization wedges: Solving the climate problems for the next 50 years with current technology. *Science, 305* (5686), 968–972.

PASSARINI, E. (1998). Sustainability and sociology. *The American Sociologist, 29* (3), 59–70.

PEARSON, L. (2008). Applying resilience thinking for sustainable development. *ECOS,* http://www.sciencealert.com.au/features/2008230417227.html.

PELLOW, D. (1994). Environmental justice and popular epidemiology: Grassroots empowerment or symbolic politics. Presented at the annual meeting of the Midwest Sociological Society, St. Louis, MO.

PELLOW, D. (2000). Environmental inequality formation. *American Behavioral Scientist, 43* (4), 581–601.

PELTO, P. (1973). *The snowmobile revolution: Technological and social change in the Arctic.* Menlo Park, CA: Cummings.

PELTO, P., and MULLER-WILLIE, L. (1972). Snowmobiles: Technological revolution in the Arctic. In H. Bernard and P. Pelto (Eds.), *Technology and cultural change.* New York: Macmillan.

PERRY, T. (2004). Water conservation is working, report says. *Los Angeles Times,* March 11; also in *The Omaha World Herald,* March 11, 2A.

PIERCE, J., DALTON, R., and ZAITSEV, A. (1999). Public perceptions of environmental conditions. In R. J. Dalton, P. Garb, N. Lovrich, J. D. Pierce, and J. M. Witely (Eds.), *Critical masses: Citizens, nuclear weapons production, and environmental destruction in the United States and Russia* (pp. 97–129). Cambridge, MA: MIT Press.

PIMENTEL, D. (1992a, October). Rural populations and the global environment. *Rural Sociology,* 12–26.

PIMENTEL, D. (1992b). Land degradation and environmental resources. In T. Miller, *Living in the Environment* (7th ed.) (pp. 330–331). Belmont, CA: Wadsworth.

PIMENTEL, D. (1997). Cited in Pearce, F. "Thirty meals that suck the well dry." *The New Scientist, 153* (2667), 7.

PIMENTEL, D. (1999, October 16). In J. Anderson, "Budding invasions costly." *The Omaha World-Herald,* pp. 1–2.

PIMENTEL, D., BERGER, B., FILBERERTO, D., NEWTON, M., WOLFE, B., KARATINAKIS, E., CLARK, S. POON, E. ABBERT, E., and HANDOGOPAL, S. (2004). Water resources: Agricultural and environmental issues. *Bioscience, 54* (10), 909–919.

PIRAGES, D. (1977). *The sustainable society: Implications for limited growth.* New York: Praeger.

PODOBNIK, B. (1999, August). Towards a sustainable energy regime: Technological forecasting and social change. Presented at the 1998 meeting of The American Sociological Association, San Francisco, CA.

POINTING, C. (1991). *A green history of the world.* London: Sinclair Stevenson.

POPE, C., and RAUBER, P. (2004). *Strategic ignorance: The Bush administration is recklerssly destroying a century of environmental progress.* San Francisco, CA: Sierra Club Books.

Population Reference Bureau. (2009). *World population: More than just numbers.* Washington, DC: Population Reference Bureau.

Population Reference Bureau. (2010). World Population Data Sheet, July 28, 2010.

POSTEL, S. (1992a). Water scarcity. *Environmental Science and Technology, 26* (12), 2332–2333.

POSTEL, S. (1992b). *The last oasis: Facing water scarcity.* New York: W. W. Norton.

POSTEL, S. (1993). Water scarcity spreading. In L. Starke (Ed.), *Vital signs 1993: The trends that are shaping our future* (pp. 106–107). New York: W. W. Norton.

POSTEL, S. (2010). Will there be enough: How to change our habits and make water last. *YES! 54* (Summer), 18–23.

POSTEL, S., and CARPENTER, S. (1997). Freshwater ecosystem services. In G. Daily (Ed.), *Nature's services: Societal dependence on natural ecosystems* (pp. 195–214). Washington, DC: Island Press.

PRUGH, T. (2006). Peak oil forum. *Worldwatch, 19* (1), 9.

PRUGH, T., COSTANZA, R, and DALY, H. (2000). *The local politics of global sustainability.* Washington, DC: Island Press.

RADFORD E., and DRIZD, T. (1982). Blood carbon monoxide levels in persons 3–74 years of age. *Advance Data, 76,* 8. Hyattsville, MD: National Center for Health Statistics.

RAPPAPORT, R. A. (1968). *Pigs for the ancestors: Ritual in the ecology of a New Guinea people.* New Haven, CT: Yale University Press.

RAVENSTEIN, E. (1889). The laws of migration, I and II. *Journal of the Royal Statistical Society, 52,* 241–305.

REDCLIFT, M. (1987). *Sustainable development: Exploring the contradictions.* London: Methuen.

REDDY, A., and GOLDEMBERG, J. (1990). Energy for the developing world. *Scientific American, 263* (3), 110–119.

REES, W. (2002). Global sustainability: Conflict or convergence? *Bulletin of Science, Technology & Society, 22* (4), 249–268.

RENNER, M. (1999). Wars increase once again. In L. Starke (Ed.), *Vital signs 1999: The environmental trends that are shaping our future* (pp. 112–133). New York: W. W. Norton.

RENNER, M. (1998). Pollution control markets expand. In L. Starke (Ed.), *Vital signs 1998: The environmental trends that are shaping our future* (pp. 144–145). New York: W. W. Norton.

RENNER, M. (2002). Breaking the link between resources and repression. In L. Starke (Ed.), *State of the world, 2002* (pp. 149–173). New York: W. W. Norton.

RENNER, M. (2007–2008). Number of violent conflicts steady. In L. Starke, (Ed.), *Vital signs 2007–2008: Trends that are shaping our future* (pp. 76–77). New York: W. W. Norton.

REPETTO, R. (1987). Population, resources, environment: An uncertain future. *Population Bulletin, 42,* 2.

REPETTO, R. (1995). *Jobs, competitivenesss, and envrionmental regulation: What are the real issues?* Washington, DC: World Resources Institute.

RESCH, R. (2009). Cited in Getting Political, *Photon* (December), 18–23.

REVKIN, A. (2006). Climate expert says NASA tried to silence him. *The New York Times.* http://www.nytimes.com/2006/01/29/science/earth/29climate.htm? Retrieved 1/29/2006.

Rijksinstituut voor Volksgesondheit en Milieuhygiene. (1991). *National environmental outlook, 1990–2010.* Bilthoven, Netherlands: RIVM.

RITZER, G. (1975). *Sociology: A multiple paradigm science.* Boston: Allyn & Bacon.

RITZER, G. (2010). *Contemporary social theory and its classical roots* (3rd ed.). New York: McGraw Hill.

ROBERTS, J. T. (1996). Predicting participation in environmental treaties: A world-system analysis. *Sociological Inquiry, 66,* 38–57.

ROBERTS, J., and GRIMES, P. (1999). Extending the world-system to the whole system. In W. Goldfrank, D. Goodman, and A. Szasz (Eds.), *The global environment and the world system.* Westport, CT: Greenwood Press.

ROBERTS, J., and GRIMES, P. (2002). World-system theory and the environment: Toward a new synthesis. In R. Dunlap, F. Buttel, P. Dickens, and A. Gijswijt (Eds.), *Sociological theory and the environment: Toward a new synthesis: Classical foundations, contemporary insights.* New York: Rowman and Littlefield.

ROBERTS, P. (2004). *The end of oil: On the edge of a perilous new world.* New York: Houghton Mifflin.

ROCKLER-GLADEN, N. (2009). America's Greenest Campuses, 2008–2009, Suite 101.com. Accessed March 20, 2011.

ROGERS, R. (1994). *Nature and the crisis of modernity.* Montreal, Canada: Black Rose Books.

ROODMAN, D. (1999). Building a sustainable society. In L. Starke (Ed.), *State of the world, 1999* (pp. 169–188). New York: W.W. Norton.

ROODMAN, D. (2000). Environmental tax shifts multiplying. In L. Starke (Ed.), *Vital signs 2000: The environmental trends that are shaping our future* (pp. 138–139). New York: W. W. Norton.

ROSA, E. (1998). Risk and environmental sociology. *Environment, Technology, and Society, 88* (8).

ROSA, E., KEATING, K., and STAPLES, C. (1981). Energy, economic growth and quality of life: A cross-national trend analysis. *Proceedings of The International Congress of Applied Systems Research and Cybernetics.* New York: Pergamon.

ROSA, E., MACHLIS, G., and KEATING, K. (1988). Energy and society. *Annual Review of Sociology, 14,* 149–172.

ROSA, E., and DIETZ, T. (2004). Reflections on the STIRPAT Research Program. *Environment, Technology, and Society,* Spring, 1–2.

ROSE, C. (2001). Common property, regulatory property, and environmental protection: Comparing community-based management to tradable environmental allowances. In Dietz, T., Dolsak, N., Ostrom, E., and Stern P. (Eds.), *The drama of the commons* (pp. 123–258). Washington, DC: National Academy Press.

ROSENBAUM, W. (1989). The bureaucracy and environmental policy. In J.P. Lester (Ed.), *Environmental politics and policy: Theories and evidence* (pp. 213–237). Durham, NC: Duke University Press.

ROSS, M., and WILLIAMS, R. (1981). *Our energy: Regaining control.* New York: McGraw-Hill.

ROSSET, P. (1997). Alternative agriculture and crisis in Cuba. *Technology and Society, 12* (2), 19–25.

Royal Society of London and the U.S. National Academy of Sciences. (1992). *Population growth, resource consumption, and a sustainable world.* Washington, DC: National Academy Press.

RUBENSTEIN, D. (1995, Winter/Spring). Environmental accounting for the sustainable corporation: Strategies and techniques. *Human Ecology Review, 2* (1), 1–21.

RUCKELSHAUS, W. (1990). Toward a sustainable world. In *Managing planet earth: Readings from Scientific American* (pp. 125–136). New York: W. H. Freeman.

RUNYAN, C., and NORDERHAUG, M. (2002). The path to the Johannesburg summit. *Worldwatch, 15,* 3.

RUSSELL, J. (2009a). Carbon emissions on the rise but policies growing up too. In L. Starke (Ed.), *Vital signs: The trends that are shaping our future* (pp. 59–61). New York: W. W. Norton.

RUSSELL, J. (2009b). Climate change accelerates. In L. Starke (Ed.), *Vital signs: Trends that are shaping our future* (pp. 56–58). New York: W.W. Norton.

RYAN, J. (1992). Conserving biological diversity. In L. Starke (Ed.), *State of the world, 1992* (pp. 9–26). New York: W. W. Norton.

SACHS, A. (1995). Population growth steady. In L. Starke (Ed.), *Vital signs 1995: The trends that are shaping our future* (pp. 94–95). New York: W. W. Norton.

SALE, K. (1993). *The green revolution: The American environmental movement, 1962–1992.* New York: Hill and Wang.

SALZMAN, J., and RUHL J. B. (2000). Currencies and the commodification of environmental law. *Stanford Law Review, 53,* 607–694.

SAMDAHL, D., and ROBERTSON, R. (1989). Social determinants of environmental concern: Specification and test of the model. *Environment and Behavior, 21,* 57–81.

SANDERSON, S. (1995). *Macrosociology: An introduction to human societies* (3rd ed.). New York: HarperCollins.

SAPP, S., ARNOT, C., FALLON, J., FLECK, T., SOORHOLTS, D., SUTTON-VERMEULEN, M., and WILSON, J. (2009). Consumer trust in the U.S. food system: An examination of the recreancy theorem. *Rural Sociology, 74* (4), 525–545.

SAWIN, J. (2005a). Climate change indicators on the rise. In L. Starke (Ed.), *Vital signs 2005: Trends that are shaping our future* (pp. 40–41). New York: W. W. Norton.

SAWIN, J. (2005b). Global wind growth continues. In L. Starke (Ed.), *Vital signs 2005: Trends that are shaping our future* (pp. 34–35). New York: W. W. Norton.

SAWIN, J. (2009a). Another sunny year for solar power. In L. Starke (Ed.), *Vital signs 2009: Trends that are shaping our future* (pp. 38–39). Washington DC: Worldwatch Institute.

SAWIN, J. (2009b). Another sunny year for solar power, *Vital signs 2009* (pp. 38–40). Washington, DC: Worldwatch Institute.

SCARCE, R. (1990). *Eco-warriors: Understanding the radical environmental movement.* Chicago: Noble Press.

SCHEINBERG, A. (2003). The proof of the pudding: Urban recycling in North America as a process of ecological modernization. *Environmental Politics, 12* (4), 49–75.

SCHELLENBERGER, M., and NORDHAUS, T. (2004). The death of environmentalism. *Http://Grist.org.*

SCHIPPER, L., and LICHTENBERG, A. J. (1976). Efficient energy use and well-being: The Swedish example. *Science, 194,* 1001–1013.

SCHMALENSEE, R., JOSKOW, P., ELLERMAN, A., MONTERO, J., and BAILEY, E. (1998). An interim evaluation of sulfur dioxide emissions trading. *Journal of Economic Perspectives, 12* (3), 53–68.

SCHNAIBERG, A., and GOULD, K. (1994). *Environment and society: The enduring conflict.* New York: St. Martin's Press.

SCHNAIBERG, A. (1980). *The environment: From surplus to scarcity.* New York: Oxford University Press.

SCHNEIDER, S. (1990b) Cooling it. *World Monitor,* Spring, 30–38.

SCHNEIDER, S. H. (1990a). The changing climate. In *Managing planet earth: Readings from* Scientific American (pp. 26–36). New York: W. H. Freeman.

SCHNEIDER, S., and LONDER, R. (1984). *The coevolution of climate and life.* San Francisco: Sierra Club Books.

SCHOR, J. (1992). *The overworked American: The unexpected decline of leisure.* New York: Basic Books.

SCHULZE, E., and MOONEY, H. (1993). *Biodiversity and ecosystem function.* Berlin: Springer-Verlag.

SCHUMACHER, E. F. (1973). *Small is beautiful: Economics as if people mattered.* New York: HarperCollins.

SCHUTZ, A. (1967). *The phenomenology of the social world.* Evanston, IL: Northwestern University Press. (Original work published 1932.)

SEN, A. (1981). *Poverty and famines.* New York: Oxford University Press.

SEN, A. (1993). The economics of life and death. *Scientific American, 208* (5), 40–47.

SHAIKO, R. (1999). *Voices and echoes for the environment: Public interest representation in the 1990s and beyond.* New York: Columbia University Press.

SHEPPARD, K. (2009). Everything you always wanted to know about the Waxman-Markey energy/climate bill—in Bullet Points. *Grist,* June 30.

SHIVA, V. (1988). *Staying alive.* London: Zed Books.

SILVER, C., and DEFRIES, R. (1990). *One earth, one future: Our changing global environment.* Washington, DC: National Academy of Sciences, National Academy Press.

SIMON, H. (1982). *Models of bounded rationality.* Cambridge, MA: MIT Press.

SIMON, J. (1990). Population growth is not bad for humanity. *National Forum: The Phi Kappa Phi Journal, 70,* 1.

SIMON, J. (1996). *Ultimate resources 2.* Princeton, NJ: Princeton University Press.

SIMON, J. (1998). There is no crisis of unsustainability. In T. Miller (Ed.), *Living in the environment* (10th ed.) (pp. 26–27). Belmont, CA: Wadsworth.

SIMON, J., and WILDAVSKY, A. (1993, May 13). Facts, not species, are periled. *The New York Times.*

SIVARD, R. (1979) *World energy survey.* Leesburg, VA: World Priorities Publications.

SIVARD, R. (1993). *World military and social expenditures.* Washington, DC: World Priorities Publications.

SMEEDING. T. (2000). Change in income equality in the OECD countries. In A. Giddens, M. Dunier, R. Applebaum, and D. Carr (Eds.), *Introduction to sociology.* New York: W. W. Norton.

SMITH, T. (1985). The polls: American's most important problems: Part I. National and international. *Public Opinion Quarterly, 46,* 38–61.

SNOW, D., and BENFORD, R. (1988). Ideology, frame resonance, and participant mobilization. In B. Klandfermans, H. Kriesi, and S. Tarrow (Eds.), *Structure to action: Comparing social movement research across cultures.* Greenwich, CT: JAI Press.

SOCOLOW, R. (1978). *Saving energy in the home: Princeton's experiments at Twin Rivers.* Cambridge, MA: Ballinger.

SODDY, F. (1926). *Wealth, virtual wealth, and debt: The solution to the economic paradox.* London: Oxford University Press.

SOUTHWICK, C. (1996). *Global ecology in human perspective.* New York: Oxford University Press.

SPEARS, J., and AYENSU, E. (1985). Resources, development, and the new century: Forestry. In R. Repetto (Ed.), *The global possible: Resources, development, and the new century* (pp. 299–335). New Haven, CT: Yale University Press.

SPETH, J. (2004). *Red sky at morning: America and the crisis of the global environment.* New Haven, CT: Yale Nota Bene. Yale University Press.

SPETH, J. (2008). *Bridge at the end of the world: Capitalism, the environment, and crossing the bridge from crisis to sustainability.* New Haven, CT: Yale Univeersity Press.

SPENCER, H. (1896). *The principles of sociology.* New York: Appleton.

STANISLAW, J., and YERGIN, D. (1993). Oil: Reopening the door. *Foreign Affairs, 72* (4), 81–93.

STARK, R. (1994). *Sociology.* Belmont, CA: Wadsworth.

STEPHAN, E. (1970). The concept of community in human ecology. *Pacific Sociological Review, 13,* 218–228.

STERN, N. (2006). What is the economics of climate change? *World Economics, 7* (2, April–June), 1–10.

STERN, N. (2007). *The economics of climate change: The Stern review.* Cambridge UK: Cambridge University Press.

STERN, P. (1992). Psychological dimensions of global environmental change. *Annual Review of Psychology, 43,* 269–302.

STERN, P., and ARONSON, E. (1984). *Energy use: The human dimension.* New York: W. H. Freeman.

STERN, P., and OSKAMP, S. (1987, March 28). Managing scarce environmental resources. In D. Stokals and I. Altman (Eds.), *Handbook of environmental psychology,* vol. 2. New York: Wiley.

STERN, P., ARONSON, E., DARLEY, D., HILL, E., HIRST, E., KEMPTON, W., and WILBANKS, T. (1986). The effectiveness of incentives for residential energy-conservation. *Evaluation Review, 10,* 147–176.

STERN, P., DIETZ, T., and KALOF, L. (1993). Value orientations, gender, and environmental concern. *Environment and Behavior, 25* (3), 322–348.

STERN, P., YOUNG, O., and DRUCKMAN, D. (Eds.) (1992). *Global environmental change: Understanding the human dimensions.* Washington, DC: National Academy Press.

STOLNITZ, G. (1964). The demographic transition from high to low birth rates and death rates. In R. Freedman (Ed.), *Population: The vital revolution.* Garden City, NJ: Anchor Books.

SWITZER, J. (1994). *Environmental politics: Domestic and global dimensions.* New York: St. Martin's Press.

SZASZ, A., and MEUSER M. (1997). Environmental inequalities: Literature review and proposals for new directions in research and theory. *Current Sociology, 45,* 99–120.

Sztompka, P. (1993). *The sociology of social change.* Cambridge, MA: Blackwell Publishers.

Tainter, J. (1988). *The collapse of complex societies.* Cambridge, England: Cambridge University Press.

Talberth. J. (2008). A new bottom line for progress. *State of the world 2008: Innovations for a sustainable economy* (pp. 18–31). New York: W. W. Norton.

Takacs, D. (1996). *The idea of biodiversity: Philosophies of paradise.* Baltimore, MD: Johns Hopkins University Press.

Taylor, B. (1992). *Our limits transgressed: Environmental political thought in America.* Lawrence, KS: University of Kansas Press.

Taylor, D. (1993). Environmentalism and the politics of inclusion. In R. Bullard (Ed.), *Confronting environmental racism: Voices from the grassroots.* Boston: South End Press.

Taylor, D. (2000). The rise of the environmental justice paradigm. *American Behavioral Scientist, 43* (4), 508–580. Available at *http://Tellus.org.*

Thomas, W. I. (1923). *The unadjusted girl.* Boston: Little Brown.

Tietenberg, T. (2002). The tradable permits approach to protecting the commons: What have we learned? In Dietz et al. (Eds.), *The drama of the commons* (pp. 197–232). Washington, DC: National Academy Press.

Tilly, C. (1984). *Big structures, large processes, huge comparisons.* New York: Russell Sage Foundation.

Tsoukalas, T. (1994). Environmental whistleblowers: A brief organization profile. *Environment, Technology, and Society, 74,* 1–5.

Tuxill, J. (1997). Death in the family tree. *Worldwatch, 10* (5), 13–21.

Tuxill, J. (1998). Vertebrates signal biodiversity losses. In L. Starke (Ed.), *Vital signs 1998: The environmental trends that are shaping our future* (pp. 128–129). New York: W. W. Norton.

Tuxill, J. (1999). Appreciating the benefits of plant biodiversity. In L. Starke. (Ed.), *State of the world, 1999* (pp. 96–114). New York: W. W. Norton.

U.S. Department of Agriculture. (1993, February). *World grain situation and outlook.* Washington, DC: Government Printing Office.

U.S. Department of Energy. (1989). *Energy conservation trends: Understanding the factors that affect conservation gains in the U.S. economy.* Washington, DC: Doe/Pe-0092.

U.S. Environmental Protection Agency. (1990). *Superfund: Environmental progress.* Washington, DC: EPA Office of Emergency and Remedial Response.

Ungar, S. (1992). The rise and (relative) decline of global warming as a social problem. *The Sociological Quarterly, 33* (4), 483–502.

Ungar, S. (1998). Bringing the issue back in: Comparing the marketability of the ozone hole and global warming. *Social Problems, 48* (4), 510–527.

Union of Concerned Scientists. (1992). *Warning to humanity.* Washington, DC: Union of Concerned Scientists.

United Nations. (1998a). *Human development report.* United Nations Development Programme. New York: Oxford University Press.

United Nations. (1998b). *World urbanization prospects: The 1996 revisions.* New York: United Nations.

United Nations. (2000). *World population prospects: The 1998 revisions.* United Nations Population Division. New York: United Nations.

United Nations Development Programme. (2005). In A. Giddens, M. Duneier, R. Aplebaum, and D.Carr, *Introduction to sociology* (7th ed., p. 213). New York: W. W. Norton.

United Nations Population Division. (2006). *World Urbanization Prospects 2005.* New York: United Nations Press.

Van Den Berghe, P. (1977–1978). Bridging the paradigms. *Society, 15,* 42–49.

Van Gelder, S., Ostrander, M., and Pible, D. (2010). Act up. Act now. *Yes!* Winter, 19.

Van Liere, K., and Dunlap, R. E., (1980). The social bases of environmental concern: A review of hypotheses, explanations, and empirical evidence. *Public Opinion Quarterly, 44,* 43–59.

VITOUSEK, P. M., EHRLICH, P. R., EHRLICH, A. H., and MATSON, P. A. (1986). Human appropriation of the products of photosynthesis. *Bioscience, 36,* 368–373.

WACKERNAGEL, M., and REES, W. (1996). *Our ecological footprint: Reducing human impact on the earth.* Gabriola Island, BC, Canada: New Society Publishers.

WACKERNAGEL, M., LINARES, D., SANCHEZ, M., FALFAN, I., and LOH, J. (2000). *Ecological footprints and ecological capacities of 152 nations: The 1996 update.* San Francisco, CA: Redefining Progress.

WACKERNAGEL, M., ONISTO, L., and BELLO, P. (1999). National natural capital accounting with the ecological footprint concept. *Ecological Economics, 29* (3), 375–390.

WACKERNAGEL, M., SCHULZ, N., DEUMLING, D., LINARES, A., JENKINS, M., KAPOS, V., MONFREDA, C., JOH, J., MYERS, N., NORGAARD, R., and RANDERS, J. (July 9, 2002). Tracking the ecological overshoot of the human economy. *Proceedings of the National Academy of Sciences of the United States of America, 99* (14), 9266–9271.

*Wall Street Journal.* (2006, July 14). Hockey stick hokum, p. A12.

WALLERSTEIN, I. (1980). *The modern world system, Vol. 2.* New York: Academic Press.

WALKER, E. (2010). Industry-driven activism. *Contexts, 9* (2), 44–49. The American Sociological Association.

WALTON, J. (1993). *Sociology and critical inquiry: The work, tradition, and purpose* (3rd ed.). Belmont, CA: Wadsworth.

WEEKS, J. R. (1994). *Population: An introduction to concepts and issues* (5th ed.). Belmont, CA: Wadsworth.

WEEKS, J. R. (2005). *Population: An introduction to concepts and issues* (9th ed.). Belmont, CA: Wadsworth.

WEEKS, J. (2008). *Population: An introduction to concepts and issues* (10th ed.). Belmont, CA: Thompson Wadsworth.

WEINBERG, A., PELLOW, D., and SCHNIBERG, A. (1998). Ecological modernization in the internal periphery of the USA: Accounting for recycling's promises and performance. Presented to the American Sociological Association, August, San Francisco, CA.

WEINBERG, A., PELLOW, D., and SCHNIBERG, A. (2000). *Urban recycling and the search for sustainable community development.* Princeton, NJ: Princeton University Press.

WHITE, G. (1980). Environment. *Science, 209* (4), 183–189.

WHITE, L. (1949). Energy and the evolution of culture. In L. White, Jr. (Ed.), *The evolution of culture* (pp. 363–393). New York: Farrar, Straus, and Giroux.

WHITE, L., JR. (1967). The historical roots of our ecological crisis. *Science, 155,* 1203–1207.

WILKINSON, R. (1996). *Unhealthy societies: The afflictions of inequality.* London: Routledge.

WILLIAMS, J. A., and MOORE, H. (1994). The rural–urban continuum and environmental concerns. *Great Plains Research: A Journal of Natural and Social Sciences, 12,* 195–214.

WILSON, A. (1992). *The culture of nature: North American landscape from Disney to the* Exxon Valdez. Cambridge, MA: Blackwell.

WILSON, E. O. (1975). *Sociobiology: The new synthesis.* Cambridge, MA: Belknap Press of Harvard University.

WILSON, E. O. (1990). Threats to biodiveristy. In *Managing planet earth: Readings from* Scientific American (pp. 49–59). New York: W. H. Freeman.

WOLF, A. (2000). Hydrostrategic territory in the Jordan basin: Water, war, and Arab–Israeli peace negotiations. In H. Amery and A. Wolf (Eds.), *Water in the Middle East: A geography of peace.* Austin, TX: University of Texas Press.

WOLF, E. (1982). *Europe and the peoples without history.* Berkeley, CA: University of California Press.

World Commission on Environment and Development. (1987). *Our common future.* Oxford: Oxford University Press.

YEARLY, S. (1996). *Sociology, environmentalism, globalization.* London: Sage.

YEOMANS, M. (2004). *Oil: A concise guide to the most important product on earth.* New York: New Press.

YORK, R., ROSA, E., and DIETZ, T. (2003a). Footprints on the earth: The environmental consequences of modernity. *American Sociological Review, 68* (2): 279–300.

YORK, R., ROSA, E., and DIETZ, T., (2003b). STIRPAT, IPAT, and ImPACT: Analytical tools for unpacking the driving forces of environmental impacts. *Environmental Economics, 46,* 351–365.

YOUNG, G. (1994). Community with three faces: The paradox of community in postmodern life with illustrations from the United States and Japan. *Human Ecology Review, 1* (1), 137–146.

ZALKE, D., ORBUCH, P., and HOUSMAN, R. F. (Eds.). (1993). *Trade and environment: Law, economics, and policy.* Washington, DC: Island Press.

# PHOTO CREDITS

# NAME INDEX

# SUBJECT INDEX